Engineering Graphics Text and Workbook

Series 2

Jerry W. Craig and Orval B. Craig

Washington University – School of Engineering

Saint Louis, MO

SDC Publications
P.O. Box 1334
Mission, KS 66222
913-262-2664
www.SDCpublications.com
Publisher: Stephen Schroff

ISBN-13: 978-1-887503-88-4
ISBN-10: 1-887503-88-9

Printed and bound in the United States of America.

CONTENTS

Preface

To Students:

Learning to think in three dimensions is a personal skill. Technical work requires reading or creating drawings as a means of communication. The only way to improve three-dimensional perception is to practice. The problems in this workbook are designed to develop visualization skills and may be very challenging. Seeing another student's answer ruins all chance to learn. Often the best approach is to work on a problem for a time - then, put it away for a while. Come back later. Your mind continues to work even though you are doing other things. Using techniques developed in this book it is possible to prove every line and surface on a drawing. There should be no question whether the answer is correct or not!

Alternate interpretations may exist. The designer had specific shapes and features in mind when the drawings were created. However, the process of representing these mental images on paper or on the computer screen may result in other ways of seeing things. This is a problem in producing real objects. Additional views or details may be needed to assure clear intent.

Professionals take great pride in their work. Sketches they produce are very neat. Drawings are clearly presented - checked and rechecked - for accuracy and clarity. Lettering is very neat and legible. The quality of the work projects the integrity of the person.

To Teachers:

The instructional approach in this book is unique. Much emphasis is placed on developing perceptional skills. Methods of analyzing surfaces and edges are presented which help to visualize surfaces and features both on paper and on the computer screen. It is possible to prove every surface and edge on an object. This is process which becomes very rapid when the mental reasoning is developed and practiced. The best way to help solve a problem is to ask questions and analyze surfaces. courage students to make clay models when they get stuck.

Each type of surface has a very limited set of rules that relate to its appearance in orthographic views and its location in space. By applying these rules, students can begin to solve problems before they can see the shape or the answer. This is a very powerful technique which can lead to far greater progress.

One of my students returned from a job interview at a large corporation. He commented that he was given a spatial perception test. He said, "I just analyzed surfaces. They were amazed at how correct I was and how fast I solved the test. They made a substantial job offer on the spot."

Acknowledgements:

Much of the theory of surface analysis was developed by **Professor Hiram Grant** at Washington University, St. Louis. Professor Grant provided valuable support and encouragement to young teachers.

In memory of
Orval B. Craig
A truly dedicated teacher who always put students first.

Engineering Drawing.

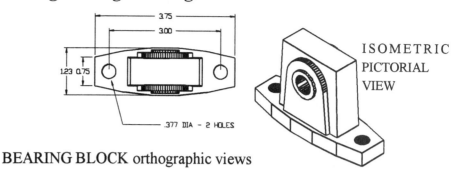

Engineering Drawings provide all design information to create objects.

ISOMETRIC PICTORIAL VIEW

BEARING BLOCK orthographic views

Drawings must show the shapes of objects. Both pictorial, and orthographic drawings are needed.

Dimensions and notes provide sizes and production information.

Engineering Drawing is very important in all phases of technical work. No object can be manufactured without the use of a drawing. Drawings are needed for construction, assembly, welding, repair -- every job relies on drawings to provide quick, clear, complete information.

Drawings are needed for advertising, catalog sheets, specification control and requests for bids. Some drawings are in the form of multiple-view (front, top and side, etc.) or in the form of pictorial views.

Drawings are used in every phase of technical work.

"The clearest form of communication"

Drawings are the clearest form of communication. People who understand the process of creating and reading drawings can quickly obtain exact information regardless of the language or country of origin.

Many drawings are created as freehand sketches. These are often the first realization of design ideas. The ability to sketch clearly with good proportion and perspective is important to all who work in technical jobs.

Freehand sketches must be clear and proportional.

A few years ago, accurate drawings were made by carefully drawing distances to scale on paper or mylar plastic film. This process was accurate to a few hundredths of an inch at best.

Computer drawings may be created with high accuracy.

Accurate drawings are now created using computers. Often, the internal accuracy is on the order of eight to fifteen decimal places. Computer data can be exported to machine tools, plate burners or laser cutters which directly manufacture objects. The accuracy is much better and the time required is much less.

DRAWING
TOOLS

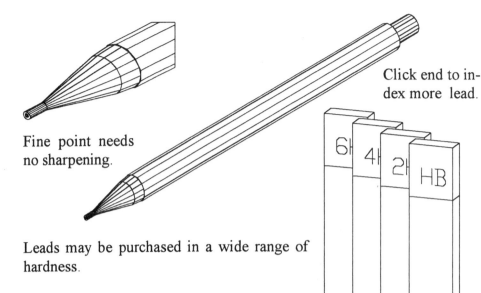

Fine point pencils are very popular with drafters. The "Pentel" type .5MM or .7MM are most often used.

Fine point needs no sharpening.

Click end to index more lead.

Use correct hardness for paper or film type.

Leads may be purchased in a wide range of hardness.

Pink erasers are used on paper. White erasers are best for plastic films

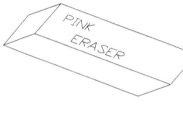

T-Squares and triangles are useful for quick layouts.

T-Squares and triangles may be used for manual drawing. They were the primary drawing tools for many years.

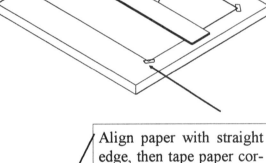

Align paper with straight edge, then tape paper corners to drawing board.

Parallel rules are popular with Architects and for work where horizontal and vertical lines are drawn.

Parallel rules run on a string and pulley system. They are inexpensive and reasonably accurate.

Drafting machines are quickly positioned for drawing. A protractor scale allows close angular settings.

Drafting machines increased productivity and accuracy. Both left-hand and right-hand models were produced.

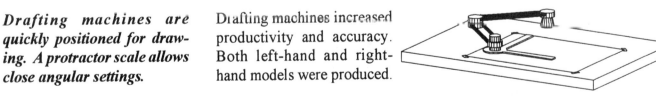

Drawing Paper

Drawings are created or plotted on transparent media.

Until the early 1900's a drawing material made of starched fine linen cloth was used. Older companies and many highway departments still have drawings of this type.

Newer materials include plasticised paper and mylar film.

Measuring

Scales

Metric units are the world standard. Most new products like automobiles and consumer items are built to metric standards.

In the United States the older (English) system of measurement is still in wide use particularly in the Archictectural field. Many existing products were built using the inch, foot, etc. measuring system. People working in technical jobs must be able to read and calculate using several different measuring units.

Manual drawings created on paper must sometimes be reduced down to fit the page. Special scales are used which have markings that allow reduction without a lot of calculation. An architectural *half scale* is shown. Note the inches to the left of the zero line.

Sheet sizes are keyed to a letter designation.

A = 8 1/2" X 11"
B = 11" X 17"
C = 17" X 22"
D = 22" X 34"

Other sizes may be used. Some drawings may be 32" or 34" wide and as long as 20 feet.

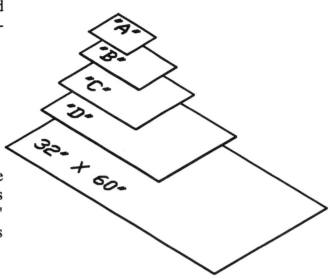

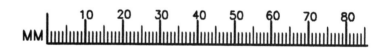

METRIC SCALE

DIVISIONS ARE MILLIMETERS

FRACTIONAL INCH SCALE

DIVISIONS ARE 1/32"

DECIMAL INCH SCALE

DIVISIONS ARE .02"
(EVEN HUNDREDTHS)

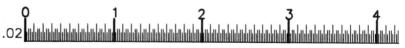

ARCHITECTURAL HALF SCALE

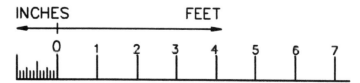

Computer Aided Drafting and Design

IBM type computers are most often used.

Extended memory
Large hard disk capacity
Math Co-processor
Large color Monitor
Mouse or Digitizer
and network connections
are common computer re-
quirements for drawing
workgroups.

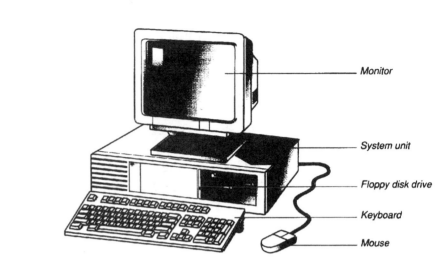

Monitor

System unit

Floppy disk drive

Keyboard

Mouse

Keyboards:

The keyboard has special key groupings which are used by CAD software.

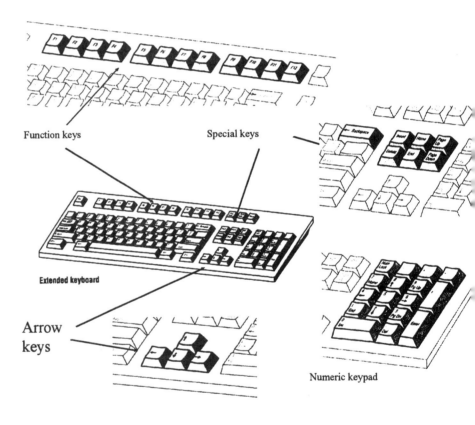

Function keys   Special keys

Extended keyboard

Arrow keys

Numeric keypad

Mouse or Digitizer

A mouse is essential for CAD drawing and menu picks.

Digitizers allow fast input.

Digitizers are often used with professional CAD systems. Commands may be selected with a single pick. This is much quicker than working through screen menus.

Large digitizers allow drawings to be traced into the computer.

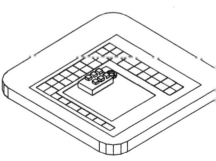

Plotters and output devices.

Pen plotters were the first type of drawing output device. Office type laser printers may be used to output up to "B" size drawings.

Pen plotters are available in many sizes. They translate computer drawings to paper or film.

Problems occur when pens skip or run out of ink.

Some plotters may be used to digitize drawings.

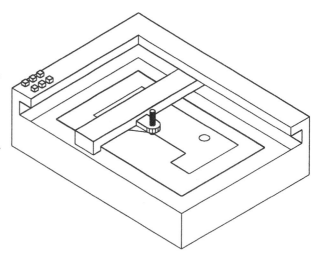

Laser plotters are used in large drawing workgroups.

Laser plotters are use in locations where there are a large number of drawings to plot. While they are very expensive, they produce more reliable plots at a much faster speed.

Laser Plotter

CAD/CAM increases productivity and accuracy in machine parts.

Drawing information may be exported to machine tools. The CAD/CAM process allows creation of parts on the computer. Drawing data is passed to a post-processor for machine tool control.

Parts which took weeks to design and manufacture a few years ago can now be produced in hours.

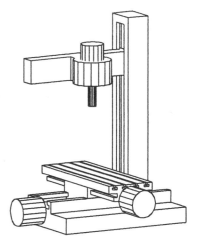

Computer networks are common in Engineering workgroups

Networks allow designers to share files, printer and plotters.

Mail may be dispatched rapidly.

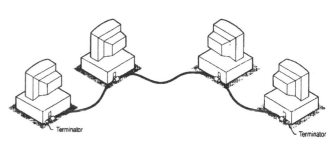

RECTANGULAR GRID

NAME

DATE

FILE NUMBER

GRADE

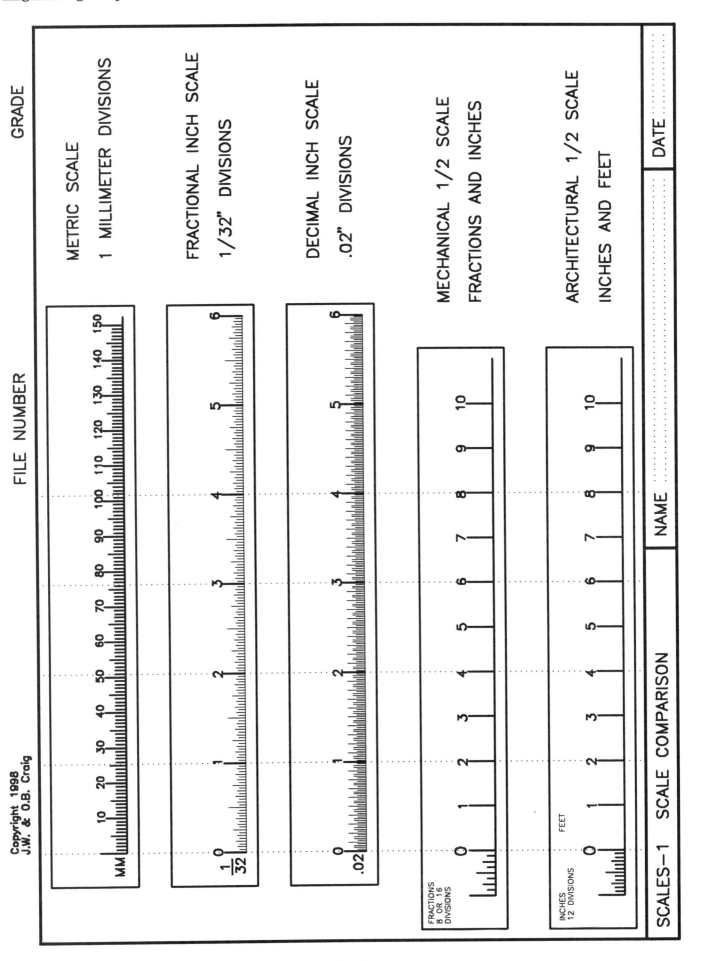

GRADE

FILE NUMBER

METRIC SCALE
1 MILLIMETER DIVISIONS

FRACTIONAL INCH SCALE
1/32" DIVISIONS

DECIMAL INCH SCALE
.02" DIVISIONS

MECHANICAL 1/2 SCALE
FRACTIONS AND INCHES

ARCHITECTURAL 1/2 SCALE
INCHES AND FEET

FRACTIONS
8 OR 16
DIVISIONS

INCHES
12 DIVISIONS

FEET

DATE

NAME

SCALES—1   SCALE COMPARISON

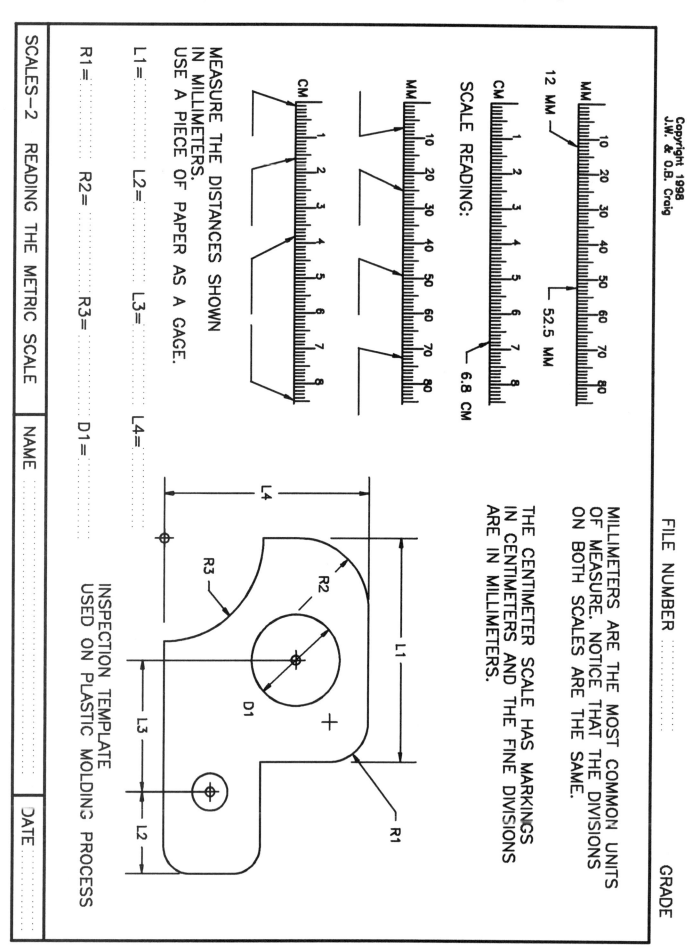

FILE NUMBER ....

GRADE

MILLIMETERS ARE THE MOST COMMON UNITS
OF MEASURE. NOTICE THAT THE DIVISIONS
ON BOTH SCALES ARE THE SAME.

THE CENTIMETER SCALE HAS MARKINGS
IN CENTIMETERS AND THE FINE DIVISIONS
ARE IN MILLIMETERS.

SCALE READING:

12 MM

52.5 MM

6.8 CM

MEASURE THE DISTANCES SHOWN
IN MILLIMETERS.
USE A PIECE OF PAPER AS A GAGE.

L1 =
L2 =
L3 =
L4 =

R1 =
R2 =
R3 =
D1 =

INSPECTION TEMPLATE
USED ON PLASTIC MOLDING PROCESS

SCALES-2   READING THE METRIC SCALE

NAME ....

DATE ....

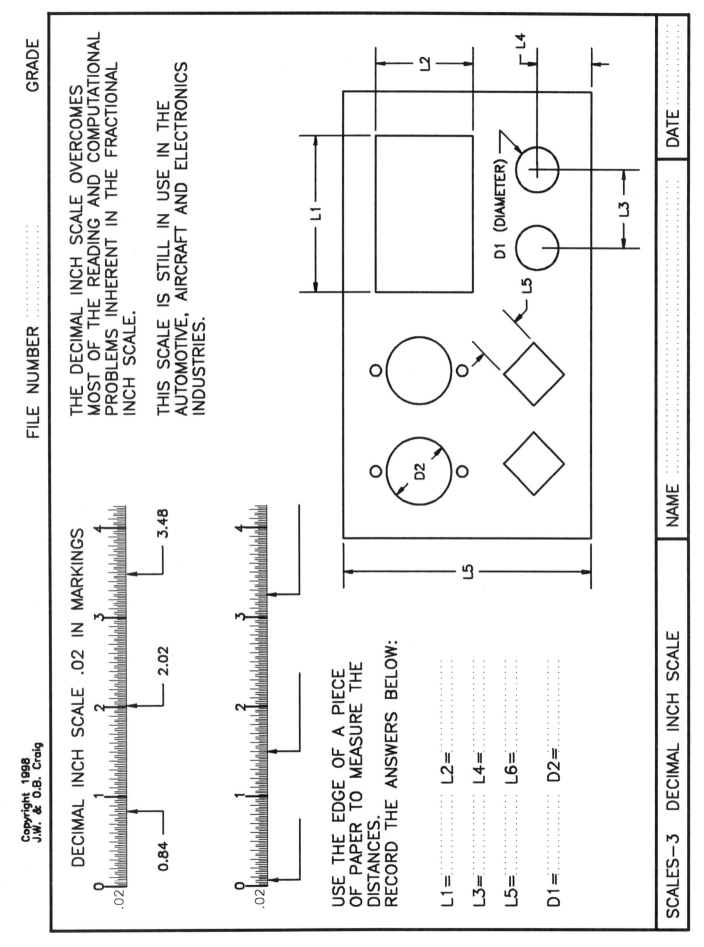

GRADE

FILE NUMBER

Copyright 1998
J.W. & O.B. Craig

THE DECIMAL INCH SCALE OVERCOMES MOST OF THE READING AND COMPUTATIONAL PROBLEMS INHERENT IN THE FRACTIONAL INCH SCALE.

THIS SCALE IS STILL IN USE IN THE AUTOMOTIVE, AIRCRAFT AND ELECTRONICS INDUSTRIES.

DECIMAL INCH SCALE .02 IN MARKINGS

0.84   2.02   3.48

USE THE EDGE OF A PIECE OF PAPER TO MEASURE THE DISTANCES.
RECORD THE ANSWERS BELOW:

L1=   L2=
L3=   L4=
L5=   L6=
D1=   D2=

D1 (DIAMETER)

L1   L2   L3   L4   L5

D2

NAME

DATE

SCALES—3   DECIMAL INCH SCALE

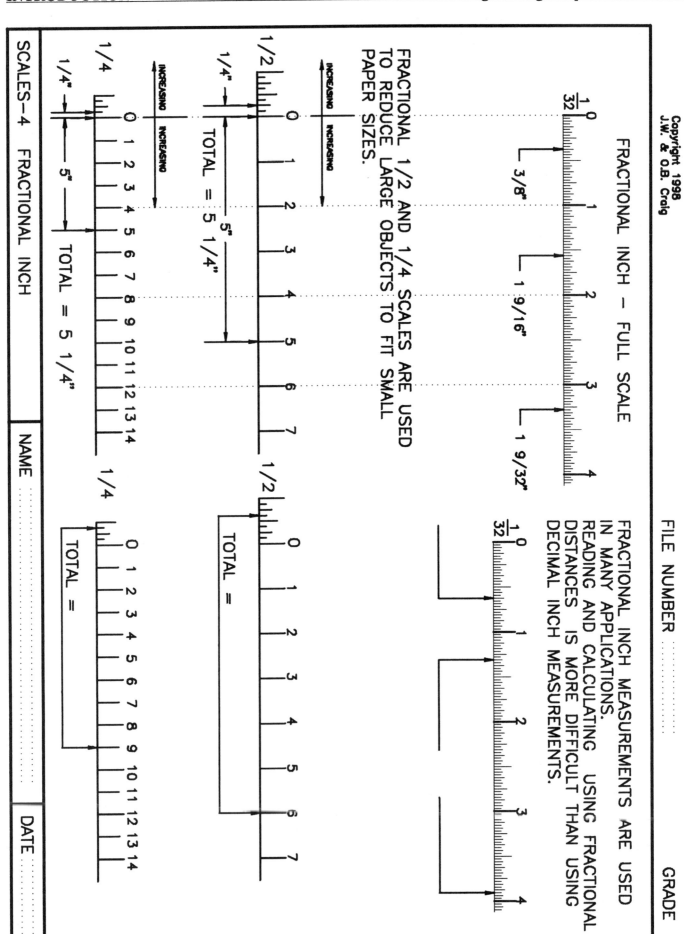

FRACTIONAL INCH — FULL SCALE

FRACTIONAL INCH MEASUREMENTS ARE USED IN MANY APPLICATIONS.
READING AND CALCULATING USING FRACTIONAL DISTANCES IS MORE DIFFICULT THAN USING DECIMAL INCH MEASUREMENTS.

FRACTIONAL 1/2 AND 1/4 SCALES ARE USED TO REDUCE LARGE OBJECTS TO FIT SMALL PAPER SIZES.

SCALES—4   FRACTIONAL INCH

Copyright 1998
J.W. & O.B. Craig

FILE NUMBER

GRADE

NAME

DATE

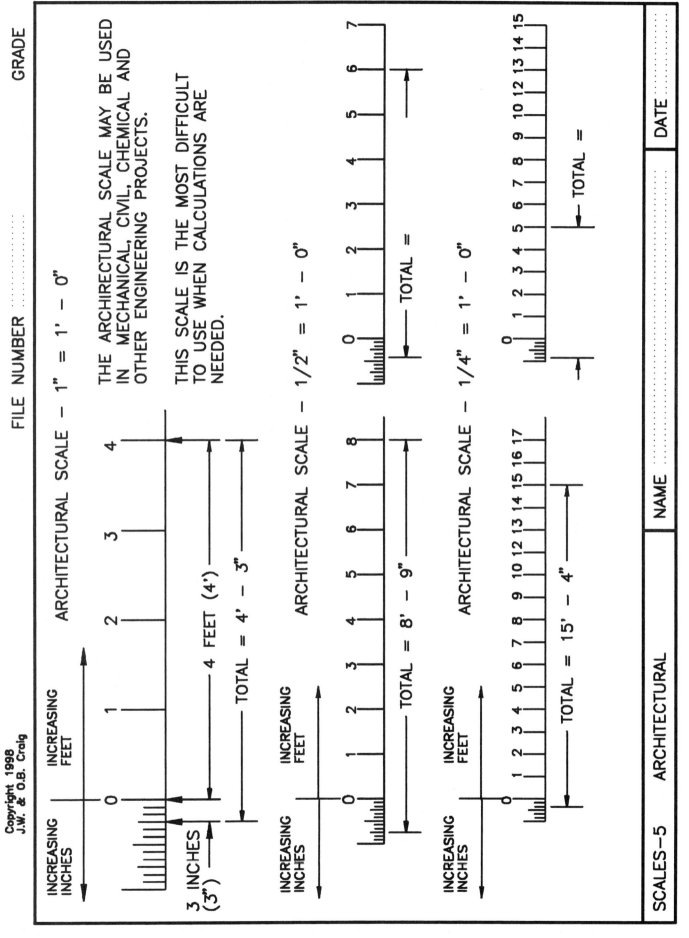

ARCHITECTURAL SCALE – 1" = 1' – 0"

THE ARCHITECTURAL SCALE MAY BE USED IN MECHANICAL, CIVIL, CHEMICAL AND OTHER ENGINEERING PROJECTS.

THIS SCALE IS THE MOST DIFFICULT TO USE WHEN CALCULATIONS ARE NEEDED.

ARCHITECTURAL SCALE – 1/2" = 1' – 0"

ARCHITECTURAL SCALE – 1/4" = 1' – 0"

INCREASING FEET

INCREASING INCHES

TOTAL = 4' – 3"

4 FEET (4')

3 INCHES (3")

TOTAL = 8' – 9"

TOTAL = 15' – 4"

TOTAL =

TOTAL =

FILE NUMBER ....

GRADE

NAME ....   DATE ....

SCALES–5   ARCHITECTURAL

Copyright 1998
J.W. & O.B. Craig

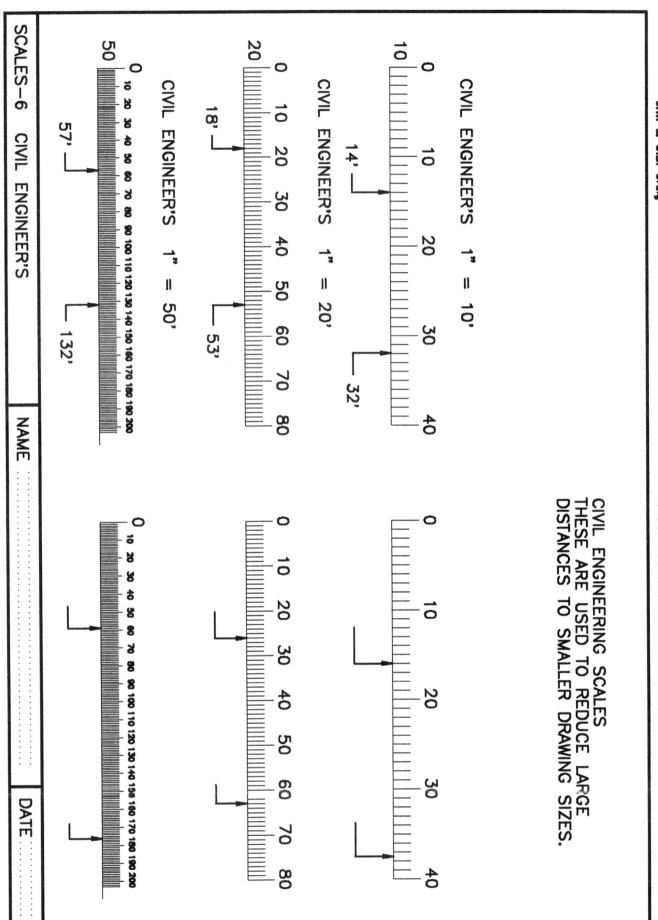

CIVIL ENGINEERING SCALES
THESE ARE USED TO REDUCE LARGE
DISTANCES TO SMALLER DRAWING SIZES.

FILE NUMBER

GRADE

SCALES—6 CIVIL ENGINEER'S

NAME

DATE

CIVIL ENGINEER'S 1" = 10'

14'

32'

CIVIL ENGINEER'S 1" = 20'

18'

53'

CIVIL ENGINEER'S 1" = 50'

57'

132'

Introduction

Freehand lettering is used in many types of technical work. Conventional drawings must have notes, instructions, materials and descriptions clearly shown. Memos must be readable.

Developing good lettering is a personal skill which takes practice. Letters must be formed properly. They must be open shaped and very legible. Clear communication is essential to avoid mistakes and reduce waste. Letter shapes are designed by standards such as the ANSI (American National Standards Institute).

Lettering may be done using a drafting type pencil, lead holder or technical pen. Whichever tool is used, the letters must be properly formed and <u>very black.</u>

Pull the pencil or pen across the paper. All lettering strokes should be a pulling motion. This avoids catching and tearing the paper. Right-handed and left-handed drafters may have to develop different styles for forming letters. Right-hand techniques are shown.

Press down hard when using a pencil.

Fine point pencils are best held nearly vertically. The fine point leads are fragile and break easily. A vertical force will produce black lines with less breakage.

Vertical capital letters are preferred for most technical work. They are formed within a 6 by 6 grid as shown. Most letters are slightly narrower than they are tall. The shapes of the letters are as open as possible. Letters with small loops and crossing strokes are avoided.

Computer fonts may be slightly different in shapes and proportions.

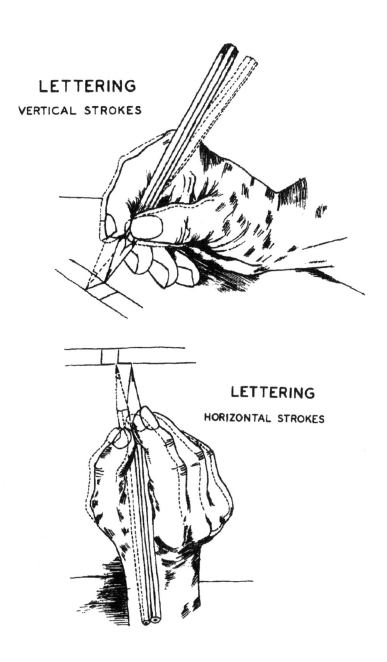

LETTERING
VERTICAL STROKES

LETTERING
HORIZONTAL STROKES

VERTICAL CAPITALS

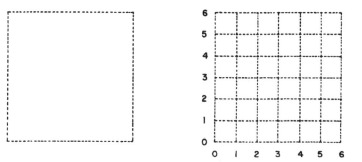

Straight Line Letters

Examples of form and proportions are shown. Letters must be as open and clear as possible for readability. Drawings and memos may be reproduced many times. Microfilm copies may be made for archiving or distribution. These copies require very legible letters.

VERTICAL CAPITALS

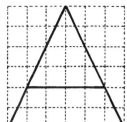
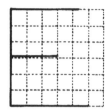

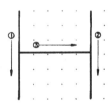
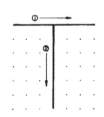
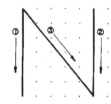

Steps for forming letters are shown. This sequence is recommended to assure that each letter is the correct width in relation to height. For example, form the two vertical sides of the "H", "N" and "M" first. Form the top of the "T" first.

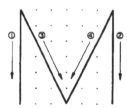

The "H" and "N" are slightly narrower than they are tall.

The "T" and the "M" are just as wide as they are tall.

Proportion: width vs. height is very important in forming letters.

Computer lettering may have slightly different proportions. In either case, be sure letters are very clear and readable.

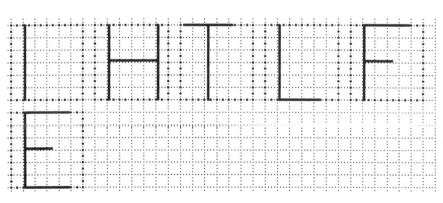

Computer letter proportions.
Straight-line letters.

Angled Line Letters

 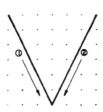 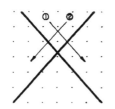 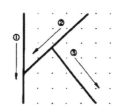 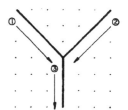

Strokes for typical angled line letters are shown. In each case the sequence is designed to set the correct proportion -- width vs. height -- for the letter.

The W is the widest letter. It is wider than it is tall.

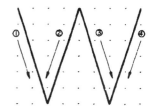

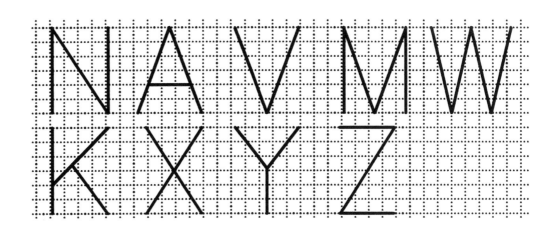

Find a comfortable position on the desk when lettering. Angle the paper so you can make a vertical stroke with a straight pull of the fingers. Be sure your elbow is on the table. It is very tiring to letter without proper arm support. Move the page occasionally as you work across.

Curved Line Letters

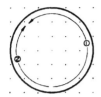 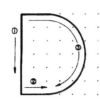 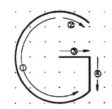 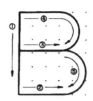 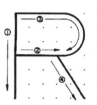

The sequence for forming typical curved line letters is shown. Use the grids to proportion the shapes.

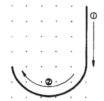

Computer generated curved line letters.

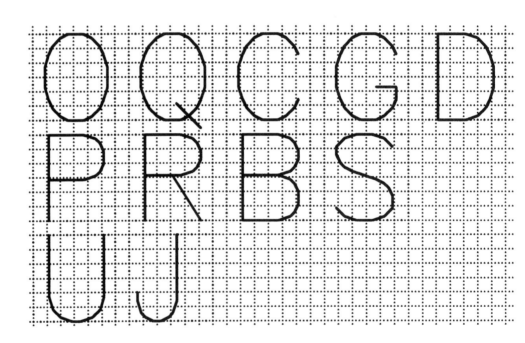

Computer generated numerals.

Notice the open form for the recommended shapes.

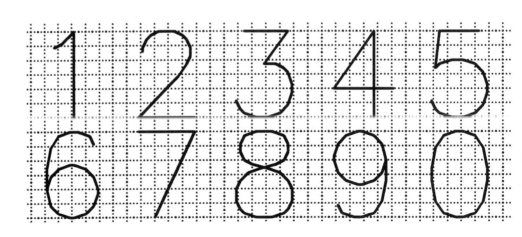

Spacing Letters and Words

The "M-A" distance is less than the "N-I-L" distance

Well - spaced lettering will have about the same <u>area</u> between each letter. This means that the distance between letters must be adjusted. Look carefully at the spacing examples shown.

Leave the space of a letter "O" as the distance between words.

These examples are computer proportional spaced text.

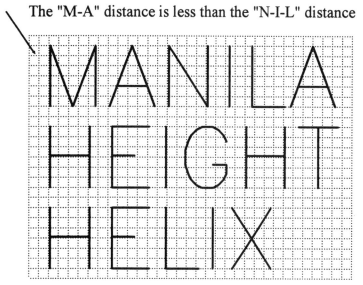

This example uses computer text with mono-spacing. Each letter is the same width and the same distance from the other letters. These words do not look as good as the previous examples.

Mono-spaced text is needed when words or numbers must line up in boxes or parts lists.

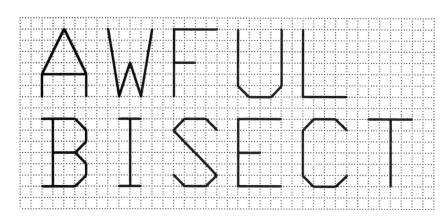

Isometric Lettering

Special lettering styles are needed for effect. In this example, the letters must "flow" with the angle of the drawing. Letters in the front actually back-slant at 30 degrees. Letters in the top and side areas forward-slant at 30 degrees.

Hold two pencils at 90 degrees and align them with the letters. Verify the slants.

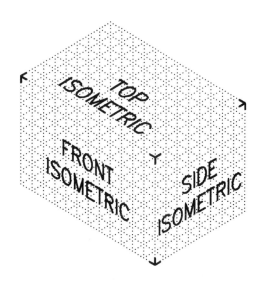

FREEHAND LETTERING

TEXT ON ENGINEERING DRAWINGS IS USUALLY LETTERED FREEHAND IN THE
FORM SHOWN ON THIS PAGE.   LETTERS ARE VERTICAL CAPITAL ROMAN
SIMPLEX FONT.   FORM MUST BE OPEN AND VERY CLEAR TO DUPLICATE AND
MICROFILM CLEARLY.   SLANTED OR "STYLIZED" LETTERS ARE AVOIDED.

MANY ENGINEERS AND DRAFTERS MAY WORK ON A PARTICULAR DRAWING SET.
TO MAINTAIN CONSISTENT APPEARANCE EACH PROFESSIONAL SHOULD USE
THE SAME LETTERING STYLE.

*ARCHITECTURAL AND CIVIL DRAWINGS MAY USE SLANTED LETTERS. AN ANGLE
OF 12.5 DEGREES   IS PREFERED.*

GUIDE LINES ARE USED TO KEEP LETTERS A CONSISTENT HEIGHT. LIGHT
LINES MAY BE DRAWN USING A 6H OR 4H LEAD. SINCE DRAWINGS ARE
USUALLY CREATED ON TRANSPARENT MYLAR OR VELLUM PAPER, A
"UNDERLAY" SHEET WITH GUIDE LINES MAY BE POSITIONED UNDER THE
AREA TO GUIDE THE LETTERING.

SPACING BETWEEN LETTERS MUST BE <u>ADJUSTED.</u>   TRY TO KEEP EQUAL
AREAS BETWEEN EACH LETTER. THE DISTANCE BETWEEN A "N" AND A "M" IS
GREATER THAN THE DISTANCE BETWEEN A "V" AND A "M", FOR EXAMPLE.

ENGINEERS MUST DEVELOP THE ABILITY TO LETTER CLEARLY, FREEHAND.
GOOD LETTERING REQUIRES PRACTICE. LETTER <u>EVERYTHING</u> — NOTES,
HOMEWORK, YOUR NAME ... ETC. WORK FOR PROFESSIONAL QUALITY.
YES, COMPUTERS CAN LETTER PERFECTLY ON DRAWINGS BUT THIS IS
ONE MANUAL SKILL THAT IS STILL ESSENTIAL.

LETTERS ARE FORMED BY A SERIES OF STROKES. PULL THE LEAD ACROSS
THE PAPER — NEVER PUSH THE LEAD AS IT WILL CATCH, TEAR, BREAK.
HOLD THE AUTOMATIC PENCIL NEARLY VERTICAL AND <u>PRESS DOWN HARD.</u>
NOTE THE STROKE SEQUENCE SHOWN IN THIS CHAPTER.
THE STROKES ARE SHOWN FOR RIGHT—HANDED PERSONS. LEFT—HANDED
PERSONS SHOULD DEVELOP THEIR OWN SEQUENCE.

STROKES ARE PROGRAMMED TO ASSURE CORRECT LETTER PROPORTIONS.
NOTE THE <u>WIDTH vs HEIGHT</u> PROPORTIONS FOR EACH LETTER AND NUMBER.

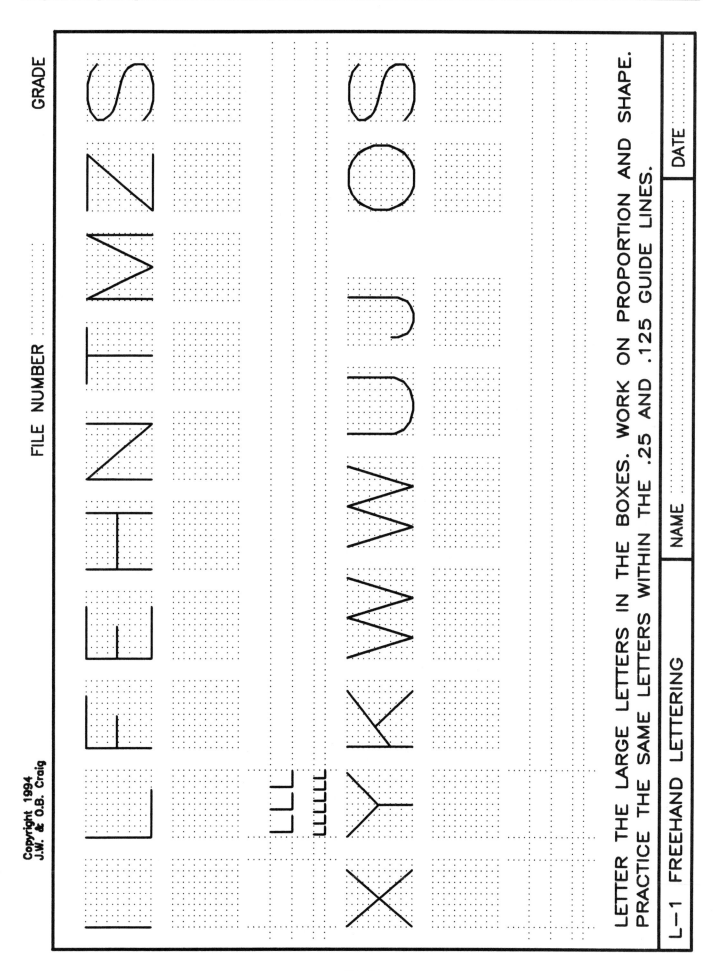

GRADE

FILE NUMBER

LETTER THE LARGE LETTERS IN THE BOXES. WORK ON PROPORTION AND SHAPE.
PRACTICE THE SAME LETTERS WITHIN THE .25 AND .125 GUIDE LINES.

| L—1 FREEHAND LETTERING | NAME | DATE |

NAME

DATE

FILE NUMBER

GRADE

FILE NUMBER   GRADE

O C G D P R B S S

1 2 3 4 5 6 7 8 9 0

LETTER THE LARGE LETTERS IN THE BOXES. WORK ON PROPORTION AND SHAPE. PRACTICE THE SAME LETTERS WITHIN THE .25 AND .125 GUIDE LINES.

L–2 FREEHAND LETTERING   NAME   DATE

NAME

DATE

FILE NUMBER

GRADE

GRADE

FILE NUMBER

DRAWING DEFINITIONS: LETTER ON THE LINES BELOW. (WEBSTERS)

ORTHOGRAPHIC PROJECTION WAS DEFINED IN 1668.

PROJECTION OF A SINGLE VIEW OF AN OBJECT ON A DRAWING SURFACE

THAT IS PERPENDICULAR TO BOTH THE VIEW AND THE LINES OF PROJECTION.

ISOMETRIC PROJECTION WAS DEFINED IN 1840

AXONOMETRIC PROJECTION IN WHICH ALL THREE FACES ARE EQUALLY

INCLINED TO THE DRAWING SURFACE SO THAT ALL THE EDGES

ARE EQUALLY FORESHORTENED.   ABBREVIATIONS: C.I. = CAST IRON

F.A.O = FINISH ALL OVER C'BORE = COUNTERBORE C'SK = COUNTERSINK

L—3	LETTERING PRACTICE	NAME	DATE

NAME

DATE

FILE NUMBER

GRADE

GRADE

FILE NUMBER

DRAWING DEFINITIONS: LETTER ON THE LINES BELOW.

A.N.S.I = AMERICAN NATIONAL STANDARDS INSTITUTE   S.I = METRIC SYSTEM

1 INCH = 25.4 MILLIMETERS   1 POUND = .45 KILOGRAMS

1 GALLON = 3.8 LITERS   1 CUBIC INCH = 16.4 CUBIC CENTIMETERS

CAD = COMPUTER AIDED DRAWING / DESIGN   I/O = INPUT - OUTPUT

DOS = DISK OPERATING SYSTEM   CRT = CATHODE RAY TUBE

RASTER SCAN = CRT WITH ELECTRON BEAM MOVING IN X-Y PATTERN

FLOPPY DISK = FLEXIBLE DISK USED TO STORE COMPUTER DATA.

CAM = COMPUTER AIDED MANUFACTURING   N/C = NUMERICAL CONTROL

L-4   LETTERING PRACTICE   NAME   DATE

NAME

DATE

FILE NUMBER

GRADE

Introduction to Freehand Sketching

Sketching is a very important technique for technical communication. Sketches can transfer ideas, instructions and information in a clear, concise form. "Thinking with a pencil" is a practice designers use to bring ideas and mental pictures to reality. Freehand sketches are often the first view of new designs. Long before formal drawings are made or computer models are created, a series of detailed sketches are analyzed and approved.

Sketching is a personal skill which everyone can improve.

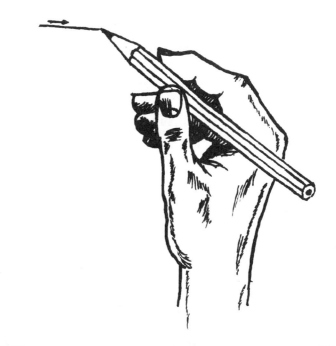

Sketching tools include:
__Pencil or leadholder.
__Leads: "H", "F" or "HB" hardness.
__Eraser: pink type preferred or white.
__Sketching paper: rectangular grid, isometric grid, vellum overlay, newsprint, etc.
__Straightedge.
__Circle and ellipse templates.
__Plastic triangles.
__Gadgets like tiny drafting machines, roller parallel tools, etc.

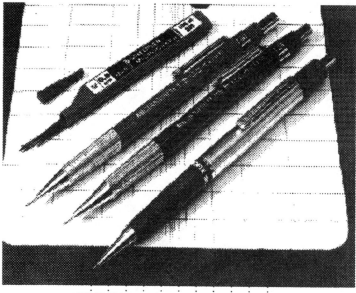

Designers may use a variety of these tools when many sketches are to be made. Since sketches may be needed quickly, it is best to rely only on pencil, paper and eraser.

Printed grids or papers with lightly ruled lines are often used for sketching. The grids are used to keep freehand lines straight. Grids may also be used to create accurately scaled sketches, keeping the drawing in correct proportion.

Grids act as guides for sketching. They help keep lines straight and in correct proportion.

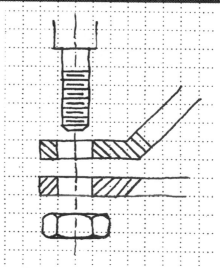

Using Sketching Grids

Grids may be used to keep features in correct X - Y scale. The rounded corner is measured three units horizontal, three units vertical and a construction point is measured half-way around the arc.

Sketches must be very neat and proportional to the real objects.

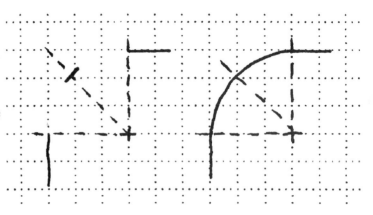

Engineering and architectural forms are available with many guide line spacings. 1/4 inch forms are common. Sketches of objects may be scaled down (or up) to fit the sheet size. The examples show several possible scale factors.

Accurately scaled sketches are needed to convey proportions.

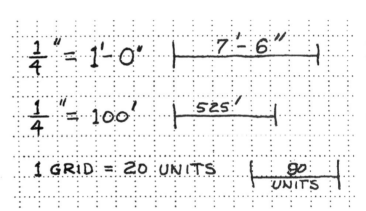

This sketch of a small room is drawn to a scale of 1/4" = 1'-0". It indicates the room is about 9'-6" wide by 11'-0" deep. The bookcase is 14" deep and 5' wide. Other furnishings are sketched to scale.

Scaled sketches are often the first step in working out the sizes and proportions for a design.

Sketches may be created anywhere and at any time with a minimum of tools. Neat sketches convey accurate information. Professionals take pride in the appearance and accuracy of their sketches.

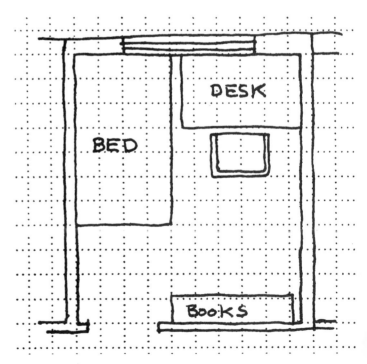

Sketching Arcs and Circles

Construction lines and points will improve the appearance of freehand circles. It takes only a few seconds to block in horizontal, vertical and 45 degree points shown. These points help when sketching the arcs for the circle.

The edge of a piece of paper may be used as a gage for measuring points on a circle.

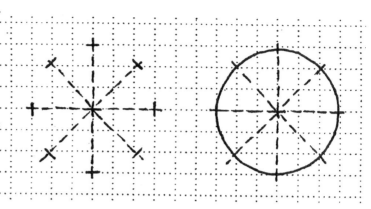

Tangent points define the extent of an arc. Tangent points are located by sketching a line from the center of the arc or circle perpendicular to the tangent line. These points show where the arc ends and the straight line begins.

Locating tangent points will improve the appearance of sketches.

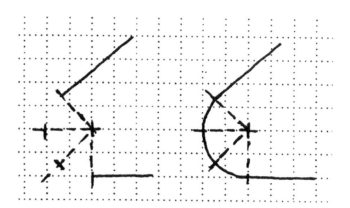

When two circles are tangent, the tangent point s on the line connecting the centers. This point shows where one arc ends and the other begins.

There are only two rules to remember when locating tangent points:
1. The point of tangency between a line and a circle is on the line perpendicular through the center of the circle.
2. The point of tangency between two circles is on the line connecting the centers of the circles.

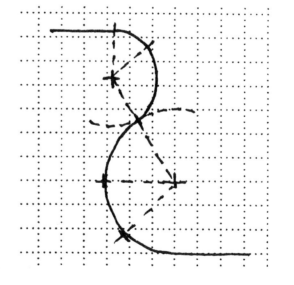

Ellipses may be sketched using four arcs. Sketch a small arc at each side and a longer arc across the top and bottom.

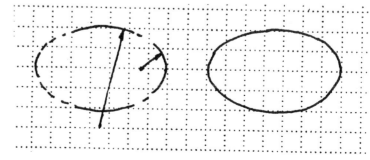

Sketching Techniques

Block in the entire circle even if only a part of the circle will be needed. This helps space the object and verify proportions.
__Sketch the three circles.
__Sketch the lines tangent to the circles.
__Sketch each radius perpendicular to each tangent line.

These constructions will locate points needed for darkening-in the final shape.

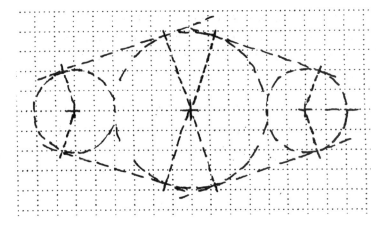

The final shape is sketched by pressing down hard on the pencil to create a smooth black outline.

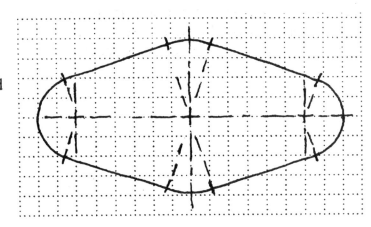

Geometric shapes like this hexagon are based on first sketching a circle. Draw the hexagon using the circle as a control surface. Construct tangent lines at approximately 60 degrees (in this case).

Blacken the lines for the final shape.

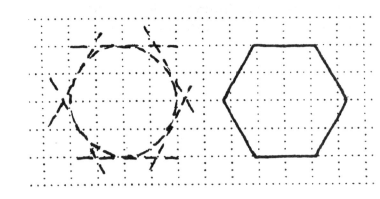

An octagon has eight sides.
__Sketch a circle.
__Sketch horizontal and vertical lines tangent to the circle.
__Sketch lines from the center of the circle at 45 degrees. (Use the diagonals of the grid boxes.)
__Sketch lines perpendicular at each diagonal.
__Blacken-in the octagonal shape.

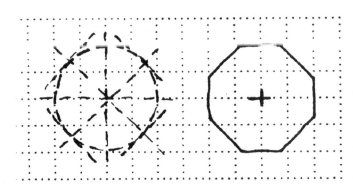

Pictorial Sketches

Pictorial sketches are easier if an isometric sketching grid is used. By following the angles of the guide lines, the shape of the front, top and side faces may be sketched.

Isometric axes are 30 degrees upward to the left (width), 30 degrees upward to the right (depth) and vertical (height).

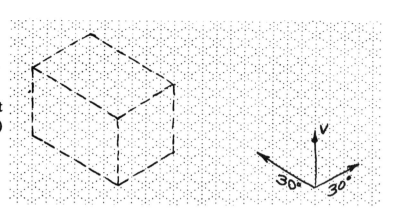

Pictorial sketches show three faces of a three dimensional object. This type of sketch helps designers and viewers portray three dimensional shapes quickly.

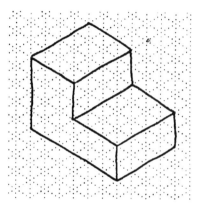

Circular shapes appear as ellipses on pictorial sketches. 4-center ellipses are often sketched or drawn. Centers are located by construction lines.

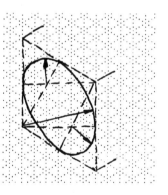

Pictorial sketch of a counter bored hole.

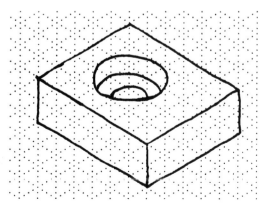

ANSI Linetypes

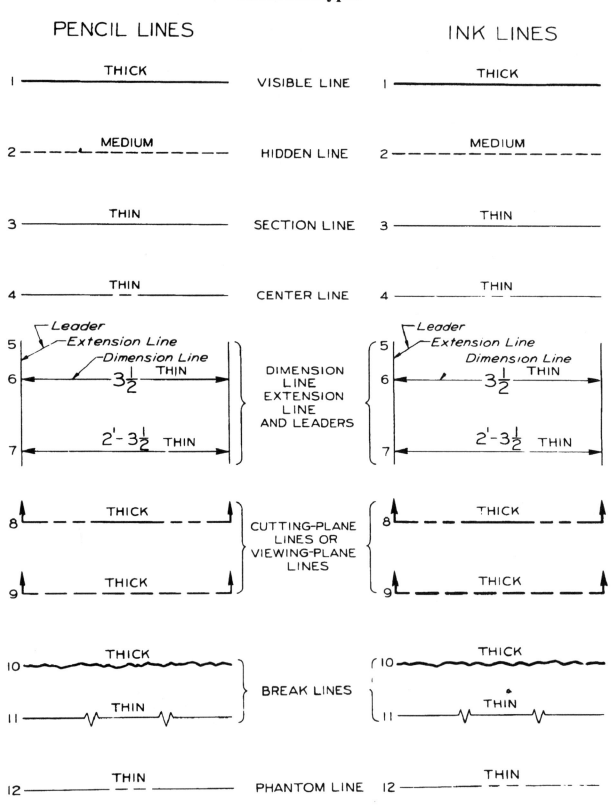

WIDTH AND CHARACTER OF LINES

FIGURE 1

Extracted from American National Standards Institute Y14.2

Drawing Sizes - Copying Large Drawings

Drawings may require very
large sheet sizes. Standard sizes
are labeled:
__A = 8 1/2 x 11
__B = 11 x 17
__C = 17 x 22 etc.

(Figure extracted from A.N.S.I
Y14.1).

Drawings are created on transparent paper or plastic film. The
reason the material is transparent relates to the copy process
used to duplicate drawings.
Many drawings are copied using
the diazo process. This process
allows large sheets to be duplicated at relatively low cost.

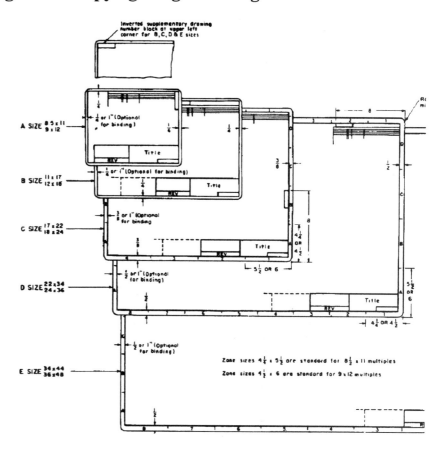

Prints are made by copying
through the original. The copy
paper is placed underneath. A
bright light shines through from
the top. Lines must be very
black to prevent light from pass-
ing through.

In commercial machines a mer-
cury-vapor light is placed inside
a glass cylinder. The original and
copy paper roll around the cylinder during exposure. Very long
drawings may be duplicated this
way.

Hot ammonia gas is used to develop the dry copy.

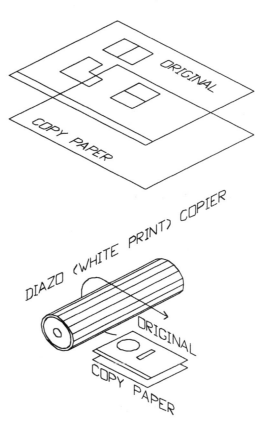

NAME

DATE

FILE NUMBER

GRADE

GRADE

FILE NUMBER

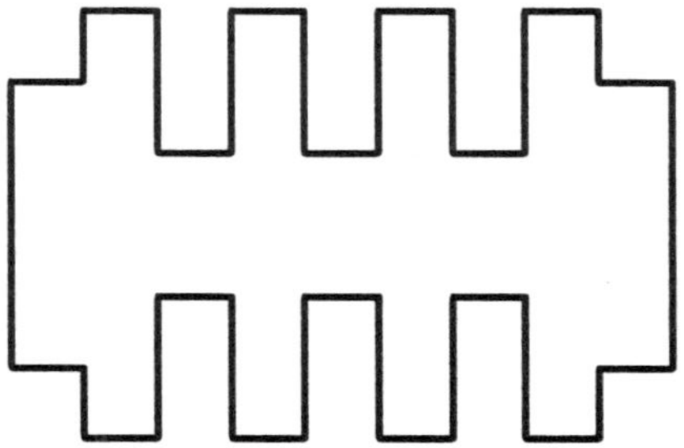

SKETCH THE SHAPE
SHOWN 2X SIZE
ON THE GRID
BELOW.
BLACKEN LINES.
(WHEN LINES ARE
BLACK, DOTS WILL
NOT SHOW).

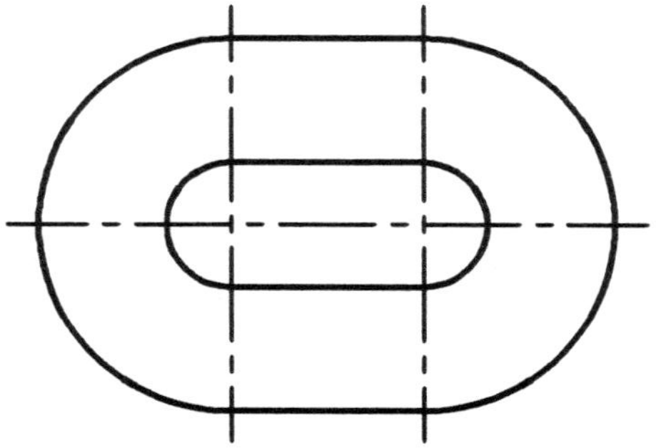

SKETCH THE SHAPE
SHOWN 2X SIZE
ON THE GRID
BELOW.
BLACKEN LINES.
(WHEN LINES ARE
BLACK, DOTS WILL
NOT SHOW).

DATE

NAME

SK—1   FREEHAND SKETCHING

SK-2 FREEHAND SKETCHING

NAME

DATE

FILE NUMBER

GRADE

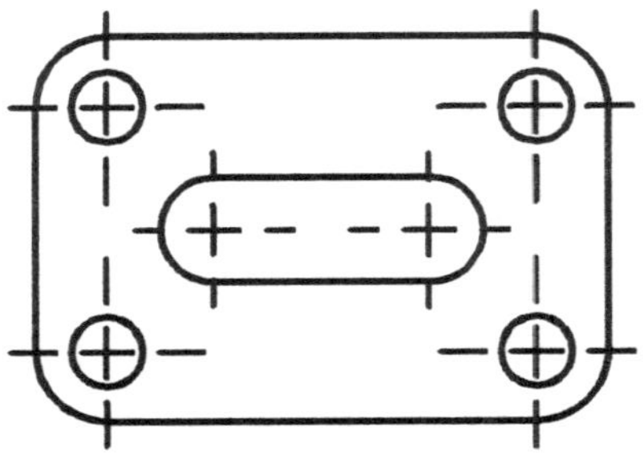

SKETCH THE SHAPE
SHOWN 2X SIZE
ON THE GRID
BELOW.
BLACKEN LINES.
(WHEN LINES ARE
BLACK, DOTS
WILL NOT SHOW).

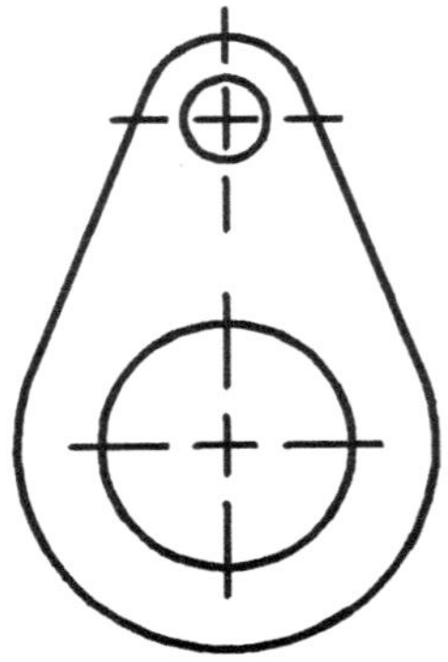

SKETCH THE SHAPE
SHOWN 2X SIZE
ON THE GRID
BELOW.
BLACKEN LINES.
(WHEN LINES ARE
BLACK, DOTS
WILL NOT SHOW).

GRADE

FILE NUMBER

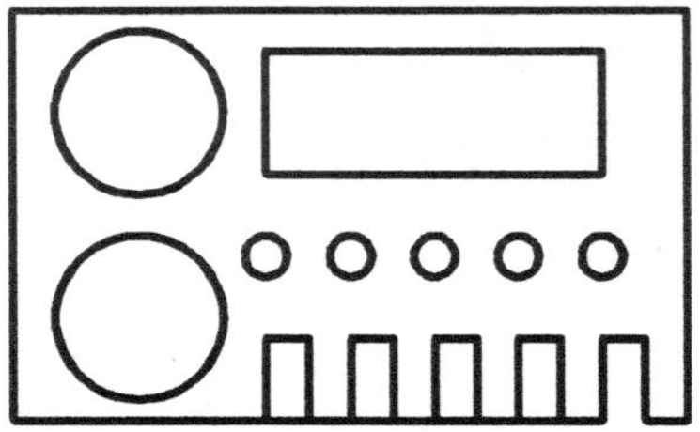

SKETCH THE
ELECTRONIC CIRCUIT
BOARD 2X SIZE
ON THE GRID.

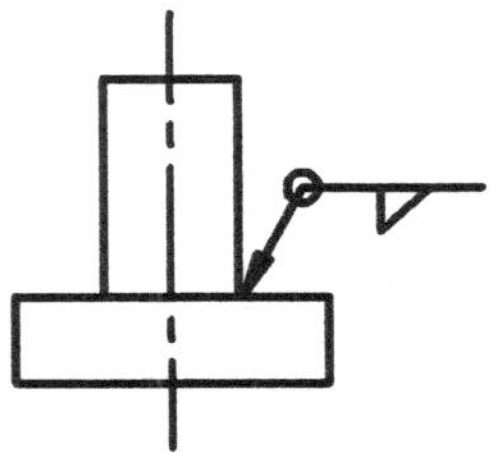

SKETCH THE DRAWING
AND WELD SYMBOL
2X SIZE ON THE GRID.
(TWO CYLINDRICAL PARTS
ARE TO BE WELDED
ALL-AROUND USING A
FILLET WELD).

(EXAMPLE. DO NOT SKETCH.)

FILLET WELD

DATE

NAME

SK-3 FREEHAND SKETCHING

BRICK

WOOD

CONCRETE

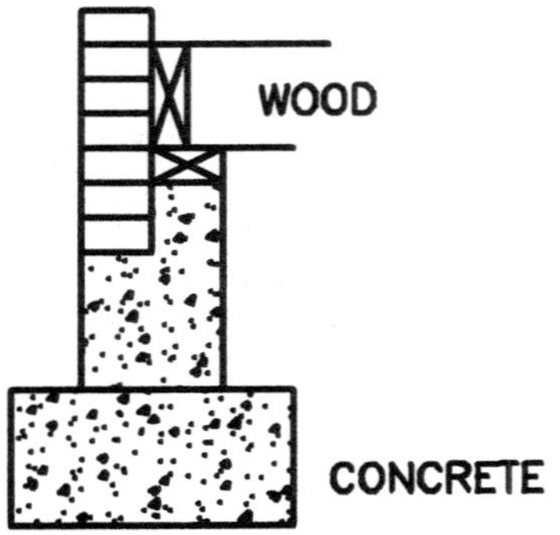

SKETCH THE FOUNDATION
DETAIL 2X SIZE ON
THE GRID.
BLACKEN LINES.
INCLUDE CONCRETE
CROSSHATCH PATTERN.

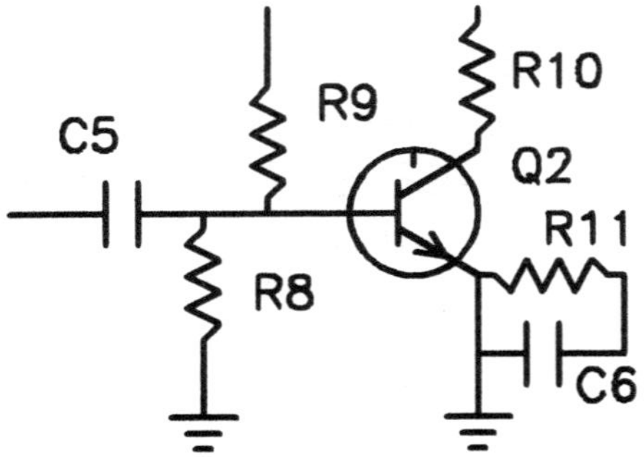

SK-4 FREEHAND SKETCHING

NAME

FILE NUMBER ....

C5

R8

R9

R10

Q2

R11

C6

SKETCH THE
SCHEMATIC 2X
SIZE ON THE
GRID.
MAKE LETTERS
1/8" HEIGHT.

DATE

GRADE

GRADE

FILE NUMBER

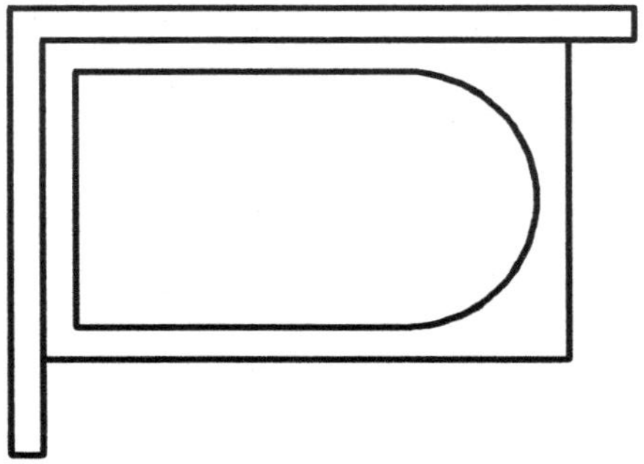

SKETCH THE
CORNER BATHTUB
2X SIZE IN THE
SPACE BELOW.
BLACKEN LINES

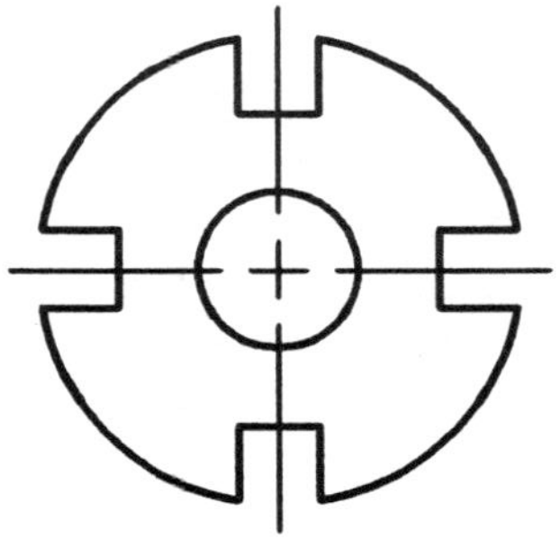

SKETCH THE SHAPE
2X SIZE IN THE
SPACE BELOW.
BLACKEN LINES.

DATE

NAME

SK—5　FREEHAND SKETCHING

SK-6 FREEHAND SKETCHING

NAME

DATE

FILE NUMBER

GRADE

HEXAGON

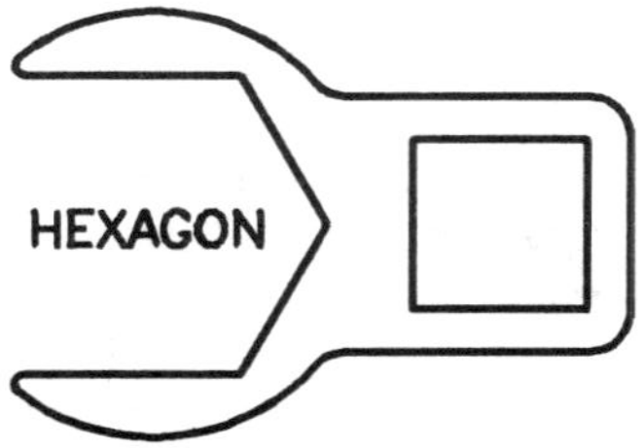

SKETCH THE
CROWS-FOOT
WRENCH 2X SIZE
IN THE SPACE
BELOW.
BLACKEN LINES.

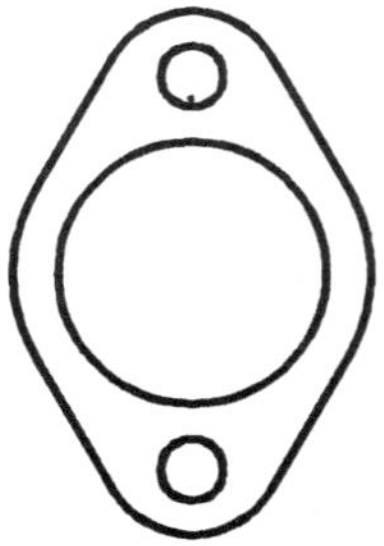

SKETCH THE
POWER TRANSISTOR
2X SIZE IN THE SPACE
BELOW.
BLACKEN LINES.

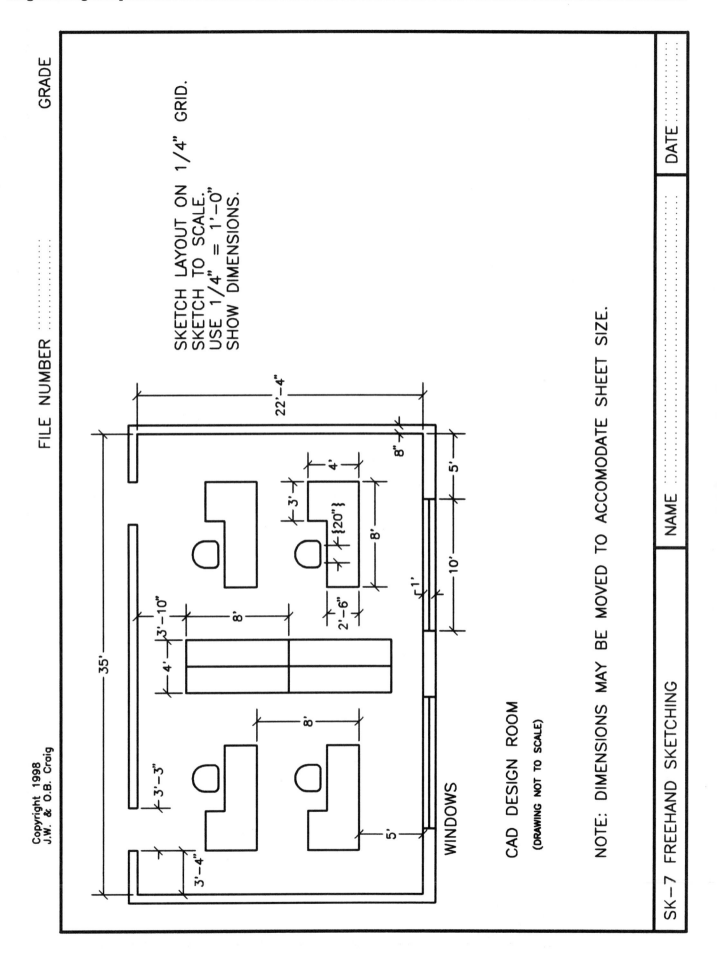

SKETCH LAYOUT ON 1/4" GRID.
SKETCH TO SCALE.
USE 1/4" = 1'-0"
SHOW DIMENSIONS.

22'-4"

8"

5'

4'

3'

{20"}

8'

2'-6"

1'

10'

35'

3'-10"

8'

4'

8'

3'-3"

WINDOWS

CAD DESIGN ROOM
(DRAWING NOT TO SCALE)

3'-4"

5'

NOTE: DIMENSIONS MAY BE MOVED TO ACCOMODATE SHEET SIZE.

GRADE

FILE NUMBER

DATE

NAME

SK-7 FREEHAND SKETCHING

NAME

DATE

FILE NUMBER

GRADE

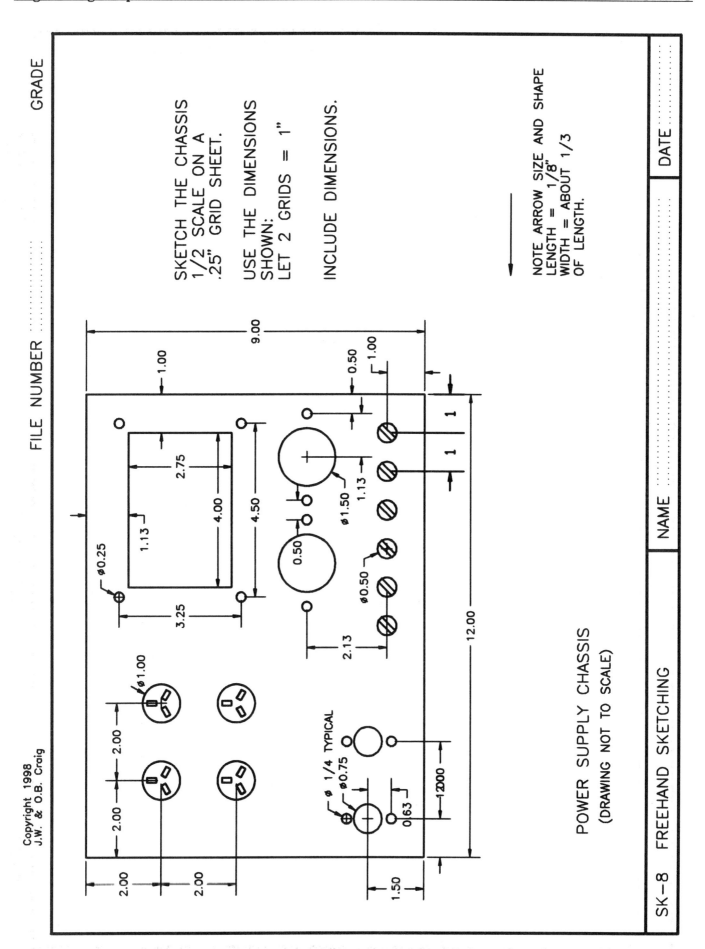

SKETCH THE CHASSIS
1/2 SCALE ON A
.25" GRID SHEET.

USE THE DIMENSIONS
SHOWN:
LET 2 GRIDS = 1"

INCLUDE DIMENSIONS.

NOTE ARROW SIZE AND SHAPE
LENGTH = 1/8"
WIDTH = ABOUT 1/3
OF LENGTH.

POWER SUPPLY CHASSIS
(DRAWING NOT TO SCALE)

SK–8   FREEHAND SKETCHING

GRADE

FILE NUMBER

NAME

DATE

Copyright 1998
J.W. & O.B. Craig

NAME

DATE

FILE NUMBER

GRADE

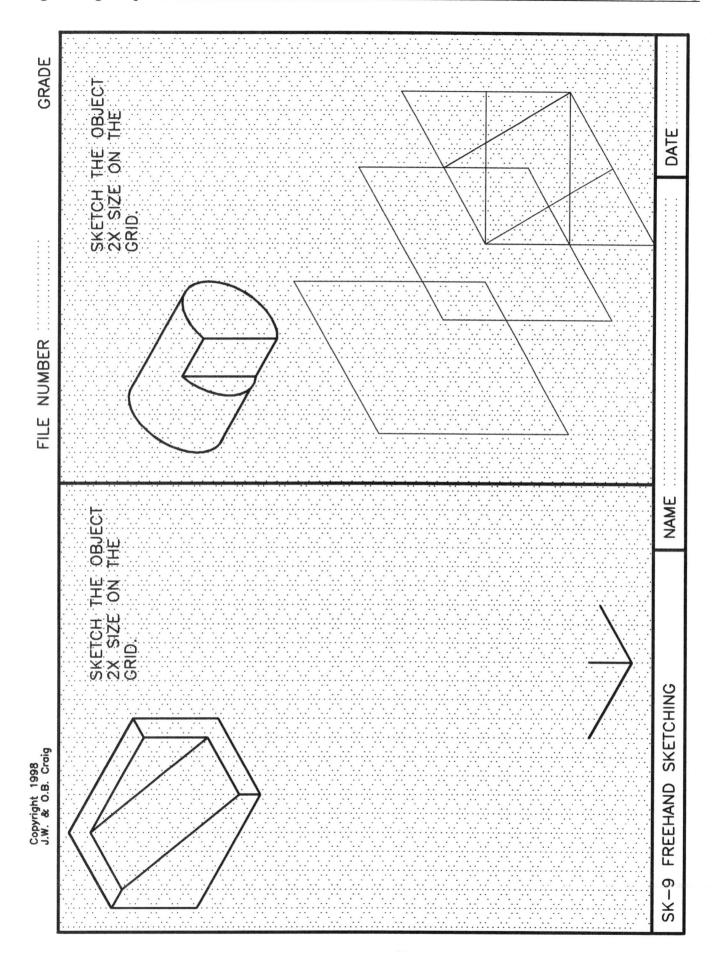

SKETCH THE OBJECT
2X SIZE ON THE
GRID.

SKETCH THE OBJECT
2X SIZE ON THE
GRID.

GRADE

FILE NUMBER

DATE

NAME

SK-9 FREEHAND SKETCHING

name

date

NOTE: Use this grid format
in horizontal direction.

FILE NUMBER

GRADE

INTRODUCTION
SURFACES AND EDGES
ORTHOGRAPHIC PROJECTION

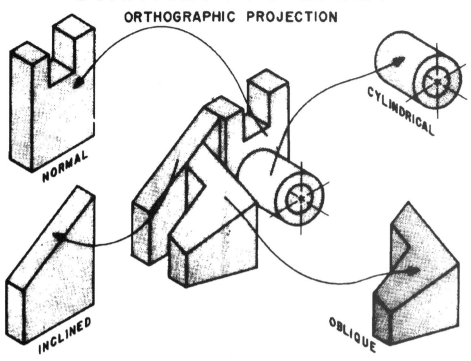

People who work with drawings develop the ability to look at lines on paper or on a computer screen and "see" the shapes of the objects the lines represent. Visualization is an essential skill when working with technical information. Architects, engineers, machinists, carpenters, welders, installers -- many types of workers create or use drawings. Technical drawings and sketches provide a clear, concise, exact method of representing three-dimensional information. Starting at the Industrial Revolution the process and theory of technical drawing has evolved into a universal graphical language.

How do people who work with drawings think about the lines they see? What is the mental process that allows skilled workers to quickly interpret abstract lines, curves and shapes to form an exact mental image of the objects represented? Part of the answer is that these people rapidly recognize and analyze basic types of surfaces. Once individual surfaces are recognized, then the interfaces -- common edges and intersections -- between the surfaces may be visualized. With practice this process becomes very rapid.

In the next four chapters much emphasis will be placed on recognizing types of plane and curved surfaces in space. Only three types of plane (flat) surfaces exist. Many types of curved surfaces -- cylinders, cones, spheres, torus, etc. -- exist. By recognizing each type of surface, rules may be applied to the appearance of the surface on drawings. Visualizing objects is a process of assembling the individual surfaces into shapes then into objects. Portions may be solved by following rules before the actual answer is apparent. Objects may be solved in much the same way a mathematical expression is solved.

Learning to visualize objects is an individual skill. Making clay models or LEGO (tm) models is an excellent step. Seeing the answer from someone else destroys all chance to learn. Problems at the end of each chapter are designed to develop visualization skills. Work on each problem for short time. If the answer is not apparent, come back to the problem later.

Pictorial vs. Orthographic Views

Pictorial drawings give quick three-dimensional views of objects. They are often used for advertising, repair manuals, and general information. Shapes are easier to visualize and intersections of surfaces can be seen.

Pictorials distort the lengths of lines and angles at corners. These drawings cannot be used for production.

This drawing is an *isometric* pictorial.

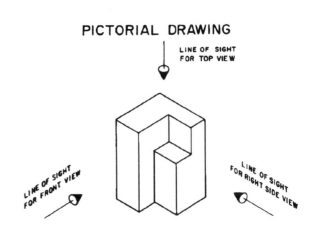

Production (detail) drawings describe the shape of the object by looking directly at the faces of the object. In this way the true length lines and true angles at corners may be seen. Multiple views are needed. These views are two-dimensional. Views are obtained by looking in the direction of the arrows shown in the isometric above.

Multiple views are needed. FRONT, TOP and RIGHT SIDE views are used here.

Dimensions and notes give size and manufacturing instructions. Dimensions are placed where the shape shows best.

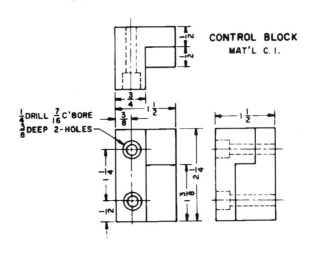

Engineers, architects and designers "see" objects in pictorial mental images. They must convert pictorial ideas into orthographic form for production. Workers and others must convert the orthographic drawings back into pictorial images in order to analyze the shapes and use the information. The transition from pictorial - to orthographic - to pictorial is a constant process.

By far, the most difficult step is converting orthographic drawings to pictorials. This process requires looking at two-dimensional images to get three-dimensional shapes.

Computer modeling is simplifying this problem.

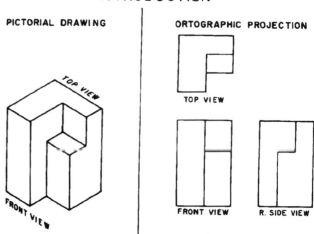

Multiple View Drawings

Orthographic views may be obtained by placing an object inside a "glass box". Faces of the box are at right angles. Surfaces on the object are aligned parallel to the faces of the box when possible. Views are drawn by projecting lines and surfaces to each face of the box.

Orthographic views are two-dimensional.

In the front view there is no way to show the difference in level (depth) between the surfaces.

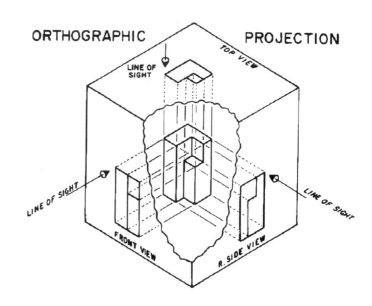

Projection planes of the glass box are perpendicular to each other. Three regular planes are shown. Left side, bottom and back planes may also be used.

These planes are also used by computer graphics systems.

The line of sight for each view is perpendicular to each projection plane. Looking perpendicular to a plane gives the true size of the plane in a particular view -- the other projection planes appear in edge-view.

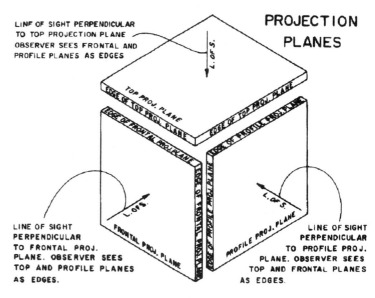

Surface 1,2,3,4 is parallel to the front projection plane. It will appear as a surface (true size) in the front view.

In the top view 1,2,3,4 appears as edge-of surface A-B.

In the side view 1,2,3,4 appears as edge-of-surface C-D.

Reading orthographic views involves integrating this type of information about every surface on the object.

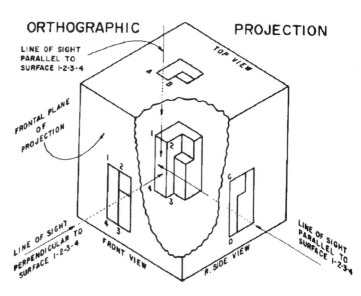

Six Regular Orthographic Views

Six regular views of an object may be projected.

Rule: Each feature of an object must be shown as visible lines in at least one view.

Drafters must decide which views to draw. Sometimes additional (auxiliary) views are needed to clarify shapes and remove ambiguities. Dimensions, for example, must be placed on the "true shape" views. Partial views may be drawn.

Notice the hinge locations when unfolding the plastic box. Observe the alignment of the views: front-top-bottom, and front-right-left-back. <u>Views must be placed on the page or computer screen in this form.</u>

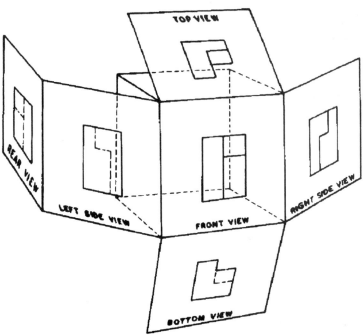

THE PLASTIC BOX

This graphic shows the AMERICAN STANDARD
 ARRANGEMENT OF VIEWS.
Views must be sketched or drawn according to this alignment.

People who work with drawings expect to find the views of objects in this form.

Front, top and bottom views <u>must be</u> aligned vertically. All corners and features must project vertically.

Front, right side, left side and back views <u>must be</u> aligned horizontally. Features and corners must project horizontally.

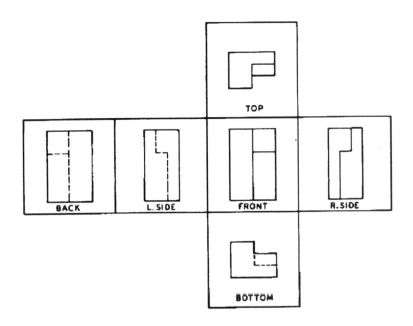

ORTHOGRAPHIC PROJECTION

Orthographic Views are Two-Dimensional

Surfaces on an object are at different levels.
__A is more to the front, then B, then C
__D is more to the top, then E
__F is more to the right, G is more to the left.

If a line separates two surfaces, there must be a
difference in level between the surfaces.

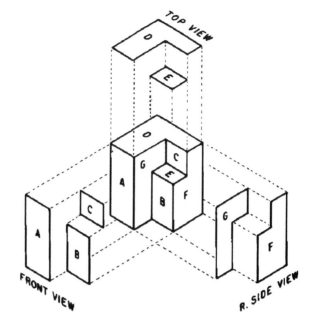

When surfaces A, B and C are projected to the
front projection plane, they appear next to
each other. The person reading the drawing
must look at an adjacent (top or side) view to
see which surface is in front.

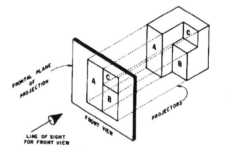

When F and G are projected to the side view,
they appear next to each other. The surfaces
are at different levels. Look at the front or top
views to see which surface is more to the right
or left.

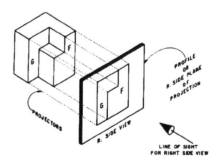

D and E appear next to each other in the top
view. Look at the front or side views to see
which surface is higher and which surface is set
down lower.

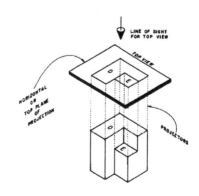

Common Dimensions Between Views

Major dimensions for objects are commonly named HEIGHT, WIDTH AND DEPTH. Orthographic views are two-dimensional so each view can show only two of the three dimensions.

In any two adjacent views, all three dimensions may be seen.

WIDTH is the common dimension between the front, top (and bottom) views.
__Top view shows width and depth
__Front view shows width and height.

Width is projected vertically between the views.

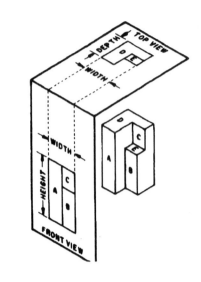

HEIGHT is the common dimension between the front, right side, (left side and back) views.
__Front view shows height and width
__Side view shows height and depth.

Height is projected horizontally between the views.

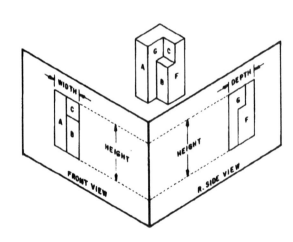

DEPTH is the common dimension between the top and side views. While DEPTH is measured in a horizontal direction in space, it must be measured in a vertical direction in the top view.
__Side view shows depth and height
__Top view shows depth and width.

Depth is measured horizontally in the side view and vertically in the top view.

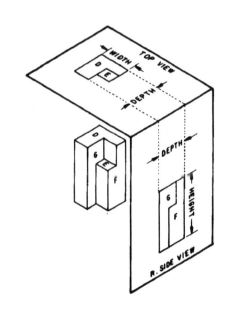

Transferring the DEPTH Dimension

Several methods of transferring depth are shown. Dividers are the quickest and most accurate tool. Use the paper method for plain paper sketches.

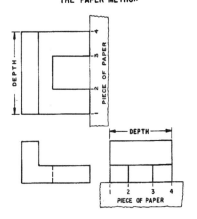

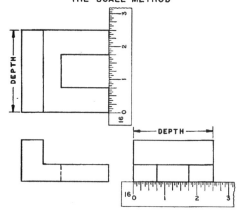

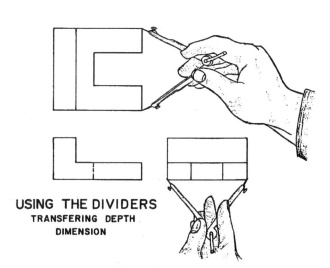

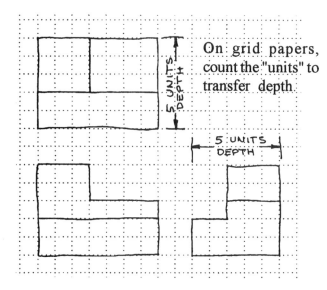

A miter line may be used to geometrically transfer depth from the side-to-top and the top-to-side views. This technique is used on drawings created with T-squares or drafting machines. This technique may be used to transfer depth measurements on computer drawings.

The miter line technique may be used on CAD drawings.

ANALYSIS OF VIEWS

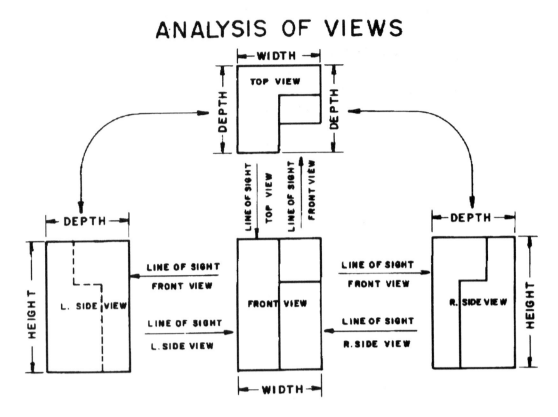

Views are shown in standard arrangement. Notice the common dimensions between the views. Also, note the line of sight between the views. For example, the arrow shows the direction to look at the front view to get the side view. And, the direction to look at the side view to get the front view.

Actually holding an object and turning it as shown will help verify the views and the projection theory on previous examples. Be sure you turn the object correctly to draw each view. At first people tend to draw some views backward!

Clay Models

Carving clay models of objects is the most effective way to experience the transition from real objects to paper drawings. Creating models from drawings will strongly reinforce the transition from abstract lines on paper to real objects.

Styrofoam packing blocks also make good modeling material.

THE DIRECT APPROACH

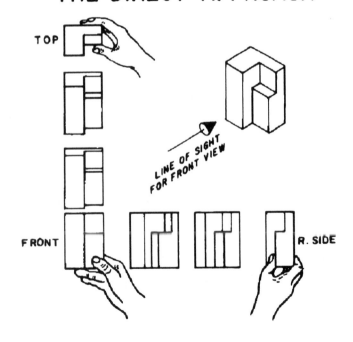

Visualizing Objects

Carving models (or just thinking through the steps) is an effective way to visualize objects. Starting with a solid block, observe the outlines of the top, front and side views. Cut away material from the object to leave the profiles shown.

No material is left in the open areas. This means that the object must be cut all the way across: top to bottom, front to back, right to left respectively.

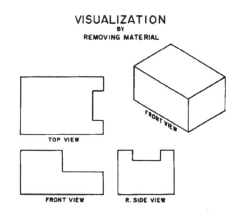

From the front view, cut away the block as shown.
This cut creates surfaces A and B.
__line 1,2 is added to the top view
__line 9,10 is added to the side view.

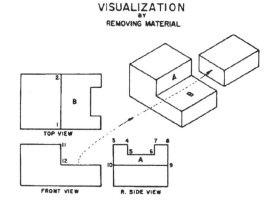

In the top view, remove the block shown. This creates surface C.
__Hidden line 1,2 is added to the front view.
__Lines 3,6 and 5,4 are added to the side view.

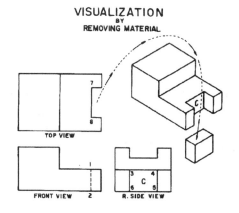

A similar process is used in computer solids modeling. "Tools" are shaped then mathematically subtracted from an object.

Cut the block from the top of the object. This completes the shape outlined in the first picture.
__Surface D is created
__line 1,2 is added to the front view
__line 3,4 and 5,6 are added to the top view.

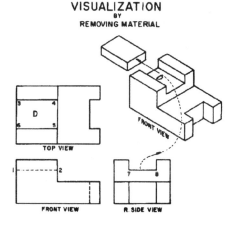

Building Objects by Joining Solids

Objects may be visualized by imagining the basic shapes which were joined.

Basic shapes include:
__cones
__rectangular solids
__cylinders
__pyramids
__torus
__spheres

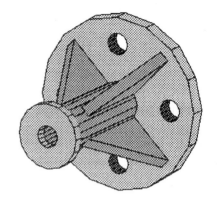

Pieces include cylinders and plates in this example.

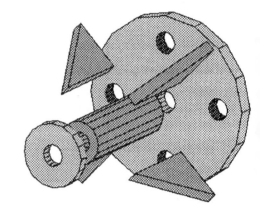

Objects are often combinations of added shapes minus subtracted shapes.

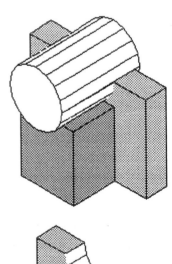

These concepts are used in computer solids modeling. Libraries of shapes may be provided which generate geometric solids. The solids may then be added together (union) or subtracted away.

Two rectangular solids are first joined together, then a cylinder is subtracted to create the final shape.

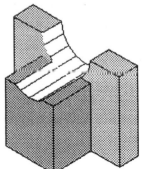

Linetypes Used on Drawings

A number of special linetypes are used on drawings. The most common line codes are shown:

__Object lines are solid lines which represent the visible edges of objects.

__Hidden lines represent features which cannot be seen. These lines must be shown to give complete information about the shape of the object. Hidden lines are short dashes- 1/8" or so.

__Center lines define the center geometry of holes or symmetry on an object. They are long-short dashed lines. 3/4" long and 1/8" short segments.

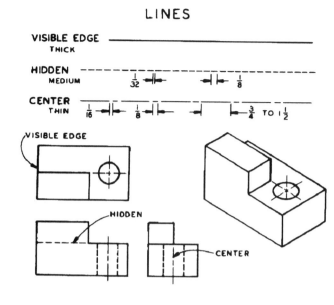

Examples of preferred hidden and center line representations are shown.

Center lines should intersect at the centers of circles.

Preferred hidden line intersections are shown.

CAD software does not always support these preferences.

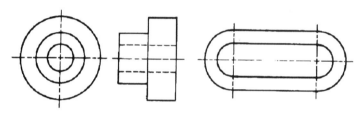

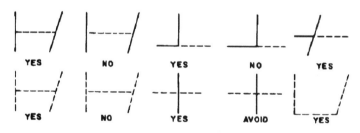

Visible edge lines are most important. They have precedence over other linetypes.

Hidden lines are second in importance. Often there are hidden lines behind visible lines on a drawing. The hidden lines cannot be shown because the visible lines are most important. This makes reading a drawing a bit harder.

Center lines have no visibility. They are least in importance.

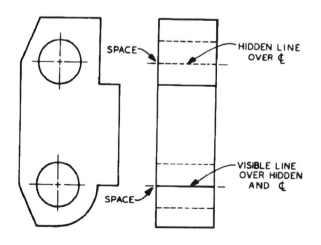

Creating Multi-view drawings from Pictorials

A pictorial shows the shape of the object for easier visualization.

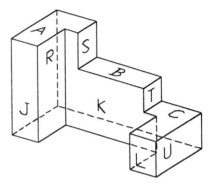

Identify the surfaces by placing a letter in each bounded area.

Sketch the top, front and side views by looking directly at each face.

__A, B and C are seen in the top view. They are at different levels to each other. (Top to bottom).

__J, K and L are seen in the front view. J and K are at different levels. L and K are at different levels. J and L are at the same level. (Front to back).

__R, S, T, and U are seen in the side view. They are all at different levels. (right to left). R extends down behind U creating the hidden line in the side view.

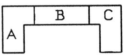

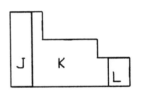

Orthographic front and top views ***must*** align vertically. Front and side views ***must*** align horizontally.

This object has normal, inclined, oblique and cylindrical surfaces.

__N1 and O are seen in the front.

__N2, N4, C (circular hole), I and O are seen in the top.

__N3, I and O are seen in the side view.

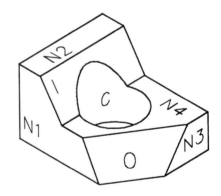

Note the location of each surface in each view:

FRONT:

__N2, N4, I and N3 appear as edge-of surface.

__N1 is a true size view, O is foreshortened.

TOP:

__N1, N3 and C (cylinder) appear as edge-of-surface. N2 and N4 are true size view.

__O and I are foreshortened.

SIDE:

__N1 and N2, N4 appear as an edge-of-surface

__O and I are foreshortened.

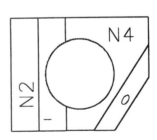

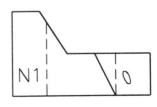

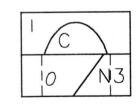

Creating Pictorial Views from Orthographic Views

Front, top and side views of an object are given. These views are complete with no missing lines.

Label surfaces by placing a letter (neatly!) in each surface. Labeling surfaces is important to assure that all surfaces are accounted for.

Sketch a box to enclose the pictorial:
__11 units width (upward to left)
__8 units height (vertical)
__8 units depth (upward to right).

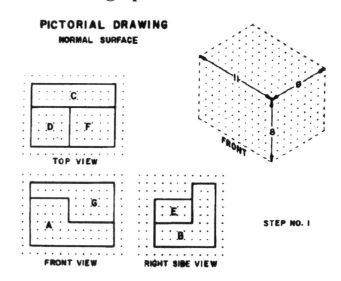

Sketch the surfaces on the outer faces of the isometric box first.

Surface A is seen from the front view.

Sketch surface A on the front face of the isometric box. Use the dimensions from the orthographic views.

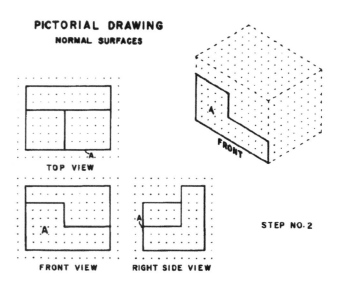

Surface B is seen in the right side view.

Sketch surface B on the right side face of the box. Surface A and surface B share an edge.

Sketching the surfaces on the faces of the isometric box helps locate corners which will be needed for other surfaces later.....

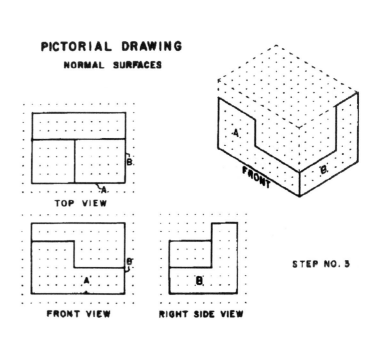

Sketching Isometric Pictorials

Surface C is seen from the top view.

Sketch C on the top plane of the isometric box.
Surface E and surface C share an edge.

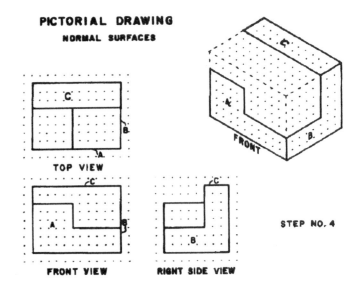

Surface D shares a horizontal edge with surface
A. D is parallel to C and two units below.

Sketch D on the pictorial starting at the top edge
of A and working back 5 units.

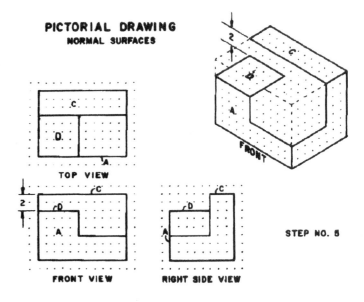

Surface E is parallel to surface B and 6 units to
the left of B. E shares a vertical edge with A.

Sketch E on the pictorial, starting at A and extending upward to the right 5 units.

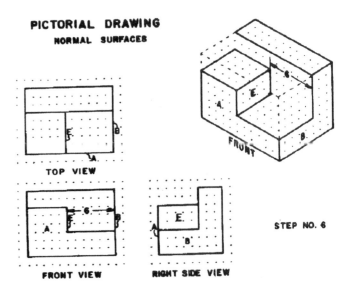

Isometric Pictorial

Surface F is seen from the top view. It is 3 units up from the bottom face. F shares an edge with A also.

Starting from A sketch F upward to the right 5 units deep and 6 units wide.

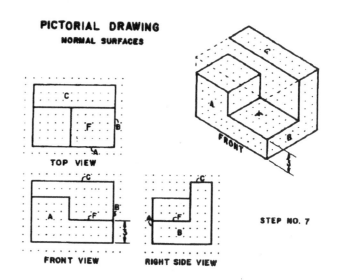

Surface G is seen from the front view. It shares edges with D, E, F, b and C.

Sketch the closed shape of surface G on the pictorial. This completes the view.

Hidden lines are usually not shown on pictorial views.

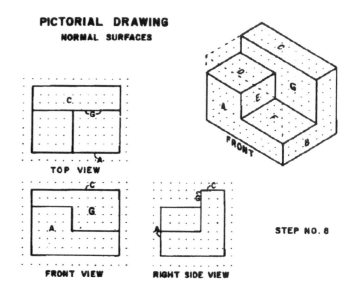

Normal Surface Pictorial

Label the surfaces on the object.

__Sketch (or draw) isometric box.
__Modify box per shape of top view.
__Locate surface A, B and C on the faces of the box.
__Sketch interior surfaces from common edges.

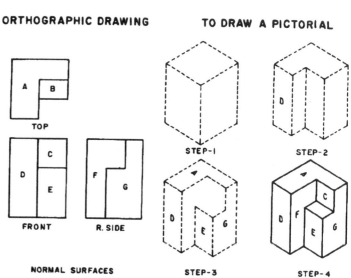

Inclined Surfaces on Pictorials

Inclined surfaces may be plotted by locating the endpoints on the inclined edges on the isometric axes. Sketch the angled lines by connecting the endpoints.

Measurements on Isometrics can only be made along the isometric axes.
__upward to the left (width)
__upward to the right (depth)
__vertical (height).

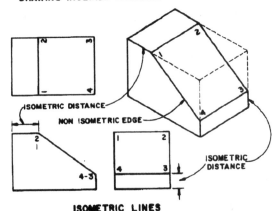

ISOMETRIC DRAWING

DRAWING INCLINED SURFACES IN ISOMETRIC

ISOMETRIC LINES

MEASUREMENTS CAN BE MADE ONLY ON THE DRAWING OF ISOMETRIC LINES
ANY LINE PARALLEL TO THE EDGE OF A CUBE IS AN ISOMETRIC LINE

Angles must be converted to coordinate measurements. Calculate (or measure) distances X and Y from the 60 degree angles. Use the distances X and Y along the isometric axes to locate point O on the pictorial.

Angular dimensions must be converted to coordinate distances.

ISOMETRIC DRAWING

INCLINED SURFACES

-X- AND -Y- ARE COORDINATE MEASUREMENTS

Measure isometric distances A and B from the orthographic view and transfer upward to the left (width) on the isometric view.

Measure distances C and D from the orthographic view and transfer vertically (height) on the isometric view.

ANGLES IN ISOMETRIC

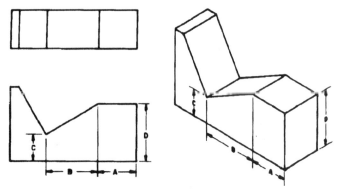

-B- AND -C- ARE COORDINATE MEASUREMENTS

Oblique Edges and Surfaces on Pictorials

Oblique edge 8 - 4 is the line of intersection between two inclined surfaces.

Sketch each inclined surface on the faces of the isometric box to locate the line of intersection.

Locate edge 6 - 7 and sketch the entire surface using parallel edges.

Locate edge 2 - 3 and sketch the entire surface using parallel edges.

Intersection line 4, 8 can be located from the common point between the two construction surfaces.

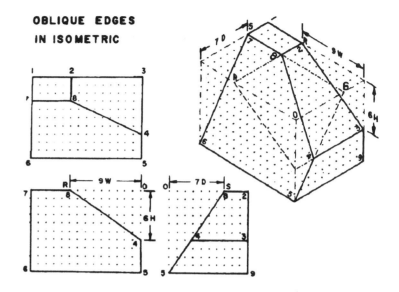

OBLIQUE EDGES IN ISOMETRIC

Locate oblique surfaces by fixing points on the edges of the isometric box.

__extend 1, 2 to locate A on the top-front edge

__plot 4 on the front-bottom edge
__plot point 5 on the side-bottom edge
__locate point 2 on the top-side-back edge.

Sketch parallel lines to locate interior points.

Locate 1 on A - 2
Locate 5 on A - 4

__5, 6 is parallel to 3, 4 and 2, A
__1, 6 is parallel to 4, A. These lines locate point 6.

OBLIQUE SURFACES IN ISOMETRIC

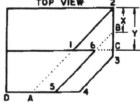

TOP VIEW

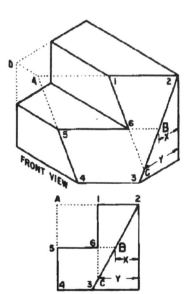

FRONT VIEW

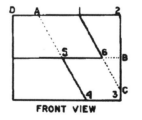

FRONT VIEW

SIDE VIEW

Circular Edges and Cylinders in Pictorial Views

Circles show as ellipses in pictorial views. Three orientations are possible.
__circle in the top face - fig. 1
__circle in the front face - fig. 3
__circle in the side face - fig. 2

"Four center" ellipses may be used for correct appearance in isometric pictorials.

Four construction lines, <u>even on sketches</u>, are needed to locate the centers for arcs which approximate true ellipses. Approximate ellipses are usually used on isometrics.

4 center ellipses

__Sketch rhombus 1,2,3,4 on the pictorial. (Use correct radius for each ellipse).
Fig 1:
__Locate mid-point for each side A,B,C,D.
__Sketch line from <u>obtuse angle</u> to opposite mid-point. (2 lines).
Fig 2:
__Sketch a small arc at corner 1 and 3 using intersection of 2-A : 4-B and 2-D : 4-C.
Fig 3:
__Sketch long arcs using 4 and 2 as centers.

Similar constructions for top or side ellipses are shown.

Four center ellipses may be used for freehand sketches or for drawings using either a compass or a computer.

Sketch an ellipse at each point along the cylinder where an intersection occurs. This will insure an accurate looking picture.

Sketch a new rhombus and new ellipse for each diameter circle in the pictorial.

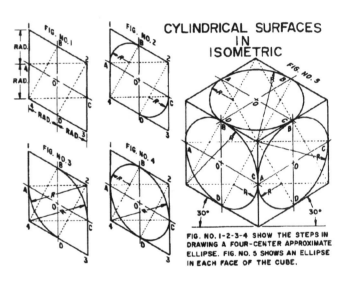

FIG. NO. 1-2-3-4 SHOW THE STEPS IN DRAWING A FOUR-CENTER APPROXIMATE ELLIPSE. FIG. NO. 5 SHOWS AN ELLIPSE IN EACH FACE OF THE CUBE.

CYLINDRICAL SURFACES IN ISOMETRIC

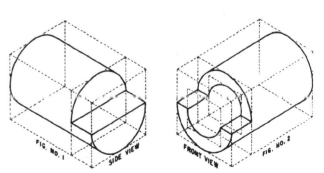

Circles and Curves in Pictorials

Correct directions for ellipses in each face are shown.

Center lines follow the isometric axis direction for each face.

Correct ellipse orientation and centerline direction is essential to produce accurate pictorial views.

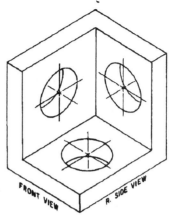

CENTER LINES IN ISOMETRIC

Other curves in pictorial views may require a number of points. Transfer X and Y distances from the orthographic view using construction lines 1 through 9 as shown.

Use parallel line constructions to locate points. Sketch a smooth curve through the points.

An irregular curve may be used on drawings to draw a smooth curve through the points. Some CAD software provides polyline constructions with curve-fitting to draw smooth curves.

CURVES IN ISOMETRIC

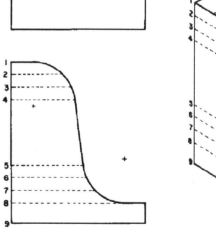

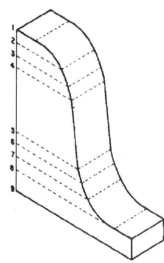

NAME

DATE

NOTE: Use this grid format in horizontal direction.

FILE NUMBER

GRADE

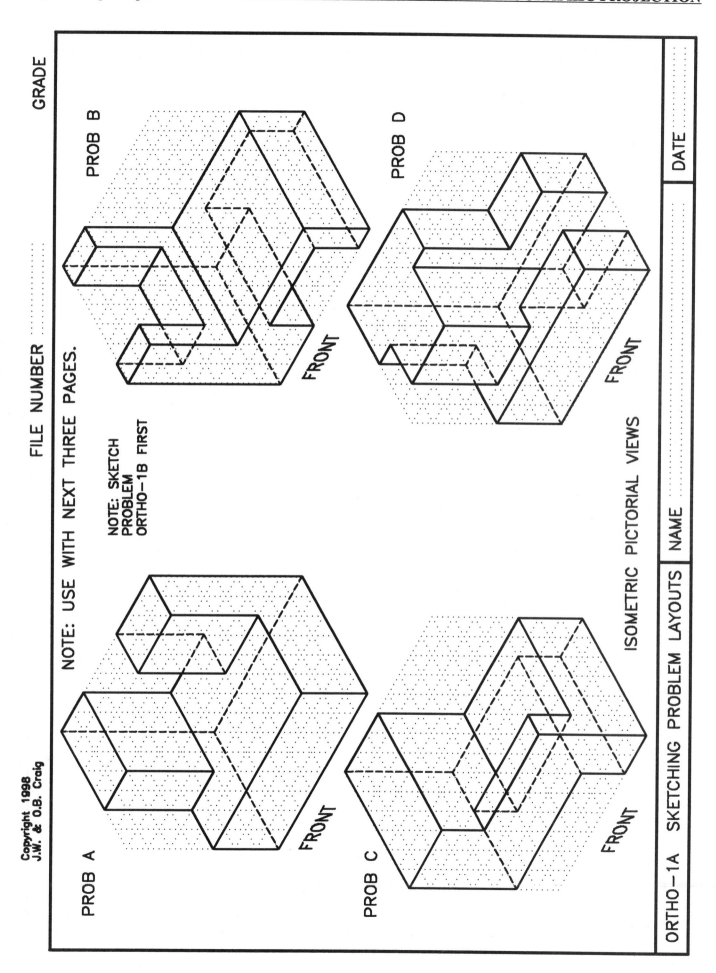

GRADE

FILE NUMBER

DATE

NAME

NOTE: USE WITH NEXT THREE PAGES.

NOTE: SKETCH
PROBLEM
ORTHO—1B FIRST

PROB B

PROB D

PROB A

PROB C

FRONT

ISOMETRIC PICTORIAL VIEWS

ORTHO—1A   SKETCHING PROBLEM LAYOUTS

ORTHO-1-C   MULTIPLE VIEWS

NAME

DATE

PROB A   BLOCK IN VIEW LOCATIONS.   CENTER VIEWS.
LEAVE 2 SPACES BETWEEN VIEWS.

TOP

FRONT   RIGHT

PROB B   BLOCK IN VIEW LOCATIONS.   CENTER VIEWS.
LEAVE 2 SPACES BETWEEN VIEWS.

TOP

FRONT   RIGHT

NOTE: TURN SHEET VERTICALLY FOR USE.

FILE NUMBER

GRADE

GRADE

FILE NUMBER

PLACE FOUR VIEWS
ON THIS PAGE

SKETCH THE PICTORIAL VIEWS FROM ORTHO–1A. BLOCK IN VIEWS. OMiT HIDDEN LINES.

NAME

DATE

ORTHO–1–B　PICTORIAL SKETCHES

PROB C   BLOCK IN VIEW LOCATIONS. CENTER VIEWS.
LEAVE 2 SPACES BETWEEN VIEWS.

PROB D   BLOCK IN VIEW LOCATIONS. CENTER VIEWS.
LEAVE 2 SPACES BETWEEN VIEWS.

ORTHO-1-D   MULTIPLE VIEWS   NAME   DATE

NOTE: TURN SHEET VERTICALLY FOR USE.

FILE NUMBER

GRADE

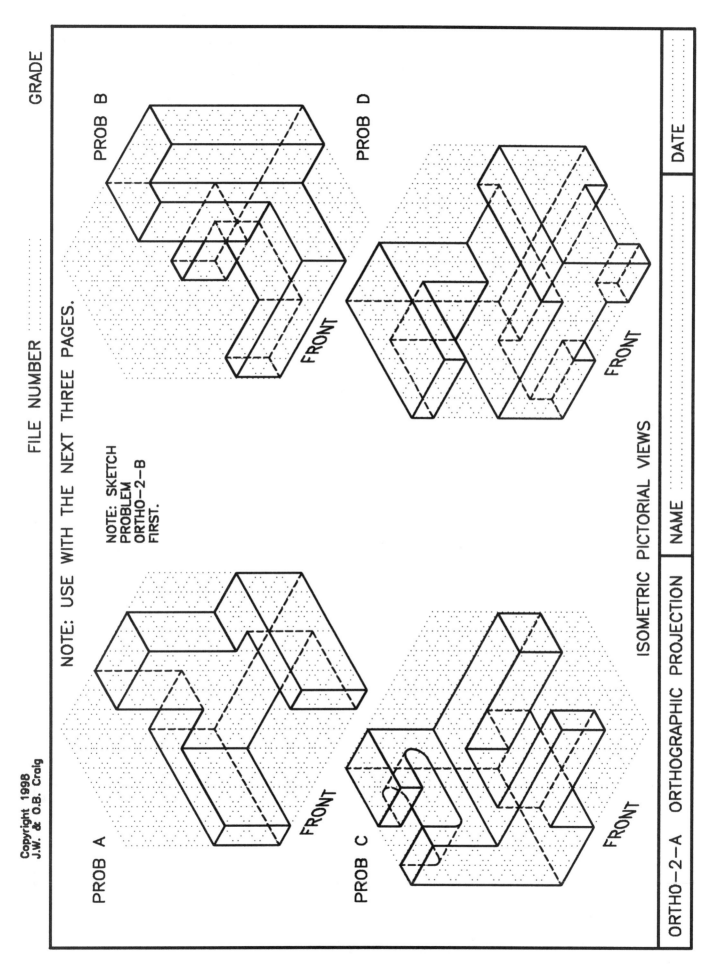

GRADE

PROB B

PROB D

FILE NUMBER

NOTE: USE WITH THE NEXT THREE PAGES.

NOTE: SKETCH
PROBLEM
ORTHO-2-B
FIRST.

FRONT

FRONT

PROB A

PROB C

FRONT

FRONT

DATE

NAME

ISOMETRIC PICTORIAL VIEWS

ORTHO-2-A   ORTHOGRAPHIC PROJECTION

PROB A   BLOCK IN VIEW LOCATIONS.   CENTER VIEWS.
                          LEAVE 2 SPACES BETWEEN VIEWS.

ORTHO-2-C   MULTIPLE VIEWS

TOP

NAME

FRONT   RIGHT

PROB B   BLOCK IN VIEW LOCATIONS.   CENTER VIEWS.
                          LEAVE 2 SPACES BETWEEN VIEWS.

DATE

NOTE: TURN SHEET VERTICALLY
FOR USE.

FILE NUMBER

GRADE

GRADE

FILE NUMBER

PLACE FOUR VIEWS
ON THIS PAGE

Copyright 1998
J.W. & O.B. Craig

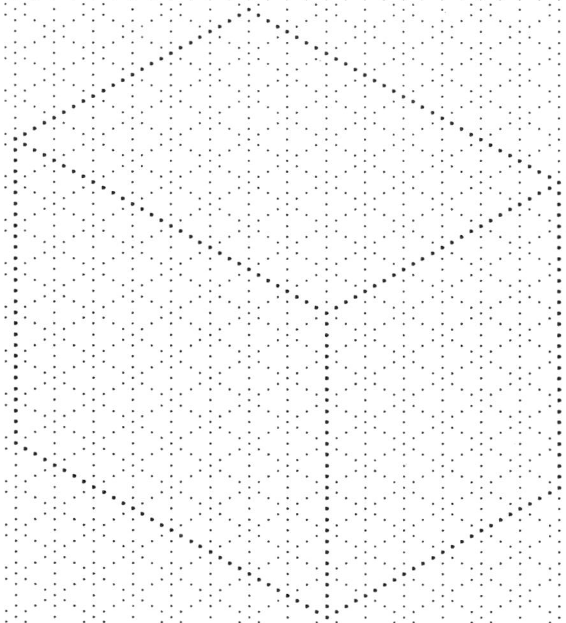

SKETCH THE PICTORIAL VIEWS FROM ORTHO-1. BLOCK IN VIEWS. OMIT HIDDEN LINES.

DATE

NAME

ORTHO-2-B   PICTORIAL SKETCHES

ORTHO–2–D   MULTIPLE VIEWS

NAME

DATE

PROB C   BLOCK IN VIEW LOCATIONS.   CENTER VIEWS. LEAVE 2 SPACES BETWEEN VIEWS.

PROB D   BLOCK IN VIEW LOCATIONS.   CENTER VIEWS. LEAVE 2 SPACES BETWEEN VIEWS.

NOTE: TURN SHEET VERTICALLY FOR USE.

FILE NUMBER

GRADE

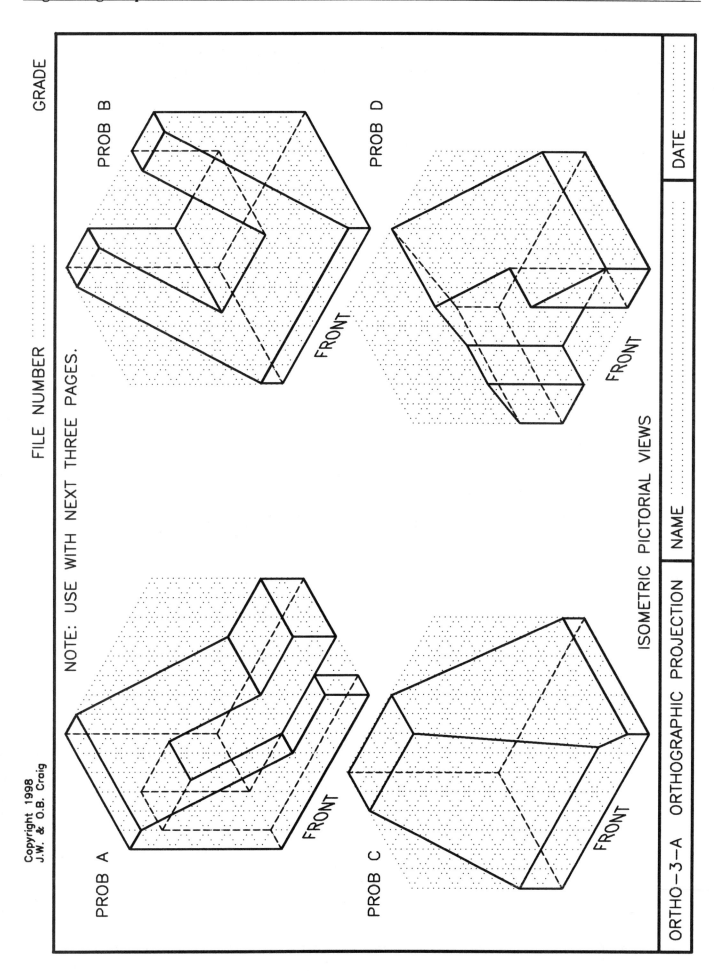

ORTHO-3-C   MULTIPLE VIEWS

NAME

DATE

Copyright 1998
J.W. & O.B. Craig

NOTE: TURN SHEET VERTICALLY FOR USE.

FILE NUMBER

GRADE

PROB A   BLOCK IN VIEW LOCATIONS.   CENTER VIEWS.
LEAVE 2 SPACES BETWEEN VIEWS.

TOP

FRONT   RIGHT

PROB B   BLOCK IN VIEW LOCATIONS.   CENTER VIEWS.
LEAVE 2 SPACES BETWEEN VIEWS.

TOP

FRONT   RIGHT

GRADE

FILE NUMBER

PLACE FOUR VIEWS
ON THIS PAGE

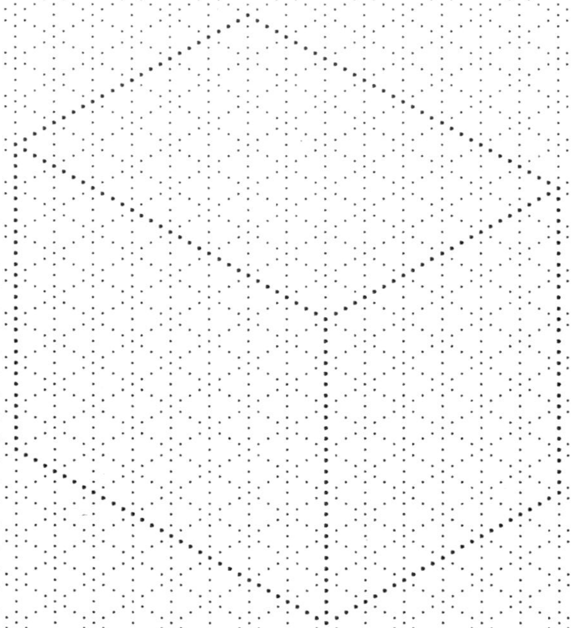

SKETCH THE PICTORIAL VIEWS FROM ORTHO-1. BLOCK IN VIEWS. OMIT HIDDEN LINES.

DATE

NAME

ORTHO-3-B   PICTORIAL SKETCHES

ORTHO–3–D MULTIPLE VIEWS

NAME

DATE

PROB C   BLOCK IN VIEW LOCATIONS.   CENTER VIEWS.
                          LEAVE 2 SPACES BETWEEN VIEWS.

PROB D   BLOCK IN VIEW LOCATIONS.   CENTER VIEWS.
                          LEAVE 2 SPACES BETWEEN VIEWS.

NOTE: TURN SHEET VERTICALLY FOR USE.

FILE NUMBER

GRADE

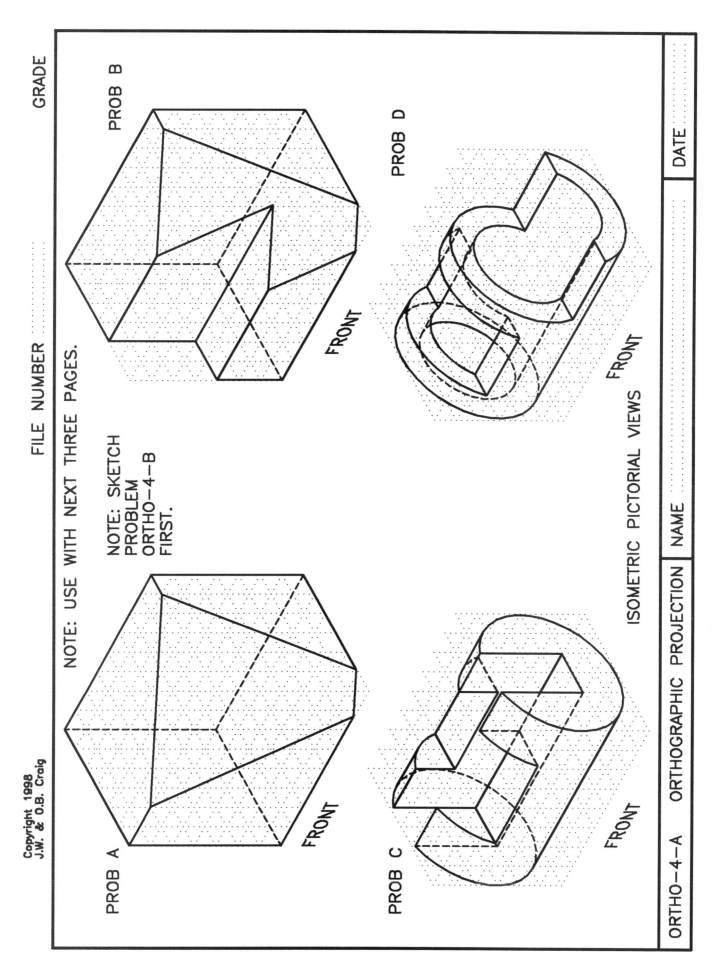

NOTE: USE WITH NEXT THREE PAGES.

NOTE: SKETCH PROBLEM ORTHO−4−B FIRST.

GRADE

PROB B

PROB D

FRONT

FILE NUMBER

Copyright 1998
J.W. & O.B. Craig

PROB A

PROB C

FRONT

FRONT

FRONT

ISOMETRIC PICTORIAL VIEWS

ORTHO−4−A   ORTHOGRAPHIC PROJECTION   NAME   DATE

ORTHO–4–C   MULTIPLE VIEWS

NAME

DATE

PROB A   BLOCK IN VIEW LOCATIONS.   CENTER VIEWS.
LEAVE 2 SPACES BETWEEN VIEWS.

TOP

FRONT   RIGHT

PROB B   BLOCK IN VIEW LOCATIONS.   CENTER VIEWS.
LEAVE 2 SPACES BETWEEN VIEWS.

TOP

FRONT   RIGHT

NOTE: TURN SHEET VERTICALLY FOR USE.

FILE NUMBER

GRADE

GRADE

FILE NUMBER

PLACE FOUR VIEWS
ON THIS PAGE

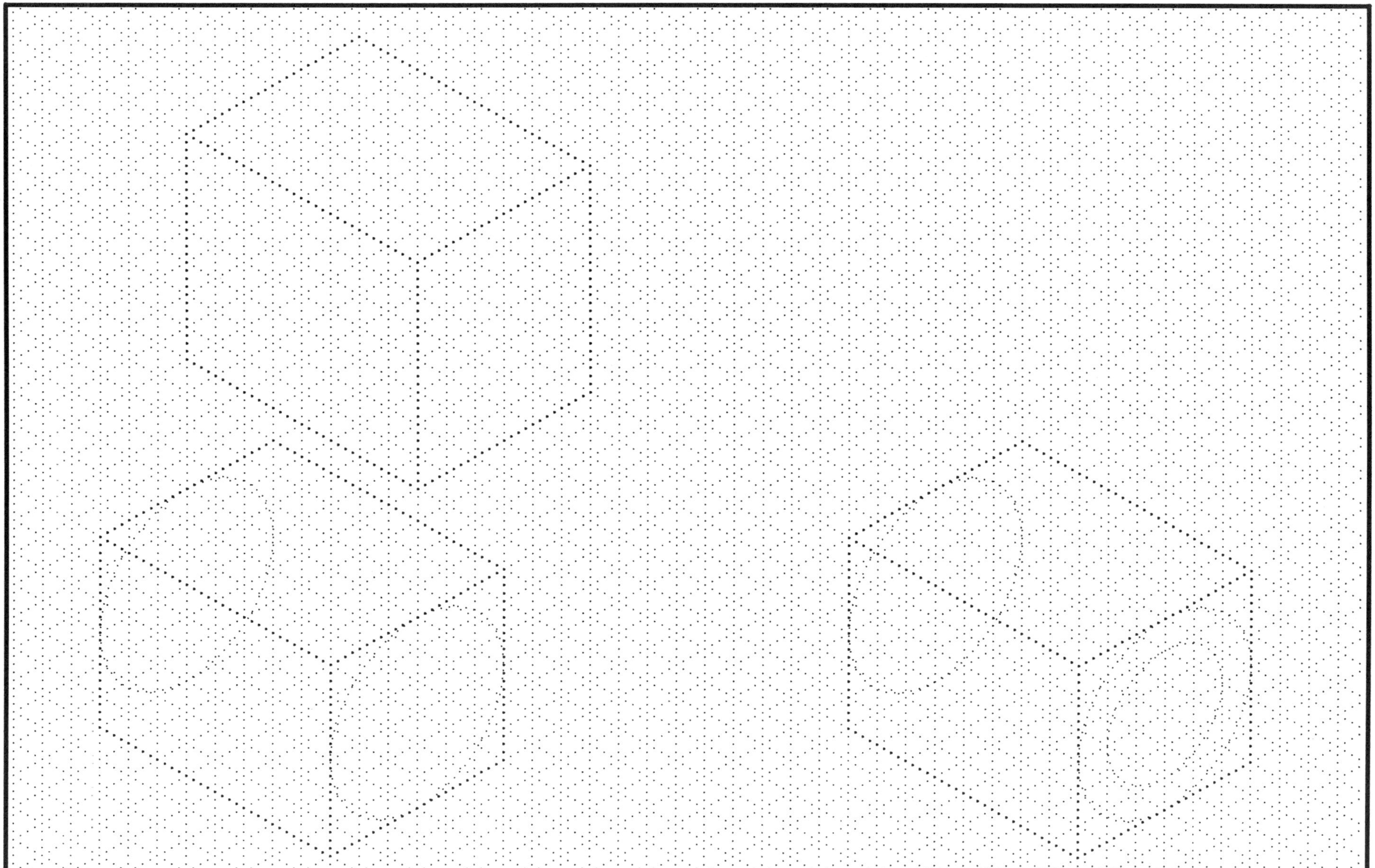

SKETCH THE PICTORIAL VIEWS FROM ORTHO-1. BLOCK IN VIEWS. OMIT HIDDEN LINES.

DATE

NAME

ORTHO-4-B   PICTORIAL SKETCHES

PROB C   BLOCK IN VIEW LOCATIONS.   CENTER VIEWS.
                LEAVE 2 SPACES BETWEEN VIEWS.

ORTHO-4-D   MULTIPLE VIEWS

NAME

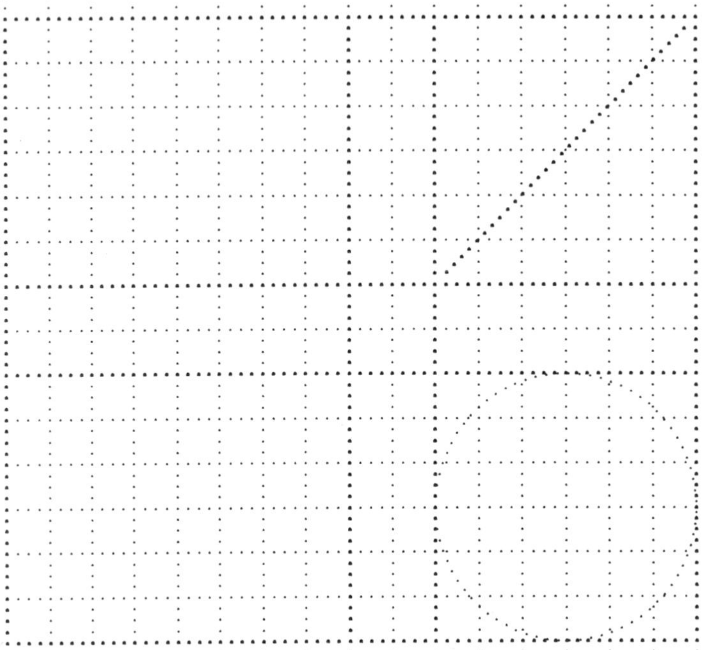

PROB D   BLOCK IN VIEW LOCATIONS.   CENTER VIEWS.
                LEAVE 2 SPACES BETWEEN VIEWS.

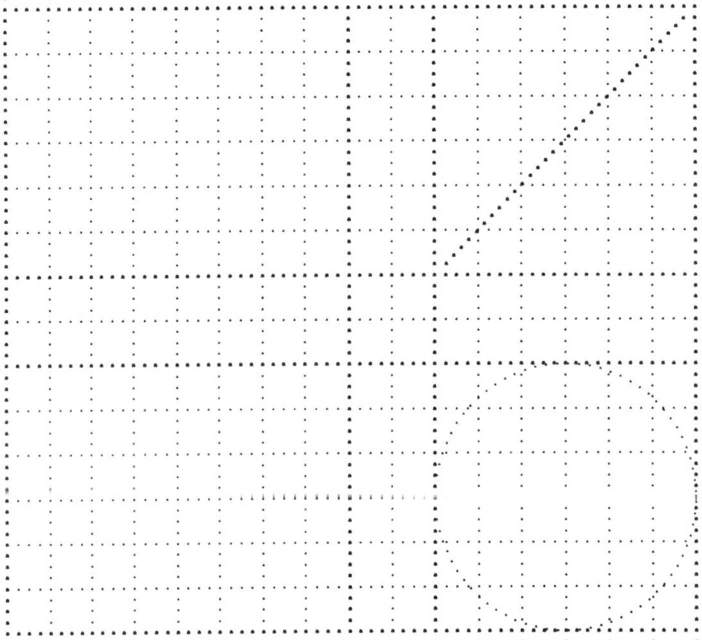

DATE

NOTE: TURN SHEET VERTICALLY FOR USE.

FILE NUMBER

GRADE

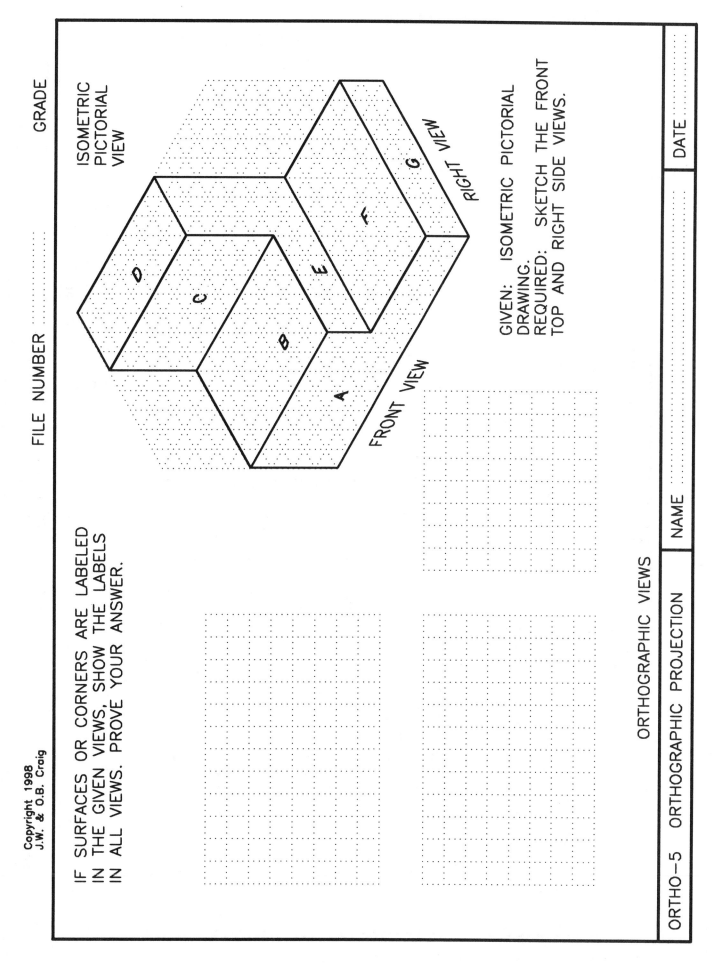

GRADE

FILE NUMBER

ISOMETRIC
PICTORIAL
VIEW

RIGHT VIEW

FRONT VIEW

GIVEN: ISOMETRIC PICTORIAL
DRAWING.
REQUIRED: SKETCH THE FRONT
TOP AND RIGHT SIDE VIEWS.

IF SURFACES OR CORNERS ARE LABELED
IN THE GIVEN VIEWS, SHOW THE LABELS
IN ALL VIEWS. PROVE YOUR ANSWER.

ORTHOGRAPHIC VIEWS

NAME

DATE

ORTHO-5   ORTHOGRAPHIC PROJECTION

Copyright 1998
J.W. & O.B. Craig

IF SURFACES OR CORNERS ARE LABELED
IN THE GIVEN VIEWS, SHOW THE LABELS
IN ALL VIEWS. PROVE YOUR ANSWER.

FILE NUMBER

GRADE

ISOMETRIC
PICTORIAL
VIEW

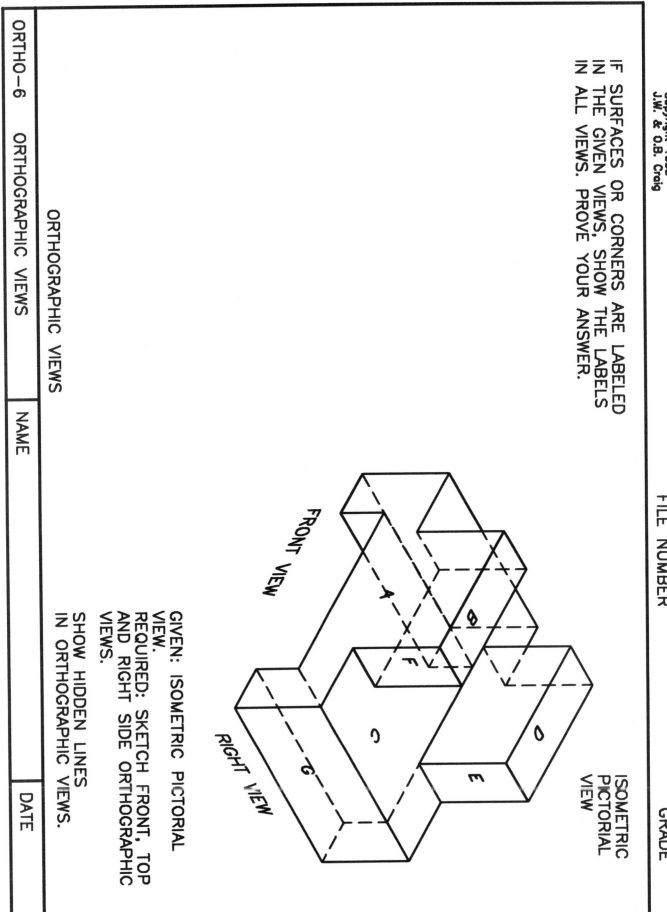

FRONT VIEW

RIGHT VIEW

GIVEN: ISOMETRIC PICTORIAL
VIEW.
REQUIRED: SKETCH FRONT, TOP
AND RIGHT SIDE ORTHOGRAPHIC
VIEWS.

SHOW HIDDEN LINES
IN ORTHOGRAPHIC VIEWS.

ORTHO—6   ORTHOGRAPHIC VIEWS

ORTHOGRAPHIC VIEWS

NAME

DATE

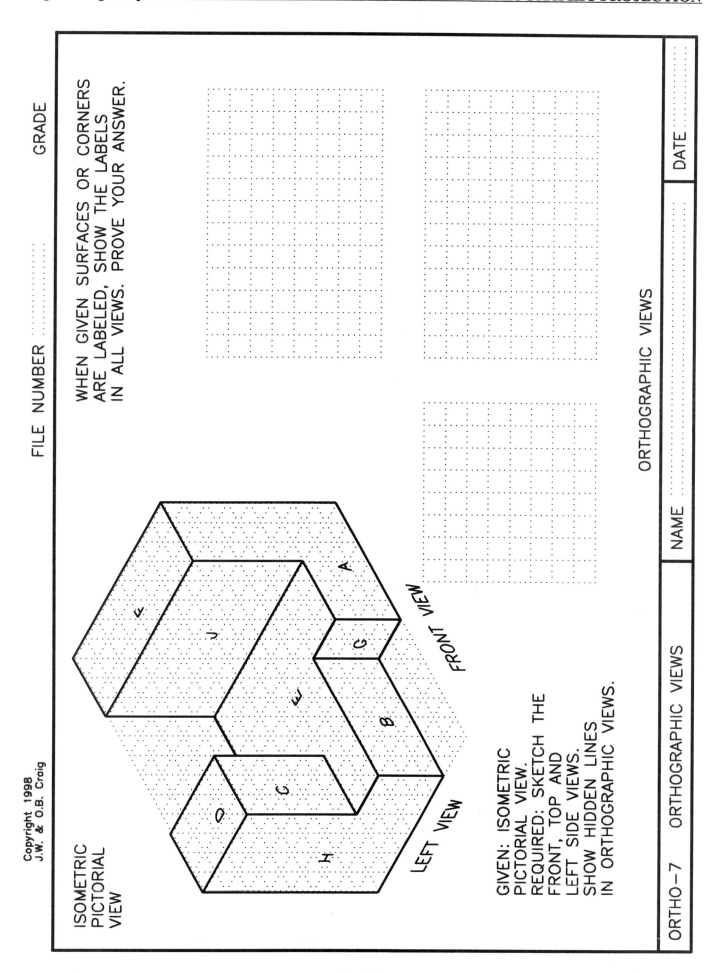

FILE NUMBER ....   GRADE

WHEN GIVEN SURFACES OR CORNERS
ARE LABELED, SHOW THE LABELS
IN ALL VIEWS. PROVE YOUR ANSWER.

Copyright 1998
J.W. & O.B. Craig

ISOMETRIC
PICTORIAL
VIEW

FRONT VIEW

LEFT VIEW

GIVEN: ISOMETRIC
PICTORIAL VIEW.
REQUIRED: SKETCH THE
FRONT, TOP AND
LEFT SIDE VIEWS.
SHOW HIDDEN LINES
IN ORTHOGRAPHIC VIEWS.

ORTHOGRAPHIC VIEWS

NAME ....   DATE ....

ORTHO-7   ORTHOGRAPHIC VIEWS

IF SURFACES OR CORNERS ARE LABELED
IN THE GIVEN VIEWS, SHOW THE LABELS
IN ALL VIEWS. PROVE YOUR ANSWER.

FILE NUMBER   GRADE

ISOMETRIC
PICTORIAL
VIEW

ORTHO-8   ORTHOGRAPHIC VIEWS

ORTHOGRAPHIC VIEWS

NAME

DATE

GIVEN: ISOMETRIC PICTORIAL
DRAWING.
REQUIRED: SKETCH THE
FRONT, TOP AND
RIGHT SIDE VIEWS.

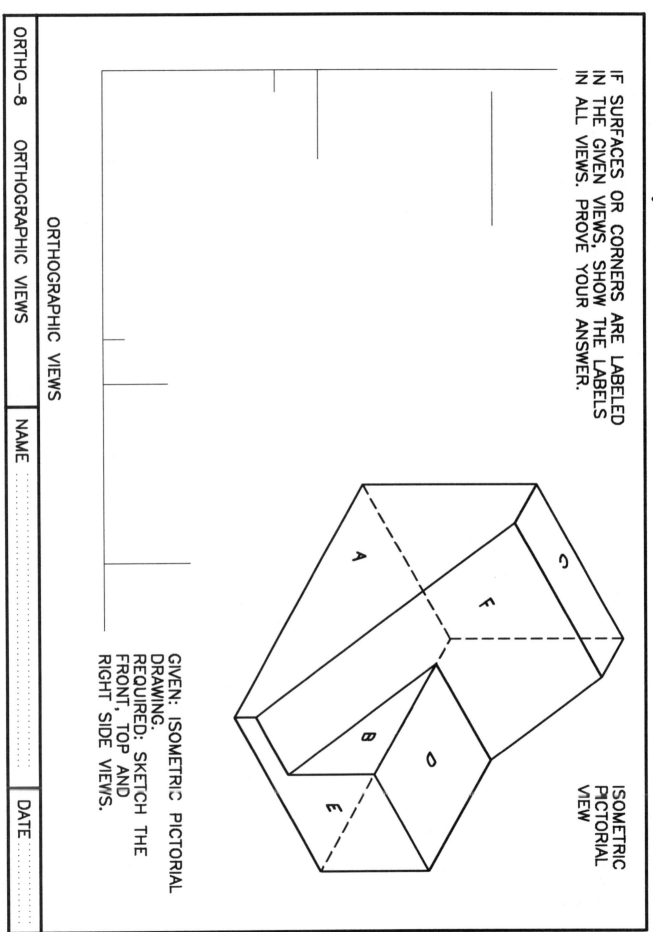

FILE NUMBER　　　　　GRADE

WHEN GIVEN SURFACES OR CORNERS
ARE LABELED, SHOW THE LABELS
IN ALL VIEWS. PROVE YOUR ANSWER.

ISOMETRIC
PICTORIAL
VIEW

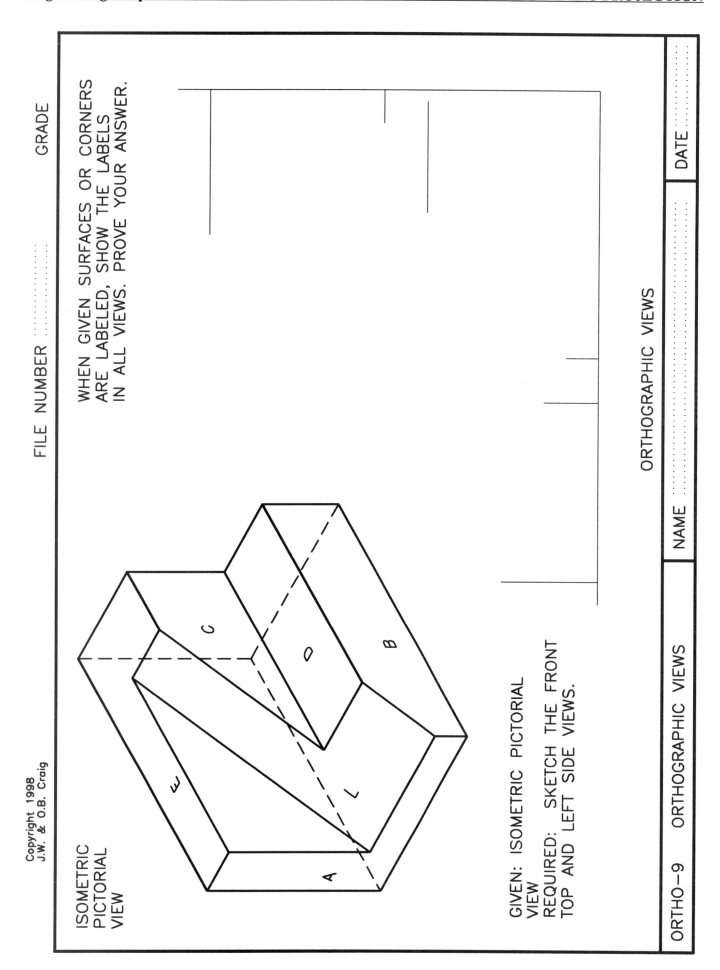

GIVEN: ISOMETRIC PICTORIAL
VIEW
REQUIRED: SKETCH THE FRONT
TOP AND LEFT SIDE VIEWS.

ORTHOGRAPHIC VIEWS

| ORTHO—9 | ORTHOGRAPHIC VIEWS | NAME | DATE |

IF SURFACES OR CORNERS ARE LABELED
IN THE GIVEN VIEWS, SHOW THE LABELS
IN ALL VIEWS. PROVE YOUR ANSWER.

FILE NUMBER ....   GRADE ....

ISOMETRIC
PICTORIAL
VIEW

C

A

B

E

D

G

F

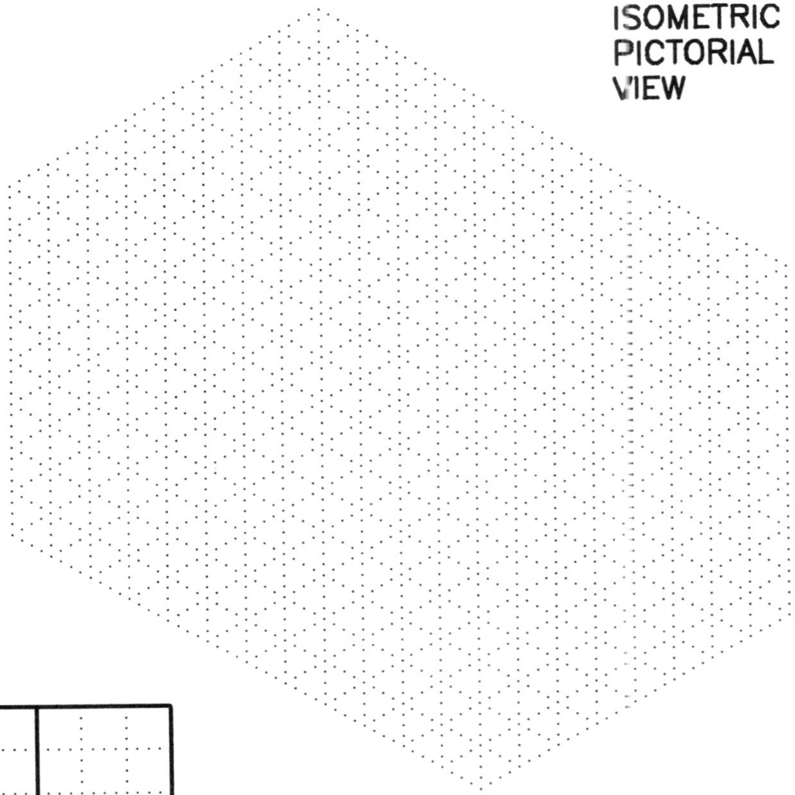

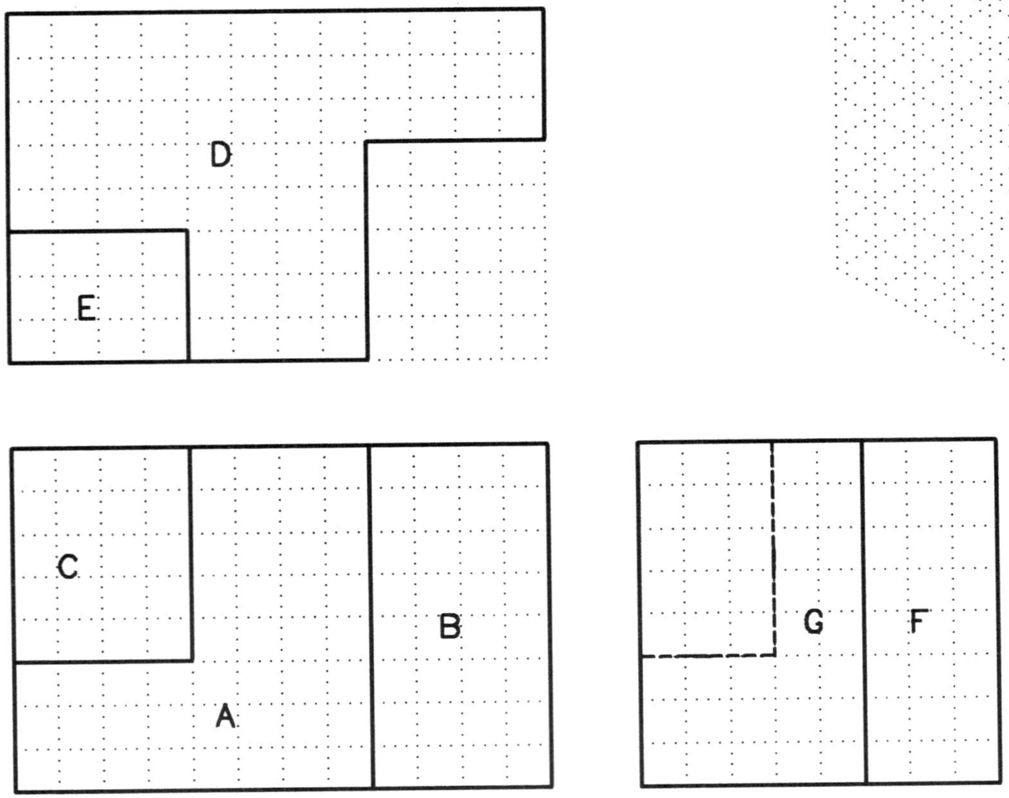

GIVEN: FRONT, TOP AND
RIGHT SIDE VIEWS
REQUIRED: SKETCH THE
ISOMETRIC PICTORIAL VIEW.
(OMIT HIDDEN LINES
IN PICTORIAL VIEWS.)

ORTHO-10   ORTHOGRAPHIC VIEWS

ORTHOGRAPHIC VIEWS

NAME ....   DATE ....

GRADE

FILE NUMBER

ISOMETRIC
PICTORIAL
VIEW

IF SURFACES OR CORNERS ARE LABELED
IN THE GIVEN VIEWS, SHOW THE LABELS
IN ALL VIEWS. PROVE YOUR ANSWER.

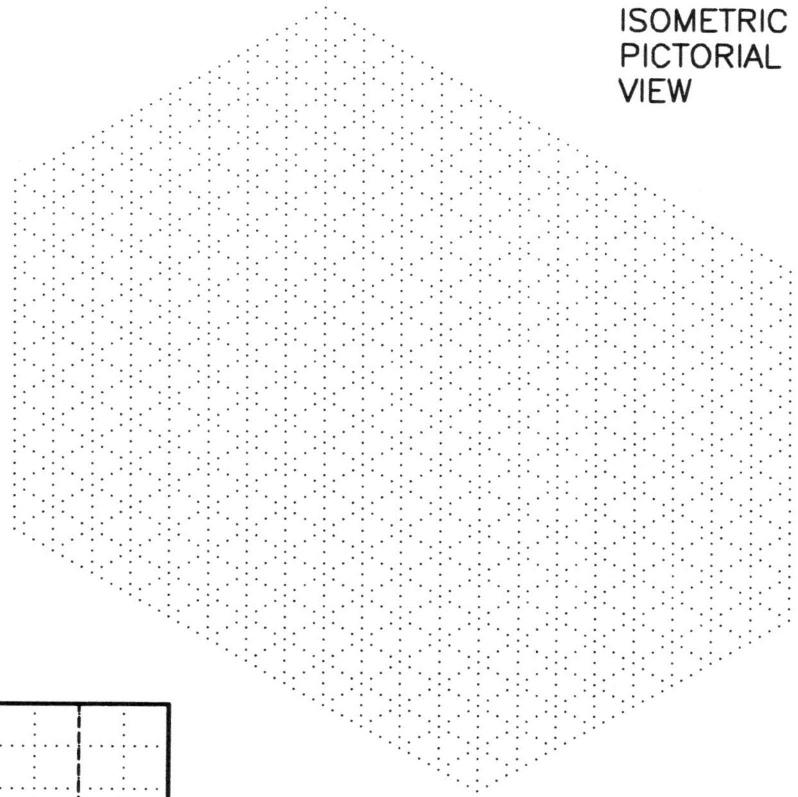

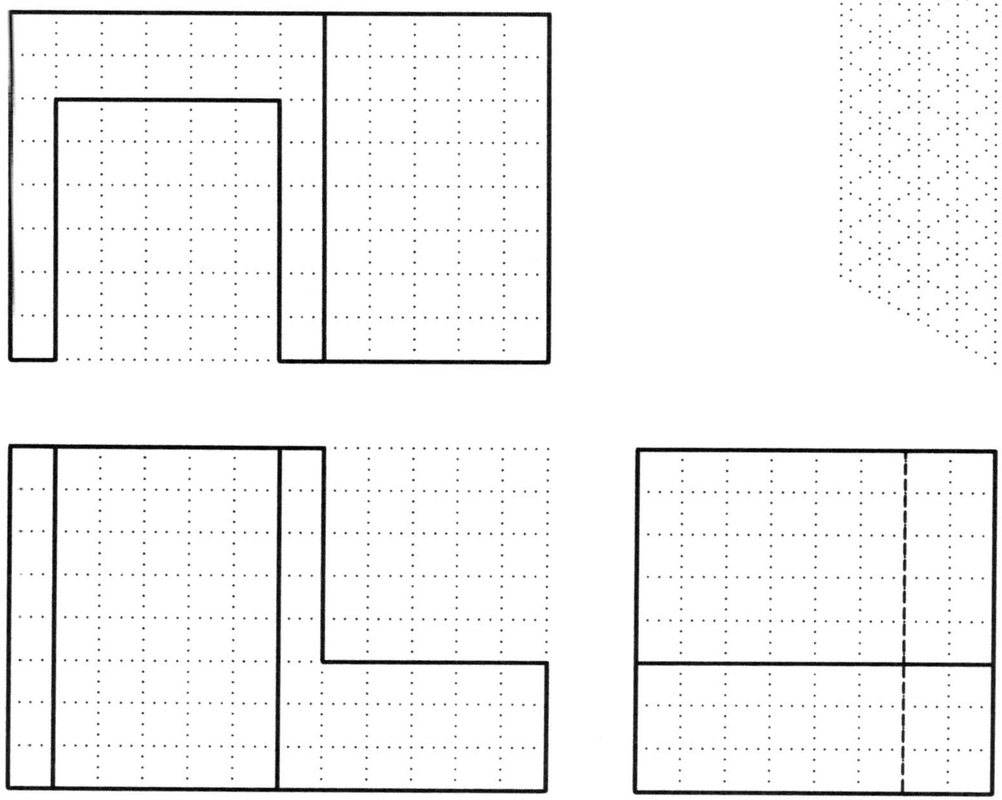

GIVEN: FRONT, TOP AND
RIGHT SIDE VIEWS.
REQUIRED: SKETCH THE
ISOMETRIC PICTORIAL VIEW.
(OMIT HIDDEN LINES
IN PICTORIAL VIEWS).

ORTHOGRAPHIC VIEWS

DATE

NAME

ORTHO−11   ORTHOGRAPHIC PROJECTION

ISOMETRIC
PICTORIAL
VIEW

FILE NUMBER

GRADE

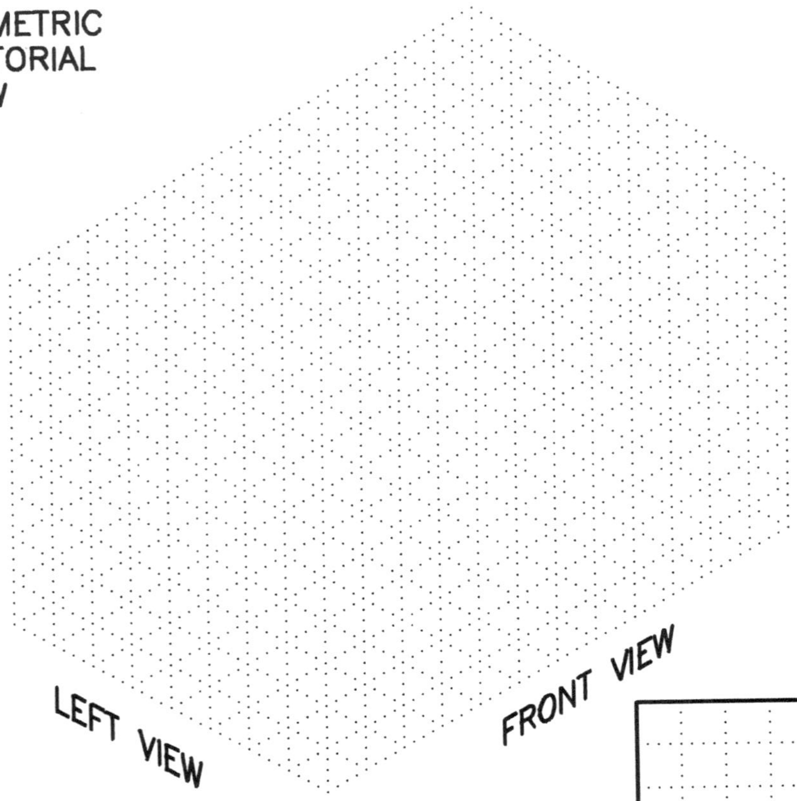

WHEN GIVEN SURFACES OR CORNERS
ARE LABELED, SHOW THE LABELS
IN ALL VIEWS. PROVE YOUR ANSWER.

LEFT VIEW

FRONT VIEW

GIVEN: FRONT, TOP AND
LEFT SIDE VIEWS.
REQUIRED: SKETCH THE
ISOMETRIC PICTORIAL VIEW.
(OMIT HIDDEN LINES
IN PICTORIAL VIEWS).

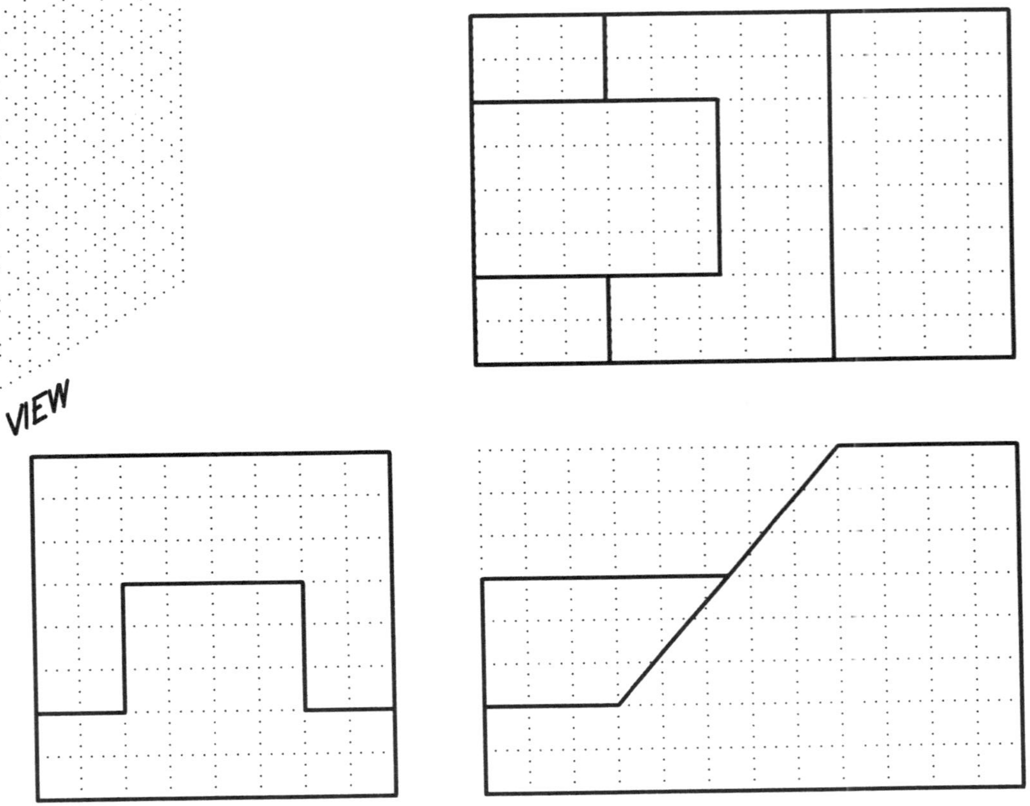

ORTHO-12   ORTHOGRAPHIC PROJECTION

NAME

ORTHOGRAPHIC VIEWS

DATE

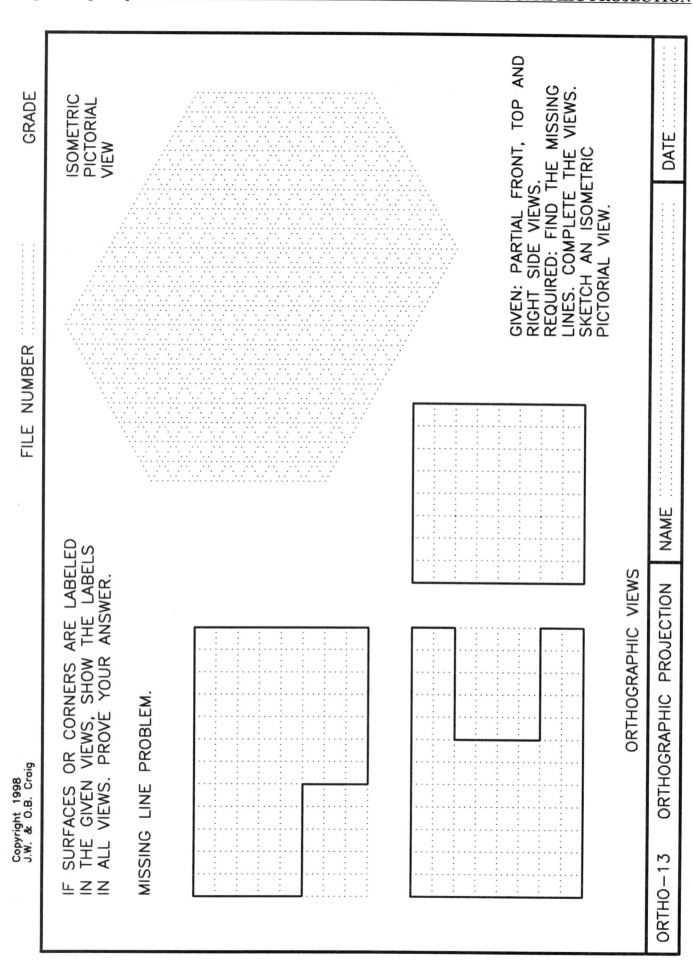

GRADE

FILE NUMBER

ISOMETRIC
PICTORIAL
VIEW

GIVEN: PARTIAL FRONT, TOP AND
RIGHT SIDE VIEWS.
REQUIRED: FIND THE MISSING
LINES. COMPLETE THE VIEWS.
SKETCH AN ISOMETRIC
PICTORIAL VIEW.

IF SURFACES OR CORNERS ARE LABELED
IN THE GIVEN VIEWS, SHOW THE LABELS
IN ALL VIEWS. PROVE YOUR ANSWER.

MISSING LINE PROBLEM.

ORTHOGRAPHIC VIEWS

DATE

NAME

ORTHO-13　　ORTHOGRAPHIC PROJECTION

IF SURFACES OR CORNERS ARE LABELED
IN THE GIVEN VIEWS, SHOW THE LABELS
IN ALL VIEWS. PROVE YOUR ANSWER.

MISSING LINE PROBLEM

FILE NUMBER

ISOMETRIC
PICTORIAL
VIEW

GRADE

ORTHO-14   ORTHOGRAPHIC VIEWS

ORTHOGRAPHIC VIEWS

NAME

DATE

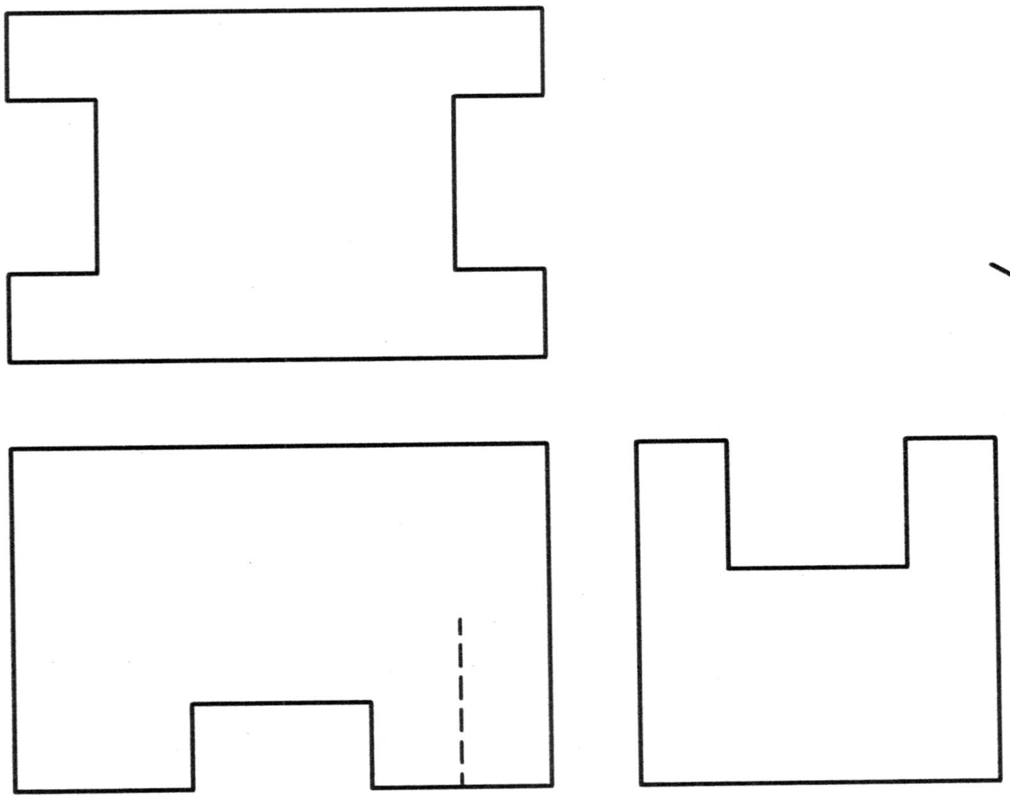

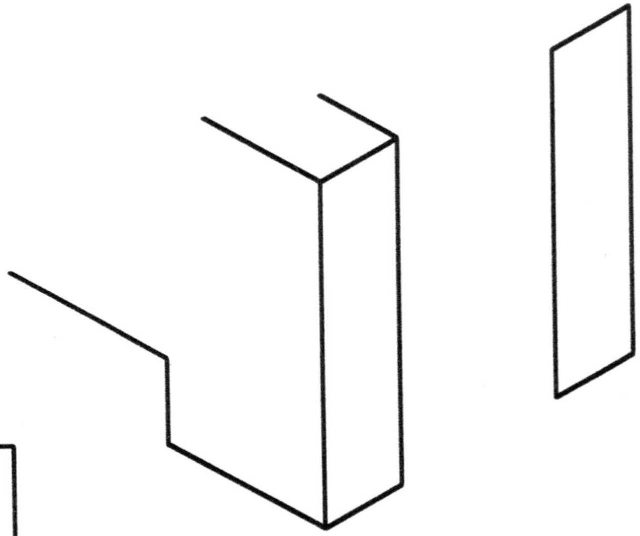

GIVEN: PARTIAL FRONT, TOP
AND RIGHT SIDE VIEWS.
REQUIRED: FIND THE MISSING
LINES AND COMPLETE
EACH VIEW.
SKETCH THE ISOMETRIC
PICTORIAL VIEW.

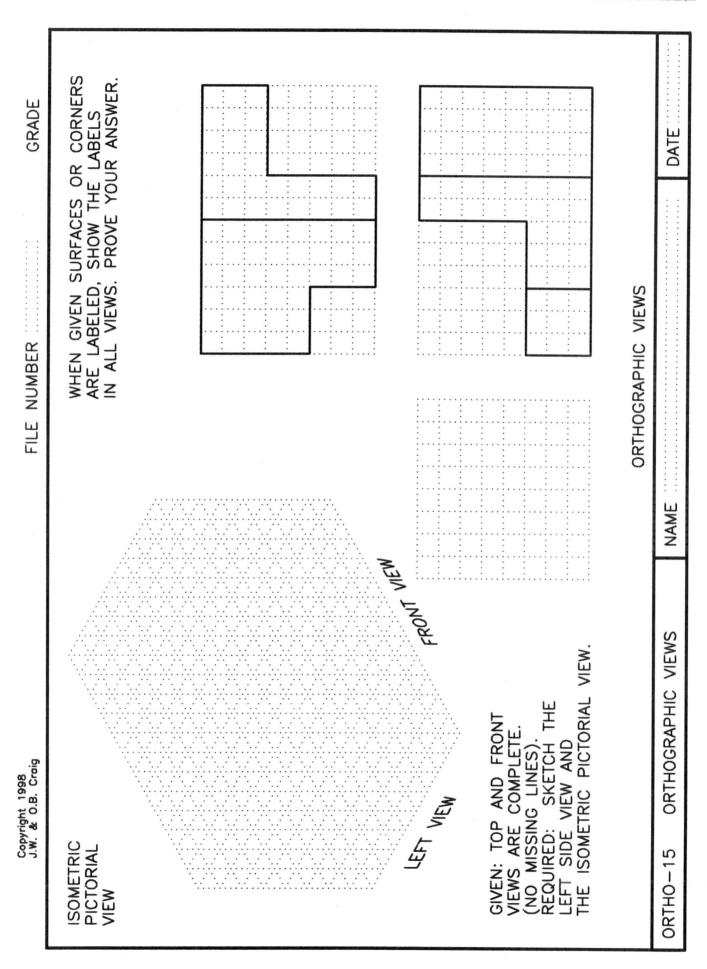

FILE NUMBER .... GRADE

WHEN GIVEN SURFACES OR CORNERS
ARE LABELED, SHOW THE LABELS
IN ALL VIEWS. PROVE YOUR ANSWER.

ISOMETRIC
PICTORIAL
VIEW

FRONT VIEW

LEFT VIEW

GIVEN: TOP AND FRONT
VIEWS ARE COMPLETE.
(NO MISSING LINES).
REQUIRED: SKETCH THE
LEFT SIDE VIEW AND
THE ISOMETRIC PICTORIAL VIEW.

ORTHOGRAPHIC VIEWS

DATE ....

NAME ....

ORTHO-15   ORTHOGRAPHIC VIEWS

NAME

DATE

FILE NUMBER

GRADE

Introduction to Normal Surfaces

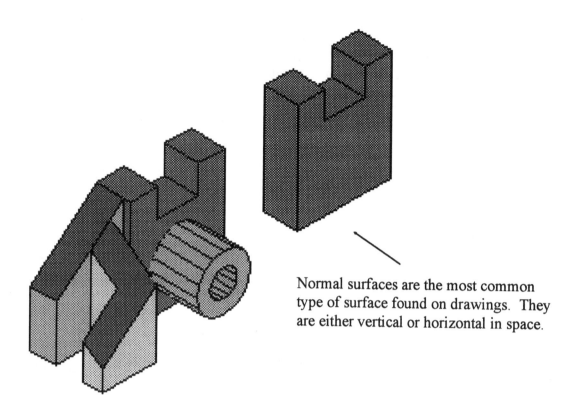

Normal surfaces are the most common type of surface found on drawings. They are either vertical or horizontal in space.

Only three types of plane surfaces exist on drawings. A surface is a closed area bounded by edges with no edges cutting across. Plane surfaces are flat with all points lying in one plane in space. Part of the process of reading or creating drawings involves recognizing unique surfaces in space and predicting the appearance of each surface in each view.

Understanding Normal Surfaces is very important for computer drawing and design. Most objects whether they already exist or are just in the visualization stage have normal surfaces. Ideas and shapes that exist in the mind must be modeled in three dimensional space.

NORMAL SURFACES are the most common type of plane surface found on drawings. They are like the walls, floor and ceiling of a room. They are either vertical or horizontal in space. Normal surfaces intersect at right angles to each other.

NORMAL EDGES may exist on almost any type of surface. They are either vertical or horizontal lines in space. Normal edges will appear as a point in one of the regular views.

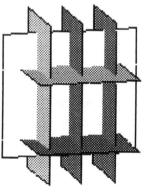

NORMAL SURFACES

Normal Surfaces in the Front View

Normal surfaces will be seen as a surface in either the front, top or side view depending on their orientation in space. These examples analyze surfaces in the front view.

Surface "A" is a surface in the front view. "A" appears as horizontal edge-of-surface 1,2 in the top view. "A" appears as vertical edge-of-surface 3,4 in the side view.

FRONT	TOP	SIDE
SURFACE	HORIZONTAL LINE	VERTICAL LINE

Surface "B" is a surface in the front view. "B" is horizontal edge-of surface 5,6 in the top view. "B" is vertical edge-of-surface 7,8 in the side view.

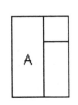

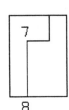

Surface "C" is a surface in the front view. "C" is horizontal edge-of-surface 9,10 in the top view. "C" is vertical edge-of-surface 11,12 in the side view.

RULE: A normal surface appearing as a surface in the front view will appear as a horizontal edge in the top view and a vertical edge in the side view.

A horizontal line in the top view will be a surface in the front view.

A vertical line in the side view will be a surface in the front view.

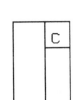

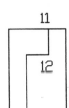

Normal Surfaces in the Top View

Surfaces in the top view will appear as a horizontal edge in both front and side views. The edges must be directly across in each view.

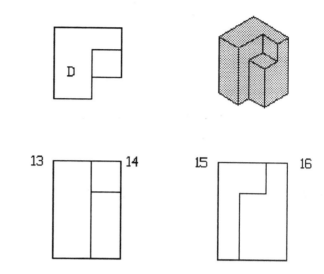

Surface "D" is a surface in the top view. "D" is edge-of-surface 13,14 in the front view. "D" is edge-of-surface 15,16 in the side view.

Notice that 13,14 is the full width of "D". And, 15,16 extends the full depth of "D".

Memorize the NORMAL SURFACE TABLE for each of the views.

A horizontal line in the front view must be a surface in the top view......

A horizontal line in the side view must be a surface in the top view.....

FRONT	TOP	SIDE
HORIZONTAL LINE	SURFACE	HORIZONTAL LINE

"E" is a surface in the top view. Surface "E" appears as horizontal edge-or-surface 17,18 in the front view. "E" is edge-of-surface 19,20 in the side view.

17,18 and 19,20 must be directly across from each other in the front and side views. 17,18 is the width of "E". 19,20 is the depth of "E".

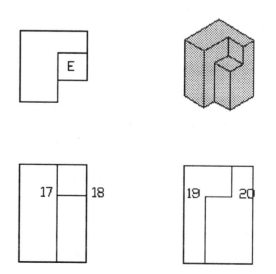

Normal Surfaces in the Side View

Normal surfaces in the side view will appear as vertical lines in the front and top views.

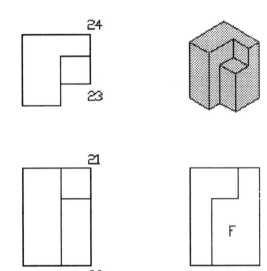

"F" is a surface in the side view. "F" appears as edge-of-surface 21,22 in the front view. "F" is edge-of surface 23,24 in the top view.

Note that 21,22 is the full height of "F" in the front view. And, 23,24 is the full depth of "F" in the top view.

Memorize the NORMAL SURFACE TABLE for the side view.

A vertical line in the front view must be a surface in the side view......

A vertical line in the top view must be a surface in the side view.

FRONT	TOP	SIDE
VERTICAL LINE	VERTICAL LINE	SURFACE

"G" is a surface in the side view. "G" is vertical edge-of-surface 25,26 in the front view. "G" is vertical edge-of-surface 27,28 in the top view.

Note that 25,26 is the full height of "G". And, 27,28 is the full depth of "G".

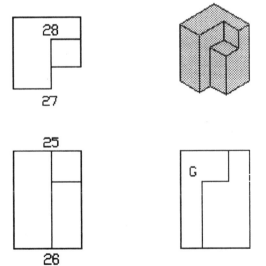

Normal surfaces are very common in objects around us. Observe architecture, furniture and everyday items close at hand. Identify normal surfaces. Imagine looking at these items from the front, top and side views. Develop the ability to break objects down into individual surfaces as a means of analyzing shapes.

Predicting Normal Surfaces

Predicting Shape

Intersection points on lines help to predict the shape of surfaces in other views.

No intersection points: the surface will be either a square or a rectangle.

Intersection points: the surface will have an irregular shape. The surface will change shape at each intersection point.

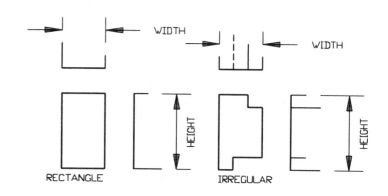

Predicting Size

The WIDTH of the surface and the width of the horizontal line in the top view must be the same.

The HEIGHT of the surface and the height of the vertical line in the side view must be the same.

Predicting appearance in the regular views.

Memorize the NORMAL SURFACE CHART.

This is the complete set of rules about normal surfaces in the regular views.

Read the chart across.

<------------------->

FRONT	TOP	SIDE
SURFACE	HORIZONTAL EDGE	VERTICAL EDGE
HORIZONTAL EDGE	SURFACE	HORIZONTAL EDGE
VERTICAL EDGE	VERTICAL EDGE	SURFACE

Using the chart to prove surfaces

"A vertical line in the side view must be a surface in the front view"

"A horizontal line in the front view must be a surface in the top view"

"A vertical line in the front view must be a surface in the side view" .... etc.

Normal Edges

Normal edges are common to two surfaces. Identifying shared edges is an important visualization tool.

A normal edge will appear as a point in one view and as either a horizontal or a vertical ***true length*** line in the other views.

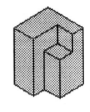

Note the point circled in the front view. This edge will be 3,4 in the side view and 1,2 in the top view. The horizontal length in the side view is the same as the vertical length in the top view.

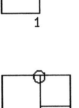
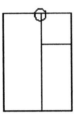
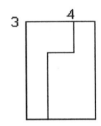

Note the point circled in the top view. This edge is 5,6 in the front view and 7,8 in the side view. The length of the line in the front view must be the same as the length of the line in the side view.

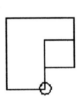
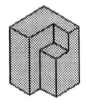

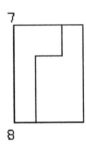

Memorize the NORMAL EDGE TABLE.

FRONT	TOP	SIDE
POINT	VERTICAL LINE	HORIZONTAL LINE
VERTICAL LINE	POINT	VERTICAL LINE
HORIZONTAL LINE	HORIZONTAL LINE	POINT

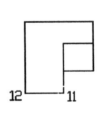
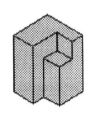

Note the circled point in the side view. This will be line 9,10 in the front view and line 11,12 in the top view.

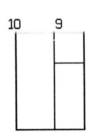
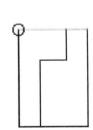

Deriving and Using Normal Surface and Edge Charts

To derive the Normal Surface and Normal Edge charts, simply sketch a box as shown.

Label the surfaces A,B and C.

Make a chart showing the appearance of A,B and C in each view.

Label edges 1,2 and 1,3 and 1,4.

Make a chart showing the appearance of the lines in each view.

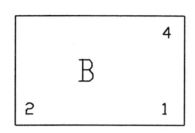

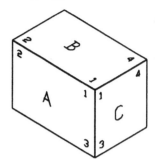

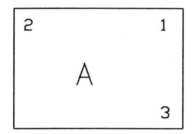

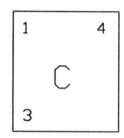

NORMAL SURFACE CHART

Verify the Normal Surface chart with the figure above.

Notice that this is a very logical organization of our knowledge about normal surfaces. You can use this to prove surfaces in the views and even to generate partial views without being able to "see" the shape.

FRONT	TOP	SIDE
SURFACE	HORIZONTAL EDGE	VERTICAL EDGE
HORIZONTAL EDGE	SURFACE	HORIZONTAL EDGE
VERTICAL EDGE	VERTICAL EDGE	SURFACE

NORMAL EDGE CHART

Verify the Normal Edge chart with the figure above.

Each normal edge is shared by two surfaces. This is a important tool in locating surfaces in the views. Also, analyzing shared edges helps to visualize the relation between surfaces.

FRONT	TOP	SIDE
POINT	VERTICAL LINE	HORIZONTAL LINE
VERTICAL LINE	POINT	VERTICAL LINE
HORIZONTAL LINE	HORIZONTAL LINE	POINT

Analyzing Normal Surfaces

*Look carefully at each surface to see
the location and extent in each view.*

Surface "C" in the front view is horizontal
line 1,2 in the top view. "C" is vertical line 10,11 in
the side view.

Surface "D" in the front view is horizontal
line 4,7 in the top view. Note the intersection
points at 5 and 6. "D" is vertical line 12,19 in the
side view.

"F" is 1,3 in the top and 17,18 in the side.

"E" is 8,9 in the top and 15,16 in the side.

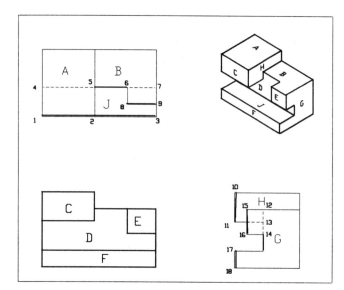

Surface "A" in the top view is 40,41 in the
front view and 50,51 in the side view.

Surface "B" is 42,43 in the front view and
52,53 in the side view.

Surface "J" in the top view is mostly hidden
by other lines. It is 44,45 in the front view and
54,55 in the side view.

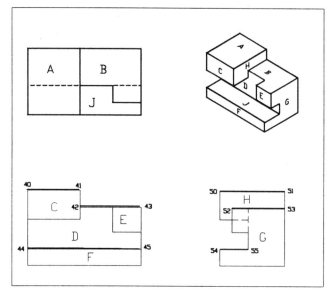

Surface "H" in the side view is partially hidden by other lines. "H" is vertical line 60,61 in the
front view and vertical line 76,74 in the top view.

Surface "G" is vertical line 62,63 in the
front view and vertical line 73,70 in the top view.

The intersection points on 73,70 and 62,63
create the irregular shape of "G".

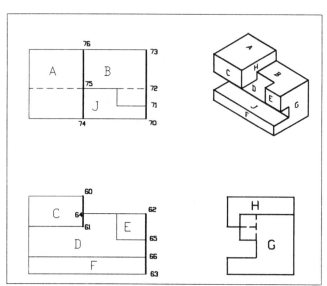

Drawing a View by Analyzing Surfaces

An effective way to analyze normal surfaces is to place a letter in each surface view. Locate the letter on the edge-of-surface lines in adjacent views.

Surface locations must be known in two views before the third view may be drawn. Using the rules for normal surfaces, surface locations may be analyzed.

When the surface location is known in two views, the surface may be plotted in the missing view as an aid to visualizing the object.

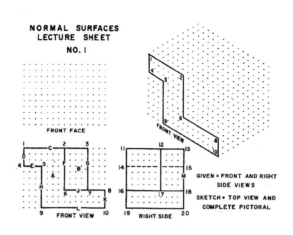

Surface "A" in the front view (1,2,6,8,10,9,5,4,1) is an area bounded by lines. It must be a vertical line in the side view. It could be 11,19,12,17 or 13,20.

12,17 is too short
13,20 is the back of the object
   (no thickness)
"A" must be 11,19 the front edge of the object in the side view.

"A" must be a horizontal line in the top view. Sketch a horizontal line the full width of "A" in the top view (21,22).

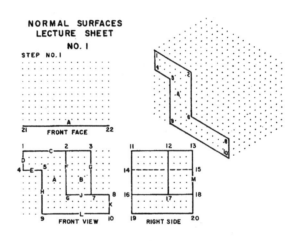

Vertical line "K" (8,10) in the front view must be a surface in the side view. The only possible surface is 16,18,20,19.

According to the Normal Surface chart "B" must be a vertical line in the top view. The line must be straight above "K" in the front view and must extend the depth of "K" from the side view. Sketch a line 10 units deep in the top view. (23,24)

Sketch surface "K" on the pictorial view. This surface extends upward to the right 10 units on the pictorial. "K" shares edge 8,10 with "A".

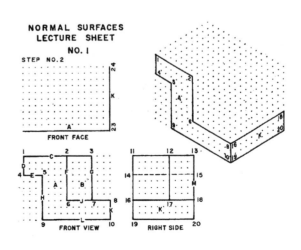

Drawing a View by Analyzing Surfaces

Vertical line "F" (2,6) in the front view must be a surface in the side view. Two possibilities: 11,12,17,16 or 12,13,18,17.

Since 2,6 is an edge of surface "A" this probably means that "F" is 11,12,17,16. It is the only surface sharing an edge with surface "A" (11,19)

"F" must be a vertical line in the top view straight above "F" in the front view and extending 5 units in depth. (25,26) It is visible because the top of "F" is the top of the object.

Sketch "F" on the pictorial view.

Surface "B" (2,3,7,6) in the front view must be a vertical line in the side view. Three possibilities: 11,16 or 12,17 or 13,18.

    11,16 is the same level as "A"
    "B" and "A" cannot share the same edge.
    13,18 is the back of the object
      (no thickness)
So, "B" must be 12,17.

Sketch a visible horizontal line in the top view straight above "B" in the front view, parallel to "A" and five units above "A" (27,28).

Vertical line 3,7 "G" in the front view must be a surface in the side view. Two possibilities: 11,12,17,16 or 12,13,18,17. Since 11,12,17,16 is "F" then "G" is 12,13,18,17.

"G" must be a visible vertical line in the top view, directly above "G" in the front and extending from "B" to the back - 5 units depth. (29,30).

Sketch "G" on the pictorial view.

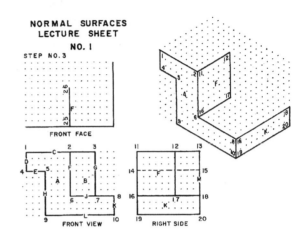

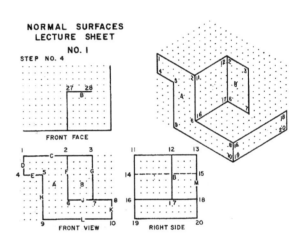

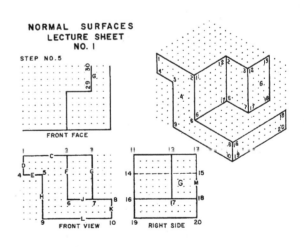

Drawing a View by Analyzing Surfaces

Horizontal line 6,8 "J" in the front view must be a horizontal line in the side view. Projecting across, it must be 16,18. According to the Normal Surface chart, "J" must be a surface in the top view. Sketch line 31,32 to close the surface.

Sketch "J" on the pictorial view.

Note the intersections on "J" at 7 and 17. These cause "J" to have an irregular shape.

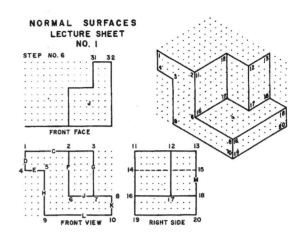

Horizontal line 1,3 "C" must be horizontal line 11,13 in the side view. Note the intersections at 2 and 12. The surface in the top view will have an irregular shape.

Sketch surface "C" in the top view. Add lines 33,34,35. Sketch "C" on the pictorial view.

The examples show how an object may be partially solved by analysis and reasoning. Part of the answer is generated before the object can be visualized.

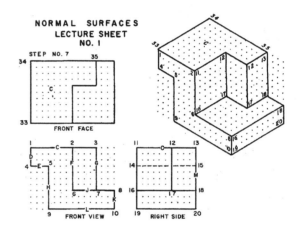

Vertical line 5,9 "H" in the front view must be a surface in the side view. Projecting across, the only possibility is 14,15,20,19 (hidden). "H" must be a vertical line in the top view.

Sketch a hidden vertical line in the top view straight above 5,9 in the front view, extending the full depth (10 units).

Using the NORMAL SURFACE and EDGE charts, it is possible to PROVE every line and surface on the drawing. This process is essential in creating accurate drawings.

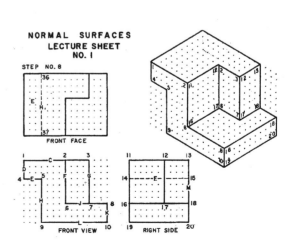

E - 11

NAME

DATE

FILE NUMBER

GRADE

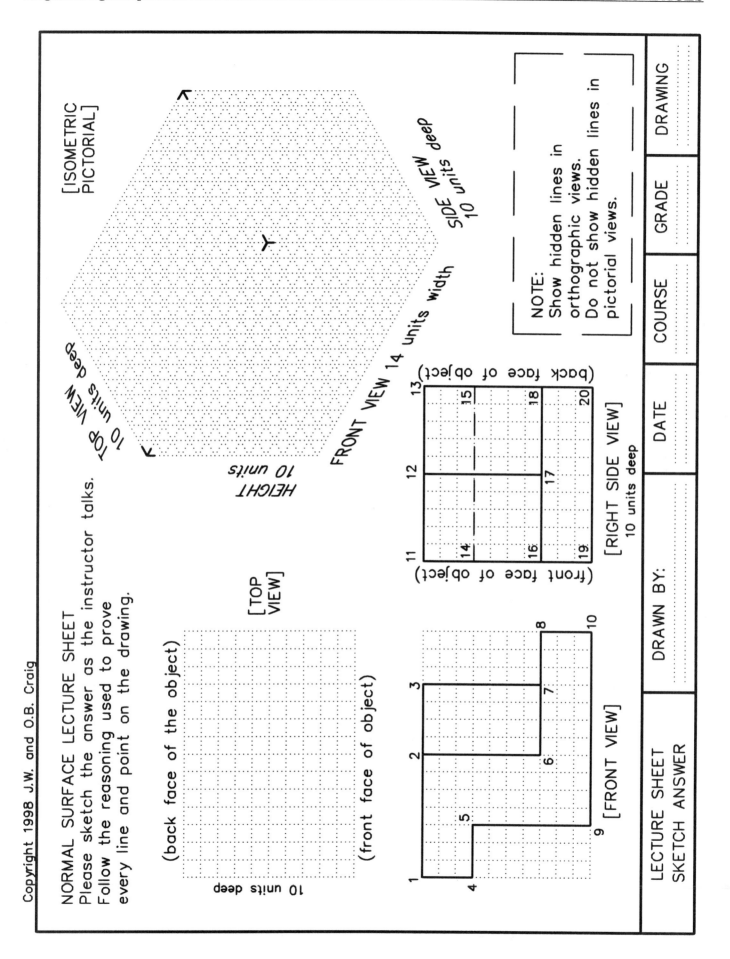

Copyright 1998 J.W. and O.B. Craig

NORMAL SURFACE LECTURE SHEET
Please sketch the answer as the instructor talks.
Follow the reasoning used to prove
every line and point on the drawing.

[ISOMETRIC PICTORIAL]

NOTE:
Show hidden lines in orthographic views.
Do not show hidden lines in pictorial views.

SIDE VIEW deep
10 units

FRONT VIEW 14 units width

TOP VIEW
10 units deep

HEIGHT 10 units

[TOP VIEW]

(back face of the object)

(front face of object)

10 units deep

[RIGHT SIDE VIEW]
10 units deep

(back face of object)

(front face of object)

[FRONT VIEW]

LECTURE SHEET
SKETCH ANSWER

DRAWN BY:

DATE

COURSE

GRADE

DRAWING

NAME

DATE

NOTE: Use this grid format
in horizontal direction.

FILE NUMBER

GRADE

FILE NUMBER

GRADE

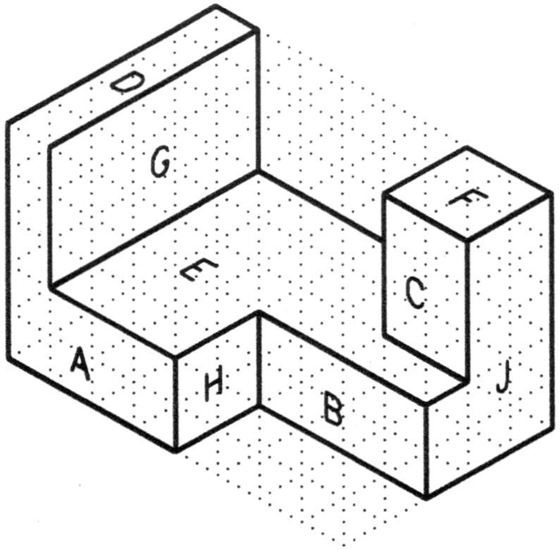

LABEL THE SURFACE VIEWS
AND THE EDGE VIEWS OF
A,B,C,D,E,F,G,H,J IN
ALL VIEWS.

TOP VIEW

RIGHT SIDE VIEW

FRONT VIEW

BOTTOM VIEW

LEFT SIDE VIEW

REAR (BACK) VIEW

GIVEN: ISOMETRIC PICTORIAL VIEW.
SKETCH THE SIX REGULAR
ORTHOGRAPHIC VIEWS.
Be sure to show hidden lines
in the orthographic views.

NAME

DATE

N-1   THE SIX REGULAR VIEWS

MEMORIZE THE NORMAL SURFACE TABLE.

NOTE: P,R,M AND N — HIDDEN

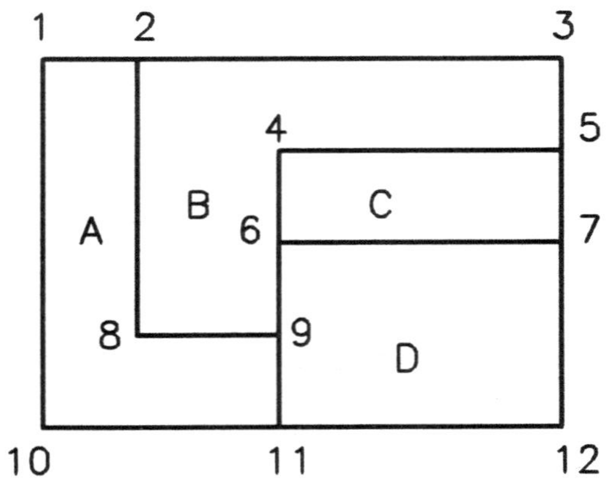

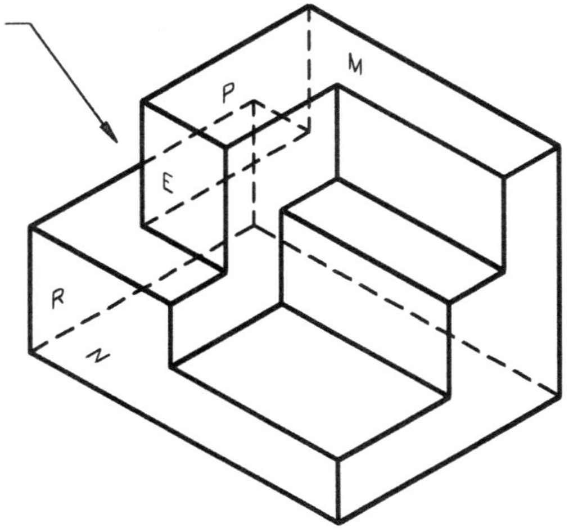

Copyright 1998
J.W. & O.B. Craig

FILE NUMBER

GRADE

NOTE: USE THE BEGINNING
AND ENDING NUMBERS ONLY
FOR EACH LINE.

FRONT		TOP		RIGHT
E		8 - 9		40-46
F				
G				
H				
M*	A			
	B			J
	C			K
	D	N*		P*
				R*

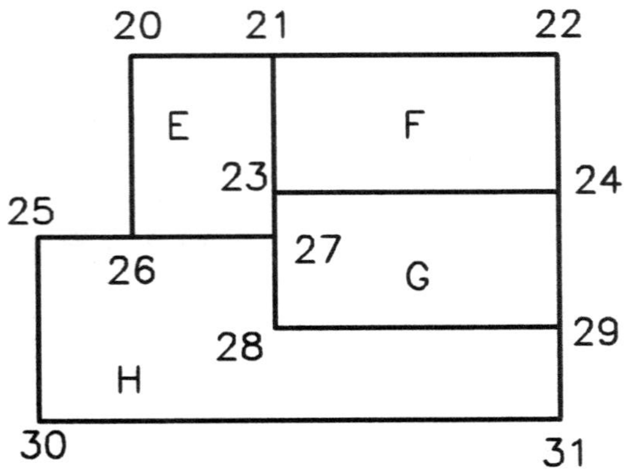

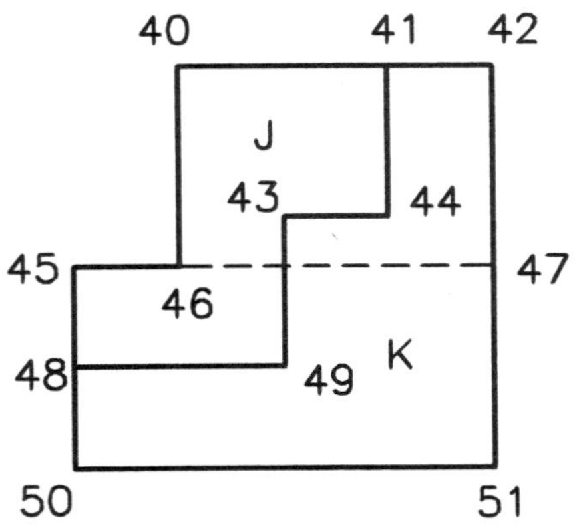

*M = 20,22,31,30,25,26,20
*N = 1,3,12,10,1
*P = 40,42,47,46,40
*R = 45,47,51,50,45

LETTER ANSWER NEATLY.

GRADE

ISOMETRIC
PICTORIAL
VIEW

FILE NUMBER

IF SURFACES OR CORNERS ARE LABELED
IN THE GIVEN VIEWS, SHOW THE LABELS
IN ALL VIEWS. PROVE YOUR ANSWER.

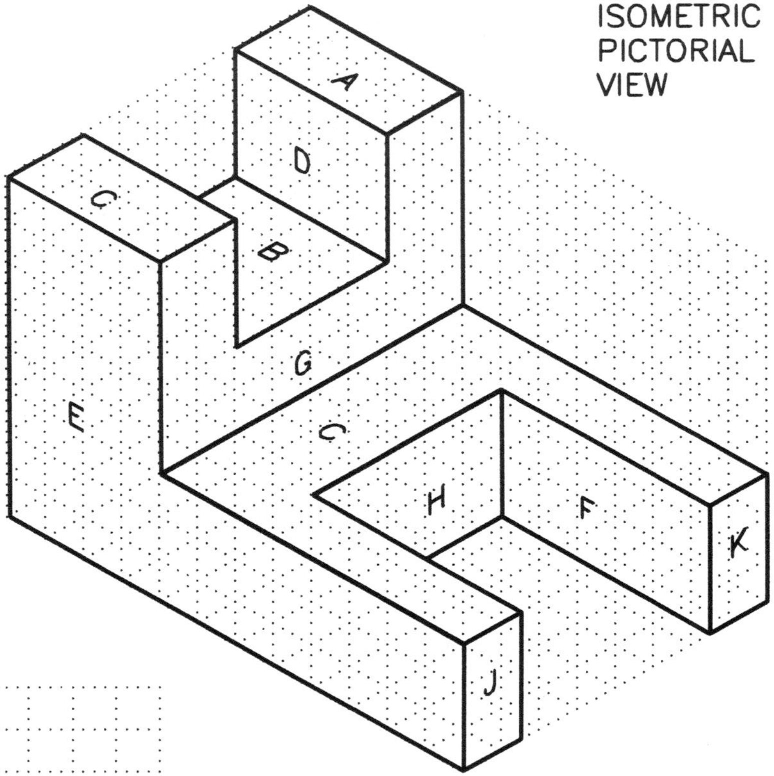

GIVEN: ISOMETRIC PICTORIAL VIEW.
REQUIRED: SKETCH THE
FRONT, TOP AND RIGHT
VIEWS.
SHOW HIDDEN LINES IN
ORTHOGRAPHIC VIEWS.

ORTHOGRAPHIC VIEWS

N-3 NORMAL SURFACES

NAME

DATE

ISOMETRIC
PICTORIAL
VIEW

Copyright 1998
J.W. & O.B. Craig

FILE NUMBER .... GRADE

WHEN GIVEN SURFACES OR CORNERS
ARE LABELED, SHOW THE LABELS
IN ALL VIEWS. PROVE YOUR ANSWER.

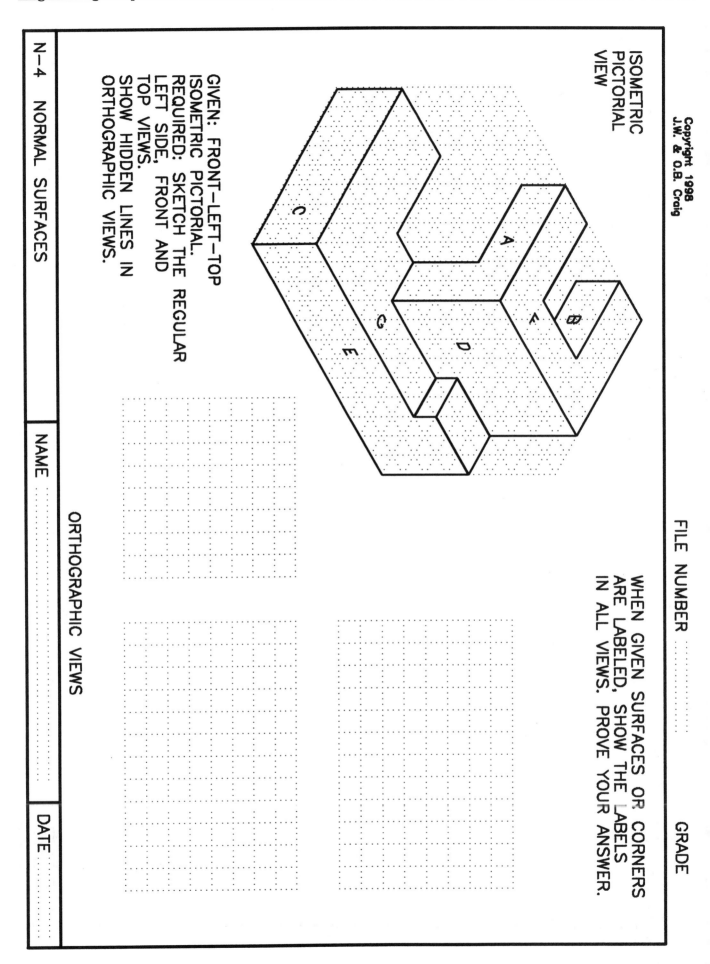

GIVEN: FRONT–LEFT–TOP
ISOMETRIC PICTORIAL.
REQUIRED: SKETCH THE REGULAR
LEFT SIDE, FRONT AND
TOP VIEWS.
SHOW HIDDEN LINES IN
ORTHOGRAPHIC VIEWS.

N–4   NORMAL SURFACES

ORTHOGRAPHIC VIEWS

NAME .... DATE ....

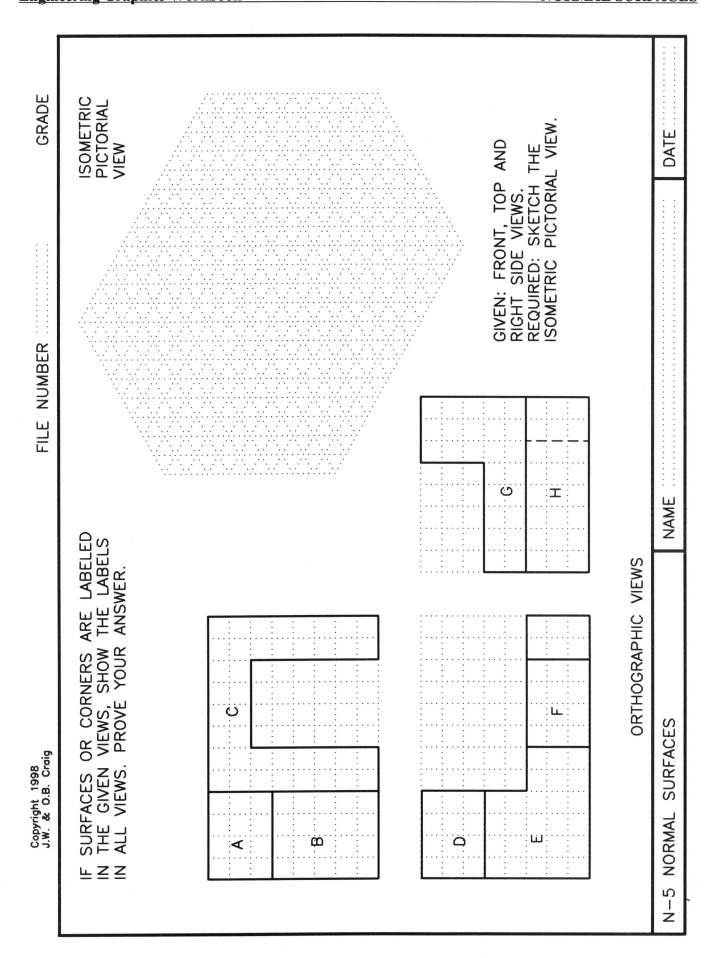

GRADE

ISOMETRIC
PICTORIAL
VIEW

GIVEN: FRONT, TOP AND
RIGHT SIDE VIEWS.
REQUIRED: SKETCH THE
ISOMETRIC PICTORIAL VIEW.

FILE NUMBER

IF SURFACES OR CORNERS ARE LABELED
IN THE GIVEN VIEWS, SHOW THE LABELS
IN ALL VIEWS. PROVE YOUR ANSWER.

Copyright 1998
J.W. & O.B. Craig

ORTHOGRAPHIC VIEWS

NAME

DATE

N-5 NORMAL SURFACES

Copyright 1998
J.W. & O.B. Craig

IF SURFACES OR CORNERS ARE LABELED
IN THE GIVEN VIEWS, SHOW THE LABELS
IN ALL VIEWS. PROVE YOUR ANSWER.

FILE NUMBER ....

GRADE

N-6 NORMAL SURFACES

ORTHOGRAPHIC VIEWS

NAME

DATE

J

K

L

M

N

P

V

W

ISOMETRIC
PICTORIAL
VIEW

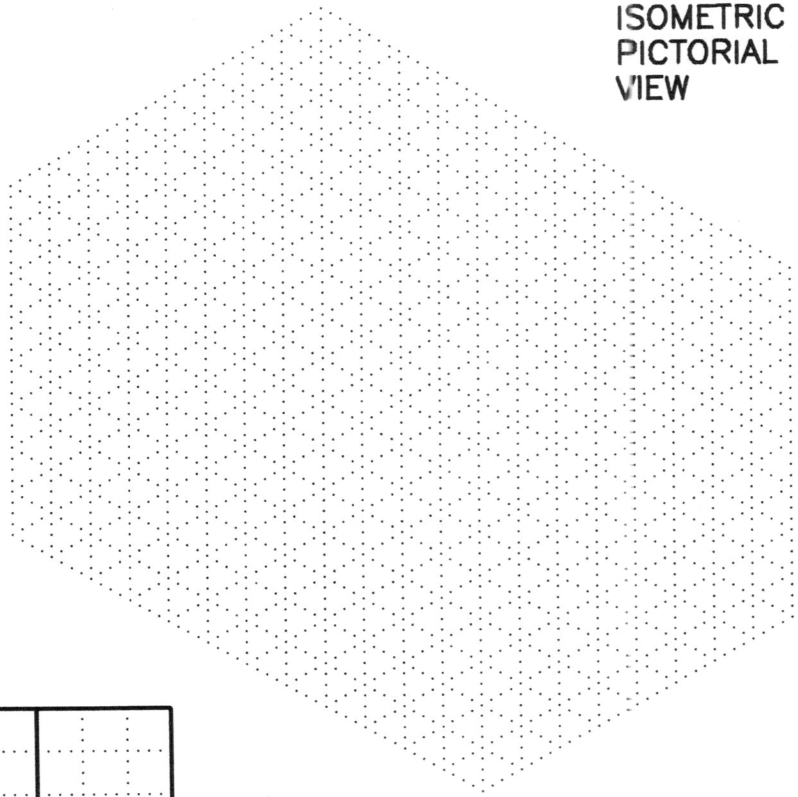

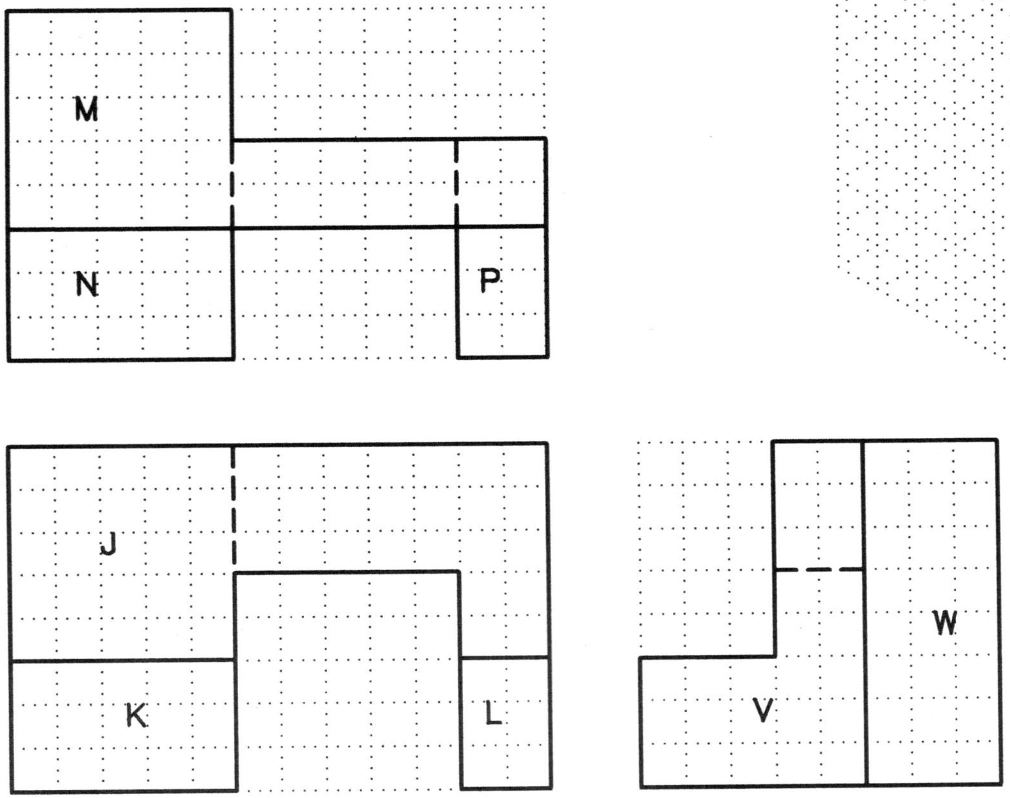

GIVEN: FRONT, TOP AND
RIGHT SIDE VIEWS.
REQUIRED: SKETCH AN
ISOMETRIC PICTORIAL
VIEW.

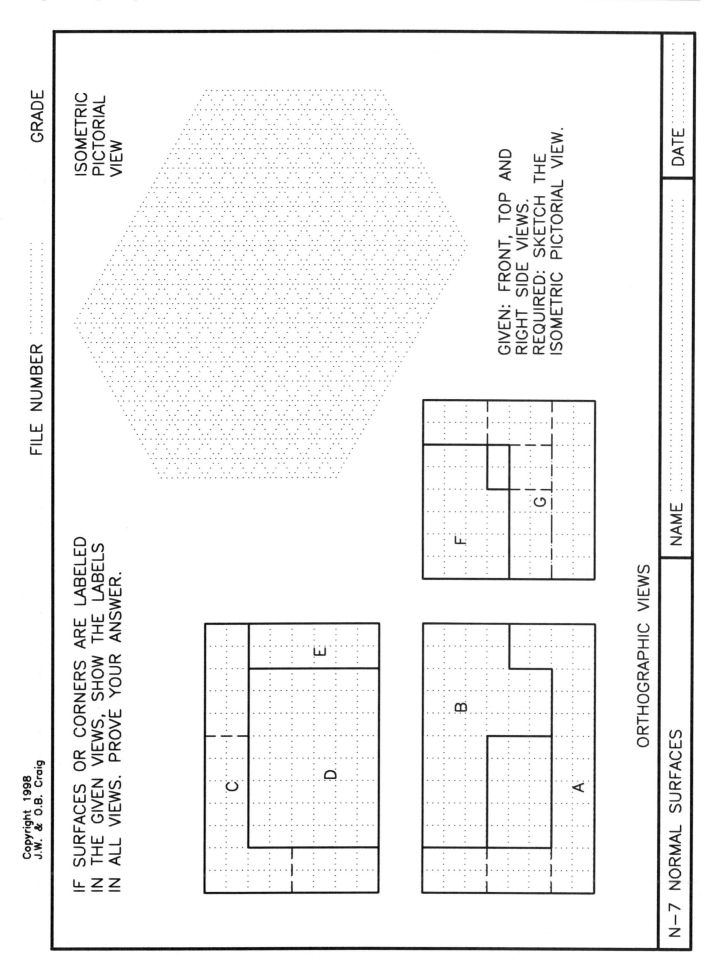

GRADE

FILE NUMBER

ISOMETRIC
PICTORIAL
VIEW

GIVEN: FRONT, TOP AND
RIGHT SIDE VIEWS.
REQUIRED: SKETCH THE
ISOMETRIC PICTORIAL VIEW.

IF SURFACES OR CORNERS ARE LABELED
IN THE GIVEN VIEWS, SHOW THE LABELS
IN ALL VIEWS. PROVE YOUR ANSWER.

F

G

C

D

E

B

A

ORTHOGRAPHIC VIEWS

NAME

DATE

N—7 NORMAL SURFACES

ISOMETRIC
PICTORIAL
VIEW

Copyright 1998
J.W. & O.B. Craig

FILE NUMBER ....   GRADE

WHEN GIVEN SURFACES OR CORNERS
ARE LABELED, SHOW THE LABELS
IN ALL VIEWS. PROVE YOUR ANSWER.

GIVEN: FRONT AND
LEFT SIDE VIEWS.
REQUIRED: SKETCH THE
TOP VIEW AND THE
ISOMETRIC PICTORIAL VIEW.

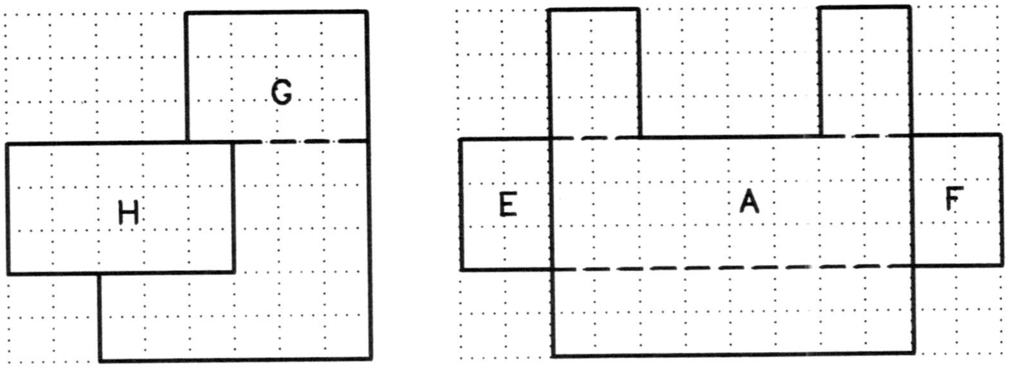

ORTHOGRAPHIC VIEWS

H

G

E

A

F

N—8 NORMAL SURFACES   NAME ....   DATE ....

GRADE

FILE NUMBER

ISOMETRIC
PICTORIAL
VIEW

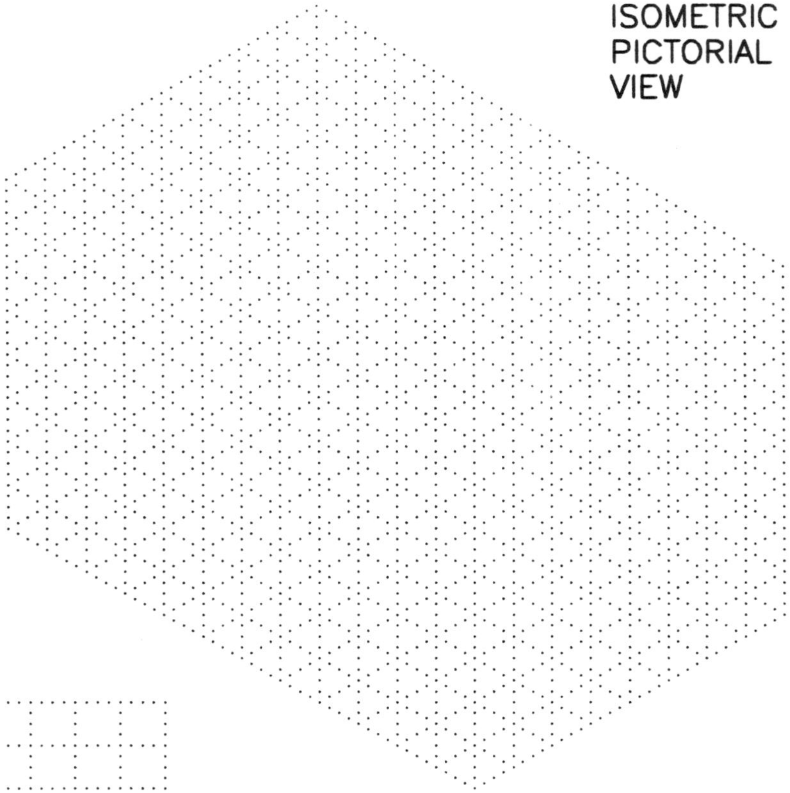

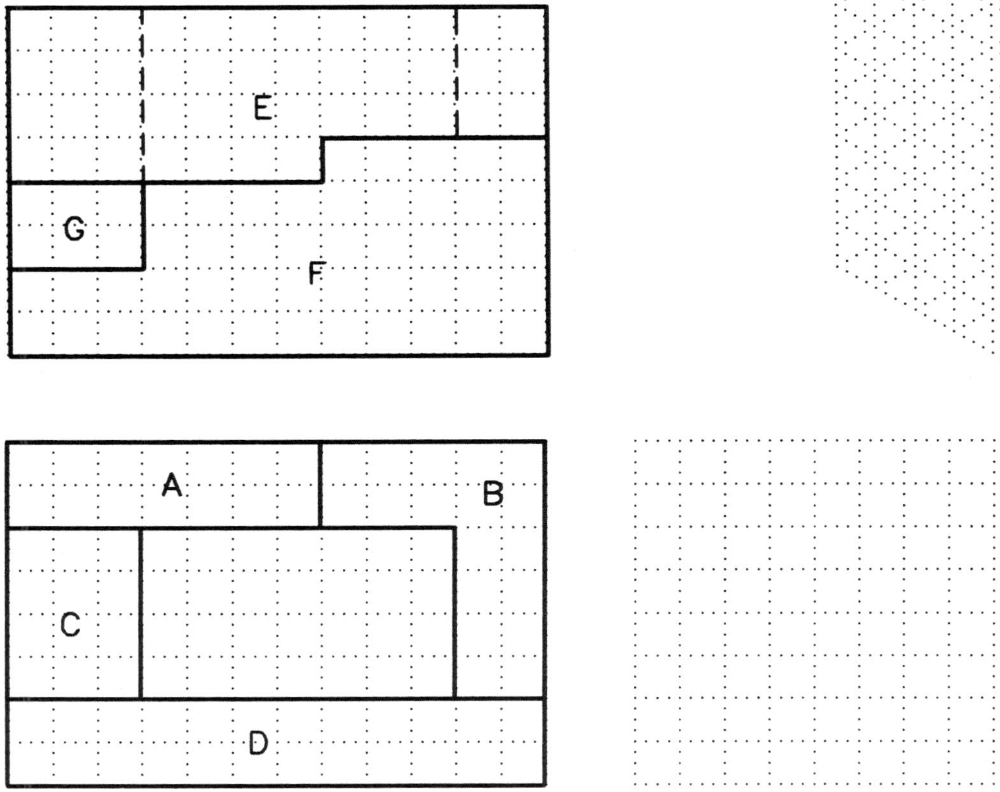

GIVEN: FRONT AND TOP
VIEWS.
REQUIRED: SKETCH THE
RIGHT SIDE VIEW
AND THE ISOMETRIC
PICTORIAL VIEW.

IF SURFACES OR CORNERS ARE LABELED
IN THE GIVEN VIEWS, SHOW THE LABELS
IN ALL VIEWS. PROVE YOUR ANSWER.

E

F

G

B

A

C

D

ORTHOGRAPHIC VIEWS

NAME

DATE

N—9 NORMAL SURFACES

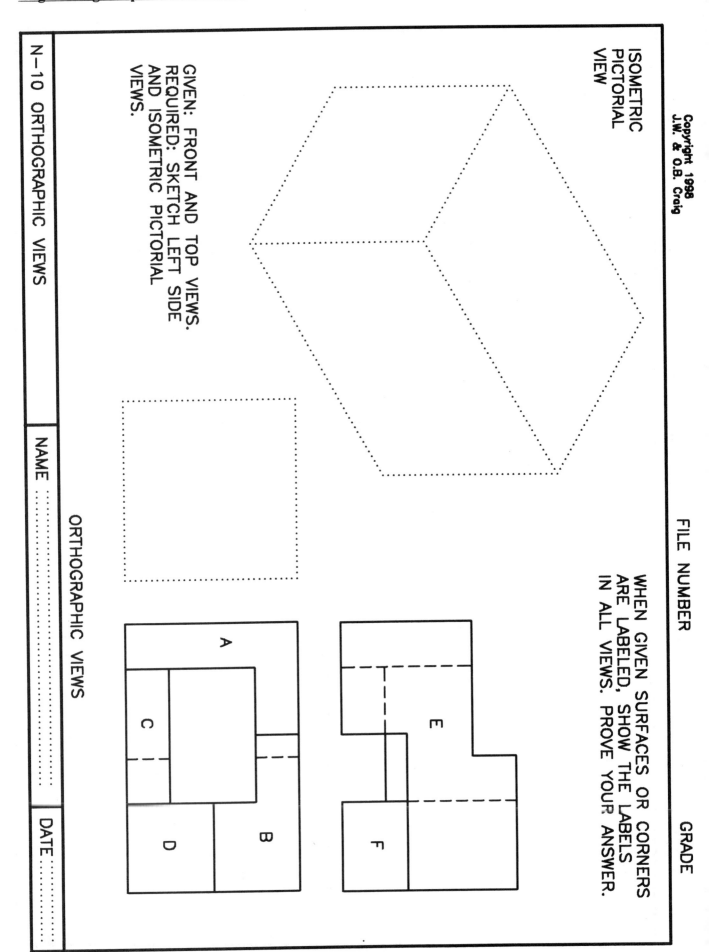

ISOMETRIC
PICTORIAL
VIEW

FILE NUMBER

GRADE

WHEN GIVEN SURFACES OR CORNERS
ARE LABELED, SHOW THE LABELS
IN ALL VIEWS. PROVE YOUR ANSWER.

GIVEN: FRONT AND TOP VIEWS.
REQUIRED: SKETCH LEFT SIDE
AND ISOMETRIC PICTORIAL
VIEWS.

ORTHOGRAPHIC VIEWS

N-10 ORTHOGRAPHIC VIEWS

NAME

DATE

GRADE

FILE NUMBER

GIVEN: FRONT AND RIGHT SIDE VIEWS.

REQUIRED: SKETCH THE TOP VIEW. LABEL SURFACES AS SHOWN.

SKETCH THE ISOMETRIC PICTORIAL ON ANOTHER SHEET.

LABEL SURFACES IN ALL VIEWS.

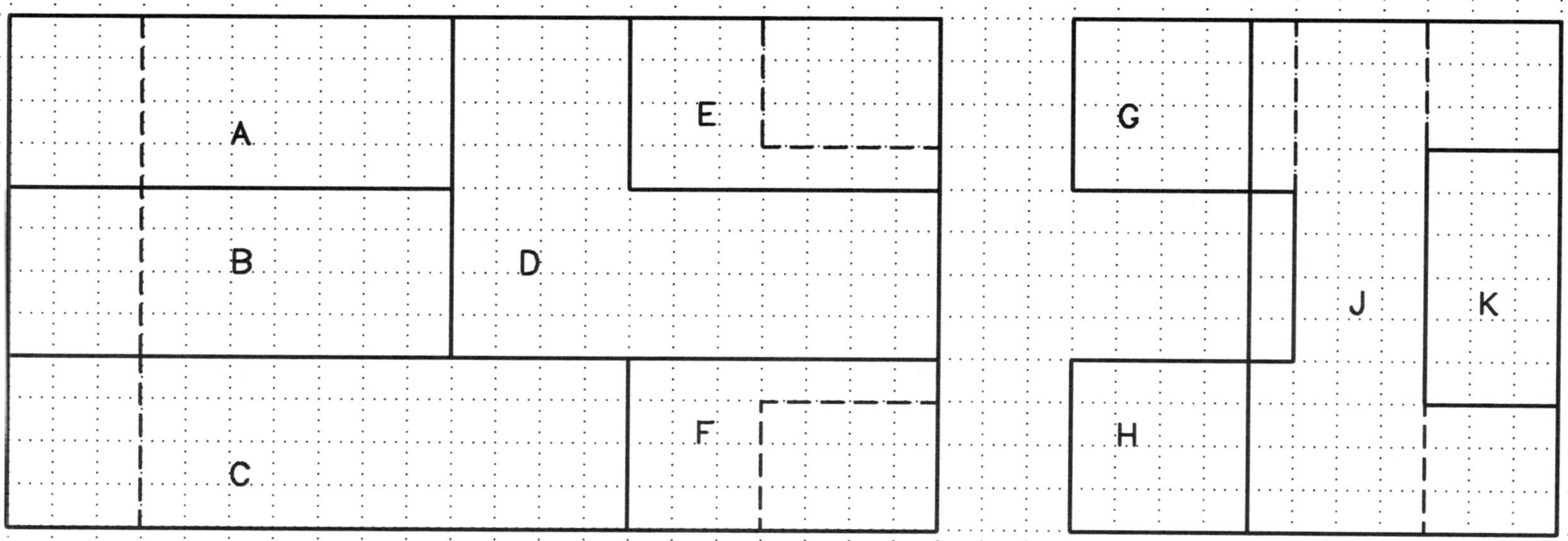

K

J

G

H

E

F

D

A

B

C

DATE

NAME

N-11 NORMAL SURFACES

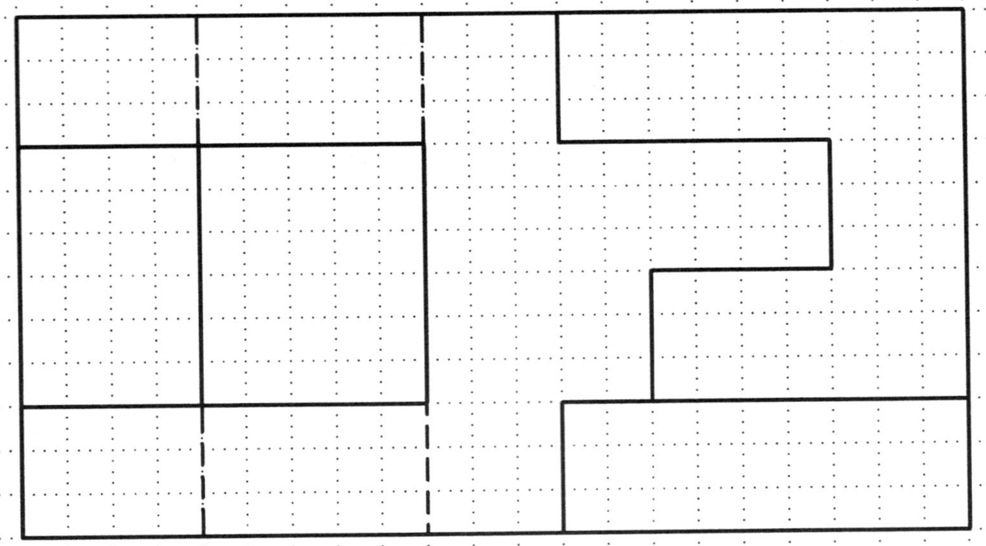

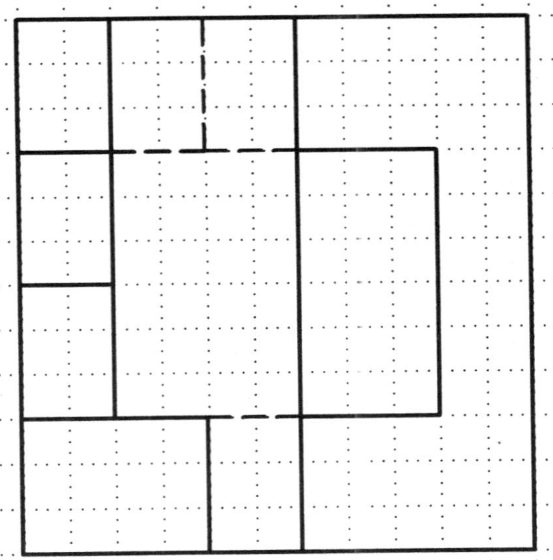

N-12 NORMAL SURFACES

NAME

DATE

FILE NUMBER

GRADE

GIVEN: FRONT AND RIGHT SIDE
VIEWS.
REQUIRED: LABEL SURFACES
SKETCH THE TOP VIEW.
SKETCH THE ISOMETRIC
PICTORIAL ON ANOTHER SHEET.

SHOW LABELS IN ALL VIEWS.

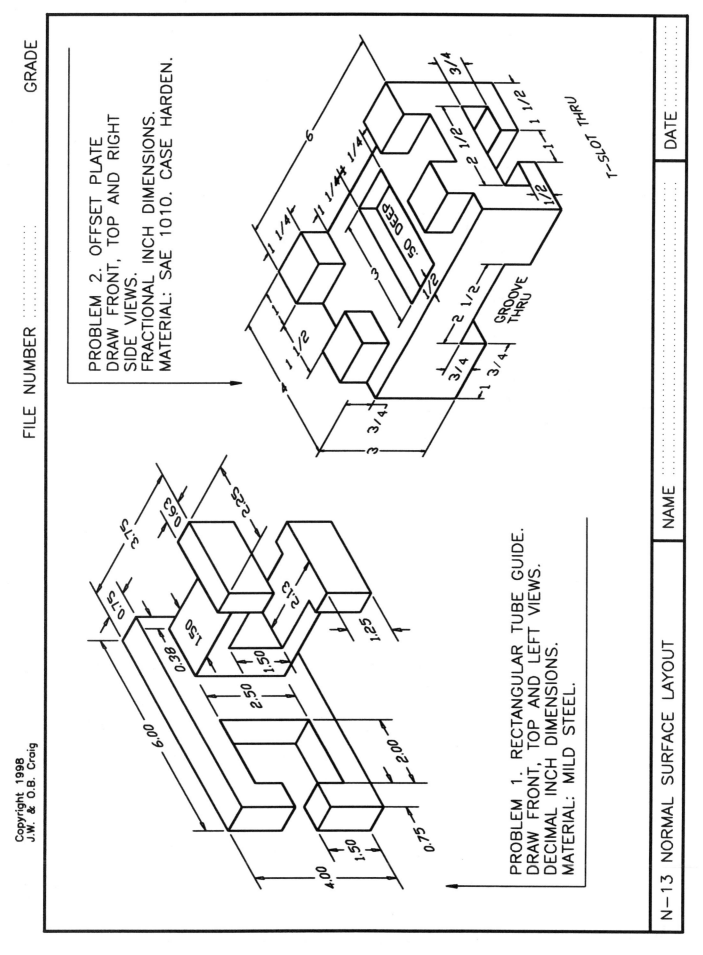

PROBLEM 2. OFFSET PLATE
DRAW FRONT, TOP AND RIGHT
SIDE VIEWS.
FRACTIONAL INCH DIMENSIONS.
MATERIAL: SAE 1010. CASE HARDEN.

PROBLEM 1. RECTANGULAR TUBE GUIDE.
DRAW FRONT, TOP AND LEFT VIEWS.
DECIMAL INCH DIMENSIONS.
MATERIAL: MILD STEEL.

Copyright 1998
J.W. & O.B. Craig

FILE NUMBER

GRADE

NAME

DATE

N-13 NORMAL SURFACE LAYOUT

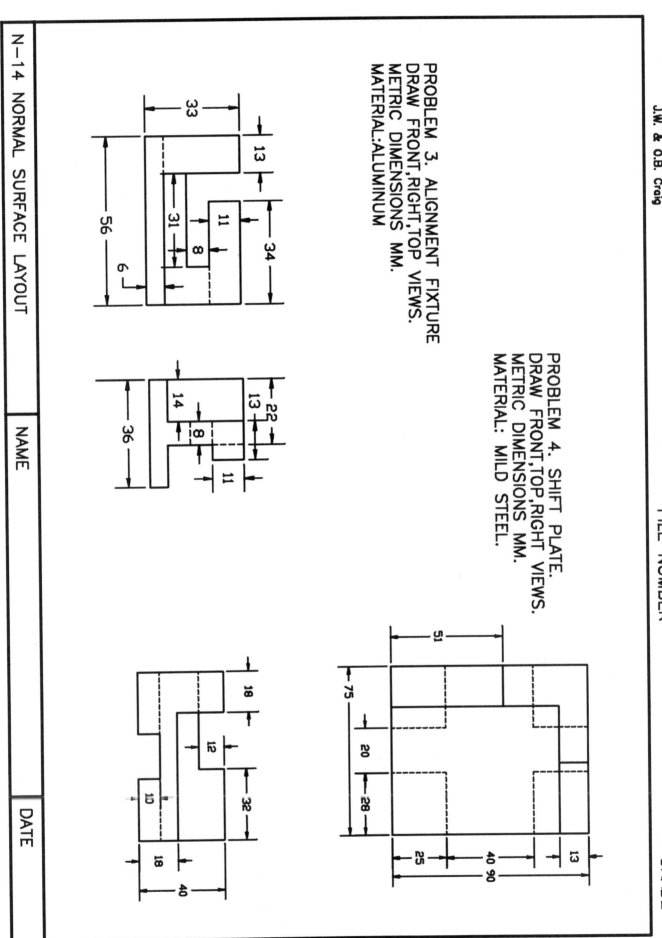

PROBLEM 3. ALIGNMENT FIXTURE
DRAW FRONT,RIGHT,TOP VIEWS.
METRIC DIMENSIONS MM.
MATERIAL:ALUMINUM

PROBLEM 4. SHIFT PLATE.
DRAW FRONT,TOP,RIGHT VIEWS.
METRIC DIMENSIONS MM.
MATERIAL: MILD STEEL.

N—14 NORMAL SURFACE LAYOUT   NAME   DATE

FILE NUMBER

GRADE

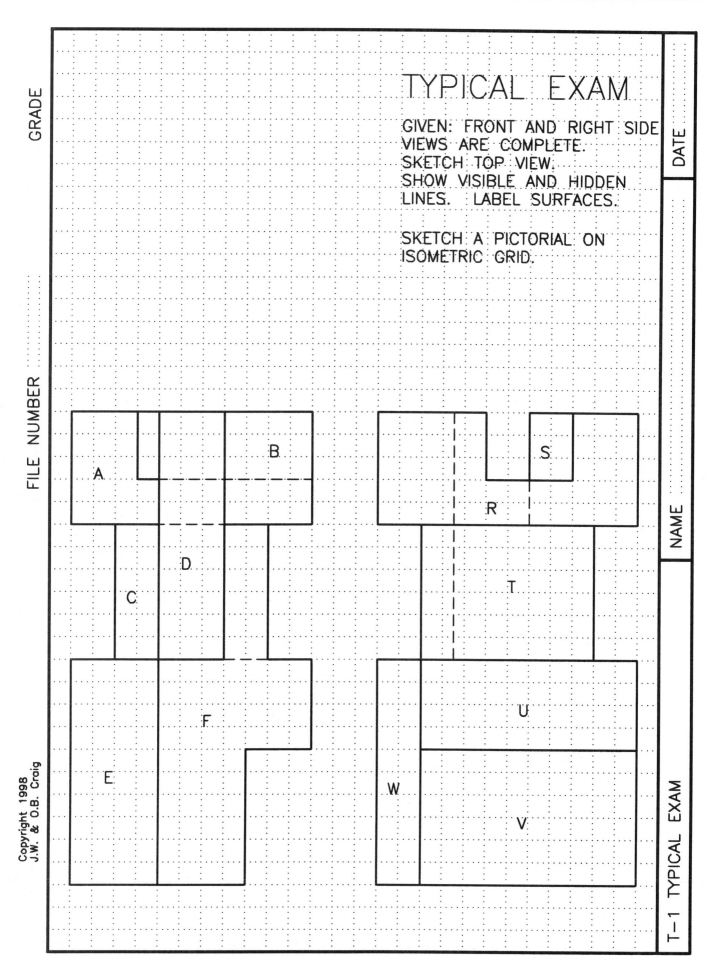

TYPICAL EXAM

GIVEN: FRONT AND RIGHT SIDE
VIEWS ARE COMPLETE.
SKETCH TOP VIEW.
SHOW VISIBLE AND HIDDEN
LINES. LABEL SURFACES.

SKETCH A PICTORIAL ON
ISOMETRIC GRID.

GRADE

DATE

FILE NUMBER

NAME

A   B

D

C

E   F

R   S

T

U

W   V

Copyright 1998
J.W. & O.B. Craig

T–1 TYPICAL EXAM

NAME

DATE

NOTE: TURN PAGE VERTICALLY
FOR USE.

FILE NUMBER

GRADE

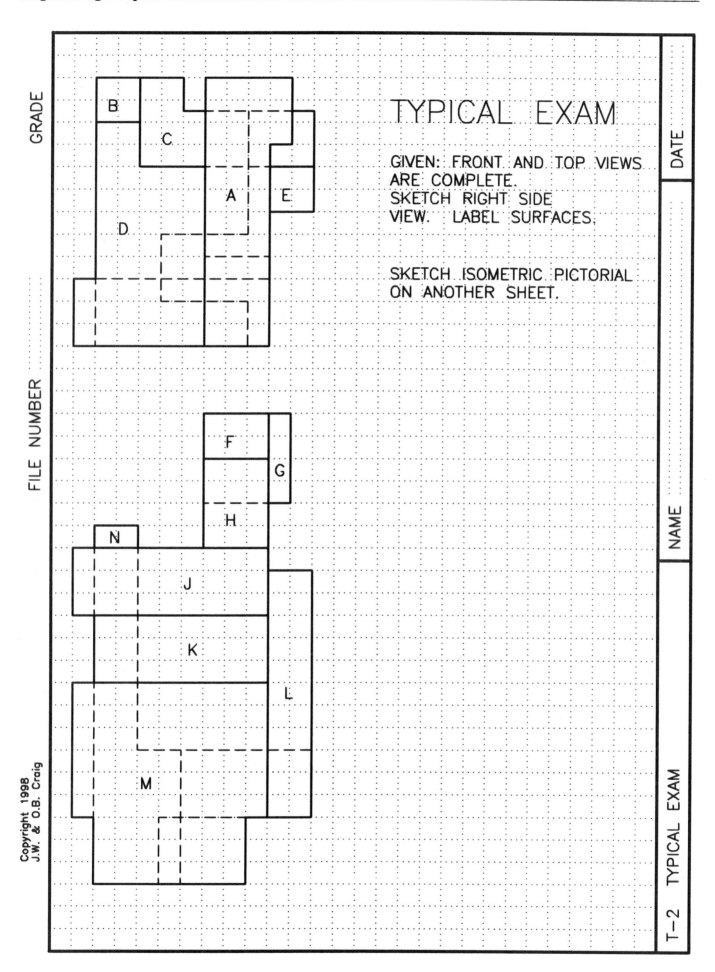

TYPICAL EXAM

GIVEN: FRONT AND TOP VIEWS
ARE COMPLETE.
SKETCH RIGHT SIDE
VIEW.   LABEL SURFACES.

SKETCH ISOMETRIC PICTORIAL
ON ANOTHER SHEET.

NAME

DATE

NOTE: TURN PAGE VERTICALLY FOR USE.

FILE NUMBER

GRADE

Introduction to Inclined Surfaces

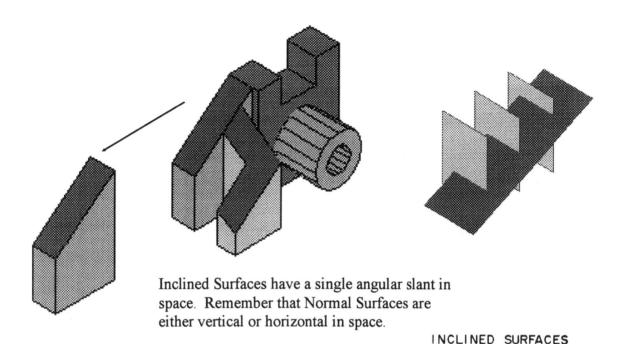

Inclined Surfaces have a single angular slant in space. Remember that Normal Surfaces are either vertical or horizontal in space.

Inclined Surfaces appear as an inclined edge-of-surface in one view. In this example, the "T" shaped surface is set parallel to the lines of sight for the front view.

Projecting surface "T" to the top view will show the surface, but it will appear shorter than its actual extent. Surface "T" is classified as foreshortened in the top view.

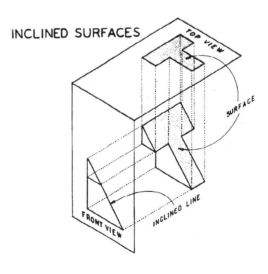

Looking at the side view, surface "T" appears as a foreshortened surface.

Analyzing Inclined surfaces starts by picking an inclined line in one view.

An Inclined line in one view <u>may be</u> the edge-of surface view of an Inclined surface on an object.

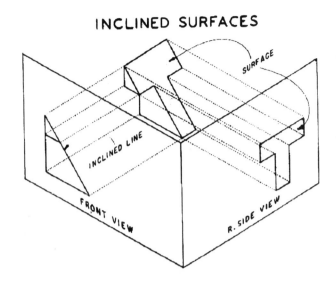

Three possible Inclined surface views.

1. Inclined edge-of-surface in the front view.

Surface "T" appears as an inclined edge-of-surface in the front view. It will appears as a foreshortened surface in the top view and as a foreshortened surface in the side view.

An Inclined surface will always have the same general shape whenever it appears as a surface.

2. Inclined edge-of-surface in the top view.

Surface "I" appears as an inclined edge-of-surface in the top view. It will appear as a foreshortened surface in the front view and a foreshortened surface in the side view.

An Inclined surface will always have the same number of corners and edges whenever it appears as a surface.

Surface "I" has 12 corners and edges in each surface view.

Numbering the corners of an Inclined surface will help assure that all corners are correctly drawn.

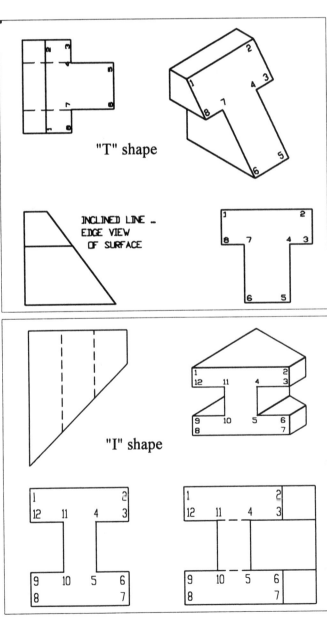

"T" shape

"I" shape

3. Inclined surface appearing as an inclined edge-of-surface in the side view.

Surface "Z" appears as an inclined line in the side view. It is a surface in the front and top views.

Inclined surfaces must have the same parallel and non-parallel edges whenever they appear as surfaces.

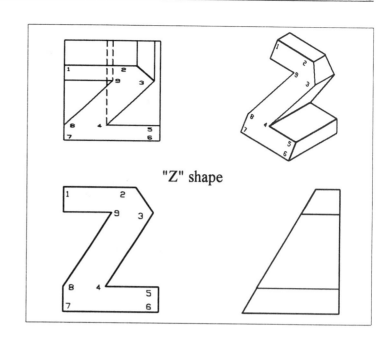

"Z" shape

This is the complete Inclined Surface Chart. It is easier to remember than the Normal Surface Chart. Usually, if there is an inclined line in one view, it will be the edge of an inclined surface appearing in the other views.

INCLINED SURFACES

FRONT	TOP	SIDE
INCLINED LINE	SURFACE	SURFACE
SURFACE	INCLINED LINE	SURFACE
SURFACE	SURFACE	INCLINED LINE

INCLINED LINES ARE TRUE LENGTH LINES
SURFACES ARE FORESHORTENED

PROVING INCLINED SURFACES

1. INCLINED LINE IN ONE VIEW — SURFACE IN THE OTHER TWO VIEWS.
2. SURFACE MUST HAVE SAME GENERAL SHAPE.
3. SURFACES MUST HAVE SAME NUMBER OF CORNERS AND EDGES.
4. SURFACES MUST HAVE THE SAME PARALLELISM AND NON PARALLELISM OF EDGES.

Analyze the surfaces on this part:

"A" (1,2,3,4,5) is an inclined line in the side view. It is a surface in the front and top views.

"B" (3,6,7,8,4) is an inclined line in the top view. It is a surface in the front and side views.

"C" (2,10,11,6,3) is an inclined line in the front view. It is a surface in the top and side views.

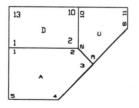
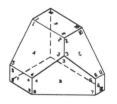
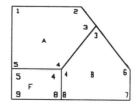
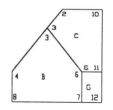

Analyzing Inclined Edges

An Inclined edge will appear as an inclined line in one view and will be either vertical or horizontal in the other views.

Line 1,2 is parallel to the front projection plane in this example. It is horizontal in the top view and vertical in the side view.

Line 1,2 is true length in the front view.

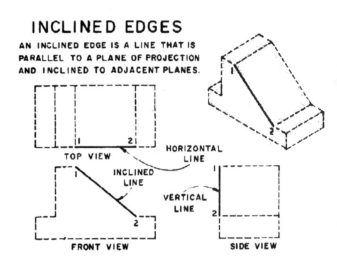

Inclined line 1,2 is parallel to the top projection plane. It is true length in the top view.

Line 1,2 is horizontal in the front and side views and is foreshortened in those views.

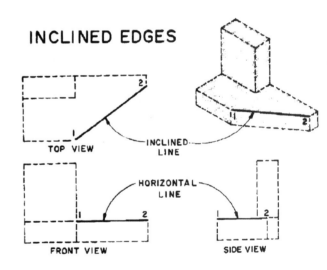

INCLINED EDGES

FRONT	TOP	SIDE
INCLINED LINE	HORIZONTAL LINE	VERTICAL LINE
HORIZONTAL LINE	INCLINED LINE	HORIZONTAL LINE
VERTICAL LINE	VERTICAL LINE	INCLINED LINE

INCLINED LINES ARE TRUE LENGTH LINES
HORIZONTAL AND VERTICAL LINES
ARE FORESHORTENED

Inclined edge chart. It is important to know when a line appears __true length__ in a view.

Inclined line 1,2 in this example is parallel to the side projection plane. It is a vertical foreshortened line in the front and top views.

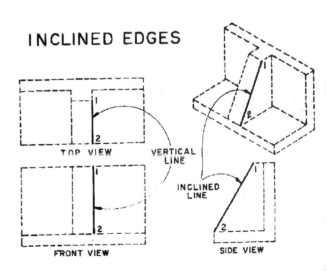

Projecting Inclined Surfaces

Given: Front and Side views are complete.

Draw: Top view.

1. Locate reference for measurements. Sketch a vertical line in the side view. Sketch a horizontal line in the top view. DEPTH is the common dimension from side to top views.

2. Identify an inclined line in the front view.
It is surface "F" in the side view.

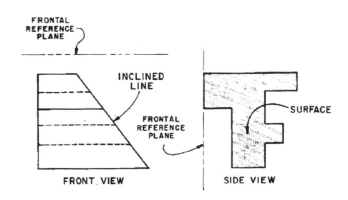

3. Number the corners of the surface in the side view. Be sure to place a number at each corner. Do not duplicate numbers.

Surface "F" has 12 corners and edges.

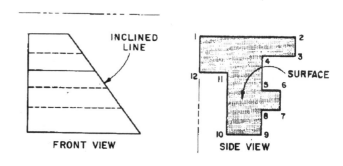

4. Locate the numbers on the inclined line in the front view.

The inclined line in the front view is the surface in the side view. All the numbers on the surface in the side view must be on the inclined line in the front view and no place else.

Drawing surface "F" in the top view becomes an automatic process.
__ Project the points from the front view.
__ Measure the points from the side view.

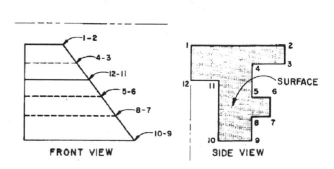

Transfer point 1 to the top view.
___1 projects up from the front view.
___1 is on the reference in the side view.
___1 is on the reference in the top view.

Transfer point 2 to the top view.
___2 projects from the front view.
___2 is the full depth (horizontal) in the side view.
___2 is the full depth (vertical) in the top view.

Put a dot and label each point in the top view.

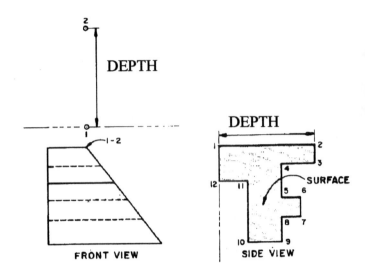

Project points 3 and 4 to the top view.

Measure the depth distances (horizontal) in the side view. Transfer the same distances (vertical) to the top view.

Place a dot and carefully label the points in the top view.

Transfer 5,6,7,8 to the top view.

Project the points from the front view.

Measure the distances from the side view.

Transfer the measurements to the top view.

Locate each point with a dot and carefully label each point in the top view.

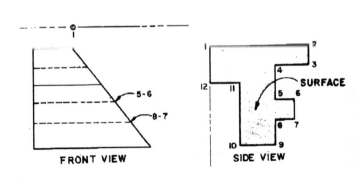

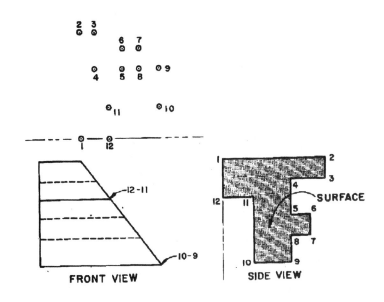

All the points have been transferred to the top view and labeled.

This process makes it possible to create portions of a missing view before the shape can be visualized. This is an excellent means of developing the ability to visualize complex shapes.

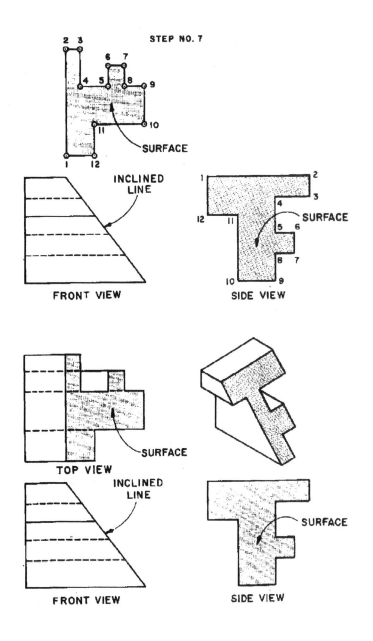

Connect the points in the same order they were connected in the side view.

Inclined surface "F" has been transferred to the top view. It must have:

__The same number of corners and edges.
__The same parallel edges.
__The same general shape in each surface view.

Thirteen surfaces must still be analyzed and drawn to complete the top view. These are all Normal Surfaces.

__Six horizontal lines in the side view must be horizontal lines in the front view and surfaces in the top view.
__Six Vertical lines in the side view must be surfaces in the front view and horizontal lines in the top view.
__A vertical line in the front view must be a surface in the side view and a vertical line in the top view.

Inclined Surfaces in Pictorial Views

Points on pictorial views may require 1, 2, or 3 measurements to locate.

Working from the lower left corner (0,0) of the object, points are measured using HEIGHT, WIDTH and DEPTH:
__point A is 3 units above O (H3).
__point B is 8 units up and 5 units back (H8,D5).
__point C is 6 units to the right, 8 units up and 5 units back. (W6, H8, D5).

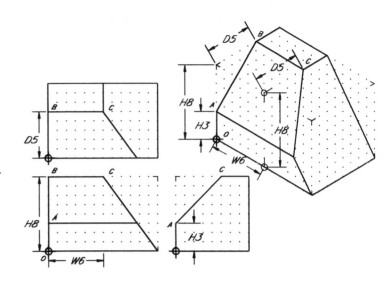

Problem Solution:

Sketch a horizontal line in the top view and a vertical line in the side view for measurements.

Inclined line 1,4 in the side view is surface 1,2,3,4,5 in the front view.
__Number the corners in the front view.
__Transfer the numbers back to the side view.

You must know exactly where each corner of the surface is .. in BOTH given views.

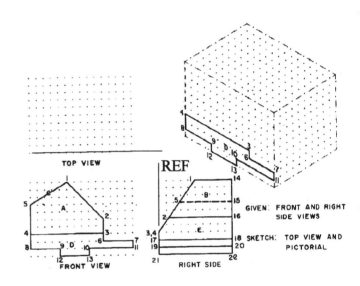

Transfer the points to the top view:
__3 and 4 project up. Both are on the front face, zero distance measurement.
__5 projects from the front. 5 is 3 units depth.
__1 projects from the front. 1 is 5 units depth,
__2 projects from the front, 2 is 1 1/2 units depth.

Transfer the points to the pictorial:
__3 and 4 are already shown.
__5 is 4 units above 4 and 3 units back. (4H and 3D relative to 4).
__1 is 5 units width, 10 units height and 5 units depth from the lower left corner of the grid. (5W, 10H and 5D)
__2 is 2 units up and 1 1/2 units back from 3. (2H and 1 1/2D relative to 3).

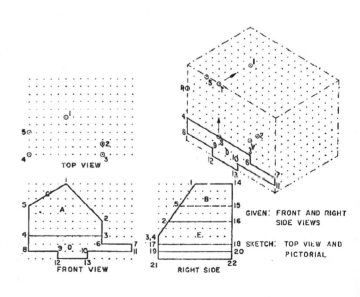

Connect the points 1,2,3,4,5,1 in order. This locates surface "A".

Inclined line "B" in the front view is surface 1,14,16,2 in the side view.
__transfer 1,14 to 1 in the front view.
__transfer 2,16 to 2 in the front view.

__project 14 to the top view. 14 measures 10 units depth (back of the object).
__project 16 to the top view. 16 also measures 10 units depth.

Plot 14 and 16 on the pictorial:
__14 is 5 units in back of 1.
(5D relative to 1).
__16 is 8 1/2 units deep relative to 2.
(8 1/2D relative to 2).
Connect 1,14,16,2,1 to complete the surface.

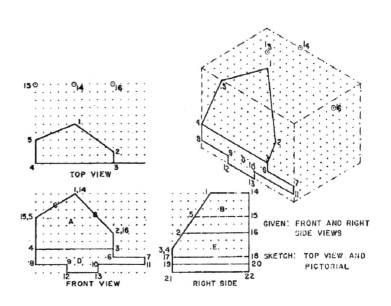

Finish the drawing.

Inclined line "C" in the front view is surface 1,14,15,5 in the side view. Project point 15 to the front view. Locate point 15 in the top view. 15 projects from the front and measures 10 units depth from the side view. Draw surface 1,14,15,5,1 in the top view.

Locate point 15 in the pictorial view. 15 is 7 units depth relative to 5. Draw surface 1,14,15,5,1 in the isometric.

Horizontal edge-of-surface 6,7 in the front view is horizontal edge-of-surface 17,18 in the side view.
__Sketch a surface in the top view 4 units wide and 10 units deep.
__Sketch the surface on the pictorial view.

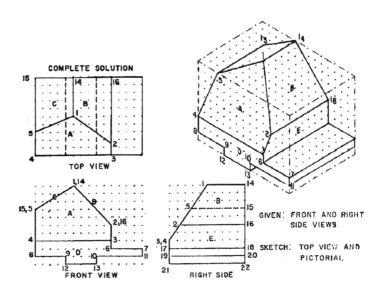

Vertical edge-of-surface 10,13 in the front view is normal surface 19,20,22,21 in the side view. Sketch a vertical hidden line in the top view directly above 10,13 and extending from front to back (10 units).

Vertical edge-of surface 9,12 in the front view is a hidden surface behind 19,20,22,21 in the side view. Sketch a vertical hidden line in the top view directly above 9,12 and 10 units deep.

NAME

DATE

FILE NUMBER

GRADE

Copyright 1998 J.W. Craig and D.B. Craig

INCLINED SURFACE LECTURE SHEET

Please sketch the answer as the instructor talks.
Follow the reasoning used to prove every line and point on the drawing.

[ISOMETRIC PICTORIAL]

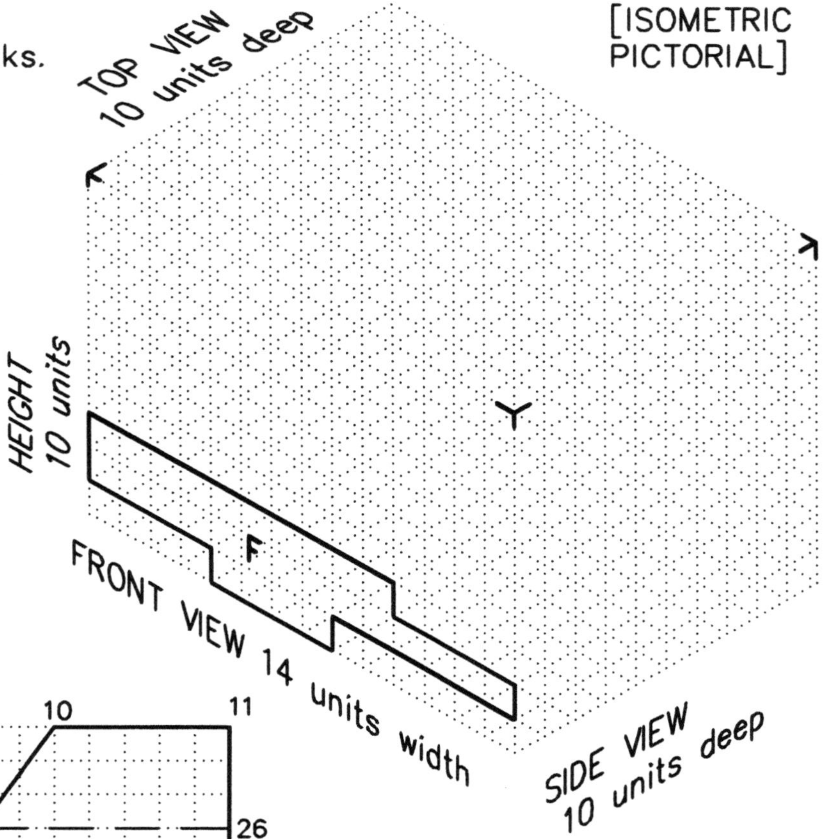

TOP VIEW 10 units deep

HEIGHT 10 units

FRONT VIEW 14 units width

SIDE VIEW 10 units deep

NOTE:
Show hidden lines in orthographic views.
Do not show hidden lines in pictorial views.

[TOP VIEW]

(back face of the object)

(front face of object)

10 units deep

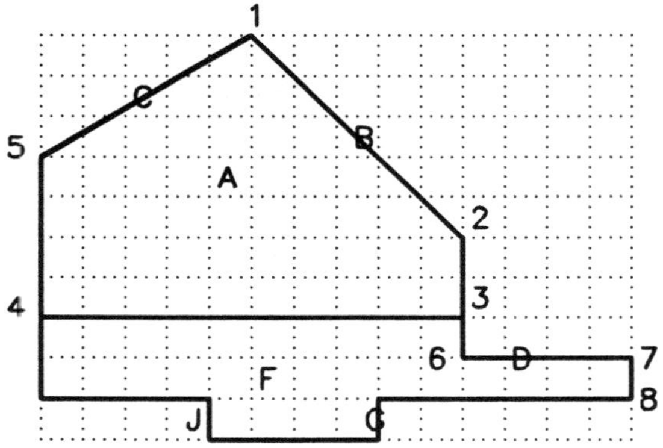

[FRONT VIEW]

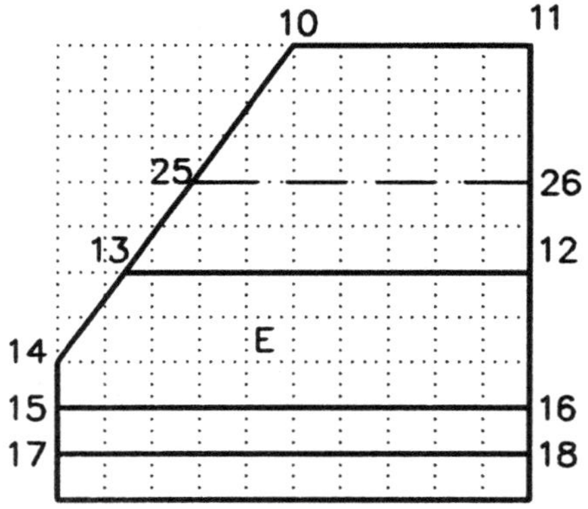

[RIGHT SIDE VIEW]
10 units deep

INCLINED SURFACE LECTURE SHEET

DRAWN BY:

DATE

COURSE

GRADE

DRAWING

FILE NUMBER ....

GRADE

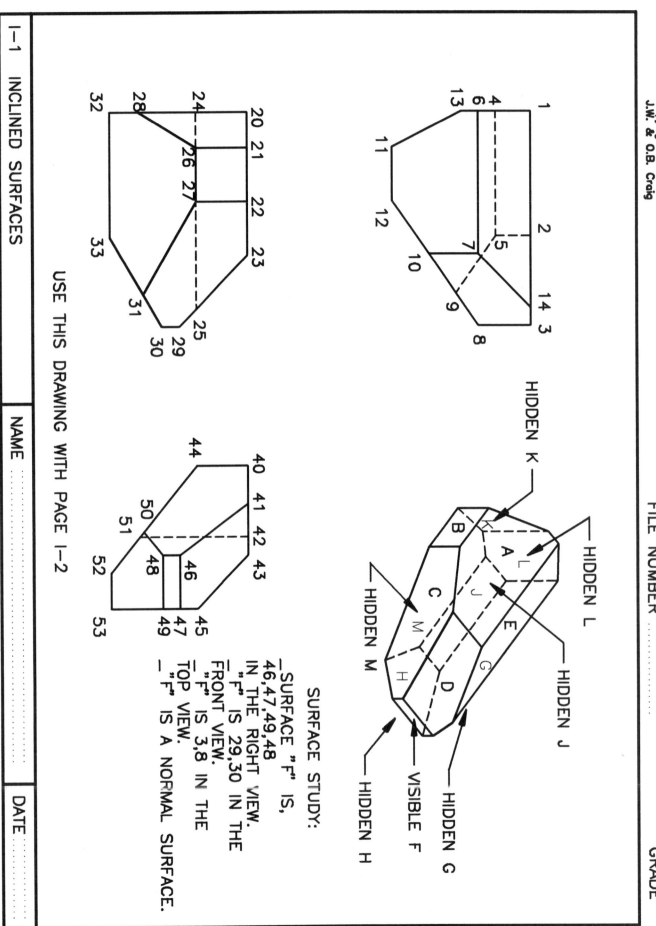

I–1

INCLINED SURFACES

USE THIS DRAWING WITH PAGE I–2

NAME ....

DATE ....

HIDDEN K

HIDDEN L

HIDDEN J

VISIBLE F

HIDDEN G

HIDDEN M

HIDDEN H

SURFACE STUDY:

SURFACE "F" IS,
46,47,49,48
IN THE RIGHT VIEW.
"F" IS 29,30 IN THE
FRONT VIEW.
"F" IS 3,8 IN THE
TOP VIEW.
"F" IS A NORMAL SURFACE.

Copyright 1998
J.W. & O.B. Craig

GRADE

FILE NUMBER

USE THIS PAGE WITH I–1. NEATLY LETTER THE ANSWERS IN THE TABLE.

SURFACE	TOP VIEW	FRONT VIEW	RIGHT SIDE VIEW	SURFACE TYPE
A				
B				
C				
D				
E				
F	3,8	29,30	46,47,49,48	NORMAL
G				
H				
J				
K				
L				
M				

SURFACE TABLES – REVIEW – FILL IN THE MISSING BLOCKS

NORMAL SURFACES

FRONT	TOP	SIDE
SURFACE		
	SURFACE	
		SURFACE

INCLINED SURFACES

FRONT	TOP	SIDE
INCLINED LINE		
	INCLINED LINE	
		INCLINED LINE

NAME

DATE

I–2　　INCLINED SURFACES

NAME

DATE

NOTE: Use this grid format
in horizontal direction.

FILE NUMBER

GRADE

GRADE

FILE NUMBER

RIGHT SIDE VIEW

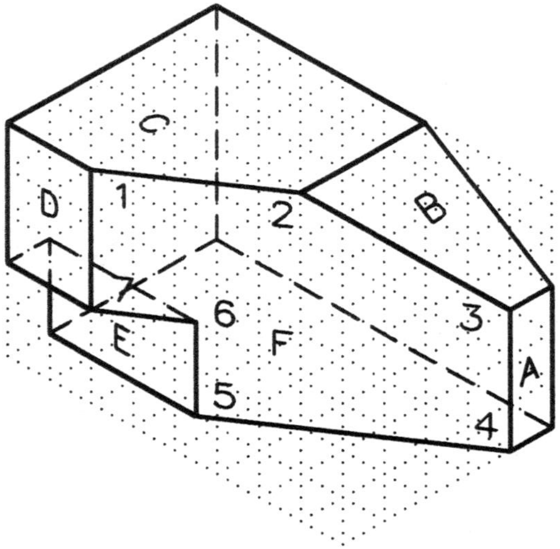

TOP VIEW

FRONT VIEW

BOTTOM VIEW

LEFT SIDE VIEW

REAR (BACK) VIEW

GIVEN: ISOMETRIC PICTORIAL VIEW.
SKETCH THE SIX REGULAR
ORTHOGRAPHIC VIEWS.
Be sure to show hidden lines
in the orthographic views.

LABEL SURFACES IN ALL VIEWS.

NAME

DATE

1-3 INCLINED SURFACES

Copyright 1998
J.W. & O.B. Craig

IF SURFACES OR CORNERS ARE LABELED
IN THE GIVEN VIEWS, SHOW THE LABELS
IN ALL VIEWS. PROVE YOUR ANSWER.

FILE NUMBER .... GRADE

ISOMETRIC
PICTORIAL
VIEW

ORTHOGRAPHIC VIEWS

GIVEN: ISOMETRIC
PICTORIAL VIEW.
REQUIRED: SKETCH THE
TOP, FRONT AND RIGHT
SIDE VIEWS.

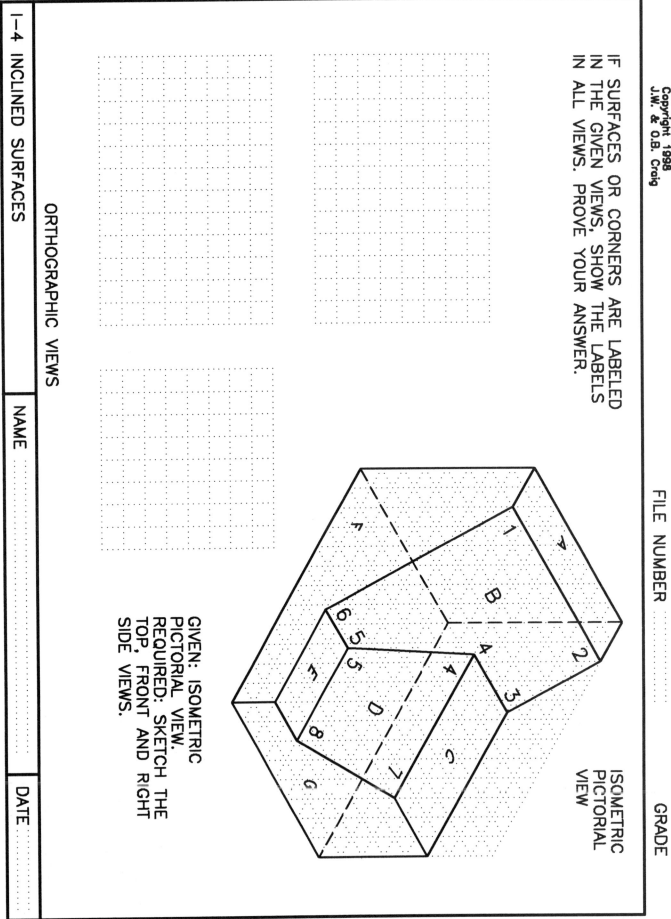

I-4 INCLINED SURFACES

NAME .... DATE ....

GRADE

FILE NUMBER

ISOMETRIC
PICTORIAL
VIEW

GIVEN: FRONT AND RIGHT SIDE
VIEWS.
REQUIRED: SKETCH THE TOP
AND ISOMETRIC PICTORIAL VIEWS.

IF SURFACES OR CORNERS ARE LABELED
IN THE GIVEN VIEWS, SHOW THE LABELS
IN ALL VIEWS. PROVE YOUR ANSWER.

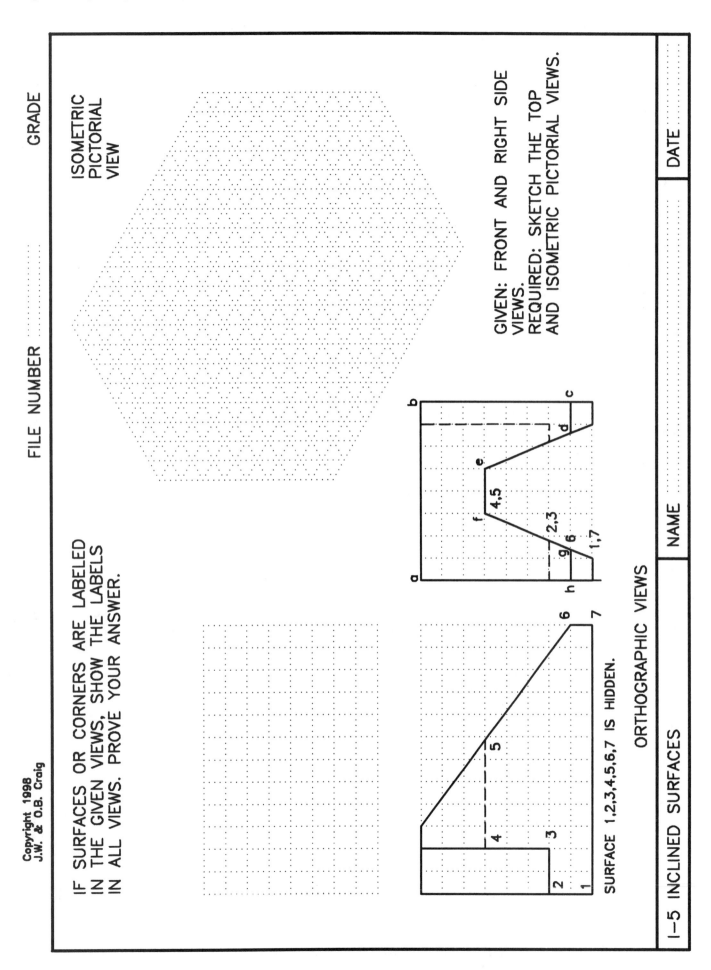

SURFACE 1,2,3,4,5,6,7 IS HIDDEN.

ORTHOGRAPHIC VIEWS

NAME

DATE

1—5 INCLINED SURFACES

Copyright 1998
J.W. & O.B. Craig

ISOMETRIC
PICTORIAL
VIEW

FILE NUMBER

GRADE

WHEN GIVEN SURFACES OR CORNERS
ARE LABELED, SHOW THE LABELS
IN ALL VIEWS. PROVE YOUR ANSWER.

GIVEN: FRONT AND LEFT SIDE
VIEWS.
REQUIRED: SKETCH THE TOP
VIEW AND ISOMETRIC
PICTORIAL VIEW.

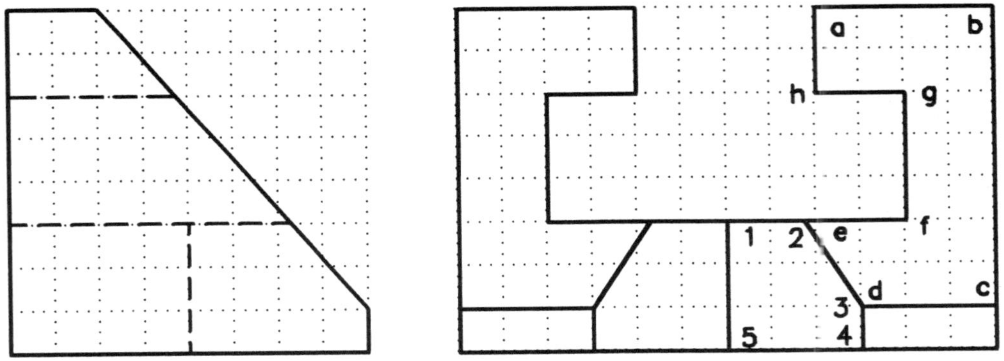

ORTHOGRAPHIC VIEWS

I–6 INCLINED SURFACES

NAME

DATE

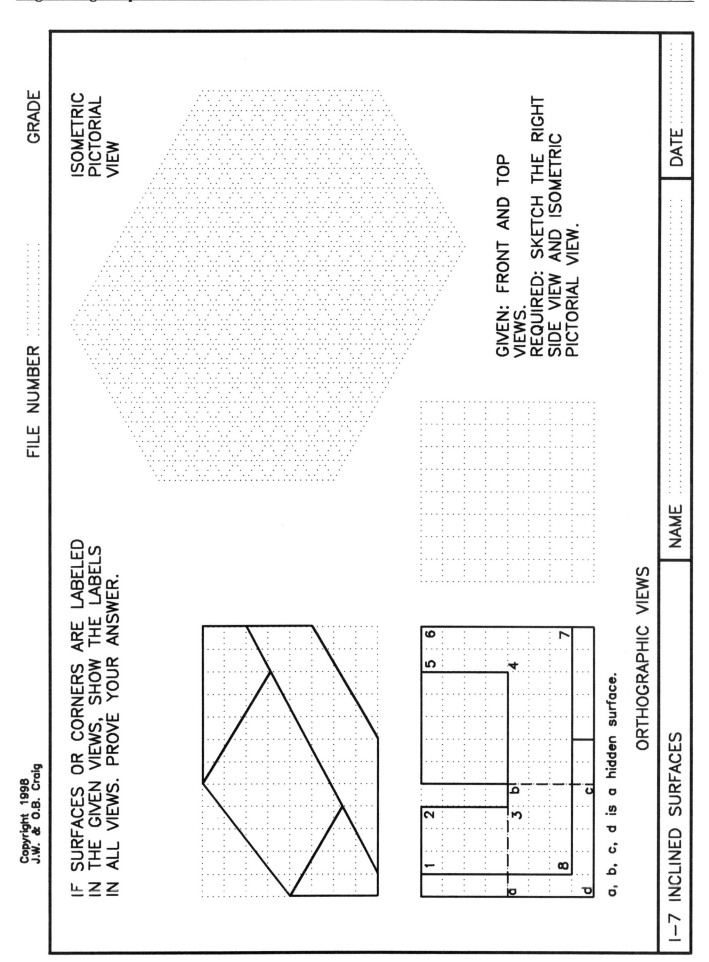

GRADE

ISOMETRIC
PICTORIAL
VIEW

FILE NUMBER

GIVEN: FRONT AND TOP
VIEWS.
REQUIRED: SKETCH THE RIGHT
SIDE VIEW AND ISOMETRIC
PICTORIAL VIEW.

IF SURFACES OR CORNERS ARE LABELED
IN THE GIVEN VIEWS, SHOW THE LABELS
IN ALL VIEWS. PROVE YOUR ANSWER.

ORTHOGRAPHIC VIEWS

a, b, c, d is a hidden surface.

NAME

DATE

I−7 INCLINED SURFACES

ISOMETRIC
PICTORIAL
VIEW

FILE NUMBER ....

GRADE

LABEL THE CORNERS OF INCLINED
SURFACES. SHOW LABELS IN ALL
VIEWS.

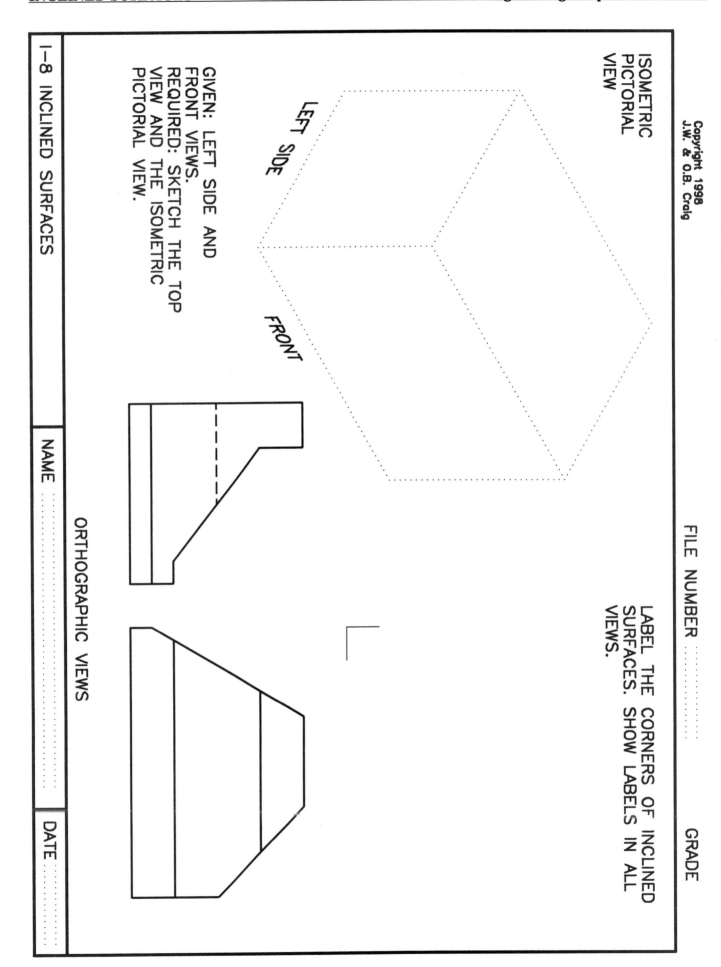

LEFT SIDE

FRONT

GIVEN: LEFT SIDE AND
FRONT VIEWS.
REQUIRED: SKETCH THE TOP
VIEW AND THE ISOMETRIC
PICTORIAL VIEW.

I–8 INCLINED SURFACES

ORTHOGRAPHIC VIEWS

NAME ....

DATE ....

F - 20

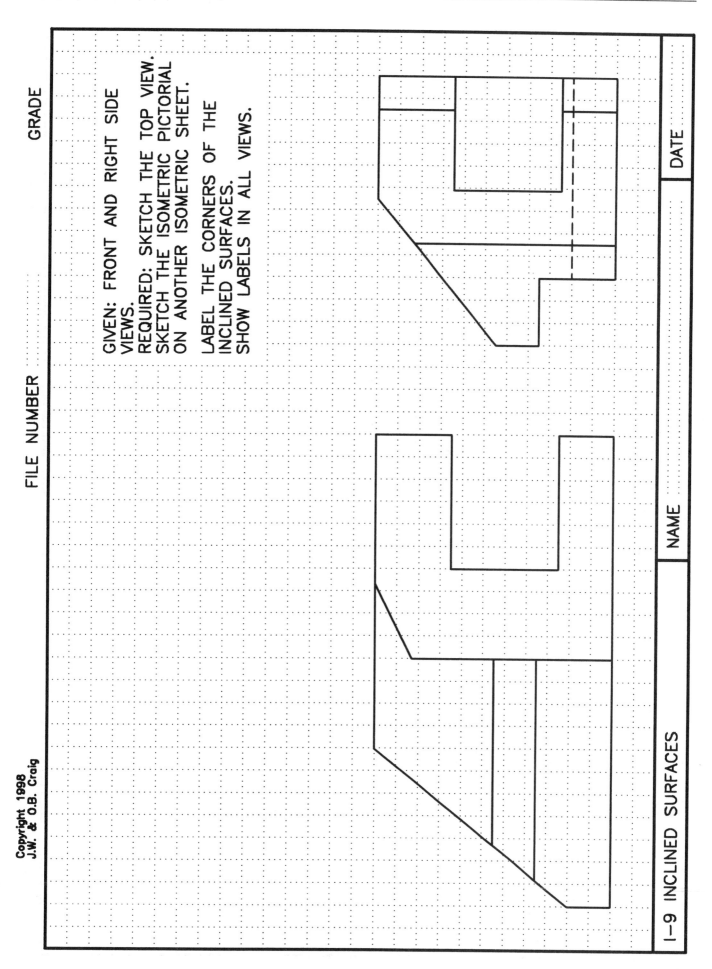

GIVEN: FRONT AND RIGHT SIDE VIEWS.

REQUIRED: SKETCH THE TOP VIEW. SKETCH THE ISOMETRIC PICTORIAL ON ANOTHER ISOMETRIC SHEET.

LABEL THE CORNERS OF THE INCLINED SURFACES. SHOW LABELS IN ALL VIEWS.

GRADE

FILE NUMBER

DATE

NAME

I-9 INCLINED SURFACES

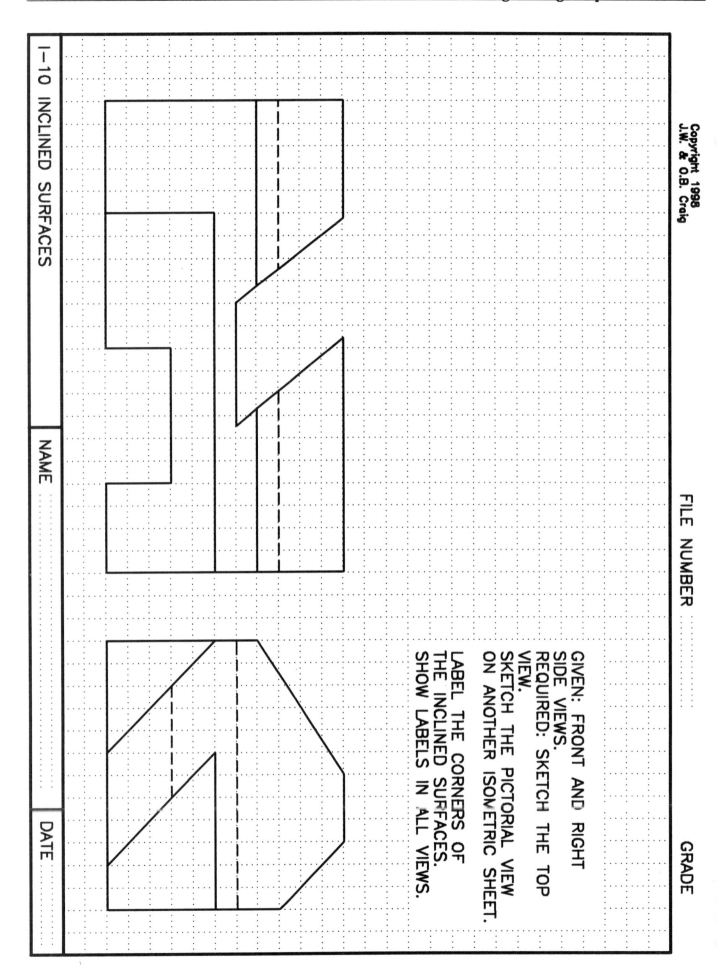

I-10 INCLINED SURFACES

NAME

DATE

FILE NUMBER

GRADE

GIVEN: FRONT AND RIGHT
SIDE VIEWS.
REQUIRED: SKETCH THE TOP
VIEW.
SKETCH THE PICTORIAL VIEW
ON ANOTHER ISOMETRIC SHEET.
LABEL THE CORNERS OF
THE INCLINED SURFACES.
SHOW LABELS IN ALL VIEWS.

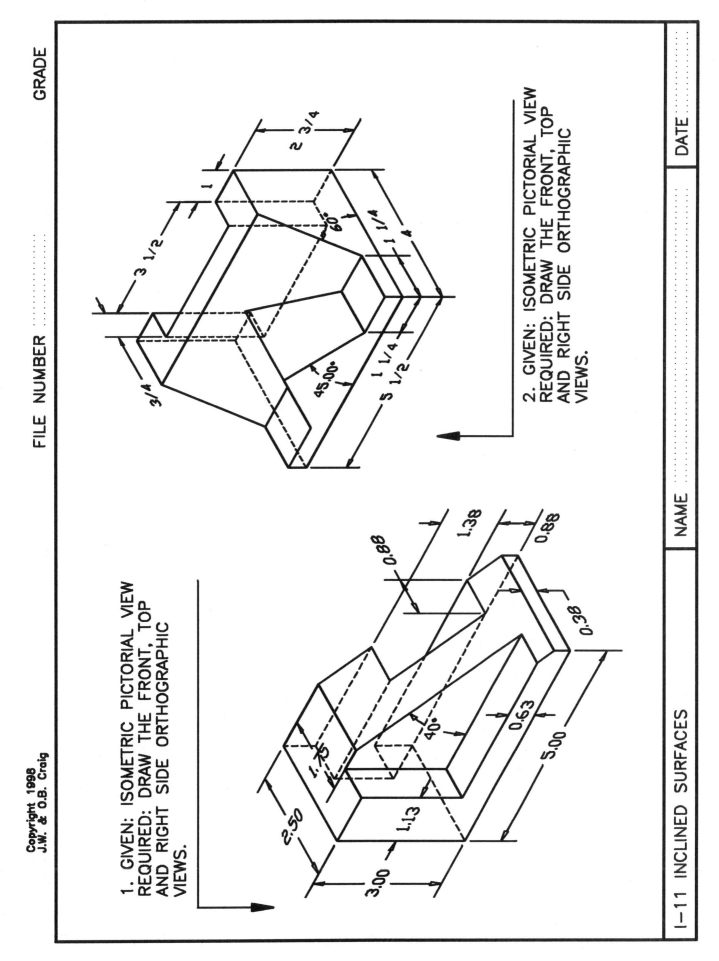

2. GIVEN: ISOMETRIC PICTORIAL VIEW
REQUIRED: DRAW THE FRONT, TOP
AND RIGHT SIDE ORTHOGRAPHIC
VIEWS.

1. GIVEN: ISOMETRIC PICTORIAL VIEW
REQUIRED: DRAW THE FRONT, TOP
AND RIGHT SIDE ORTHOGRAPHIC
VIEWS.

GRADE

DATE

FILE NUMBER

NAME

I-11 INCLINED SURFACES

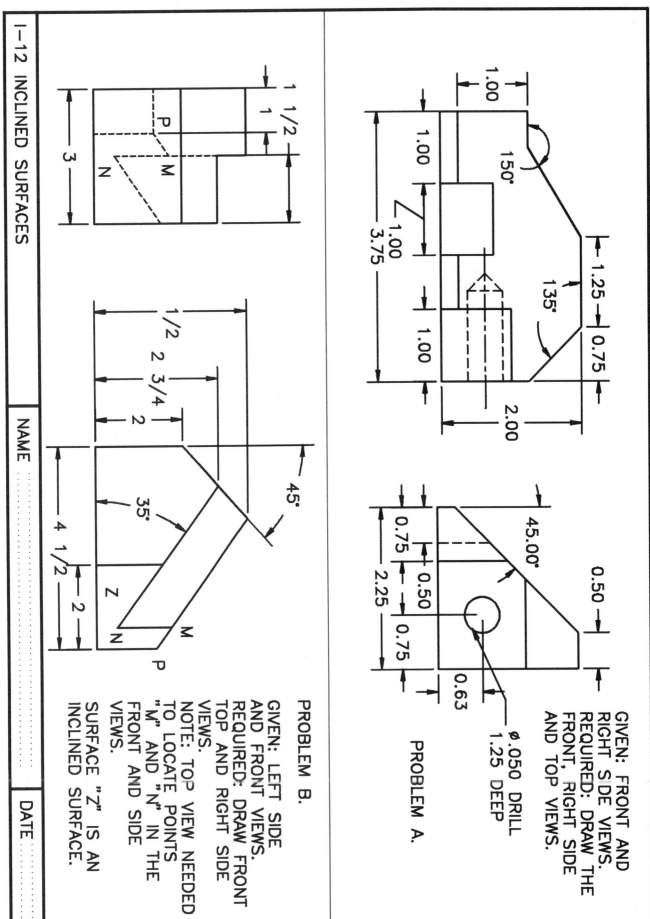

FILE NUMBER   GRADE

GIVEN: FRONT AND
RIGHT SIDE VIEWS.
REQUIRED: DRAW THE
FRONT, RIGHT SIDE
AND TOP VIEWS.

PROBLEM A.

PROBLEM B.

GIVEN: LEFT SIDE
AND FRONT VIEWS.
REQUIRED: DRAW FRONT
TOP AND RIGHT SIDE
VIEWS.
NOTE: TOP VIEW NEEDED
TO LOCATE POINTS
"M" AND "N" IN THE
FRONT AND SIDE
VIEWS.
SURFACE "Z" IS AN
INCLINED SURFACE.

Ø.050 DRILL
1.25 DEEP

I–12   INCLINED SURFACES   NAME   DATE

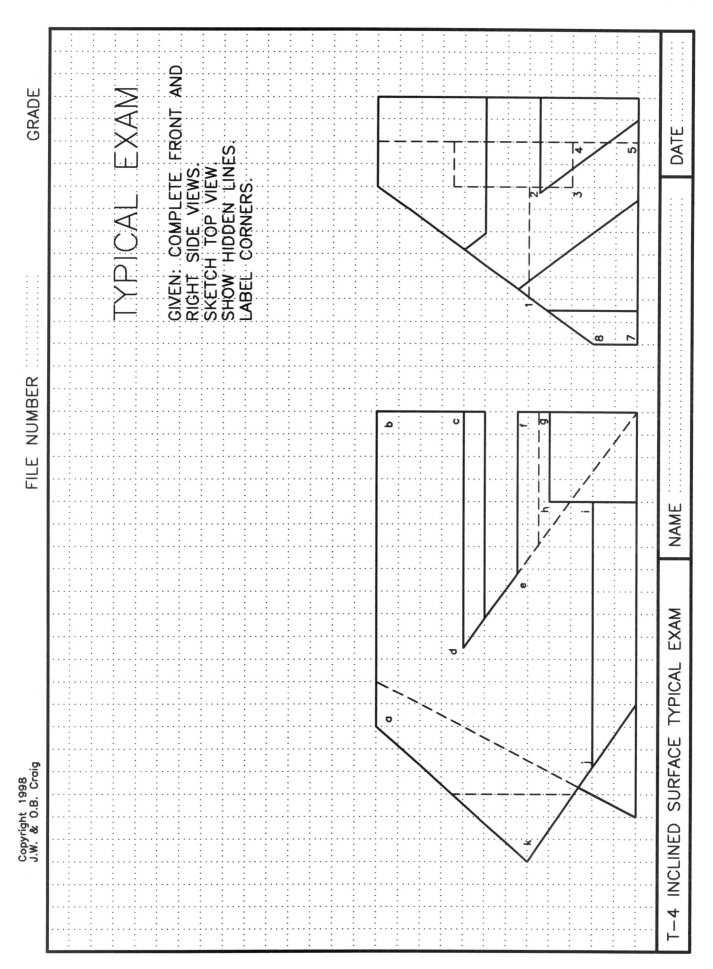

TYPICAL EXAM

GIVEN: COMPLETE FRONT AND
RIGHT SIDE VIEWS.
SKETCH TOP VIEW.
SHOW HIDDEN LINES.
LABEL CORNERS.

GRADE

FILE NUMBER

DATE

NAME

T-4 INCLINED SURFACE TYPICAL EXAM

Copyright 1998
J.W. & O.B. Craig

NOTE: TURN PAGE VERTICALLY FOR USE.

FILE NUMBER

NAME

DATE

GRADE

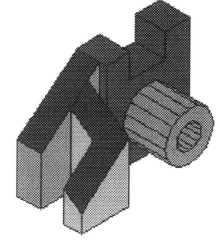

Oblique surfaces have a double slant in space. They are compound-angle surfaces.

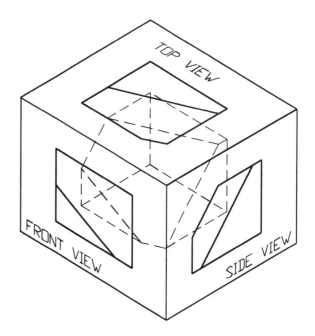

Oblique surfaces are the third type of plane surface. They slant at an angle to the front, top and side picture planes. Oblique surfaces appear as foreshortened surfaces in all regular views.

Oblique surfaces are not as common as other surface types. Architects and product designers may use these surfaces to create interesting and unique shapes. Since oblique surfaces do not appear as an edge in any regular view, designers must be sure the surfaces drawn are truly flat (plane) surfaces.

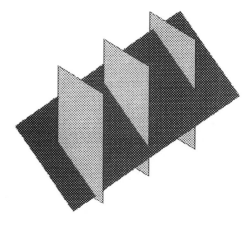

Machining oblique surfaces requires special set-up calculations and positioning tools. Compound angle calculations require three-dimensional trigonometry. Compound angle vises or machine tables are used to position parts for oblique surface machining.

Oblique Surface Theory

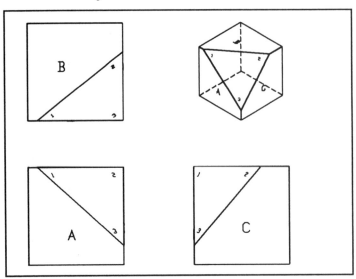

An oblique surface may be created by cutting a block as shown. The cutting plane contains points 1,2 and 3. 1 is on the front-top edge, 2 is on the top-side edge and 3 is on the front-side edge.

A true PLANE surface passes through three points not in the same straight line.

Surface 1,2,3 appears as a foreshortened surface in the front, top and side views.

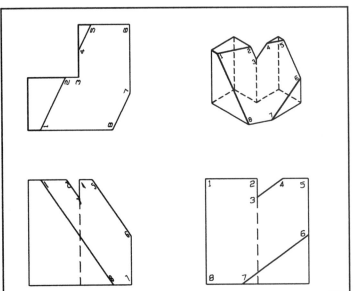

Oblique surfaces must have the same general shape in each regular view.

Study the shape of surface 1,2,3,4,5,6,7,8 in the drawing. Sometimes the shape is somewhat distorted or turned around, but the same shape may be seen in each view.

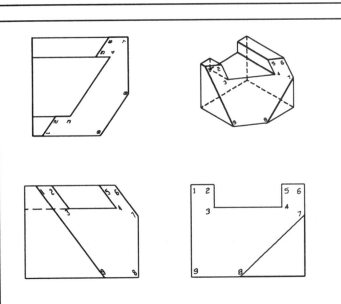

Oblique surfaces must have the same number of corners and edges in each regular view.

Note surface 1,2,3,4,5,6,7,8,9 in the example. It has 9 corners and edges in each view. Numbering corners and transferring points is a very effective way of drawing oblique surfaces in missing views. Use the same process as was used for inclined surfaces.

Oblique Surfaces and Edges

Oblique surfaces must have the same parallel and non-parallel edges in every view.

Note parallel lines:
__1,2 // 5,6 and 3,4
__1,6 // 5,4
These lines must be parallel in every view.

Parallelism is an effective way to locate points in missing views.

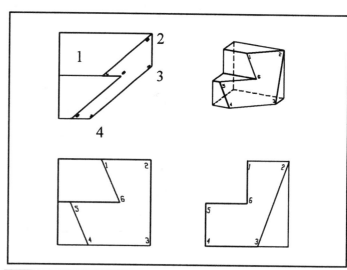

Oblique edges are foreshortened in all regular views.

Line 1,2 is not true length in any of the regular views. The true length of the line may be calculated using algebra or trigonometry. The true length may be seen in an auxiliary view looking perpendicular to 1,2.

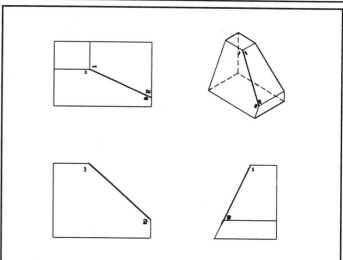

OBLIQUE SURFACES

FRONT	TOP	SIDE
SURFACE	SURFACE	SURFACE

SURFACES ARE NOT TRUE SIZE

OBLIQUE EDGES

FRONT	TOP	SIDE
INCLINED LINE	INCLINED LINE	INCLINED LINE

INCLINED LINES ARE FORESHORTENED

Intersecting lines between corners of oblique surfaces may be used to prove whether points are on or off the surface. Choose three points then test the remaining points. Intersecting lines must intersect at the same point in every view. (Point of intersection must project.)

OBLIQUE SURFACES

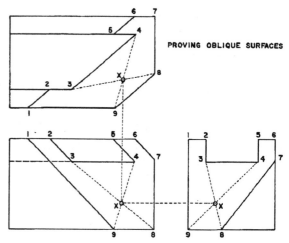

PROVING OBLIQUE SURFACES

ANALYZING PLANE SURFACES

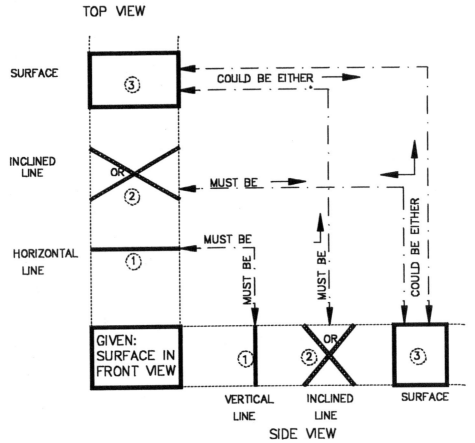

ANALYSIS PROCESS FOR PLANE SURFACES WITH SURFACE
GIVEN IN FRONT VIEW.

Example: Front and Top views are given.

A surface in the front view may appear one of three ways in the top view:
  __1. Horizontal edge-of-surface.
  __2. Inclined edge-of-surface.
  __3. Foreshortened surface with the same shape, same number of corners and edges, and same parallel edges.

Based on the appearance in the top view, the appearance in the side view is known...
  __If (1), then it must be a vertical edge-of-surface in the side view.
  __If (2), then it must be a foreshortened surface in the side view.
  __If (3), then the surface may project as an inclined line in the side view or it may project as a foreshortened surface in the side view.

Solving Oblique Surfaces

Front and top views of the object are complete. Sketch the side and pictorial views.

__ Locate the front view surfaces in the top view.

Remember that the location of each surface must be known in the given views **_before_** the third view can be solved.

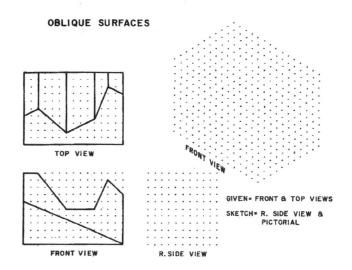

Surface "A" in the front view is a horizontal edge-of-surface in the top view. Locate "A" on the pictorial view.

Label the corners of the other surface 1,2,3,4,5,6,7,8 as shown. From the shape, width, number of corners etc. , surface 1---8 is also a surface in the top view.

Label the common point 7 and 8 on the pictorial.

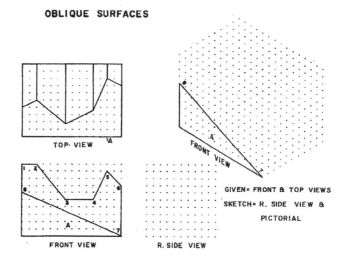

Locate corners 1,2,3,4,5,6,7 and 8 in the top view. Placing point 1 or 8 or 6 or 7 in the top view is a problem. Since these points all project vertically, there are multiple locations possible.

The key to locating some corners of oblique surfaces is to find one corner that is known for sure.

In this example, corners 2,3,4 and 5 can be located. Knowing these points will find 1.
__1 must connect to 2. And, 8 must connect to 1.
__6 must connect to 5, etc.

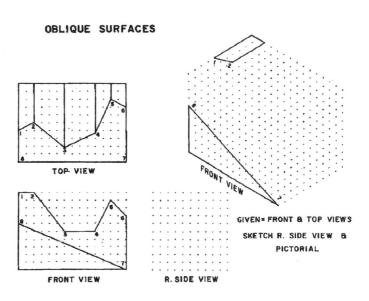

Solving Oblique Surfaces (continued)

Label the corners 1,2,3,4,5,6,7 and 8 in the top view. It takes only a few seconds to place the labels.

Carefully labeling corners will help assure that the points will be plotted correctly in the side view.

Sketch the top surface "T" on the pictorial. This technique often helps locate points which are otherwise difficult to plot. Drawing surface "T" locates points 1 and 2.

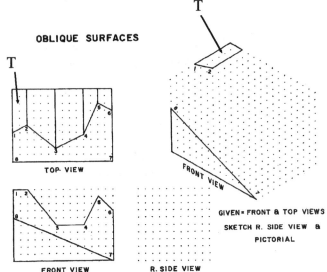

Project the points from the front view.

Measure the points from the top view. Depth is the common measurement.

Place a dot and label the point as each corner is located. This will assure the points will be connected correctly.

Sketch the right side surface on the pictorial. Locate points 6 and 5 as shown.

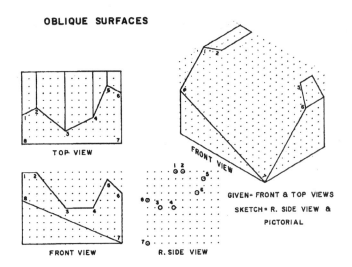

Connect point 1,2,3,4,5,6,7,8 to 1 in the side view.

The surface should have the same number of corners and edges, the same general shape and the same parallel edges.

On the pictorial view from the lower left:
   3 is 6 Width, 5 Height and almost 2 Depth.
   4 is 10 Width, 5 Height, about 4 Depth.

Sketch 1,2,3,4,5,6,7,8 to 1 on the pictorial. The surface should have the same shape, number of corners, and parallel edges.

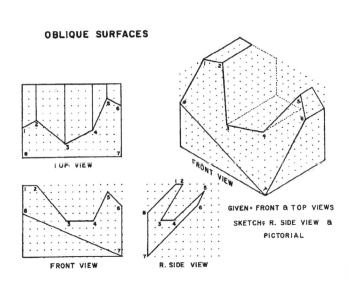

Solving Oblique Surfaces (continued)

Five more surfaces must be plotted. These are the other Normal and Inclined surfaces in the view. Check Inclined lines:

___5,6 in the front is a surface in the top view.

___4,5 in the front is a surface in the top view.

___2,3 in the front is a surface in the top view.

___7,8 in the front view is NOT a surface in the top view. 7,8 is just a common edge between surfaces -- it is not an edge-of-surface.

___3,4 and 1,2 are Normal surfaces in the top view.

Transfer these surfaces to the side and pictorial views.

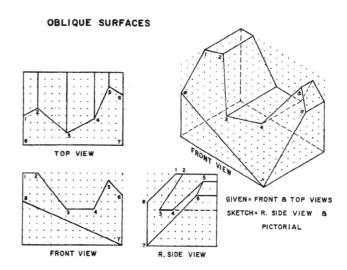

OBLIQUE SURFACES

TOP VIEW

FRONT VIEW

FRONT VIEW

R. SIDE VIEW

GIVEN= FRONT & TOP VIEWS
SKETCH= R. SIDE VIEW &
PICTORIAL

This graphic lists the steps in solving oblique surfaces.

Using a process similar to this will allow surfaces to be solved and plotted ***before the shape can be visualized!*** This is a very powerful tool for solving complex shapes.

Drafters with many years experience carefully label corners to assure correct surfaces are drawn.

These rules are true for both Inclined and Oblique surfaces.

ANALYZATION OF OBLIQUE SURFACES

1. FIND SURFACE IN ONE OF THE GIVEN VIEWS AND PLACE NUMBER IN EACH CORNER OF SURFACE.

2. FIND SURFACE IN OTHER GIVEN VIEW THAT HAS =
   A. SAME SIMILARITY IN OUTLINE.
   B. SAME NUMBER OF CORNERS AND EDGES.
   C. SAME PARALLELISM AND NON PARALLELISM OF EDGES.

3. PLACE NUMBERS IN CORNERS OF SURFACE IN SECOND VIEW.

4. TRANSFER THE POINTS OF SURFACE TO THE THIRD VIEW.

5. COMPLETE THE SURFACE BY CONNECTING POINTS.

PROVING OBLIQUE SURFACES

1. OBLIQUE SURFACES WILL APPEAR AS A SURFACE IN ALL REGULAR VIEWS.

2. SURFACES IN ALL REGULAR VIEWS MUST BE SIMILAR IN SHAPE.

3. SURFACES IN EACH VIEW MUST HAVE THE SAME NUMBER OF CORNERS AND EDGES.

4. SURFACES IN EACH VIEW MUST HAVE THE SAME PARALLELISM AND NON PARALLELISM OF EDGES.

NAME

DATE

FILE NUMBER

GRADE

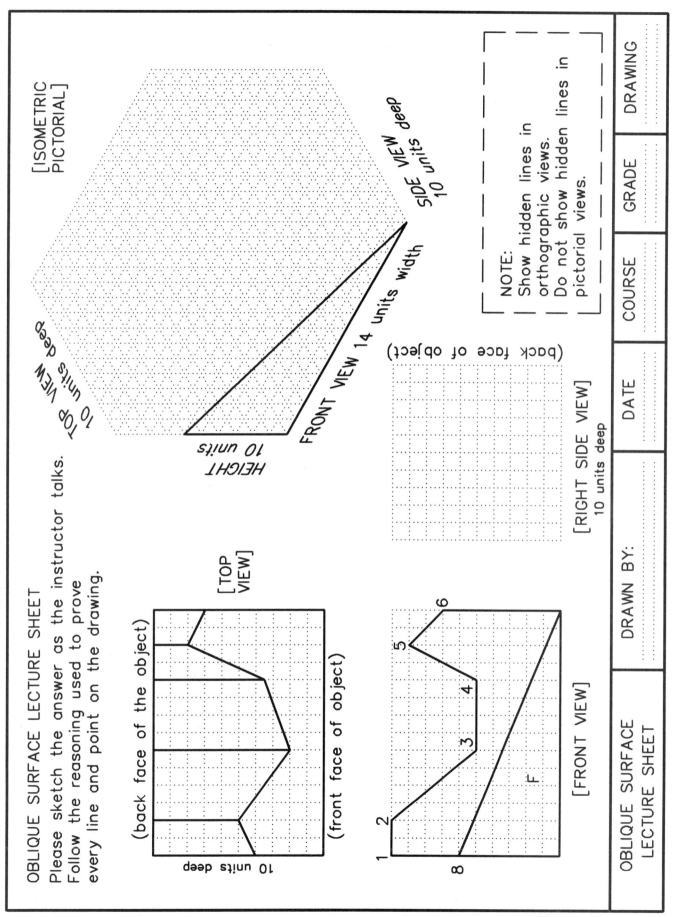

O-1 OBLIQUE SURFACES

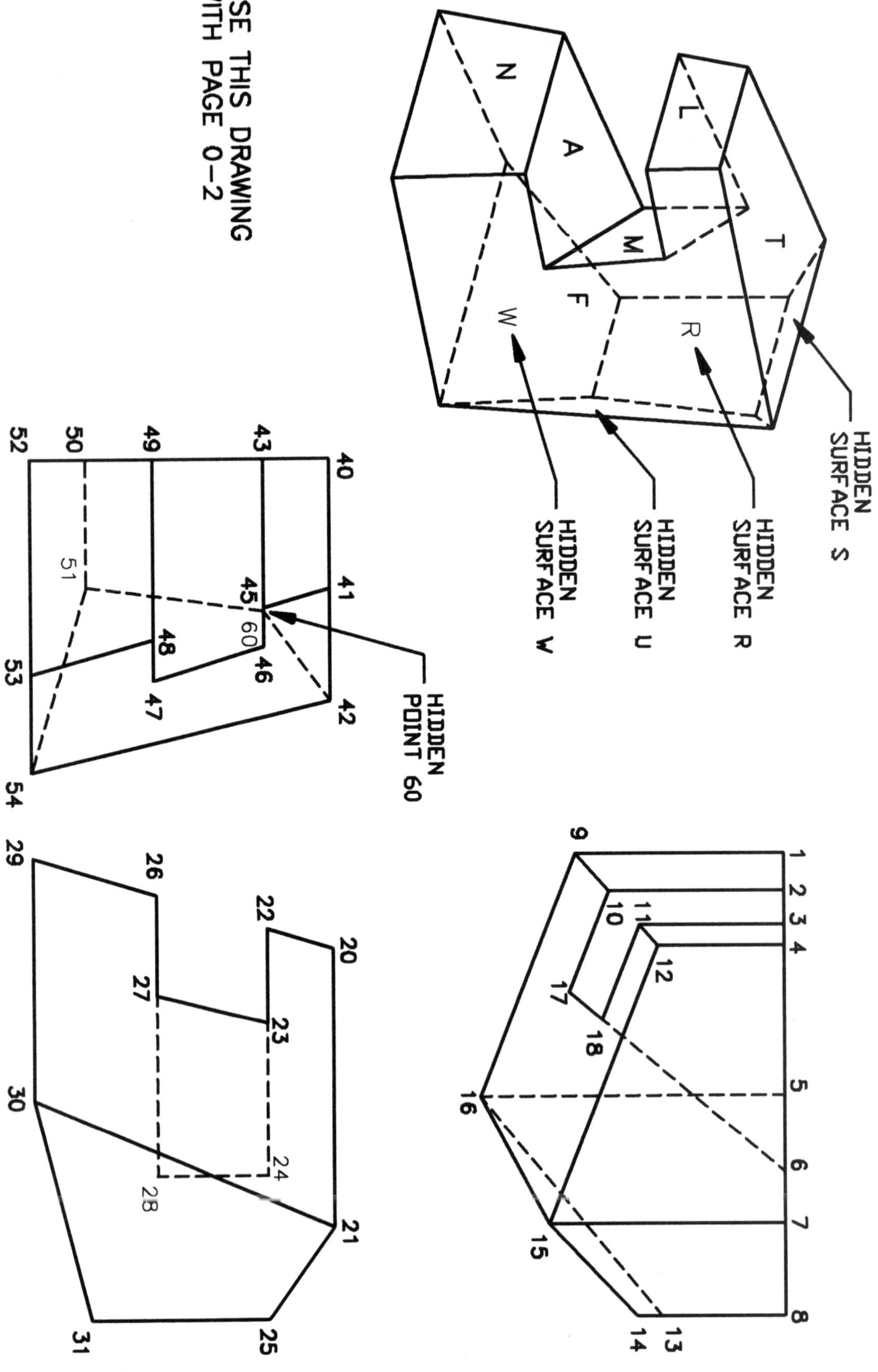

USE THIS DRAWING
WITH PAGE O-2

NAME

DATE

FILE NUMBER

GRADE

HIDDEN
SURFACE S

HIDDEN
SURFACE R

HIDDEN
SURFACE U

HIDDEN
SURFACE W

HIDDEN
POINT 60

GRADE

FILE NUMBER

USE THIS PAGE WITH O-1. NEATLY LETTER THE ANSWERS IN THE TABLE.

SURFACE	TOP VIEW	FRONT VIEW	LEFT SIDE VIEW	SURFACE TYPE
A	2,6,17,10	26,28	49,47	NORMAL
F				
L				
M				
N				
R				
S				
T				
U				
W				

SURFACE TABLES – REVIEW – FILL IN THE MISSING BLOCKS

NORMAL SURFACES

FRONT	TOP	SIDE
SURFACE	SURFACE	
	SURFACE	SURFACE

INCLINED SURFACES

FRONT	TOP	SIDE
INCLINED LINE		INCLINED LINE
	INCLINED LINE	

OBLIQUE SURFACE TABLE

FRONT	TOP	SIDE

NAME

DATE

O-2 OBLIQUE SURFACES

NAME

DATE

NOTE: Use this grid format
in horizontal direction.

FILE NUMBER ....

GRADE

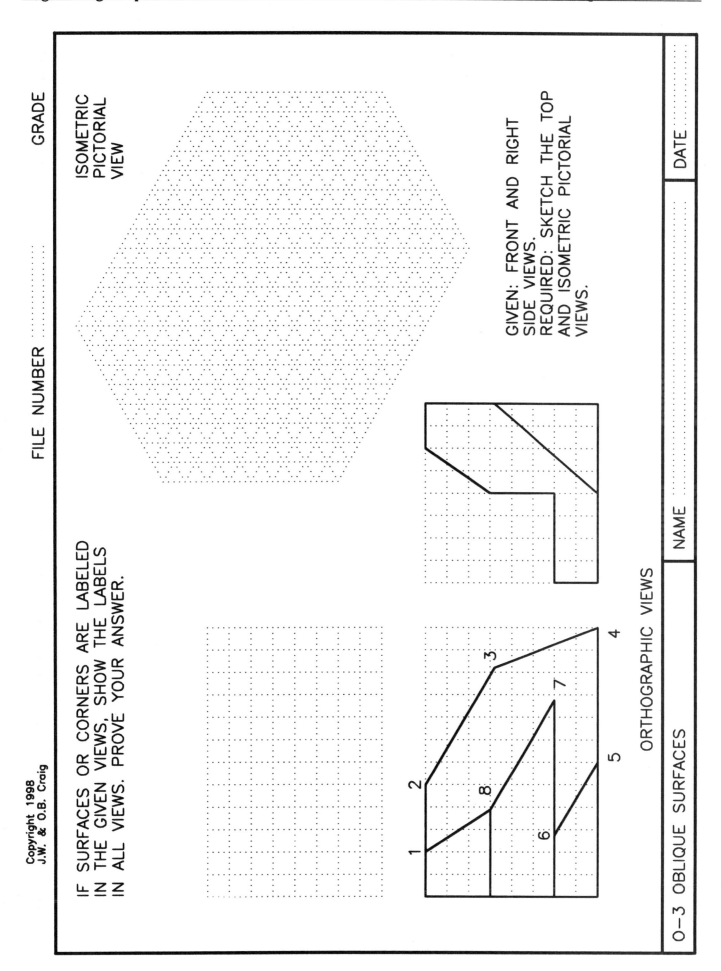

GRADE

ISOMETRIC
PICTORIAL
VIEW

FILE NUMBER

GIVEN: FRONT AND RIGHT
SIDE VIEWS.
REQUIRED: SKETCH THE TOP
AND ISOMETRIC PICTORIAL
VIEWS.

IF SURFACES OR CORNERS ARE LABELED
IN THE GIVEN VIEWS, SHOW THE LABELS
IN ALL VIEWS. PROVE YOUR ANSWER.

ORTHOGRAPHIC VIEWS

DATE

NAME

O-3 OBLIQUE SURFACES

Copyright 1998
J.W. & O.B. Craig

IF SURFACES OR CORNERS ARE LABELED
IN THE GIVEN VIEWS, SHOW THE LABELS
IN ALL VIEWS. PROVE YOUR ANSWER.

FILE NUMBER

GRADE

ISOMETRIC
PICTORIAL
VIEW

O–4 OBLIQUE SURFACES

ORTHOGRAPHIC VIEWS

NAME

DATE

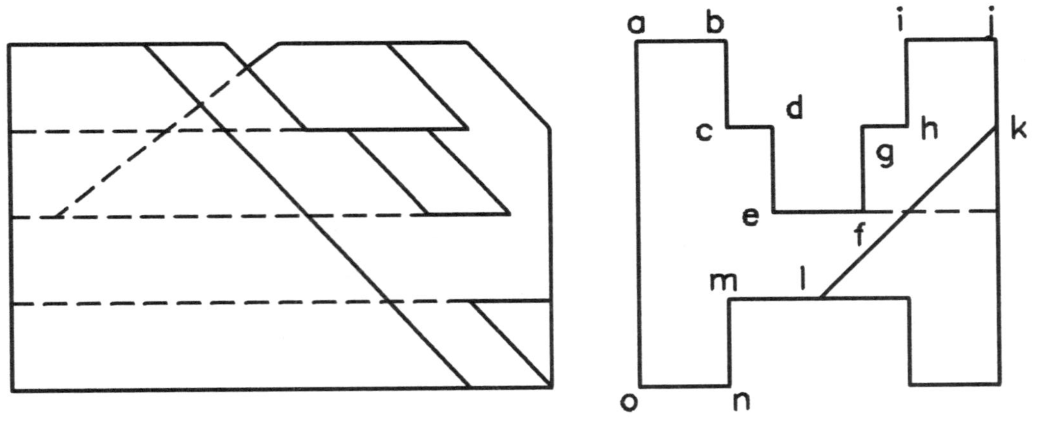

GIVEN: FRONT AND RIGHT
SIDE VIEWS.
REQUIRED: SKETCH THE TOP
VIEW AND THE ISOMETRIC
PICTORIAL VIEW.

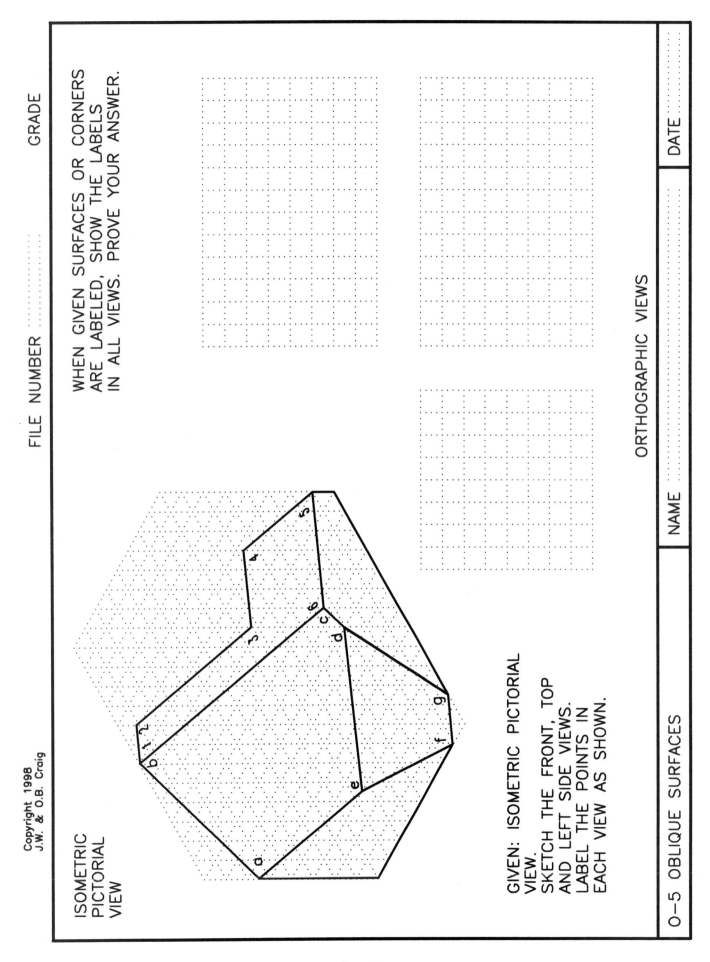

FILE NUMBER   GRADE

WHEN GIVEN SURFACES OR CORNERS ARE LABELED, SHOW THE LABELS IN ALL VIEWS. PROVE YOUR ANSWER.

ISOMETRIC PICTORIAL VIEW

ORTHOGRAPHIC VIEWS

GIVEN: ISOMETRIC PICTORIAL VIEW.
SKETCH THE FRONT, TOP AND LEFT SIDE VIEWS.
LABEL THE POINTS IN EACH VIEW AS SHOWN.

NAME   DATE

O-5 OBLIQUE SURFACES

Copyright 1998
J.W. & O.B. Craig

IF SURFACES OR CORNERS ARE LABELED
IN THE GIVEN VIEWS, SHOW THE LABELS
IN ALL VIEWS. PROVE YOUR ANSWER.

FILE NUMBER   GRADE

ISOMETRIC
PICTORIAL
VIEW

O-6 OBLIQUE SURFACES

ORTHOGRAPHIC VIEWS

NAME   DATE

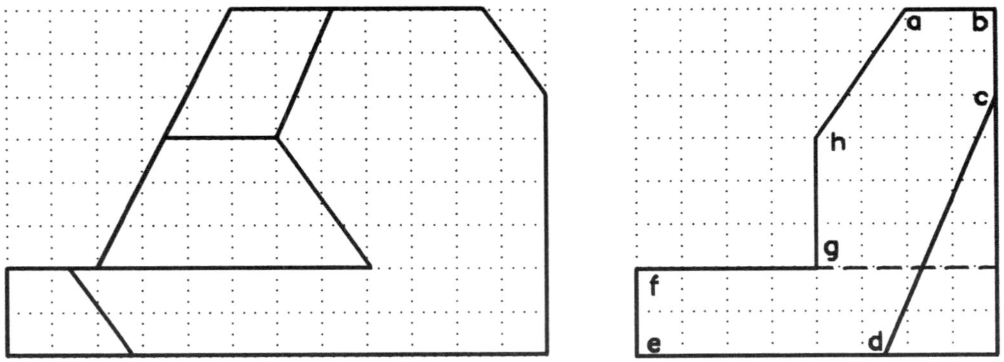

GIVEN: FRONT AND RIGHT
SIDE VIEWS.
SKETCH: TOP AND ISOMETRIC
PICTORIAL VIEWS.

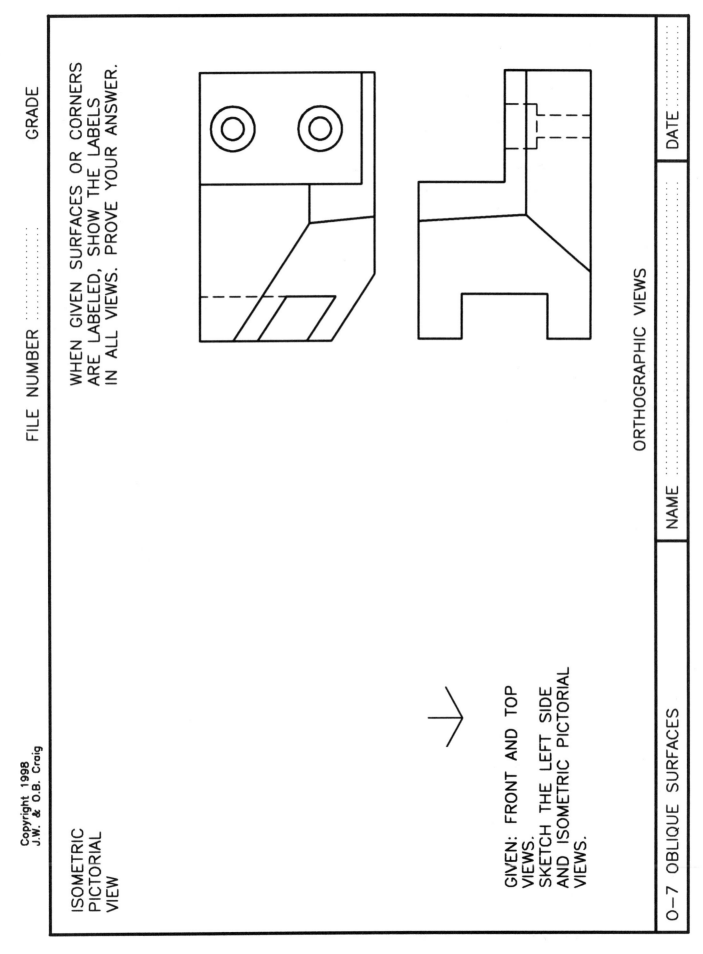

GRADE

FILE NUMBER

WHEN GIVEN SURFACES OR CORNERS
ARE LABELED, SHOW THE LABELS
IN ALL VIEWS. PROVE YOUR ANSWER.

Copyright 1998
J.W. & O.B. Craig

ISOMETRIC
PICTORIAL
VIEW

ORTHOGRAPHIC VIEWS

GIVEN: FRONT AND TOP
VIEWS.
SKETCH THE LEFT SIDE
AND ISOMETRIC PICTORIAL
VIEWS.

NAME

DATE

O-7 OBLIQUE SURFACES

WHEN THE GIVEN SURFACES OR CORNERS ARE LABELED.
SHOW THE LABELS IN ALL VIEWS. PROVE YOUR ANSWER.

FILE NUMBER

GRADE

WELD FIXTURE BLOCK
FOR DOUGH MIXER PADDLE.

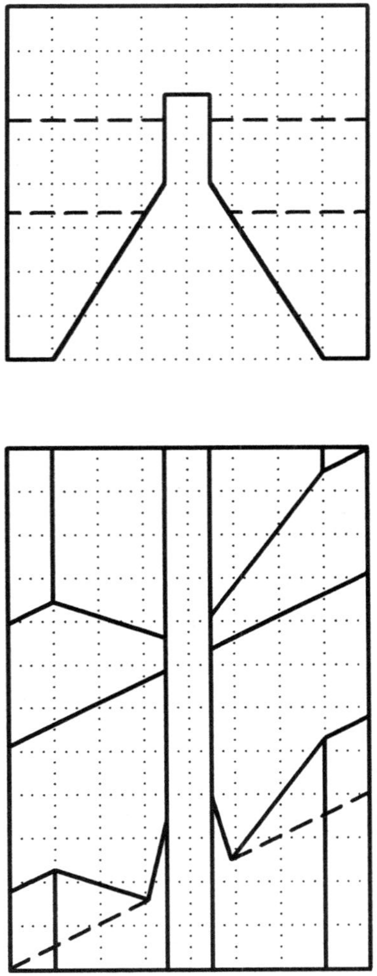

ISOMETRIC
PICTORIAL
VIEW

O-8 OBLIQUE SURFACES

ORTHOGRAPHIC VIEWS

GIVEN: FRONT AND TOP VIEWS.
SKETCH RIGHT SIDE AND
ISOMETRIC PICTORIAL VIEWS.

NAME

DATE

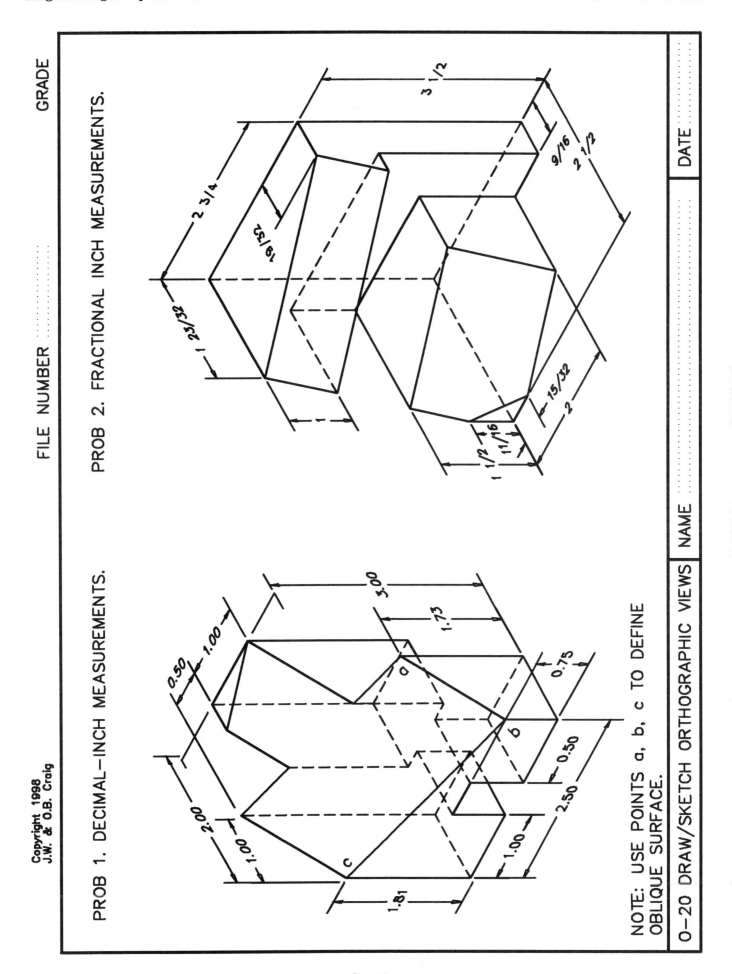

PROB 2. FRACTIONAL INCH MEASUREMENTS.

PROB 1. DECIMAL–INCH MEASUREMENTS.

GRADE

FILE NUMBER

DATE

NAME

O–20 DRAW/SKETCH ORTHOGRAPHIC VIEWS

NOTE: USE POINTS a, b, c TO DEFINE
OBLIQUE SURFACE.

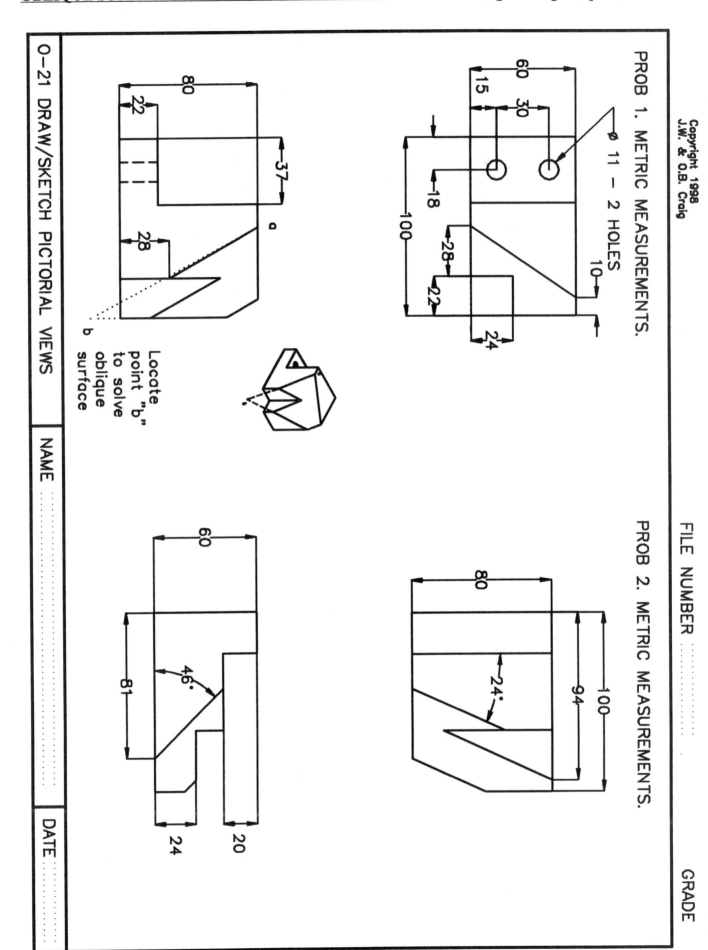

PROB 1. METRIC MEASUREMENTS.

ø 11 — 2 HOLES

PROB 2. METRIC MEASUREMENTS.

FILE NUMBER

GRADE

O-21 DRAW/SKETCH PICTORIAL VIEWS

NAME

DATE

Locate
point "b"
to solve
oblique
surface

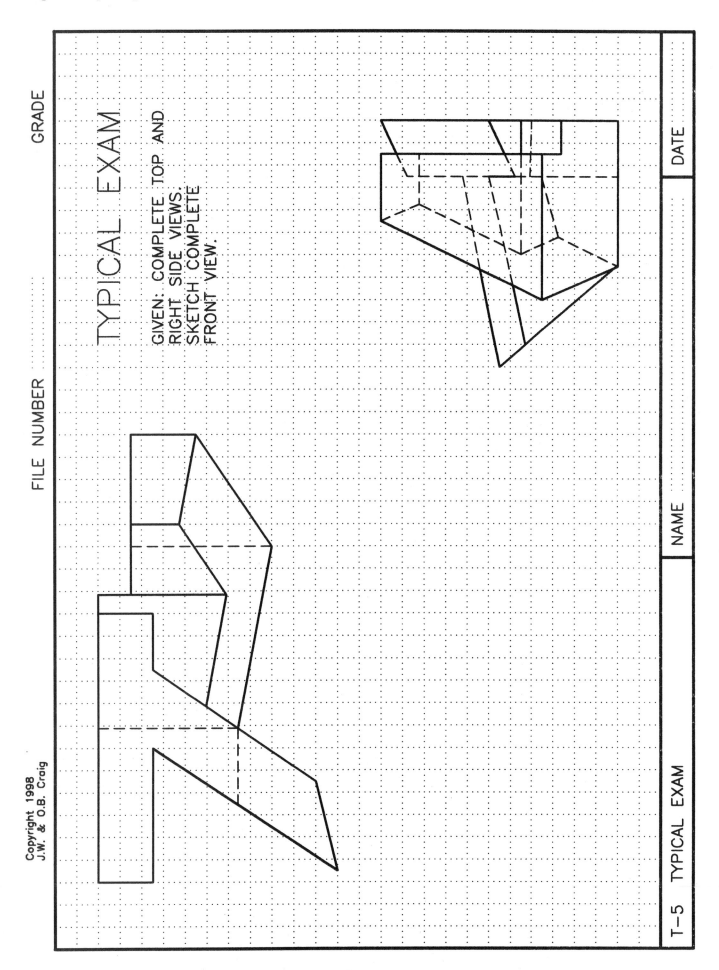

TYPICAL EXAM

GIVEN: COMPLETE TOP AND
RIGHT SIDE VIEWS.
SKETCH COMPLETE
FRONT VIEW.

GRADE

FILE NUMBER

DATE

NAME

T–5　TYPICAL EXAM

NAME

DATE

NOTE: Use this grid format in horizontal direction.

FILE NUMBER

GRADE

Introduction to Cylindrical Surfaces

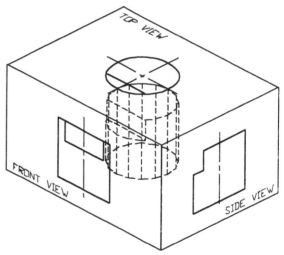

Cylindrical surfaces may be shown in two forms:

__Positive Cylinders that have mass.

__Negative Cylinders or holes.

Cylindrical Surfaces are the most common curved surface. Cylinders or partial cylinders are found on nearly every item in sight. Take a close look -- try to identify cylinders on objects. From small pens and pencils to giant storage tanks, cylinders may be seen.

One view of a cylinder shows the circular shape. (Top view in this example.) Other views show only a rectangular outline. From the front or side view it is impossible to identify the object as cylindrical. Placing center lines in the views helps the reader to identify some type of symmetry on the object.

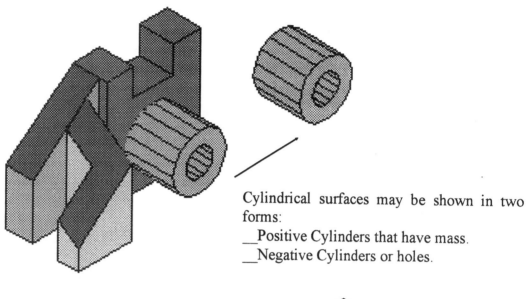

Center lines are very important for interpreting cylindrical shapes. Fig. 1 -- Center lines are repeating long-short dashed lines. Center lines have no visibility. Crossed center lines should be drawn at the centers of circles(Fig. 2). Circular center lines may be drawn (Fig. 4). Center lines are often needed for dimensioning.

Center lines are the least important type of line on a drawing. Visible lines take precedence. Then hidden lines. Then center lines. (Fig. 5).

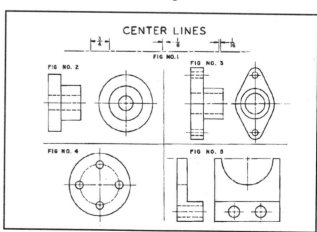

Features of Cylinders

Positive Cylinders are solid shapes. Note the top view points A,C and D,B. These are the extreme left, right and front, back points respectively. They define the boundaries of the other views:

__A is left contour element 2,4 in the front view.
__C is right contour element 3,5 in the front view.
__D is front contour element 6,8 in the side view.
__B is back contour element 7,9 in the side view.
Also,
__D and B fall along the axis E,F in the front view.
__A and C fall along the axis G,H in the side view.

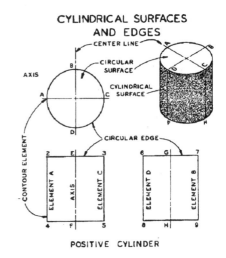

CYLINDRICAL SURFACES AND EDGES

POSITIVE CYLINDER

A drilled hole is a negative cylinder where mass has been removed. Similar features are seen. Contour elements are hidden lines.

Extreme points A, C and D, B define the boundaries for the other views.

__A is left contour element 2,4 in the front view.
__C is right contour element 3,5 in the front view.
__D is front contour element 6,8 in the side view.
__B is back contour element 7,9 in the side view.
Also,
__D and B fall along the axis E,F in the front view.
__A and C fall along the axis G,H in the side view.

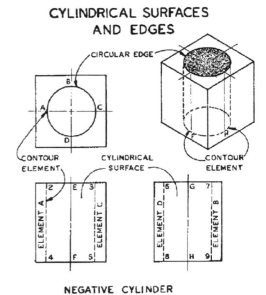

CYLINDRICAL SURFACES AND EDGES

NEGATIVE CYLINDER

Cuts on the cylinder must be carefully drawn or sketched in each view.

Normal edge-of-surface 11,12 in the top view cuts at the center of the cylinder so the width of the cut is the full width of the cylinder.

Normal edge-of-surface 9, 10 in the top view cuts away considerable material from the cylinder.
__Point 9 projects to line 1,4 in the front.
__Point 10 projects to line 2,5 in the front.
This is the maximum width of the surface.
__Contour lines above 3 and 6 no longer exist, giving the offset shape in the front view.

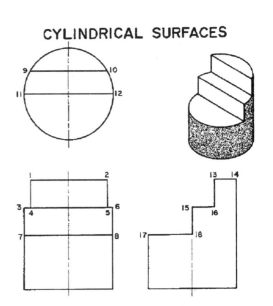

CYLINDRICAL SURFACES

Normal and Inclined Surface Intersections with Cylinders

Normal edge-of-surface 9,10 in the top view creates surface 1,2,4,3 in the front view. Point 9 projects to line 1,3 and point 10 projects to line 2,4. Contour lines exist to the left of 1,3 and to the right of 2,4.

Inclined edge-of-surface 11,12 in the top view creates inclined surface 5,6,7,8 in the front view. There is no contour line to the right of 6,7.

In the side view the contour line above 14 is not there. The front contour line to the left of 16,19 is removed.

This example is a hollow pipe with a groove cut through the middle at 19,22,21,20. Since the centerline area in the side view is cut, this removes portions of the left and right contour lines for the front view. Note the offset intersections due to curvature of the cylinder.

__18 in the top projects to 1,10 in the front.
__17 in the top projects to 2,8 in the front.
Same for 16 and 15 in the top view.

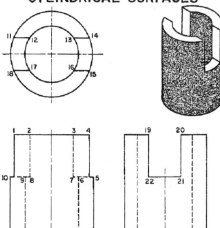

Normal edge-of-surface 1,4 in the front view and 13,15 in the side view cuts across two cylinders. This creates surface 11,8,7,5,6,10,9,12,11 in the top view.

Left and right contour elements for the cylinders must be shown since the cut was above the center of the cylinders.

Surface "C" extends the full width. Hidden line 8,9 must be shown in the top view.

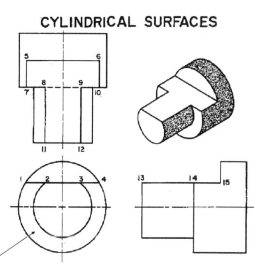

Surface "C"

Cylindrical Intersections

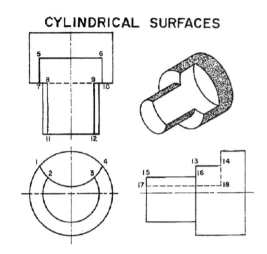

CYLINDRICAL SURFACES

Analysis of cylindrical surfaces is similar to inclined surfaces. A cylinder will appear as a circular edge-of-surface in one view and as a foreshortened surface in the other two views.

Cylinder 1,2,3,4 in the front view is surface 7,5,6,10,9,12,11,8 in the top view and surface 15,16,13,14,18,17 in the side view

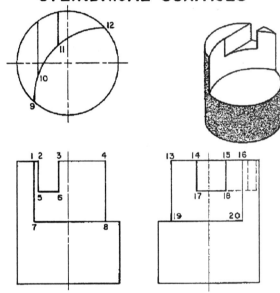

CYLINDRICAL SURFACES

Cylindrical surface 9,10,11,12 in the top view is surface 1,2,5,6,3,4,8,7 in the front view and surface 13,14,17,18,15,16,20,19 in the side view.

Note the similar outline, same number of corners and edges in the surface views.

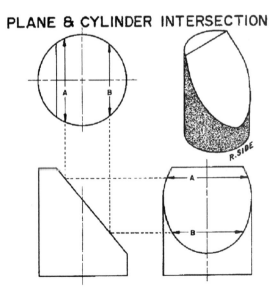

PLANE & CYLINDER INTERSECTION

Cutting a cylinder on an angle to the axis will result in an elliptical curve. Points must be plotted as shown to define the curve. Many locations similar to "A" and "B" are projected to the inclined cut in the front view. These points are projected to the side view. Measurements are transferred from the top view to the side view. Points are connected using an irregular curve to produce a smooth line.

Curves and intersections like this are quickly solved using computer solid modeling techniques.

Analyzing Contour Lines

Top and bottom contour points in the side view fall along the center line A,B in the top view. These are contour lines C,D and E,F in the front view.

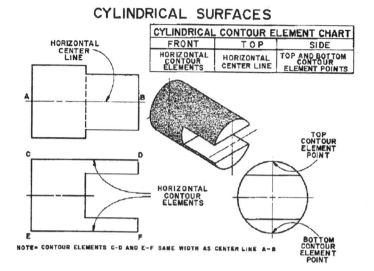

CYLINDRICAL SURFACES

CYLINDRICAL CONTOUR ELEMENT CHART		
FRONT	TOP	SIDE
HORIZONTAL CONTOUR ELEMENTS	HORIZONTAL CENTER LINE	TOP AND BOTTOM CONTOUR ELEMENT POINTS

NOTE: CONTOUR ELEMENTS C-D AND E-F SAME WIDTH AS CENTER LINE A-B

Front contour point G and back contour point H fall along center line E,F in the front view. This line is cut short.

Contour lines A,B and C,D in the top view are cut short.

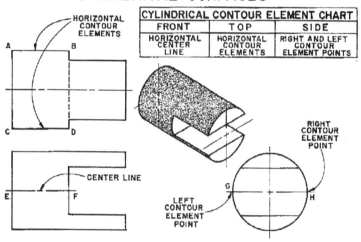

CYLINDRICAL SURFACES

CYLINDRICAL CONTOUR ELEMENT CHART		
FRONT	TOP	SIDE
HORIZONTAL CENTER LINE	HORIZONTAL CONTOUR ELEMENTS	RIGHT AND LEFT CONTOUR ELEMENT POINTS

NOTE: CONTOUR ELEMENT A-B AND C-D SAME WIDTH AS CENTER LINE E-F

Left and right contour points A,B and C,D in the top view fall along center line N,O in the side view. These lines are cut short.
__A is E,J in the front
__B is F,K
__C is G,L and
__D is H,M.

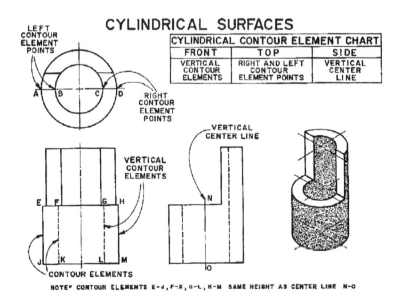

CYLINDRICAL SURFACES

CYLINDRICAL CONTOUR ELEMENT CHART		
FRONT	TOP	SIDE
VERTICAL CONTOUR ELEMENTS	RIGHT AND LEFT CONTOUR ELEMENT POINTS	VERTICAL CENTER LINE

NOTE: CONTOUR ELEMENTS E-J, F-K, G-L, H-M SAME HEIGHT AS CENTER LINE N-O

Analyzing Contour Lines

Front contour points C and D in the top view are cut short. Their length is F-G in the front view and H-J in the side view. C is K-L in the side view.

Back contour points A and B in the top view are the full length E-G in the front view. A is contour line O-P in the side view. B is contour line M-N in the side view.

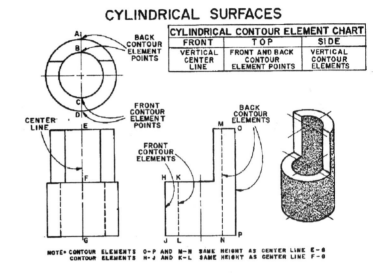

CYLINDRICAL SURFACES

CYLINDRICAL CONTOUR ELEMENT CHART		
FRONT	TOP	SIDE
VERTICAL CENTER LINE	FRONT AND BACK CONTOUR ELEMENT POINTS	VERTICAL CONTOUR ELEMENTS

NOTE: CONTOUR ELEMENTS O-P AND M-N SAME HEIGHT AS CENTER LINE E-G
CONTOUR ELEMENTS H-J AND K-L SAME HEIGHT AS CENTER LINE F-G

Left and right contour points E and F in the front view fall along center line G-H in the side view. These lines extend the full depth of the cylinder.

E is contour line A-B in the top view. F is contour line C-D in the top view.

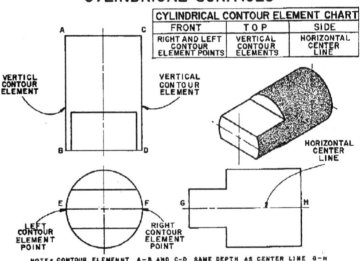

CYLINDRICAL SURFACES

CYLINDRICAL CONTOUR ELEMENT CHART		
FRONT	TOP	SIDE
RIGHT AND LEFT CONTOUR ELEMENT POINTS	VERTICAL CONTOUR ELEMENTS	HORIZONTAL CENTER LINE

NOTE: CONTOUR ELEMENT A-B AND C-D SAME DEPTH AS CENTER LINE G-H

Top and bottom contour points C and D in the front view fall along center line B-A in the top view. These lines are cut short.

C is contour line E-F in the side view. D is contour line G-H in the side view.

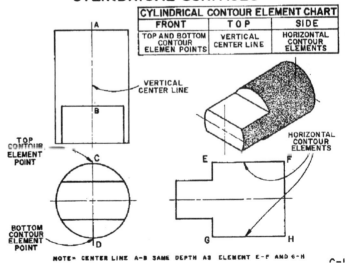

CYLINDRICAL SURFACES

CYLINDRICAL CONTOUR ELEMENT CHART		
FRONT	TOP	SIDE
TOP AND BOTTOM CONTOUR ELEMEN POINTS	VERTICAL CENTER LINE	HORIZONTAL CONTOUR ELEMENTS

NOTE: CENTER LINE A-B SAME DEPTH AS ELEMENT E-F AND G-H

C-15

Cylindrical Intersections, Tangencies and Runouts

__No. 1. The rounded (filleted) corner in the front view does not produce intersection lines in the top or side views.

__No. 2. Cylindrical intersection creates lines in front and top views.

__No. 3. Transitions in the front view from normal to cylindrical to inclined to cylindrical to normal does not produce any intersection lines in the top or side views.

__No. 4. The cylindrical curves in the front view produce a contour line in the top view, but no intersection line in the side view.

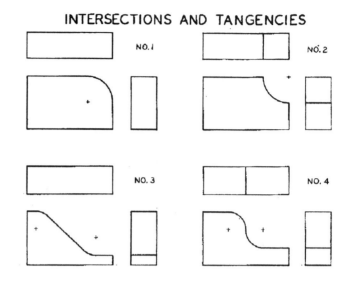

Tangency points often define the intersection or end-point of surfaces.

__No.1. Intersection point "A" projects from the top view to locate the width of the normal surface in the front view.

__No.2. Tangency point "B" in the top view locates the extent of the normal surfaces in the front view. In this situation, a line shows in the front view with no connection to the end point.

__No. 3. Tangency point "C" in the top view locates end point "E" in the front view. Again, there is no connecting line to point "E".

_No. 4. "G" in the front view locates a contour line in the top view. "F" locates the end of the line in the top view.

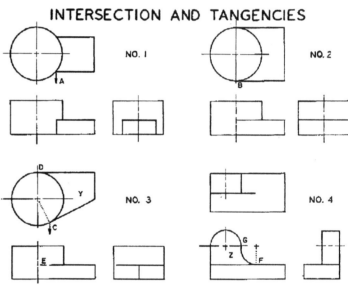

Runouts occur when rounded edges or filleted corners intersect. These features are found on most parts where sharp edges must be rounded for safety. Parts which are cast or forged to shape often have filleted corners to reduce stress or metallurgical problems.

Examples of common intersections are shown.

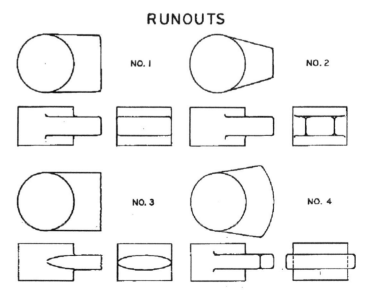

Solving Cylindrical Surfaces

Front and right side views are complete.

Sketch the pictorial and top views.

Sketch construction ellipses in the pictorial view at each location where the object changes shape.

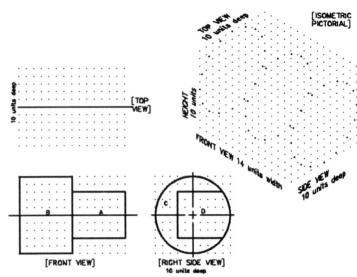

Label the surfaces in the front and side views.
__A is a vertical edge-of-surface in the side view.
__Locate horizontal lines E and F in the side view.
__B is a cylindrical edge-of-surface in the side view.
__D and C are vertical edge-of-surfaces in the front view.

Plot surface D on the pictorial. Use the center of the ellipse as a reference.

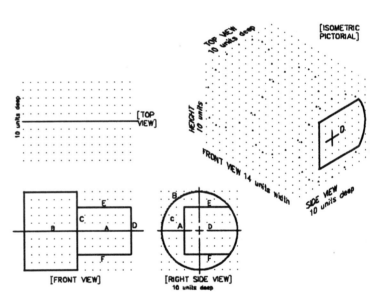

Draw surfaces A and E using "D" as a reference.

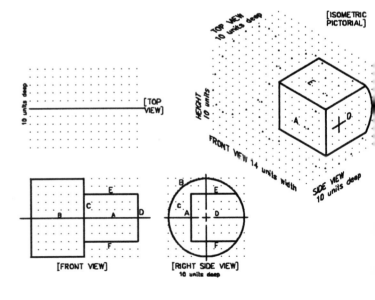

Sketching Cylindrical Surfaces

Sketch surface "C" on the pictorial. Use the middle construction ellipse as a guide to get the correct curvature.

Sketch cylindrical surface "B". Use the end face construction ellipse to get the correct curvature. Sketch lines at the extreme contour points to define the cylinder.

Sketch the top view. Locate the Normal surfaces D, A, E, and C. Sketch the contour lines for the cylindrical surface "B".

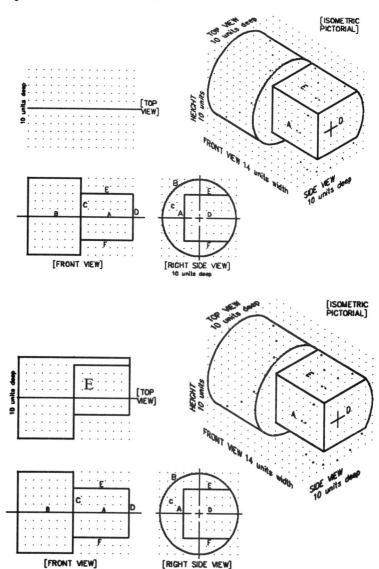

NAME

DATE

FILE NUMBER

GRADE

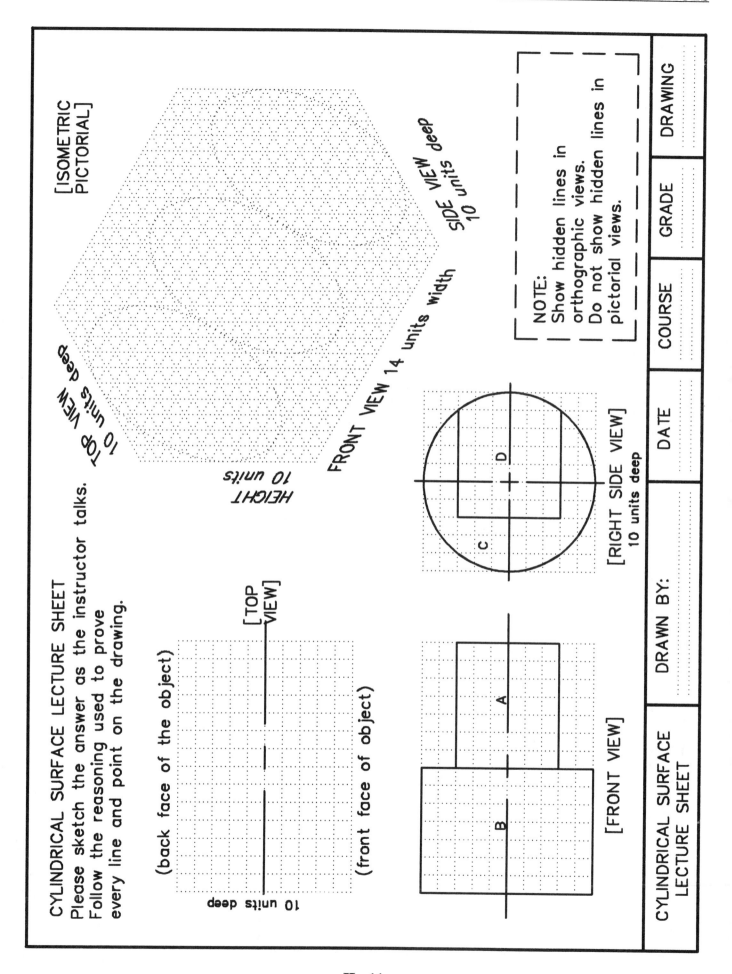

CYLINDRICAL SURFACE LECTURE SHEET
Please sketch the answer as the instructor talks.
Follow the reasoning used to prove every line and point on the drawing.

[ISOMETRIC PICTORIAL]

TOP VIEW 10 units deep

SIDE VIEW 10 units deep

FRONT VIEW 14 units width

HEIGHT 10 units

(back face of the object)

[TOP VIEW]

10 units deep

(front face of object)

[FRONT VIEW]

A

B

[RIGHT SIDE VIEW]
10 units deep

C

D

NOTE:
Show hidden lines in orthographic views.
Do not show hidden lines in pictorial views.

CYLINDRICAL SURFACE LECTURE SHEET

DRAWN BY:

DATE

COURSE

GRADE

DRAWING

NAME

DATE

NOTE: Use this grid format
in horizontal direction.

FILE NUMBER

GRADE

FILE NUMBER

GRADE

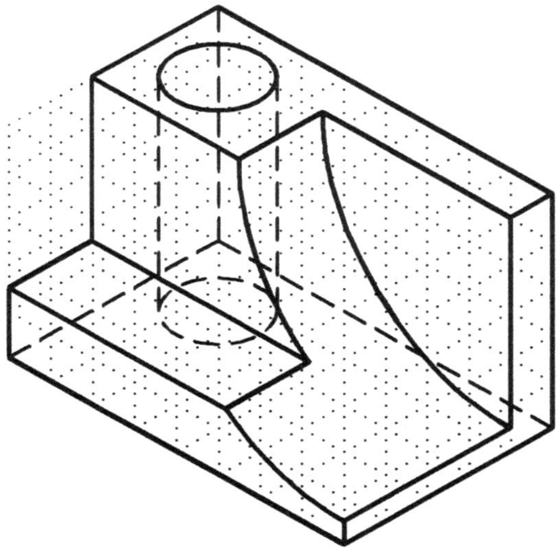

TOP VIEW

FRONT VIEW

RIGHT SIDE VIEW

LEFT SIDE VIEW

REAR (BACK) VIEW

BOTTOM VIEW

GIVEN: ISOMETRIC PICTORIAL VIEW.
SKETCH THE SIX REGULAR
ORTHOGRAPHIC VIEWS.
Be sure to show hidden lines
in the orthographic views.

LABEL SURFACES IN ALL VIEWS.

C–1 SKETCH SIX VIEWS

NAME

DATE

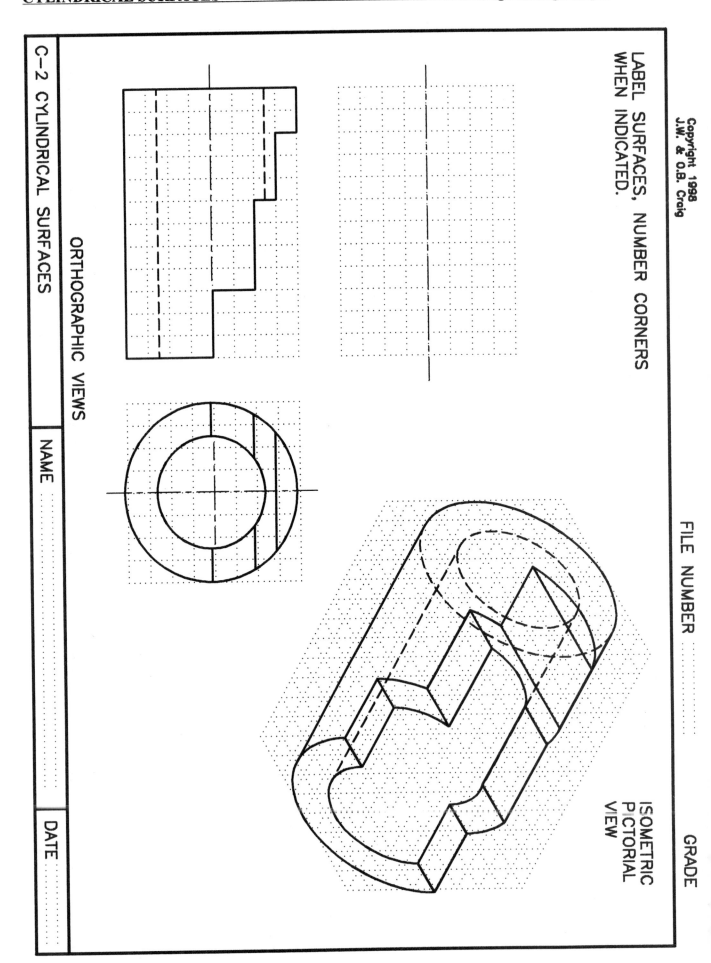

LABEL SURFACES, NUMBER CORNERS
WHEN INDICATED.

FILE NUMBER

GRADE

C-2 CYLINDRICAL SURFACES

ORTHOGRAPHIC VIEWS

NAME

DATE

ISOMETRIC
PICTORIAL
VIEW

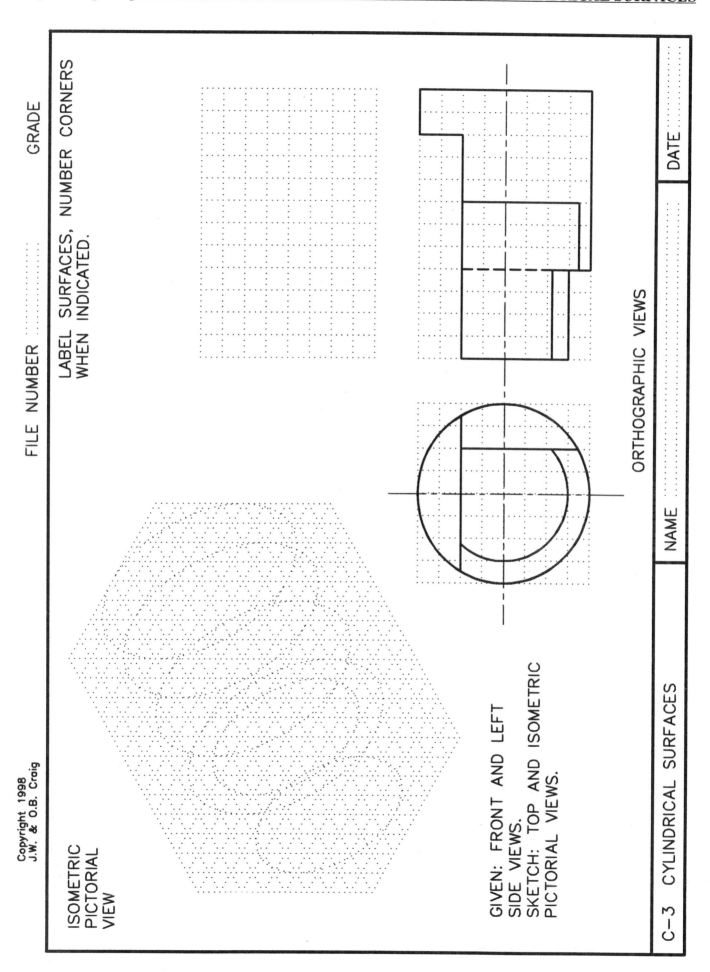

FILE NUMBER ....　　　　GRADE

LABEL SURFACES, NUMBER CORNERS
WHEN INDICATED.

ISOMETRIC
PICTORIAL
VIEW

GIVEN: FRONT AND LEFT
SIDE VIEWS.
SKETCH: TOP AND ISOMETRIC
PICTORIAL VIEWS.

ORTHOGRAPHIC VIEWS

Copyright 1998
J.W. & O.B. Craig

C—3　CYLINDRICAL SURFACES

NAME ....

DATE ....

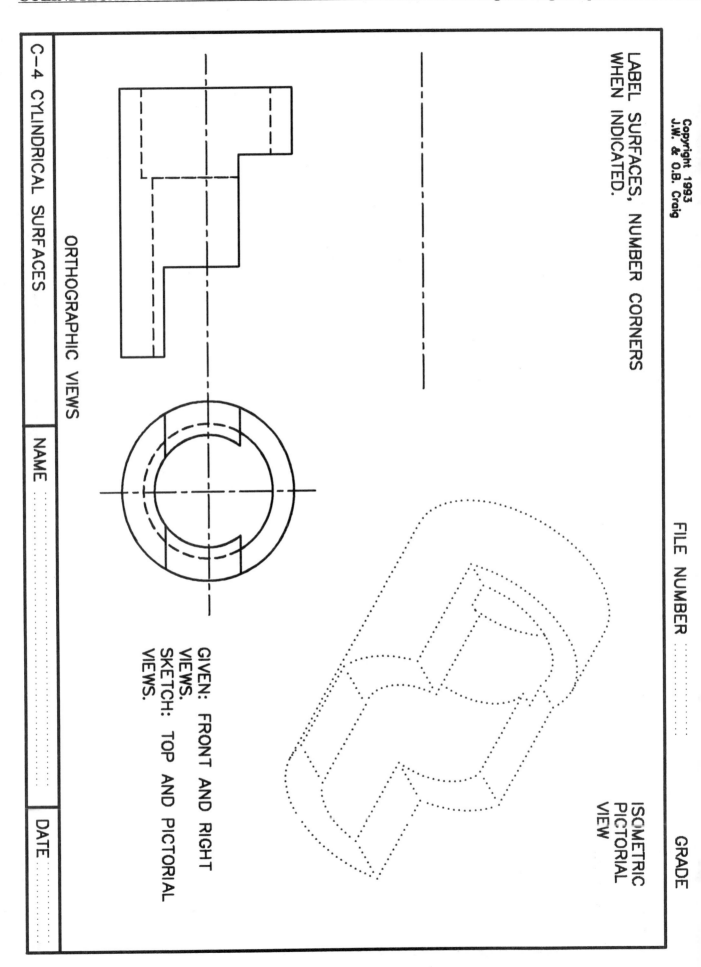

LABEL SURFACES, NUMBER CORNERS
WHEN INDICATED.

FILE NUMBER

GRADE

ISOMETRIC
PICTORIAL
VIEW

ORTHOGRAPHIC VIEWS

GIVEN: FRONT AND RIGHT
VIEWS.
SKETCH: TOP AND PICTORIAL
VIEWS.

C-4 CYLINDRICAL SURFACES

NAME

DATE

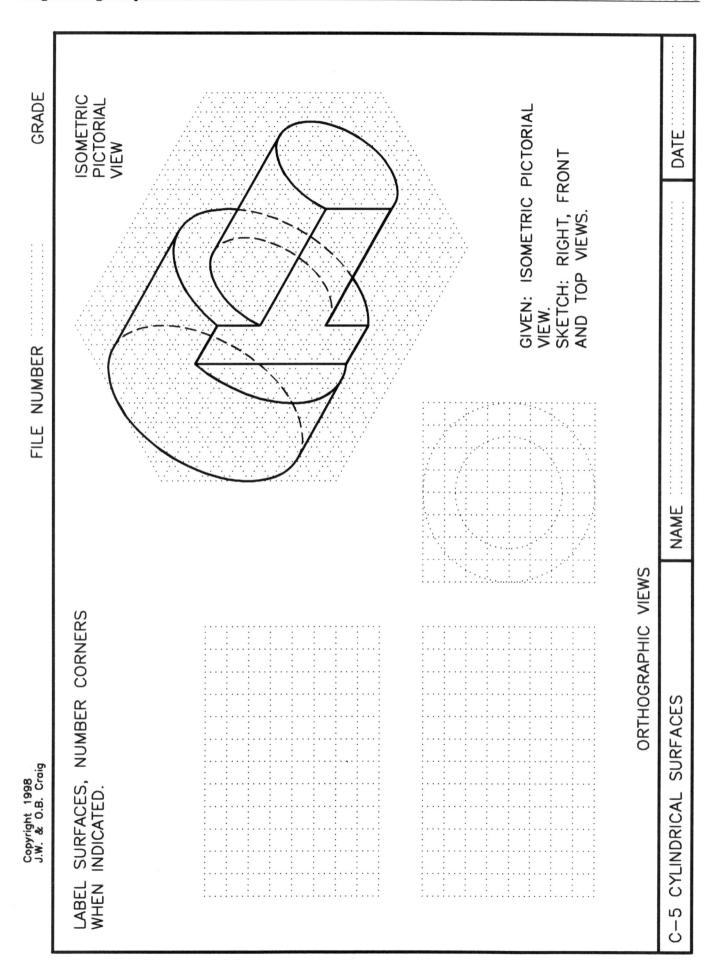

GRADE

ISOMETRIC
PICTORIAL
VIEW

FILE NUMBER

LABEL SURFACES, NUMBER CORNERS
WHEN INDICATED.

GIVEN: ISOMETRIC PICTORIAL
VIEW.
SKETCH: RIGHT, FRONT
AND TOP VIEWS.

ORTHOGRAPHIC VIEWS

DATE

NAME

C—5 CYLINDRICAL SURFACES

Copyright 1993
J.W. & O.B. Craig

ISOMETRIC
PICTORIAL
VIEW

FILE NUMBER

GRADE

LABEL SURFACES, NUMBER CORNERS
WHEN INDICATED.

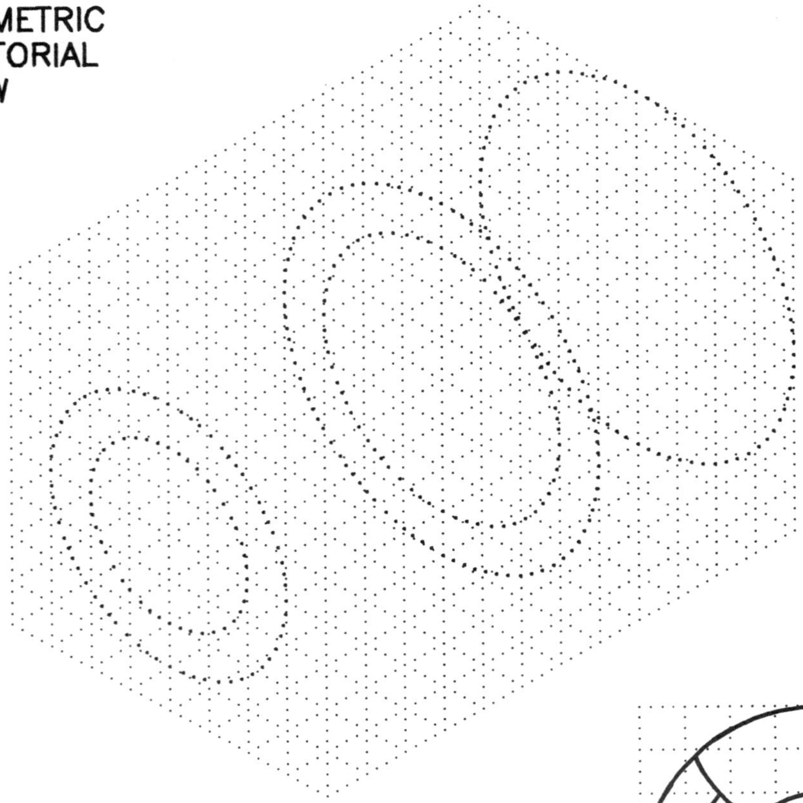

GIVEN: LEFT SIDE AND
FRONT VIEWS.
SKETCH: TOP VIEW AND
ISOMETRIC PICTORIAL VIEWS.

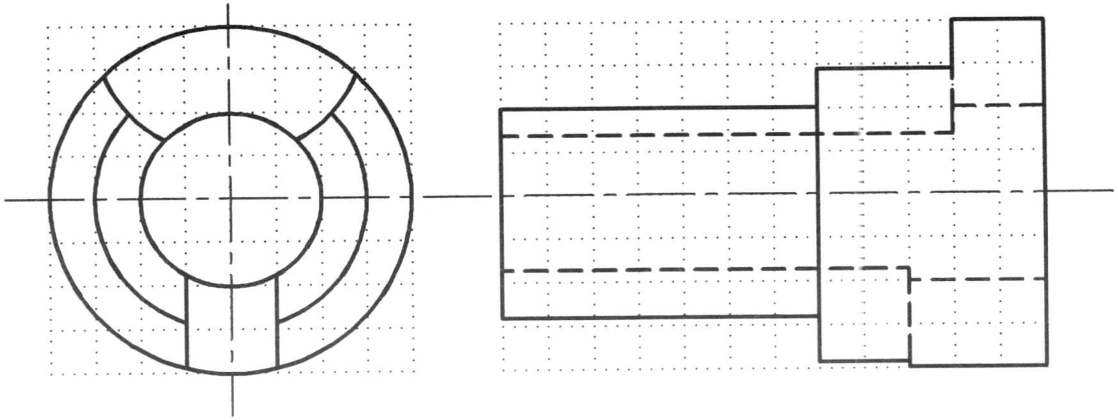

ORTHOGRAPHIC VIEWS

C-6 CYLINDRICAL SURFACES

NAME

DATE

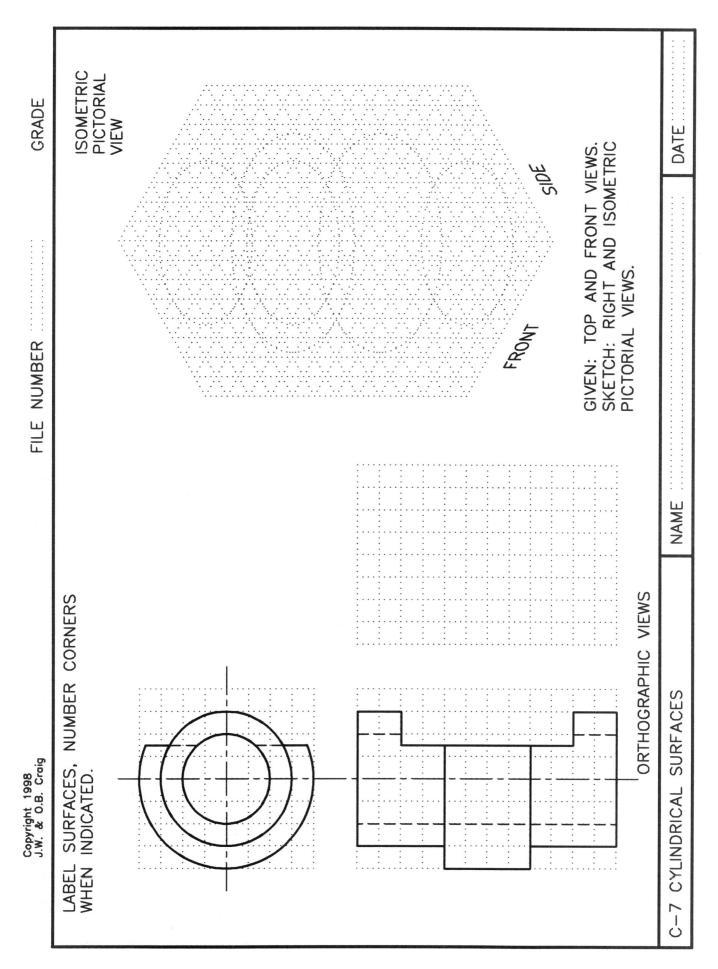

GRADE

ISOMETRIC
PICTORIAL
VIEW

FILE NUMBER

SIDE

FRONT

GIVEN: TOP AND FRONT VIEWS.
SKETCH: RIGHT AND ISOMETRIC
PICTORIAL VIEWS.

Copyright 1998
J.W. & O.B. Craig

LABEL SURFACES, NUMBER CORNERS
WHEN INDICATED.

ORTHOGRAPHIC VIEWS

NAME

DATE

C—7 CYLINDRICAL SURFACES

LABEL SURFACES, NUMBER CORNERS
WHEN INDICATED.

FILE NUMBER

GRADE

ORTHOGRAPHIC VIEWS

C-8 CYLINDRICAL SURFACES

NAME

DATE

ISOMETRIC
PICTORIAL
VIEW

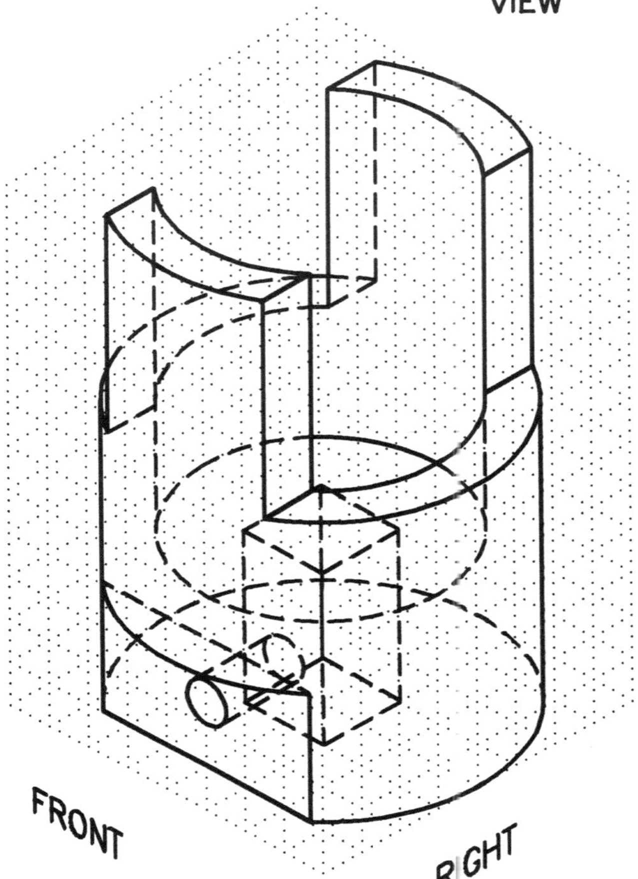

GIVEN: ISOMETRIC PICTORIAL VIEW.
SKETCH: TOP, FRONT AND
RIGHT SIDE VIEWS.

FRONT

RIGHT

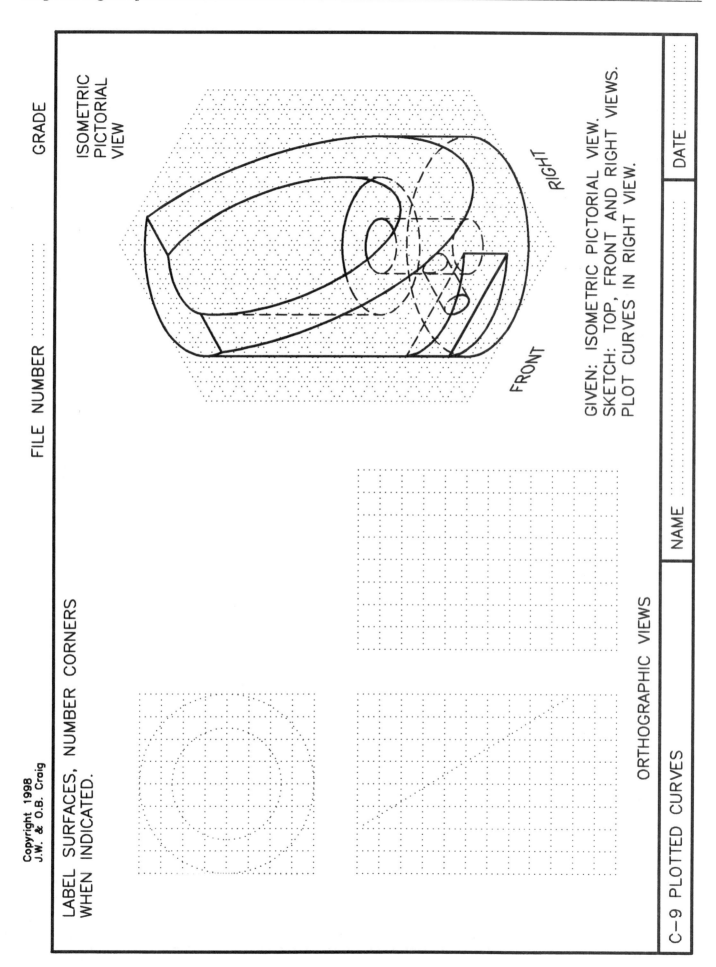

GRADE

FILE NUMBER

ISOMETRIC PICTORIAL VIEW

RIGHT

FRONT

GIVEN: ISOMETRIC PICTORIAL VIEW.
SKETCH: TOP, FRONT AND RIGHT VIEWS.
PLOT CURVES IN RIGHT VIEW.

LABEL SURFACES, NUMBER CORNERS
WHEN INDICATED.

ORTHOGRAPHIC VIEWS

NAME

DATE

C-9 PLOTTED CURVES

LABEL SURFACES, NUMBER CORNERS WHEN INDICATED.

FILE NUMBER

GRADE

ISOMETRIC PICTORIAL VIEW

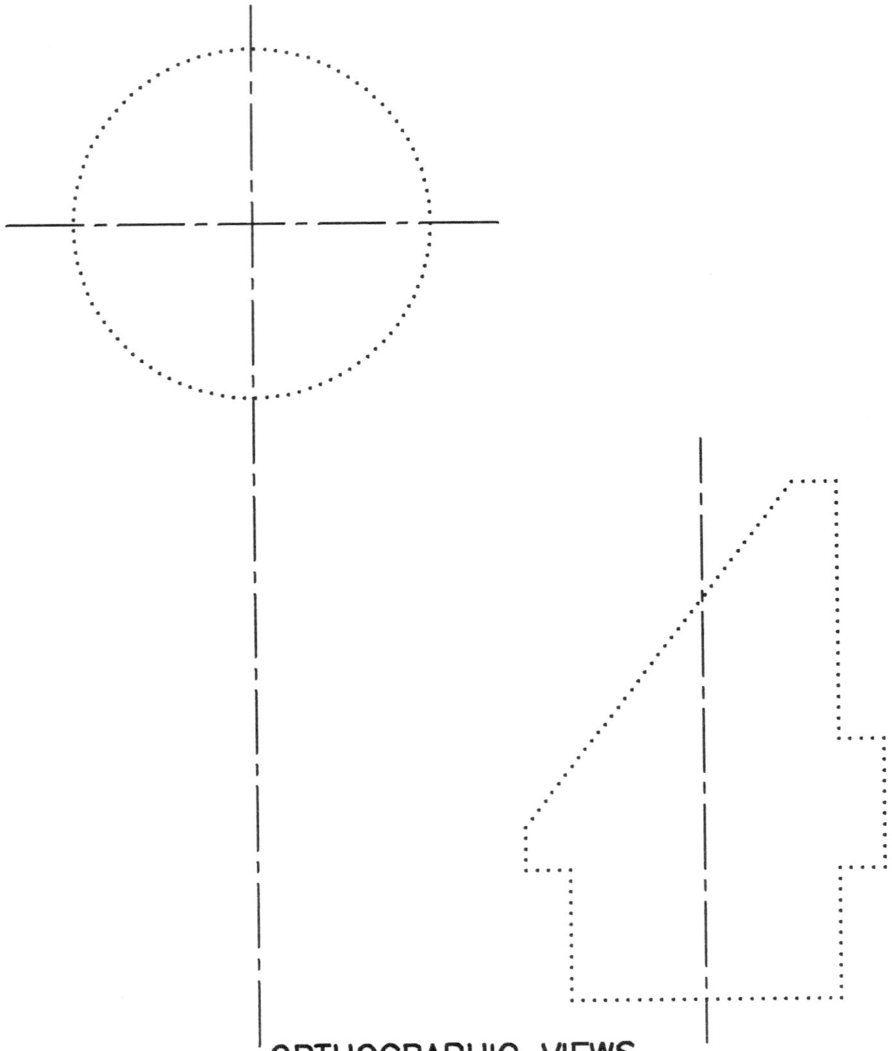

C-10 PLOTTED CURVES

ORTHOGRAPHIC VIEWS

NAME

DATE

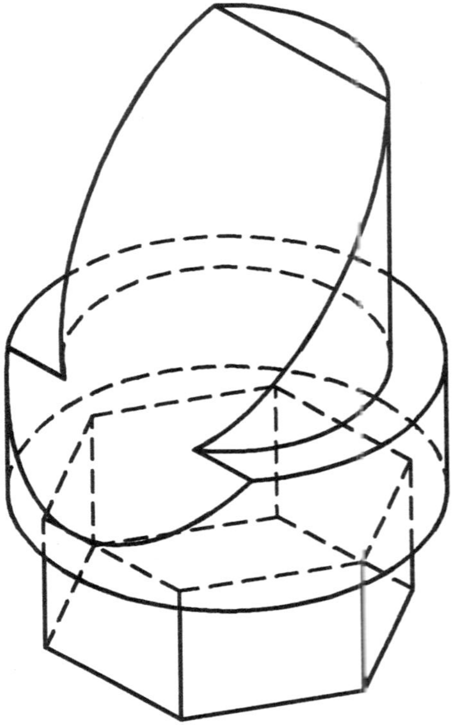

GIVEN: ISOMETRIC PICTORIAL VIEW.
SKETCH: TOP, FRONT AND RIGHT VIEWS.
PLOT CURVES.

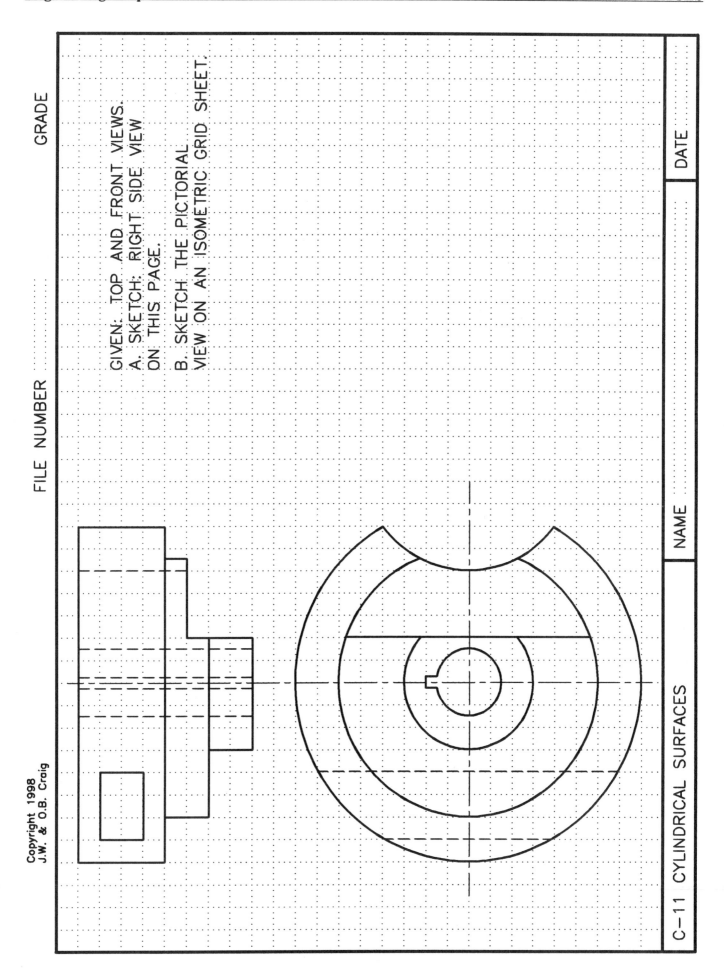

GRADE

FILE NUMBER

GIVEN: TOP AND FRONT VIEWS.
A. SKETCH: RIGHT SIDE VIEW
ON THIS PAGE.

B. SKETCH THE PICTORIAL
VIEW ON AN ISOMETRIC GRID SHEET.

DATE

NAME

C—11 CYLINDRICAL SURFACES

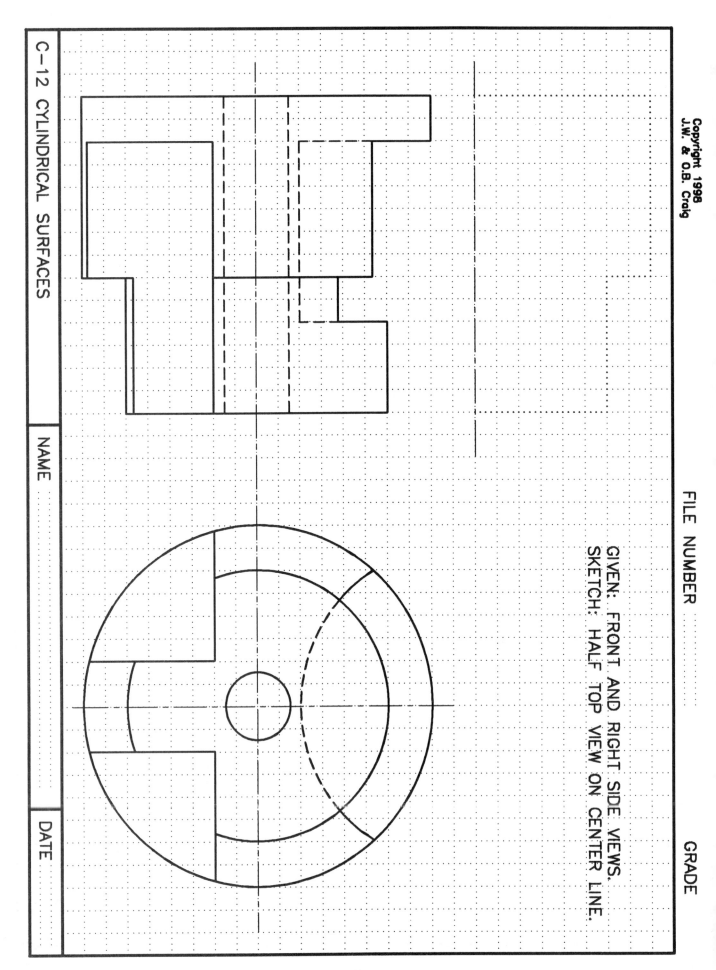

C-12 CYLINDRICAL SURFACES

NAME

DATE

FILE NUMBER

GRADE

GIVEN: FRONT AND RIGHT SIDE VIEWS.
SKETCH: HALF TOP VIEW ON CENTER LINE.

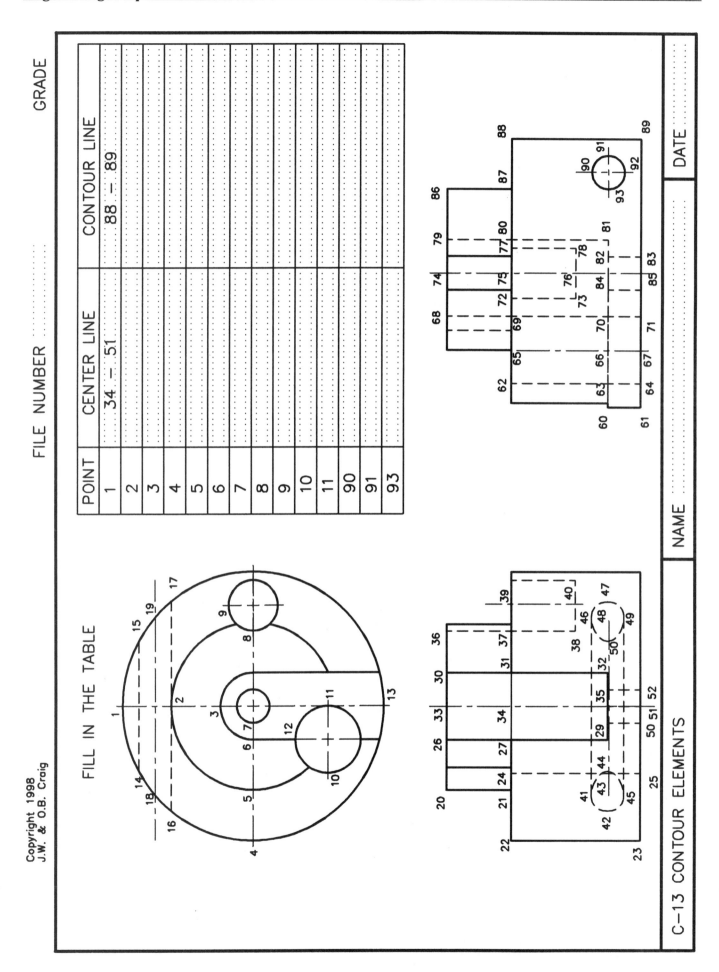

POINT	CENTER LINE 34 – 51	CONTOUR LINE 88 – 89
1		
2		
3		
4		
5		
6		
7		
8		
9		
10		
11		
90		
91		
93		

GRADE

FILE NUMBER

FILL IN THE TABLE

NAME

DATE

C—13 CONTOUR ELEMENTS

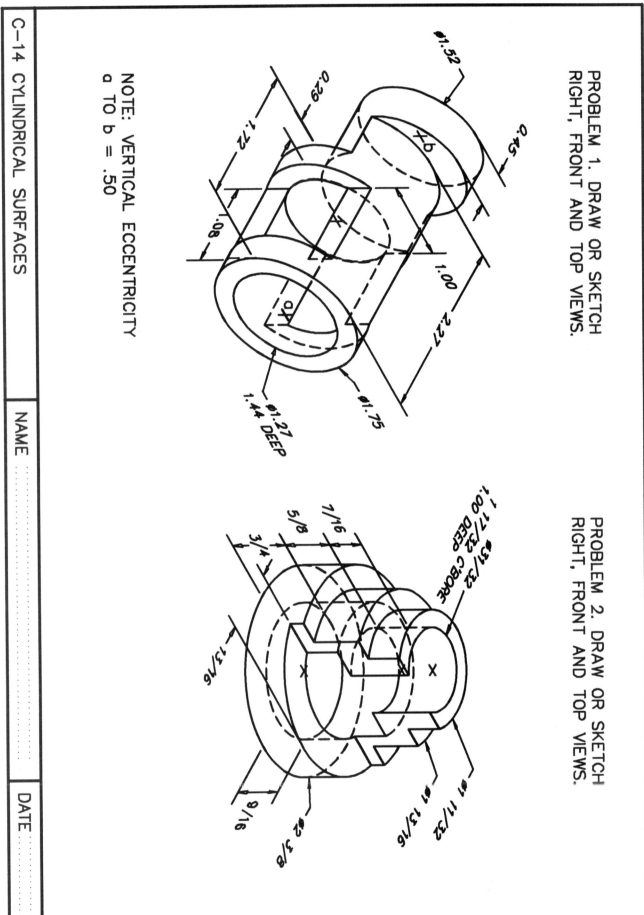

PROBLEM 1. DRAW OR SKETCH
RIGHT, FRONT AND TOP VIEWS.

PROBLEM 2. DRAW OR SKETCH
RIGHT, FRONT AND TOP VIEWS.

FILE NUMBER

GRADE

NOTE: VERTICAL ECCENTRICITY
a TO b = .50

C-14 CYLINDRICAL SURFACES

NAME

DATE

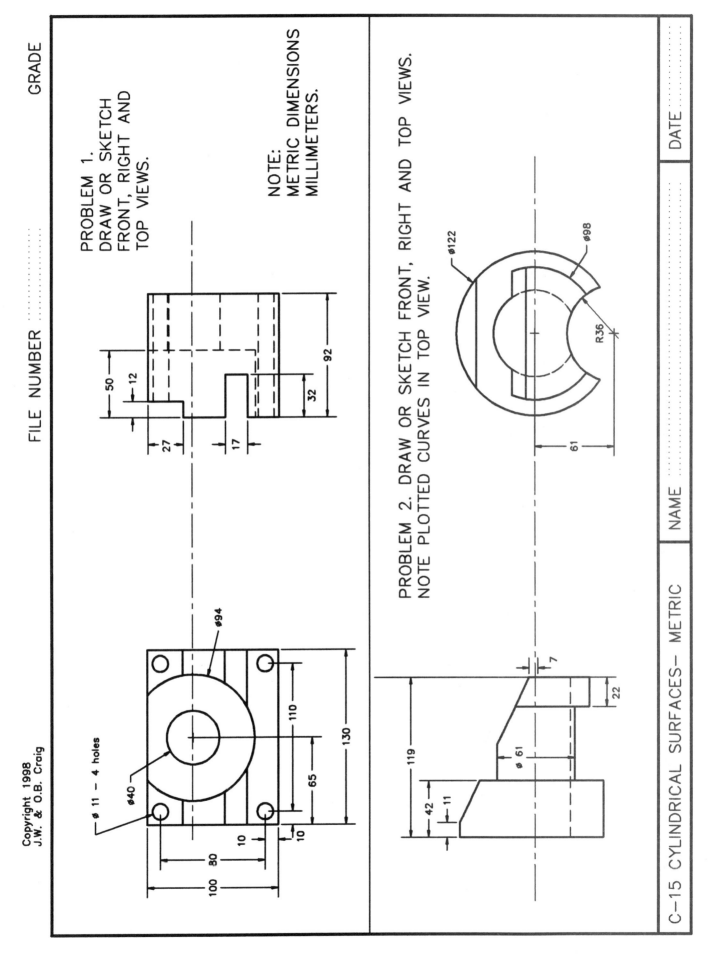

GRADE

FILE NUMBER

PROBLEM 1.
DRAW OR SKETCH
FRONT, RIGHT AND
TOP VIEWS.

NOTE:
METRIC DIMENSIONS
MILLIMETERS.

PROBLEM 2. DRAW OR SKETCH FRONT, RIGHT AND TOP VIEWS.
NOTE PLOTTED CURVES IN TOP VIEW.

DATE

NAME

C-15 CYLINDRICAL SURFACES- METRIC

Copyright 1998
J.W. & O.B. Craig

PROBLEM 1. DRAW OR SKETCH
ISOMETRIC PICTORIAL VIEW.

PROBLEM 2. DRAW OR SKETCH
ISOMETRIC PICTORIAL VIEW.

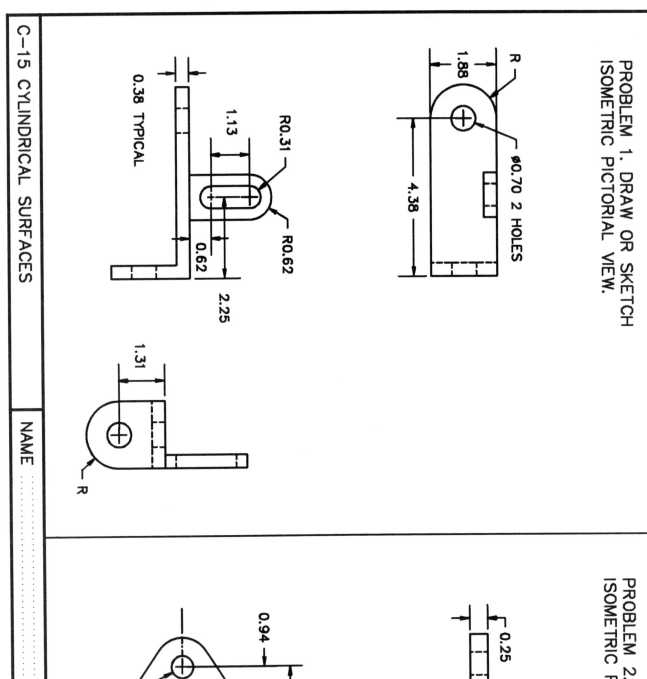

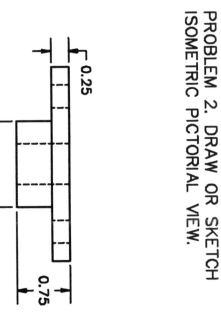

FILE NUMBER

GRADE

C-15 CYLINDRICAL SURFACES

NAME

DATE

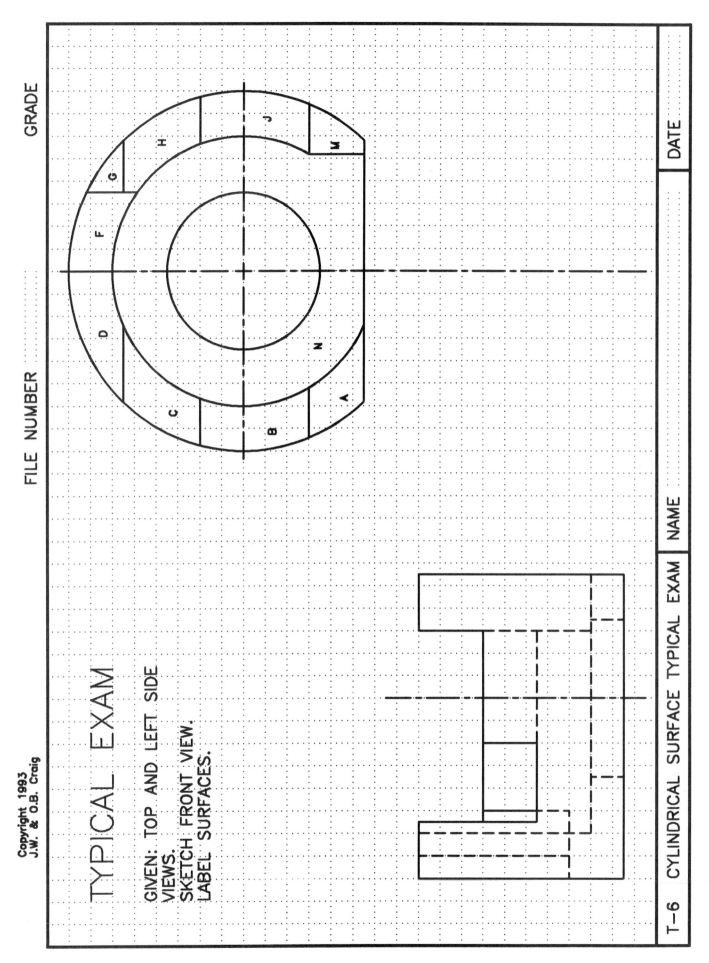

GRADE

FILE NUMBER

DATE

NAME

Copyright 1993
J.W. & O.B. Craig

TYPICAL EXAM

GIVEN: TOP AND LEFT SIDE
VIEWS.
SKETCH FRONT VIEW.
LABEL SURFACES.

T−6　CYLINDRICAL SURFACE TYPICAL EXAM

NAME

DATE

FILE NUMBER

GRADE

Introduction to Auxiliary Views

Regular views of objects show only normal surfaces in true size and shape. The oblique surface in this example is foreshortened in all views. When features must be measured or dimensioned the actual size must be seen.

Auxiliary views are needed to show features that cannot be seen in the regular views.

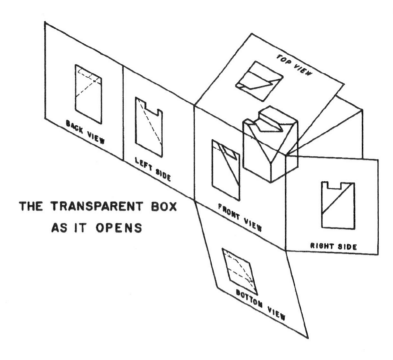

THE TRANSPARENT BOX
AS IT OPENS

Auxiliary views are projected onto picture planes which are at angles to the regular views. The auxiliary plane is at an angle to the horizontal (top) and profile (side) planes. Note:
__The horizontal plane is perpendicular to the frontal plane.
__The profile plane is perpendicular to the frontal plane.
__The auxiliary plane is perpendicular to the frontal plane.

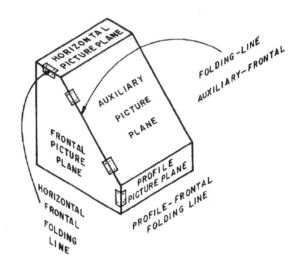

When the auxiliary glass box is opened onto a flat surface, the views are placed as shown.
__The top view is rotated 90 degrees from the front view.
__The side view is rotated 90 degrees from the front view.
__The auxiliary view is rotated 90 degrees from the front view

Auxiliary views may be projected from any view -- front, top, side or another auxiliary.

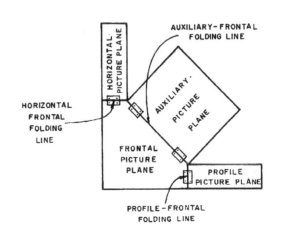

Typical Reasons for Drawing Auxiliary Views

True size of surface.
True size of holes.
True location of holes.

True view of groove.
True angle of groove.

True size of surface.
True shape of rectangular
hole.
True location of hole.

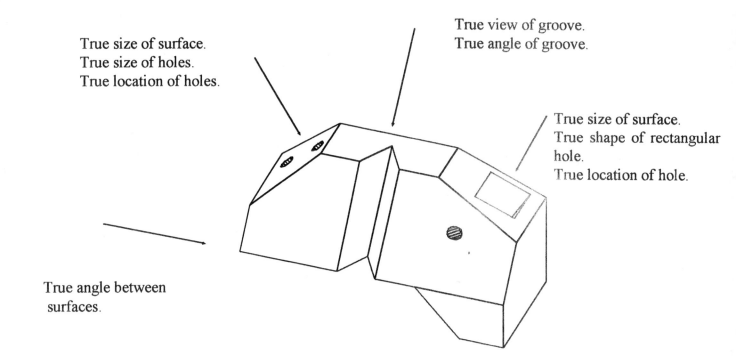

True angle between
 surfaces.

The true size of the inclined surface is to be drawn. A view must be drawn looking perpendicular to the inclined surface to see its true size. An auxiliary picture plane is set parallel to the inclined surface.

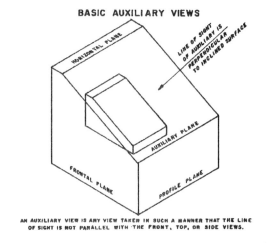

BASIC AUXILIARY VIEWS

AN AUXILIARY VIEW IS ANY VIEW TAKEN IN SUCH A MANNER THAT THE LINE
OF SIGHT IS NOT PARALLEL WITH THE FRONT, TOP, OR SIDE VIEWS.

Views are projected to the picture planes. Notice that the inclined surface is foreshortened in the top and side views. The auxiliary view shows the surface's true size.

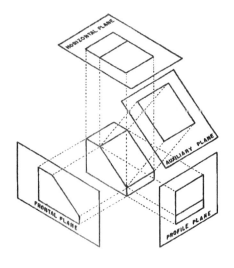

Auxiliary Views Projected from the Front View
These views have depth as the common dimension.

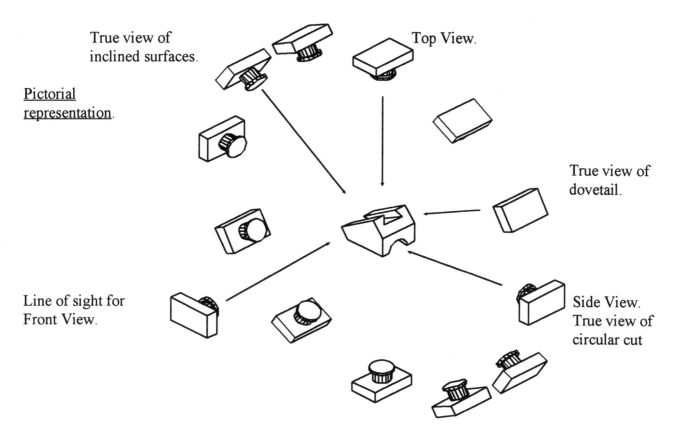

True view of
inclined surfaces.

Top View.

Pictorial
representation.

True view of
dovetail.

Line of sight for
Front View.

Side View.
True view of
circular cut

Orthographic representation.

Depth (front to back) is the common dimension. Views are projected from the front view.

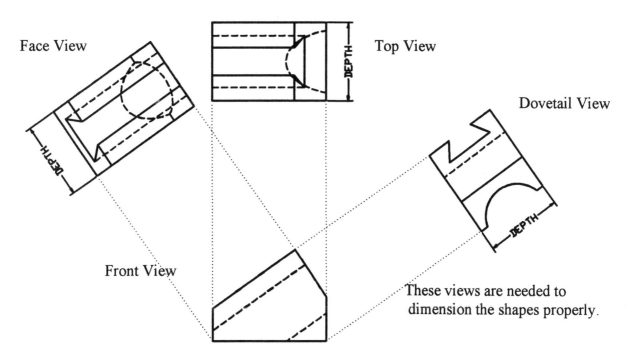

Face View

Top View

DEPTH

Dovetail View

DEPTH

DEPTH

Front View

These views are needed to
dimension the shapes properly.

Auxiliary View Projected From the Front View - continued

Select a line of sight to show the inclined surface true size.

Project all corners parallel to the line of sight.

Measure the depth from the side view and transfer the depth to the auxiliary view. Depth is measured parallel to the line of sight.

Block in the shape of the auxiliary view. Locate the outer corners and edges.

Identify surfaces. Be sure every surface -- visible and hidden -- is shown.

Complete the view. Be sure to include all hidden lines. Verify the extent and shape of every surface.

This corner is often forgotten when projecting features.

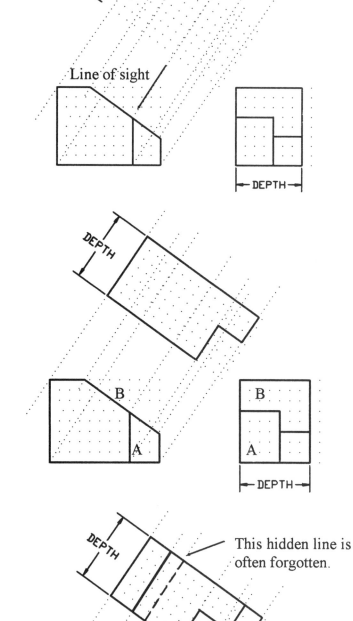

Auxiliary Views Projected from the Top View
These auxiliary views have height as the common dimension.

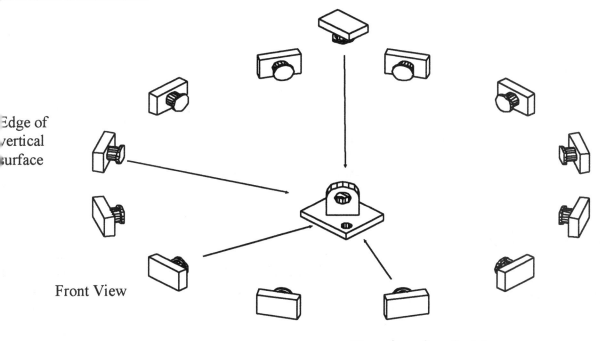

Line of sight for Top View

Pictorial representation.

Edge of vertical surface

Front View

True size of vertical face

Orthographic representation

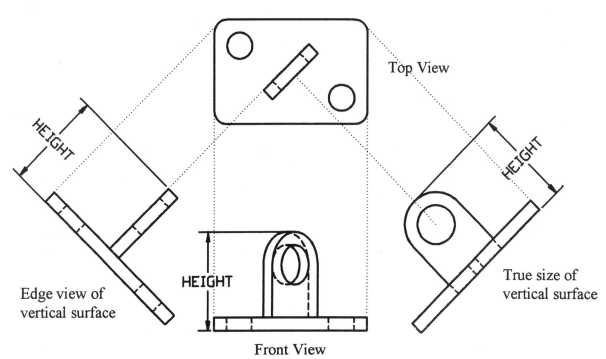

Top View

HEIGHT

HEIGHT

HEIGHT

Edge view of vertical surface

HEIGHT

True size of vertical surface

Front View

Height (top to bottom) is the common dimension between any views projected off the top view.

Auxiliary View Projected From the Top View - continued

Select a line of sight.

Project all corners parallel to the line of sight.

Height is the common dimension. Measure height from the front view and transfer the distance to the auxiliary view.

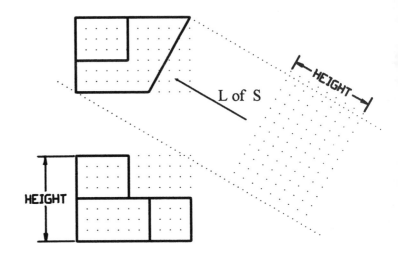

Project all the corners from the top view. Block in surfaces.

Measure height distances from the front view.

Inclined surface A is true size in the auxiliary view.

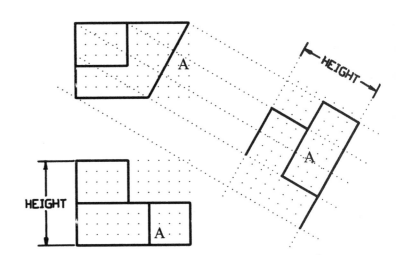

Complete the view. Verify the extent and visibility of every surface.

Be sure to show all hidden lines.

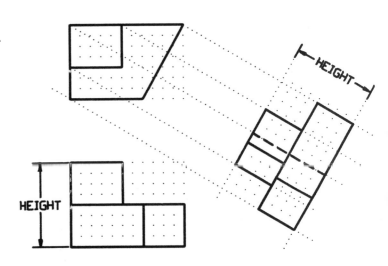

Auxiliary View Projected From the Side View.

True size of surface view.

Pictorial Representation

Top View

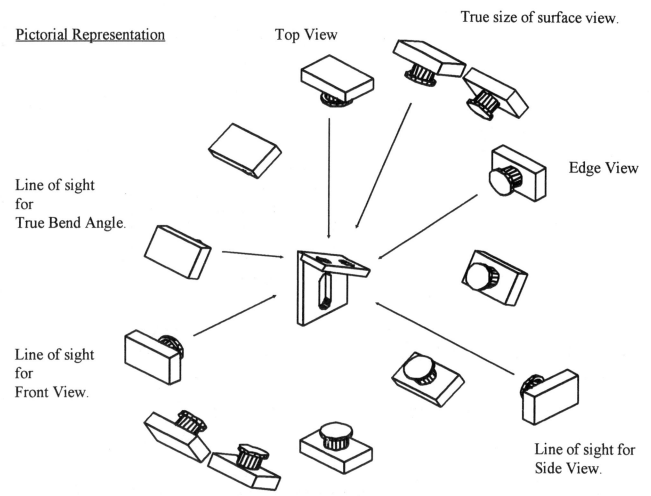

Edge View

Line of sight
for
True Bend Angle.

Line of sight
for
Front View.

Line of sight for
Side View.

Auxiliary views projected from the side view have width (right to left) as the
common dimension.

Orthographic representation.

True view of
inclined surface.

True view of
bend angle.

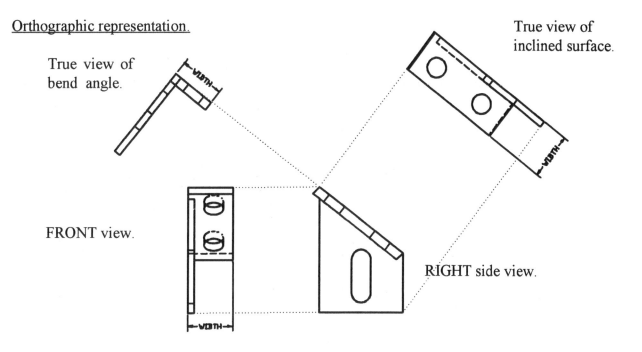

FRONT view.

RIGHT side view.

Auxiliary View Projected From the Side View - continued
These views have width as the common dimension.

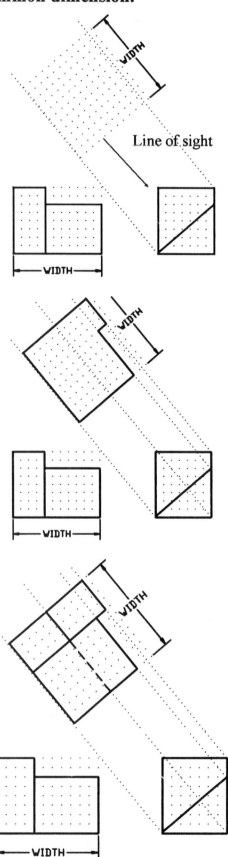

Select a line of sight. Project all corners and features parallel to the line of sight.

Measure width from the front view and transfer this distance to the auxiliary view.

Block in the outline of the auxiliary view. Locate outer corners and edges.

Identify surfaces. Be sure all surfaces are projected and measured accurately.

Complete the view. Be sure to include all hidden lines. Verify the extent and shape of every surface.

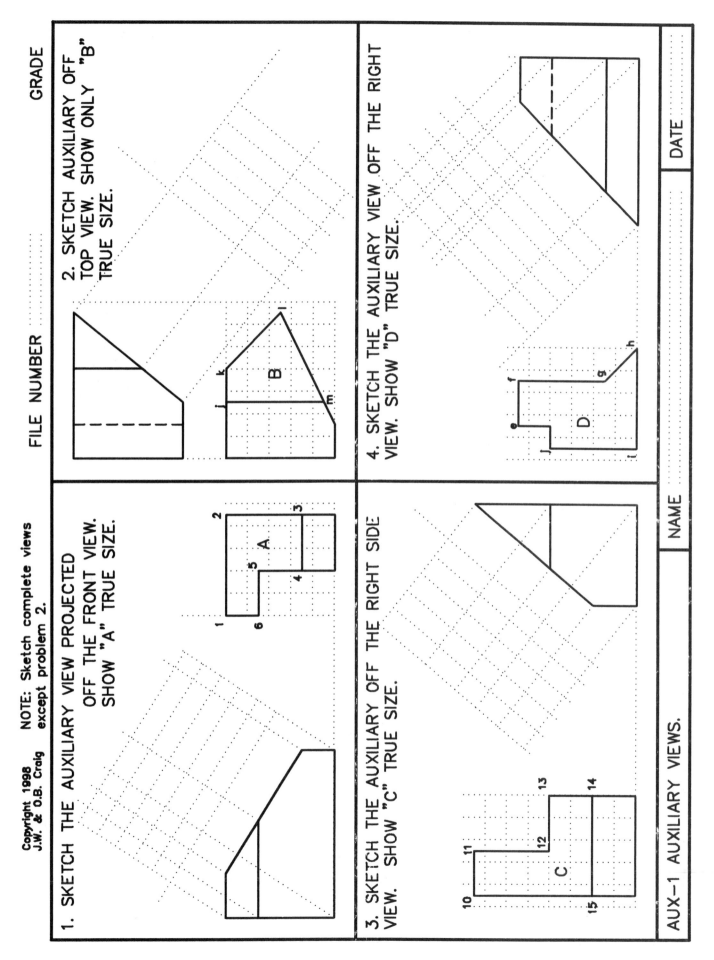

Copyright 1998
J.W. & O.B. Craig

NOTE: Sketch complete views
except problem 2.

FILE NUMBER

GRADE

1. SKETCH THE AUXILIARY VIEW PROJECTED
OFF THE FRONT VIEW.
SHOW "A" TRUE SIZE.

2. SKETCH AUXILIARY OFF
TOP VIEW. SHOW ONLY "B"
TRUE SIZE.

3. SKETCH THE AUXILIARY OFF THE RIGHT SIDE
VIEW. SHOW "C" TRUE SIZE.

4. SKETCH THE AUXILIARY VIEW OFF THE RIGHT
VIEW. SHOW "D" TRUE SIZE.

AUX-1 AUXILIARY VIEWS.

NAME

DATE

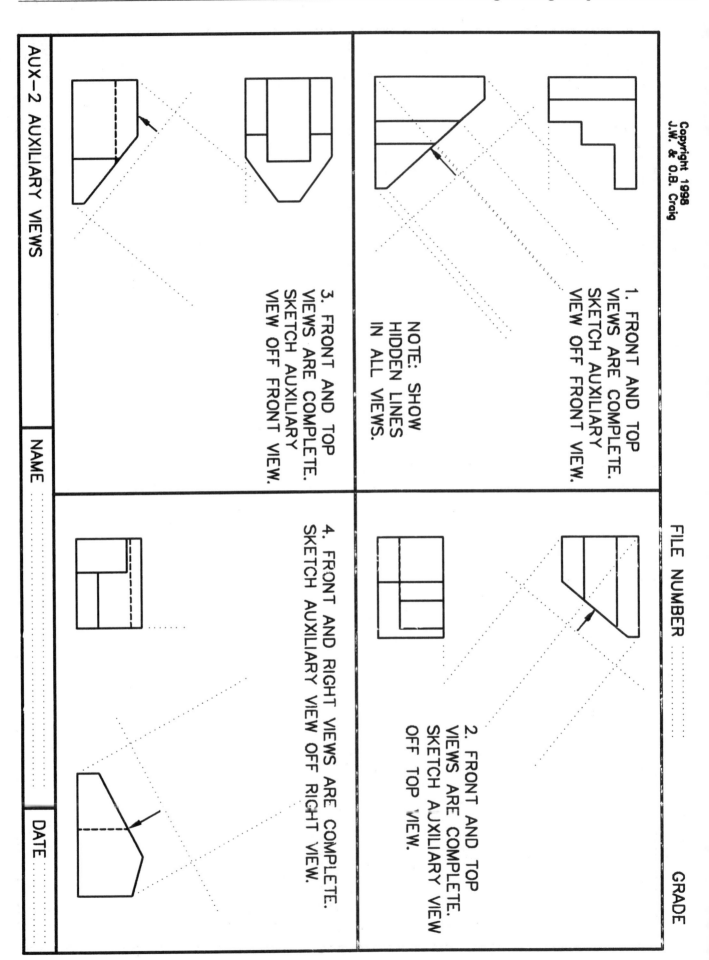

AUX-2 AUXILIARY VIEWS

FILE NUMBER

GRADE

NAME

DATE

1. FRONT AND TOP
VIEWS ARE COMPLETE.
SKETCH AUXILIARY
VIEW OFF FRONT VIEW.

NOTE: SHOW
HIDDEN LINES
IN ALL VIEWS.

2. FRONT AND TOP
VIEWS ARE COMPLETE.
SKETCH AUXILIARY VIEW
OFF TOP VIEW.

3. FRONT AND TOP
VIEWS ARE COMPLETE.
SKETCH AUXILIARY
VIEW OFF FRONT VIEW.

4. FRONT AND RIGHT VIEWS ARE COMPLETE.
SKETCH AUXILIARY VIEW OFF RIGHT VIEW.

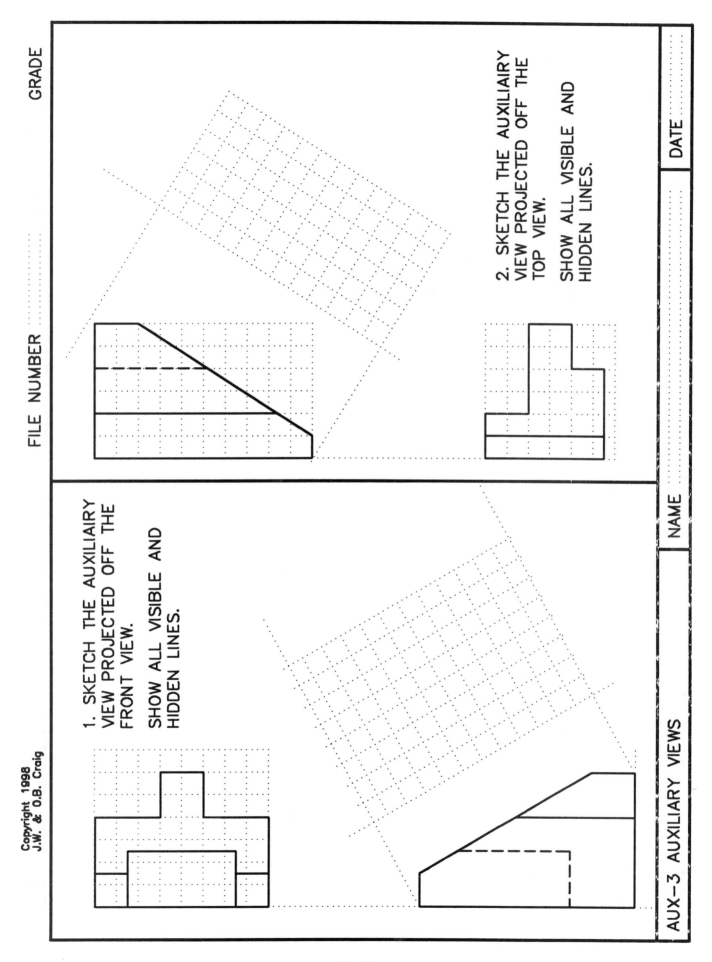

GRADE

FILE NUMBER

DATE

NAME

Copyright 1998
J.W. & O.B. Craig

2. SKETCH THE AUXILIAIRY
VIEW PROJECTED OFF THE
TOP VIEW.

SHOW ALL VISIBLE AND
HIDDEN LINES.

1. SKETCH THE AUXILIAIRY
VIEW PROJECTED OFF THE
FRONT VIEW.

SHOW ALL VISIBLE AND
HIDDEN LINES.

AUX-3 AUXILIARY VIEWS

GIVEN: FRONT AND LEFT SIDE VIEWS.
SKETCH: AUXILIARY VIEW PROJECTED
OFF THE FRONT VIEW.
SHOW VISIBLE AND HIDDEN LINES.

Surfaces H & J
are Inclined.

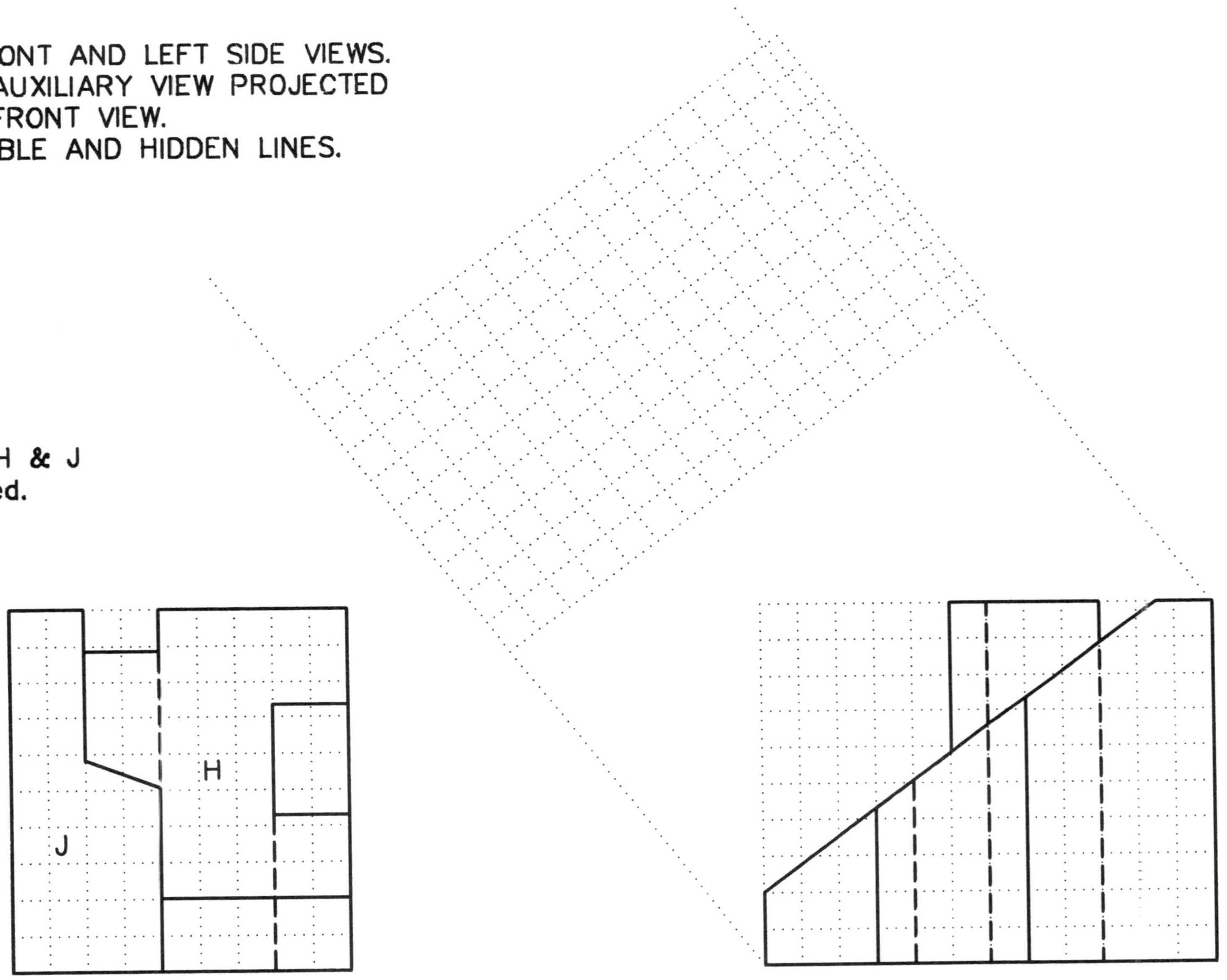

FILE NUMBER

GRADE

AUX-4   AUXILIARY VIEWS

NAME

DATE

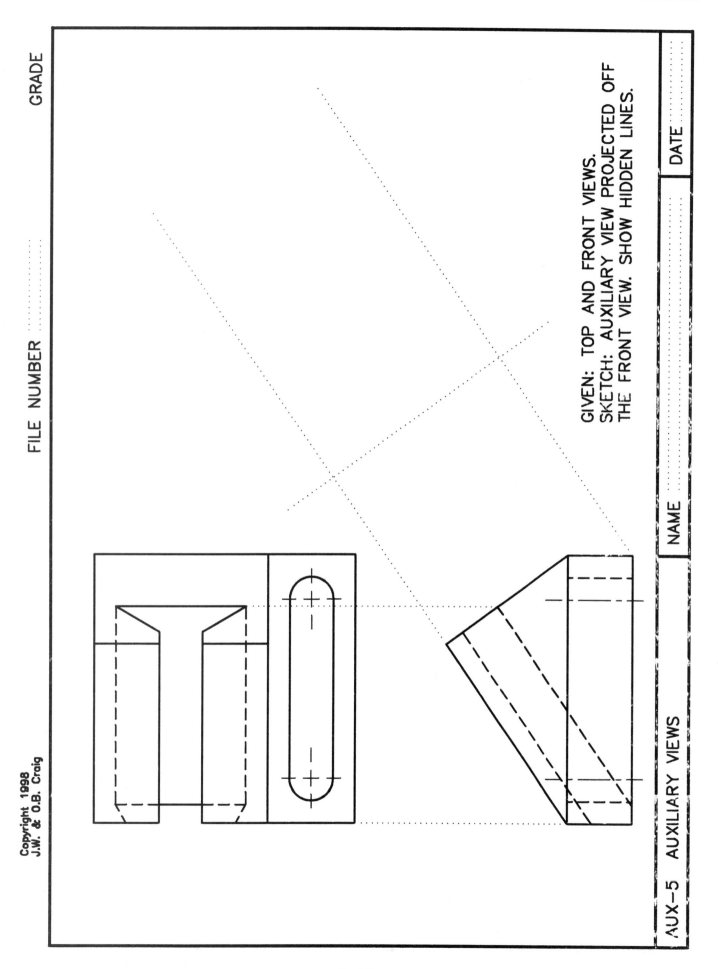

GRADE

FILE NUMBER

GIVEN: TOP AND FRONT VIEWS.
SKETCH: AUXILIARY VIEW PROJECTED OFF
THE FRONT VIEW. SHOW HIDDEN LINES.

NAME

DATE

AUX-5   AUXILIARY VIEWS

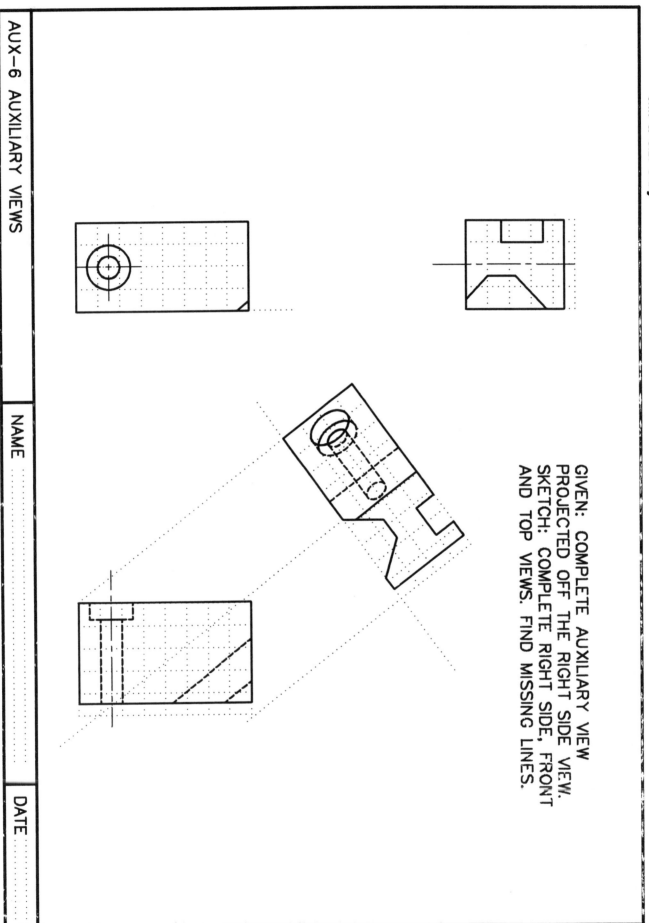

GIVEN: COMPLETE AUXILIARY VIEW PROJECTED OFF THE RIGHT SIDE VIEW.
SKETCH: COMPLETE RIGHT SIDE, FRONT AND TOP VIEWS. FIND MISSING LINES.

AUX–6 AUXILIARY VIEWS

NAME

DATE

FILE NUMBER

GRADE

GRADE

FILE NUMBER

GIVEN: FRONT AND RIGHT VIEWS ARE COMPLETE.
SKETCH: COMPLETE AUXILIARY VIEW OFF RIGHT
SIDE VIEW.
ADD MISSING LINES TO TOP VIEW.

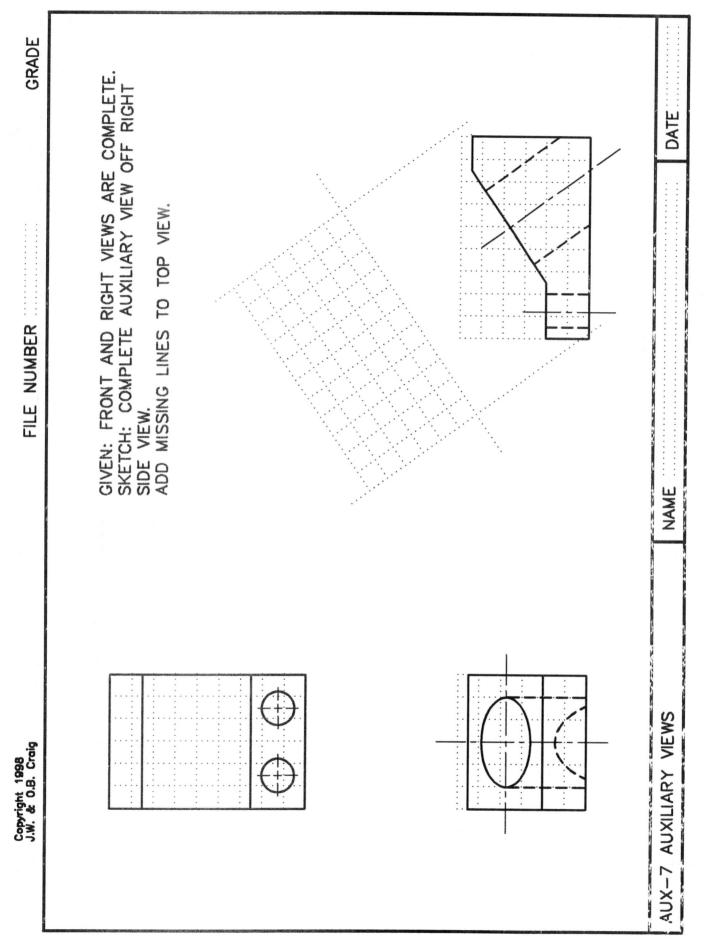

AUX-7 AUXILIARY VIEWS

NAME

DATE

Copyright 1998
J.W. & O.B. Craig

PROBLEM 1. DRAW FRONT, AUXILIARY
OFF FRONT VIEW AND TOP VIEWS.

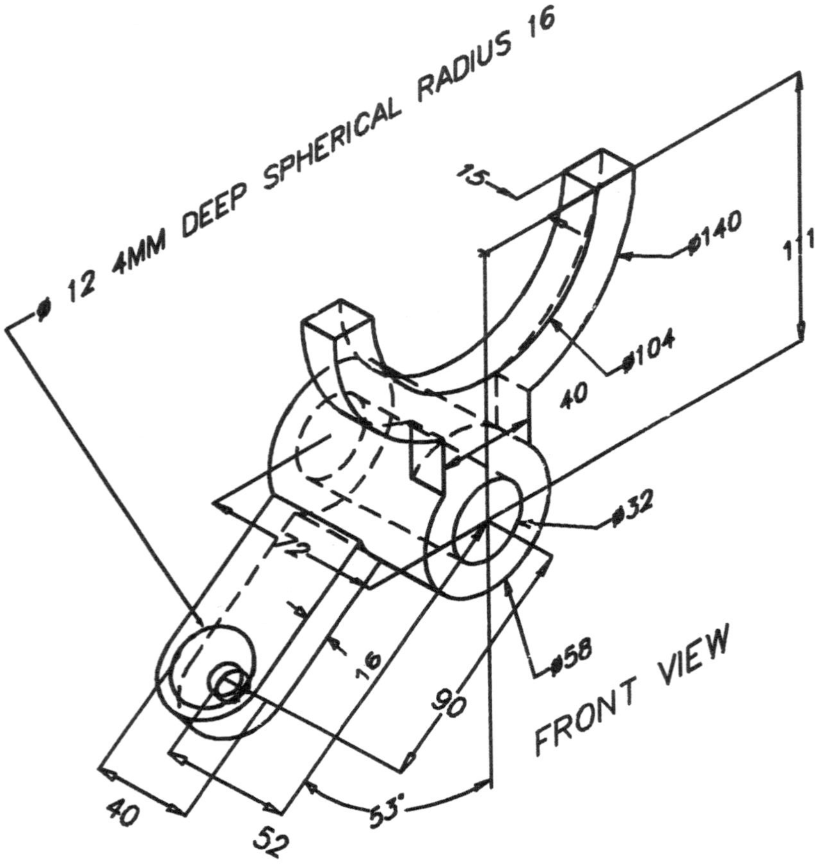

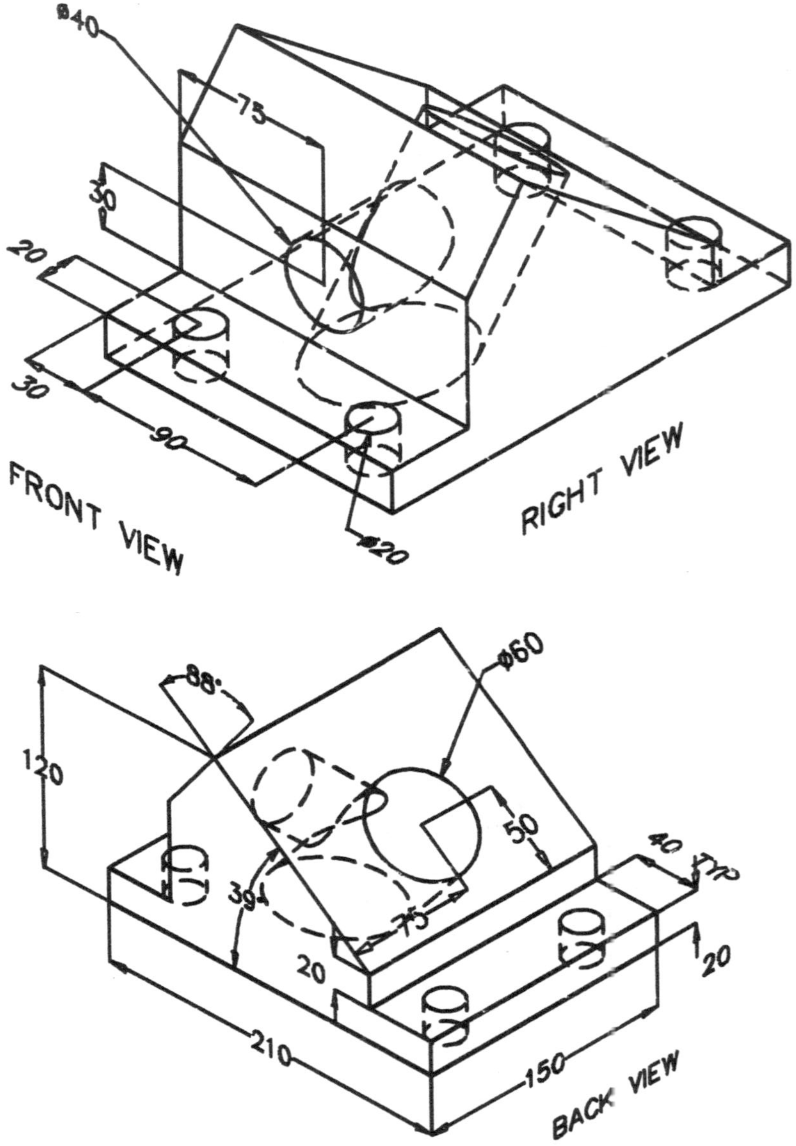

PROBLEM 2. DRAW FRONT, RIGHT AND
AUXILIARY VIEW OFF RIGHT VIEW.
NOTE: ALL DIMENSIONS METRIC (mm).

AUX-8 AUXILIARY VIEWS.

NAME

DATE

FILE NUMBER

GRADE

Ø 12 4MM DEEP SPHERICAL RADIUS 16

40
52
53°
90
16
72
Ø58
Ø32
40
Ø104
Ø140
111
15

FRONT VIEW

120
88°
394
20
210
75
50
Ø60
150
BACK VIEW
20
40

FRONT VIEW
30
20
90
50
75
Ø40
Ø20

RIGHT VIEW

GRADE

FILE NUMBER

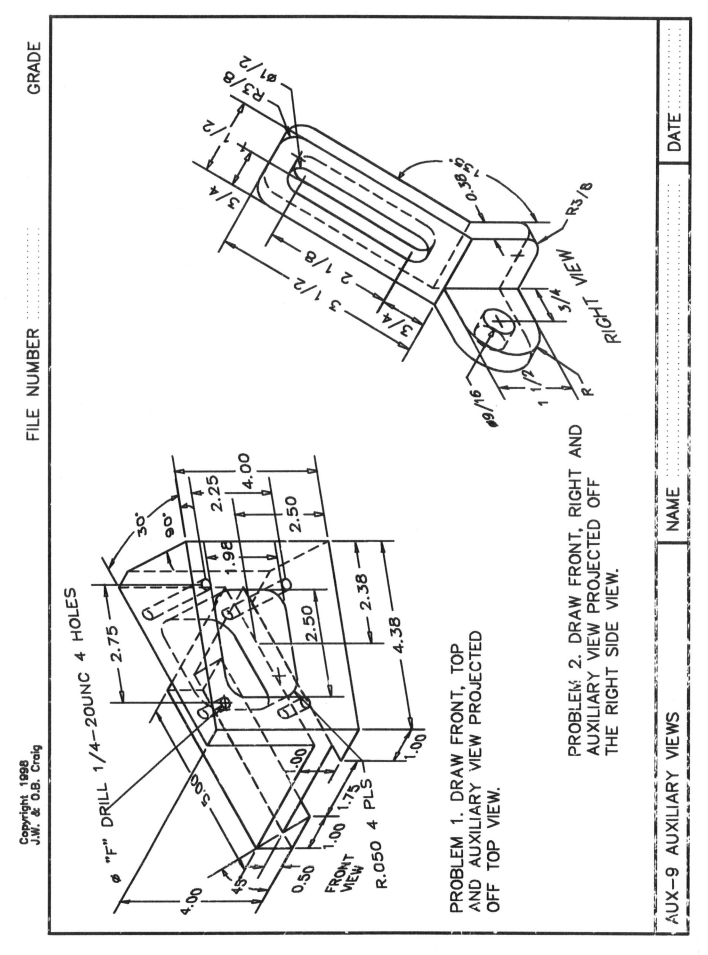

Ø "F" DRILL 1/4—20UNC 4 HOLES

R.050 4 PLS

FRONT VIEW

RIGHT VIEW

PROBLEM 1. DRAW FRONT, TOP AND AUXILIARY VIEW PROJECTED OFF TOP VIEW.

PROBLEM 2. DRAW FRONT, RIGHT AND AUXILIARY VIEW PROJECTED OFF THE RIGHT SIDE VIEW.

NAME

DATE

AUX—9 AUXILIARY VIEWS

NAME

DATE

FILE NUMBER

GRADE

SECTIONAL VIEWS

Section views are cut-away views of objects. Often, objects have complex shapes inside. These shapes are difficult to visualize from hidden lines. By taking an imaginary cut through an object and removing a portion, hidden features may be shown as visible lines.

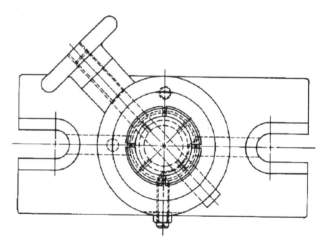

Section views require a good ability to visualize the internal shapes of objects. These views are sometimes difficult to draw, but they help anyone reading the drawing. Graphical communication should be as clear as possible.

Many types of section views are used. The engineer or drafter must decide which view is best for a particular use. Some section views are not exactly true projections as some elements may be omitted or translated before projecting.

Hidden lines are often omitted in section views.

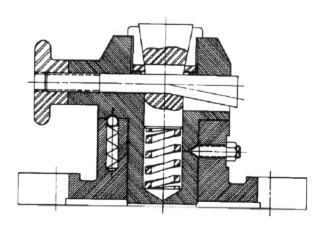

ASSEMBLY SECTION views are often used by designers to show how parts fit together. This type of view is used on the first page of a set of production drawings.

Assembly section view of a holding fixture.

Full Section Views

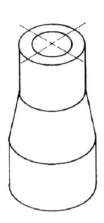

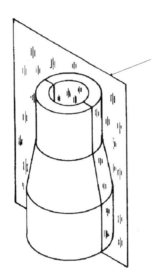

CUTTING PLANE

Front half is discarded.
View from center to back.

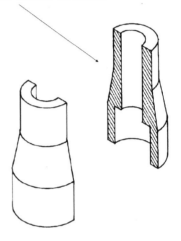

Full section views show the FULL VIEW in SEC-
TION. A cutting plane is located at the middle of
the object. The front half of the part is discarded.
The view shows features from the middle on back.

Sketch the shape of solid area. Then, add visible
lines.

First, outline the solid material that is cut. Imagine a saw cutting through. Decide where material
exists -- hard to cut. And, where open areas exist -
- easy to cut.

SECTIONAL VIEWS
FULL SECTION

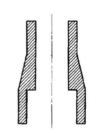 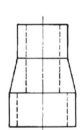

Add the visible lines to the view. Hidden lines are
usually not shown in full section views.

Add center lines.

Show cutting plane lines and labels if needed. Cutting plane lines may be omitted if there is only one
section view on the object and if the cut is taken at
the middle. If any confusion exists then the cutting
plane line should be shown. Labels must be used if
more than one section view is drawn. The arrows
on the cutting plane lines show the direction of
sight.

SECTIONAL VIEWS
FULL SECTION

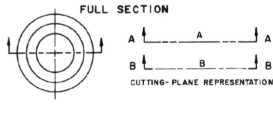

CUTTING- PLANE REPRESENTATION

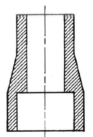 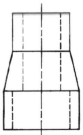

Section Line types and Orientation.

SYMBOLS FOR SECTION LINING

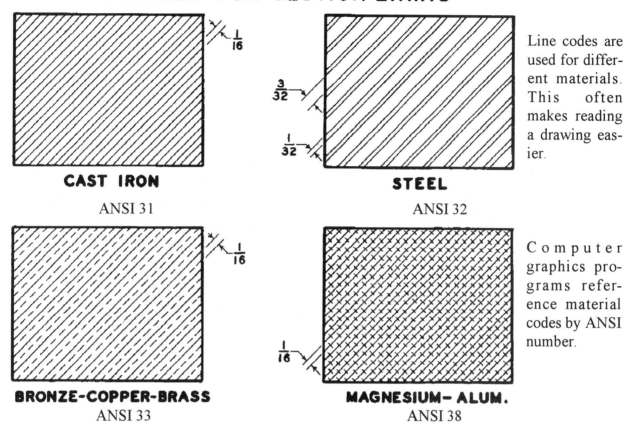

CAST IRON

ANSI 31

STEEL

ANSI 32

Line codes are used for different materials. This often makes reading a drawing easier.

BRONZE-COPPER-BRASS

ANSI 33

MAGNESIUM– ALUM.

ANSI 38

Computer graphics programs reference material codes by ANSI number.

Many line codes exist for architectural drawing, map drawing, machine parts etc. The default line type is equally spaced lines (cast iron). Section lines are draw as thin lines on drawings, but they must be very dark in order to print clearly.

Section lines on the same part should be drawn at the same angle.

Section lines are drawn at 45 degrees if possible. If many parts are shown then other angles should be used for each separate part. Using different angles makes the individual parts easier to see.

SECTION LINING ON ASSEMBLY DRAWINGS

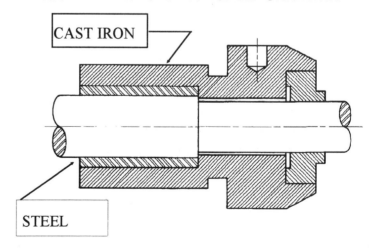

CAST IRON

STEEL

Note: Standards vary on the required use of crosshatch line codes. Also, some companies prefer to use only ANSI 31 for all materials. In some cases, no crosshatch lines are used in sectional views.

Phantom Section Views

PHANTOM SECTIONING

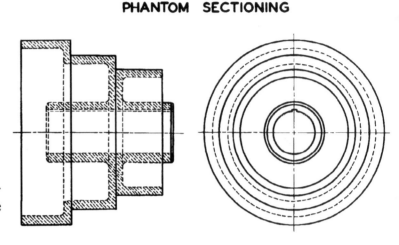

Phantom sections are regular views with a full section view super-imposed as a hidden section. These views are very effective for hollow parts. In the example, the part is mostly hollow to reduce weight and material use. The phantom section gives a very clear picture of where solid material exists.

Phantom section views are also known as hidden section views. Material types cannot be shown.

Two phantom sections are used. Cutting plane A-A is shown in the front view. B-B is shown in the side view.

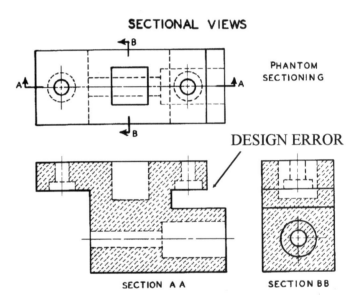

Look at the design error on this part. How can the counter-bored hole be machined? How do you get a bolt into the hole? If a nut is used here why design a counter-bore?

Features of objects may be rotated then projected to section views. The purpose is to make the section view as useful as possible. This may be done to show a true distance from a center or to show a feature that would not otherwise be seen.

This practice is not limited to sectional views. Features may also be rotated or aligned in regular drawings.

VIOLATIONS OF PROJECTION

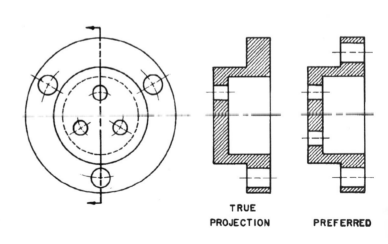

Half Section Views

A Half Section view shows HALF of the VIEW in SECTION. This type of view is very useful on parts which are symmetrical. The drawing may show both outer and inner features in the same view.

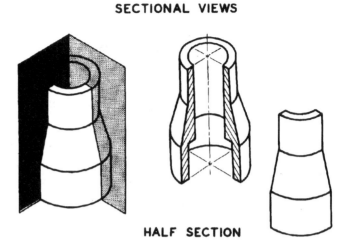

Hidden lines may be shown in the un-sectioned half of the view to provide clarity. Hidden lines are not shown in the sectioned portion of the view.

A CENTER LINE is used to separate the sectioned half view from the un-sectioned half.

Half Section views are not a good choice when dimensions must be applied. Dimension standards do not allow hidden lines to be dimensioned except when only a single view is drawn.

Half Section views are a good choice for symmetrical parts.

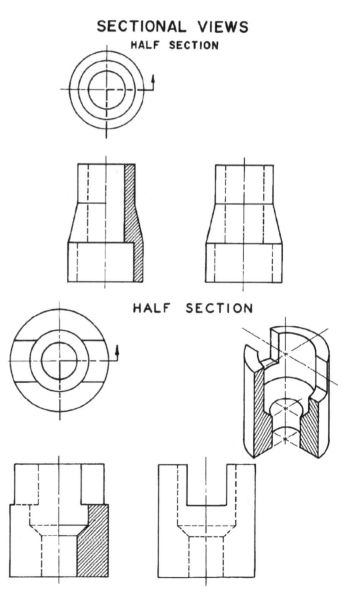

Offset Sections

An Offset Section may be used to pick up features that are not on a regular cutting plane. To show more about the part, the cutting plane was offset through the small hole and boss.

No line is drawn at the point of the offset in the sectional view.

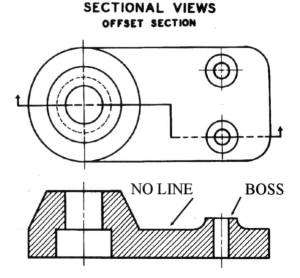

Thin Webs in Section

Thin areas that occur near the cutting plane may be alternate-hatched. Every other crosshatch line is drawn making the sectioned area appear less dense. This practice gives a clearer picture of the thickness of the hatched area. Alternate hatching clearly shows thin and thick material sections along the cutting plane.

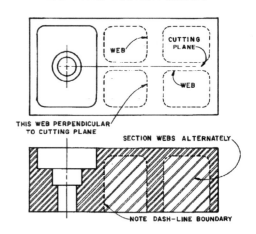

Webs are thin features on parts that are added for strength or rigidity. Webs may be outlined with hidden lines and alternate-hatched. This is one instance where hidden lines are used in a sectional view.

Thin areas may be outlined with hidden lines and alternate hatched.

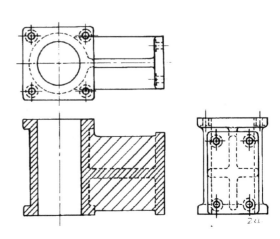

Revolved Section Views

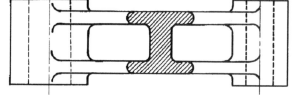

REVOLVED SECTIONS

Revolved Sections are used to show cross-sectional areas on elongated parts. Structural drawings use this technique to show material shapes.

Cut a thin slice across the part and revolve it into the plane of view.

The section view is super-imposed on the regular view.

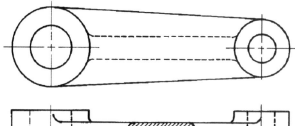

REVOLVED SECTIONS

This representation uses a broken-out area to separate the regular view from the section view. Broken lines are sketched freehand.

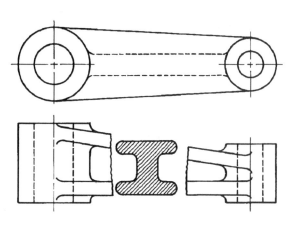

SECTIONAL VIEWS

REVOLVED SECTIONS

Revolved Sections give a quick, clear view of the cross-sectional area at a point on the part. Information that would be hard to show or visualize from hidden lines may be seen.

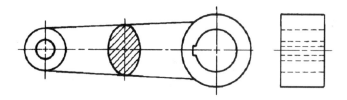

The drawing shows the cross-section at the point where the revolved section was cut.

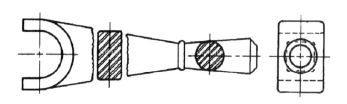

Detail (Removed) Sections

Thin sections are cut along a part. Each section is identified A-A, B-B, etc. The sectional views are placed wherever space permits. Each view is identified with the cut label. On large drawings the views may be on another page. Zone numbering may also be used to identify cut and view locations.

Detail Sections show only lines that are on (or very near to) the cutting plane.

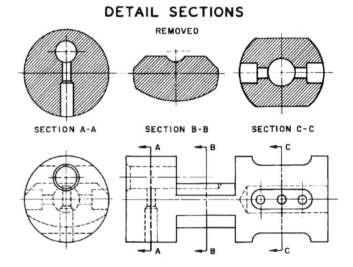

Aligned Section Views

Section views must be true views of the cut. Foreshortened section views are not allowed. Whenever a cut must be taken on an angle, the view must be aligned then projected as a true view.

Foreshortened section views are not allowed.

In the example, notice that the front view is wider than the actual projection from the top view.

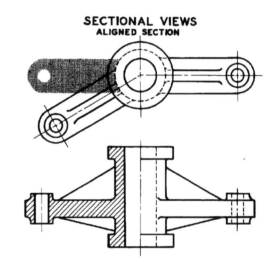

Combinations of section view types may be used. An Offset, Full and Aligned section cut is used in this example.

Points behind the cutting plane must be projected perpendicular to the cutting plane before revolving.

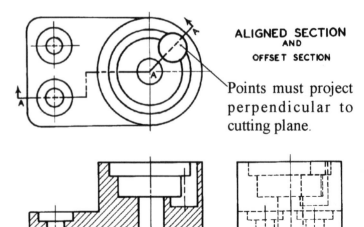

Points must project perpendicular to cutting plane.

Broken-out Sections and Conventional Breaks

"D" is a Broken-Out section cut. These may also be called detail sections. They are used to show a limited section area. (Places where a full section would be too extensive.)

"B" and "E" show conventional breaks. These are used to shorten the width of the drawing for very long parts.

The taper pin at "C" is not sectioned.

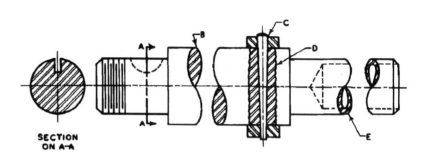

SECTIONAL VIEWS

Pictorial Sections

Pictorial section views may provide clear information on part shape and cross-sectional areas.

Note the preferred angle for cross-hatch lines in the front, top and side planes.

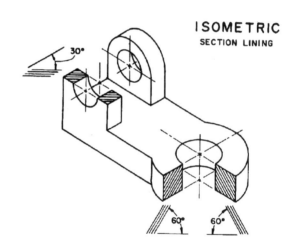

ISOMETRIC
SECTION LINING

Simplified Threads in Section

Simplified threads are preferred on drawings. Examples of external and internal section views are shown. The major diameter should be drawn accurately. Minor diameter sizes may be approximated.

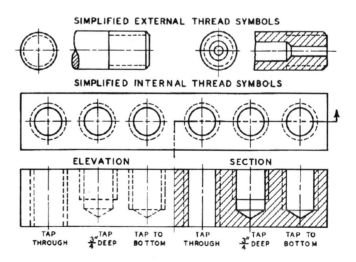

CONVENTIONAL THREADS

What Not to Section

MACHINE ELEMENTS NOT SECTIONED

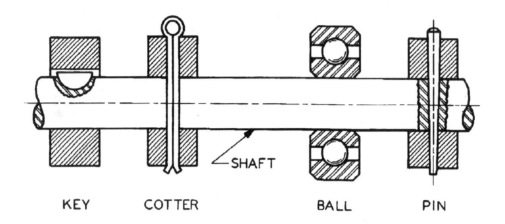

KEY   COTTER   SHAFT   BALL   PIN

Sectioning all elements of a drawing would not
add to the clarity. Center shafts or other features
at the center of the design are not sectioned.

Hardware, nuts and bolts, pins, keys, bearings,
etc. are not sectioned.

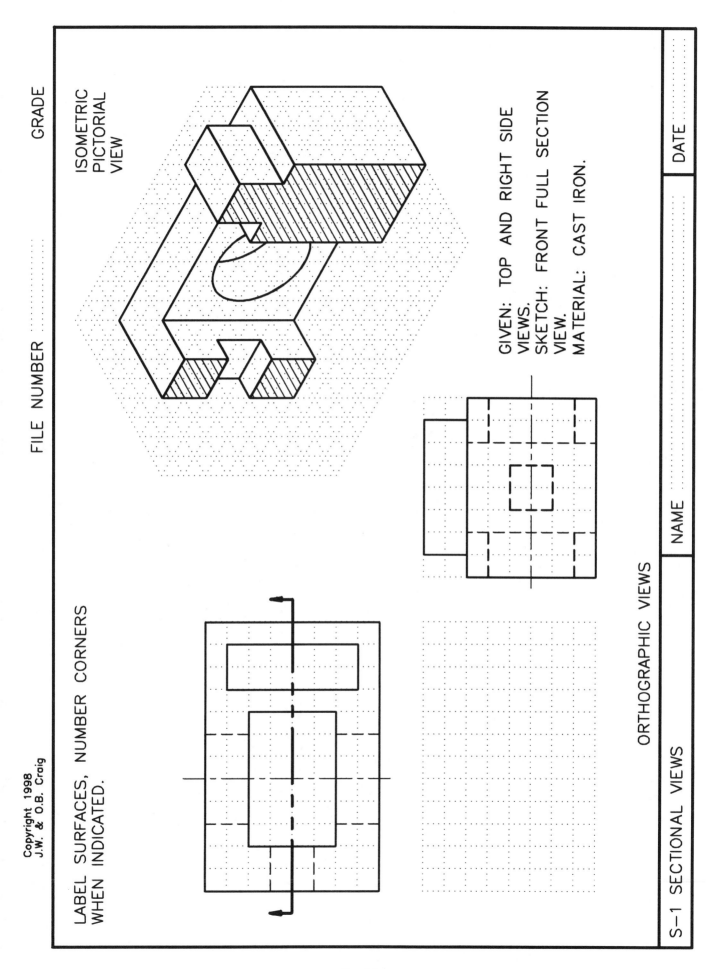

GRADE

FILE NUMBER

ISOMETRIC
PICTORIAL
VIEW

GIVEN: TOP AND RIGHT SIDE
VIEWS.
SKETCH: FRONT FULL SECTION
VIEW.
MATERIAL: CAST IRON.

LABEL SURFACES, NUMBER CORNERS
WHEN INDICATED.

ORTHOGRAPHIC VIEWS

DATE

NAME

S-1 SECTIONAL VIEWS

Copyright 1998
J.W. & O.B. Craig

IF SURFACES OR CORNERS ARE LABELED
IN THE GIVEN VIEWS, SHOW THE LABELS
IN ALL VIEWS. PROVE YOUR ANSWER.

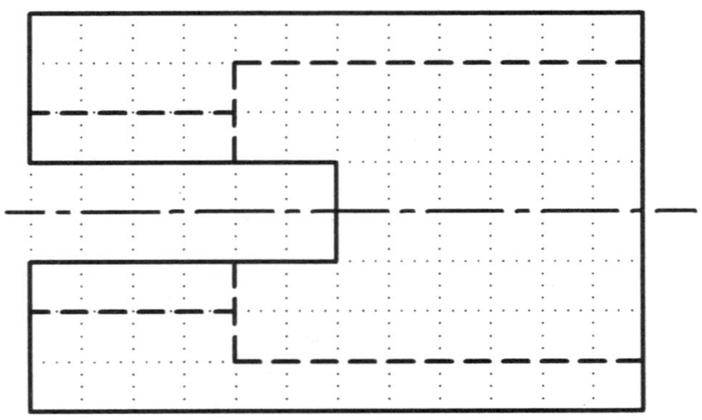

FILE NUMBER .... GRADE ....

ISOMETRIC
PICTORIAL
VIEW

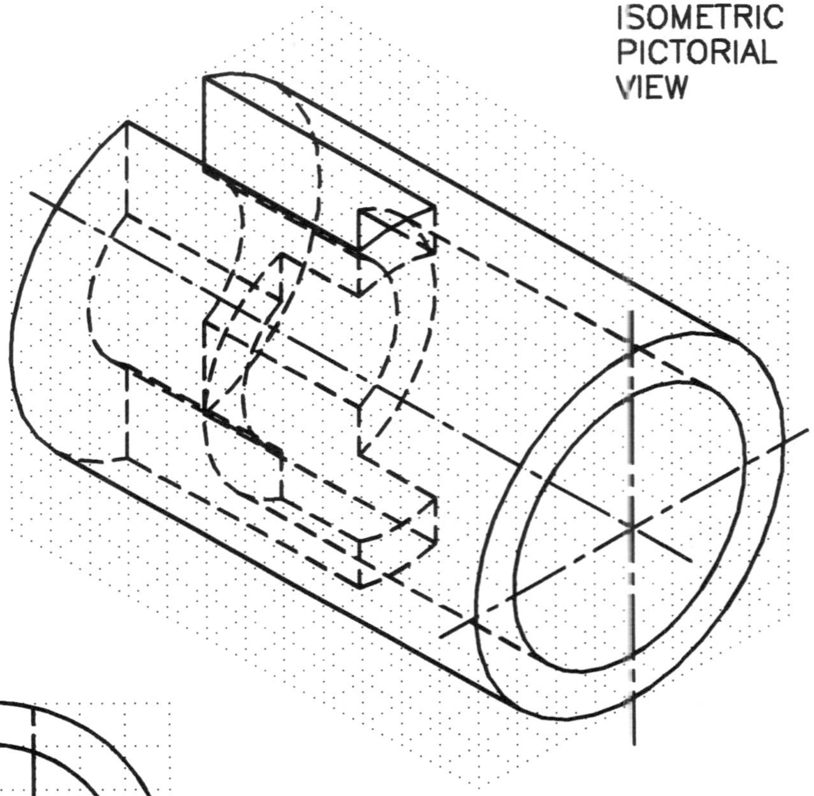

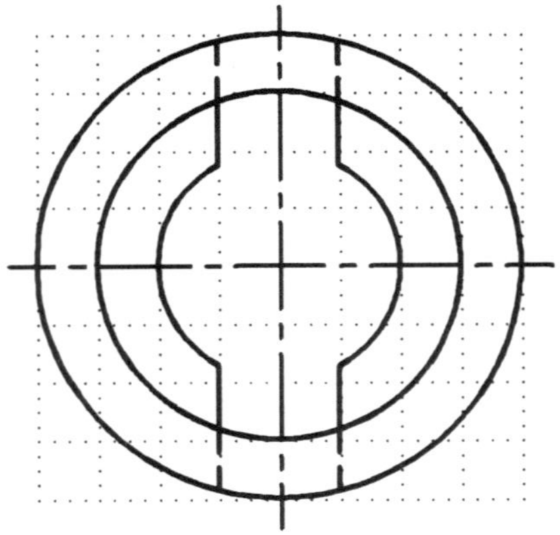

S–2

SECTIONAL VIEWS

ORTHOGRAPHIC VIEWS

NAME	DATE
....	....

GIVEN: TOP, SIDE AND
ISOMETRIC VIEWS.
PROBLEM: SKETCH THE FRONT
FULL SECTION VIEW.
MATERIAL: STEEL

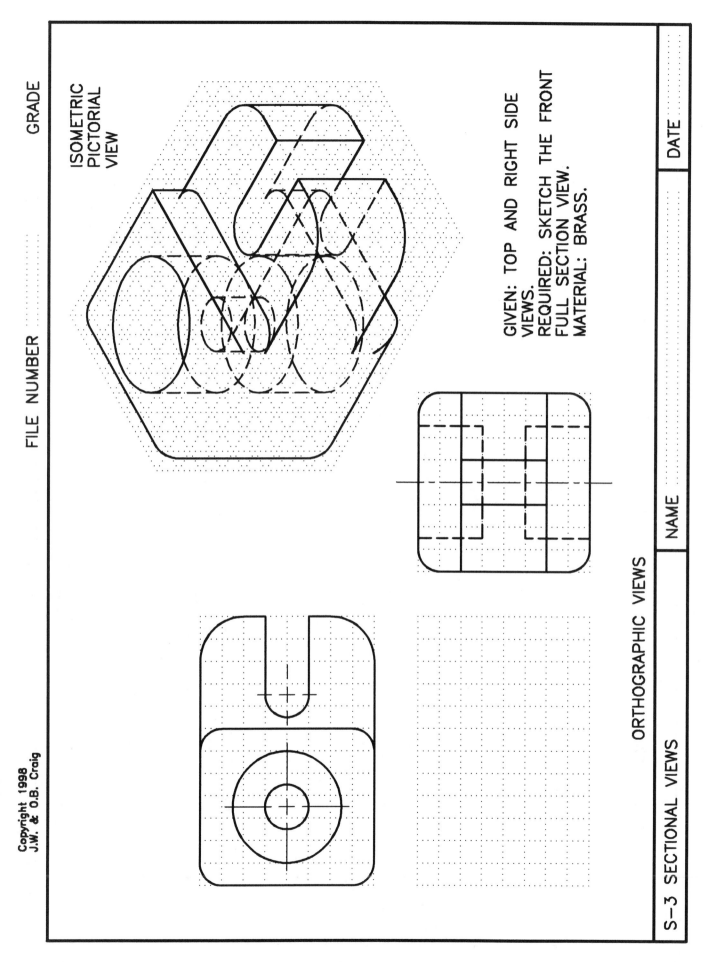

GRADE

ISOMETRIC
PICTORIAL
VIEW

GIVEN: TOP AND RIGHT SIDE
VIEWS.
REQUIRED: SKETCH THE FRONT
FULL SECTION VIEW.
MATERIAL: BRASS.

FILE NUMBER

ORTHOGRAPHIC VIEWS

DATE

NAME

S–3 SECTIONAL VIEWS

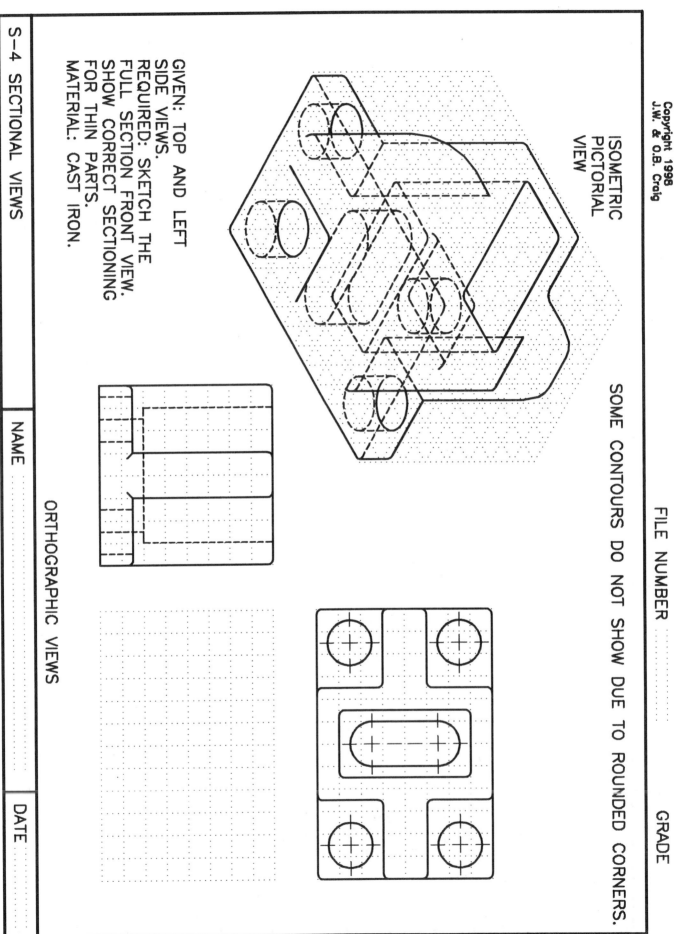

ISOMETRIC
PICTORIAL
VIEW

FILE NUMBER

GRADE

SOME CONTOURS DO NOT SHOW DUE TO ROUNDED CORNERS.

GIVEN: TOP AND LEFT
SIDE VIEWS.
REQUIRED: SKETCH THE
FULL SECTION FRONT VIEW.
SHOW CORRECT SECTIONING
FOR THIN PARTS.
MATERIAL: CAST IRON.

S-4 SECTIONAL VIEWS

NAME

DATE

ORTHOGRAPHIC VIEWS

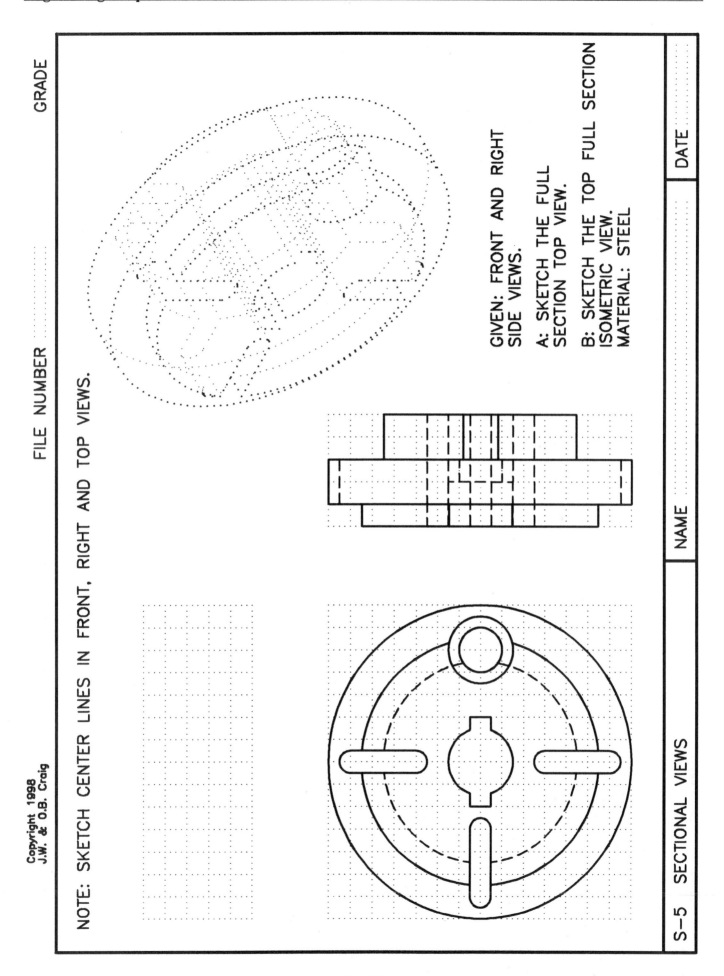

GRADE

FILE NUMBER

DATE

GIVEN: FRONT AND RIGHT
SIDE VIEWS.

A: SKETCH THE FULL
SECTION TOP VIEW.

B: SKETCH THE TOP FULL SECTION
ISOMETRIC VIEW.
MATERIAL: STEEL

NOTE: SKETCH CENTER LINES IN FRONT, RIGHT AND TOP VIEWS.

NAME

S—5   SECTIONAL VIEWS

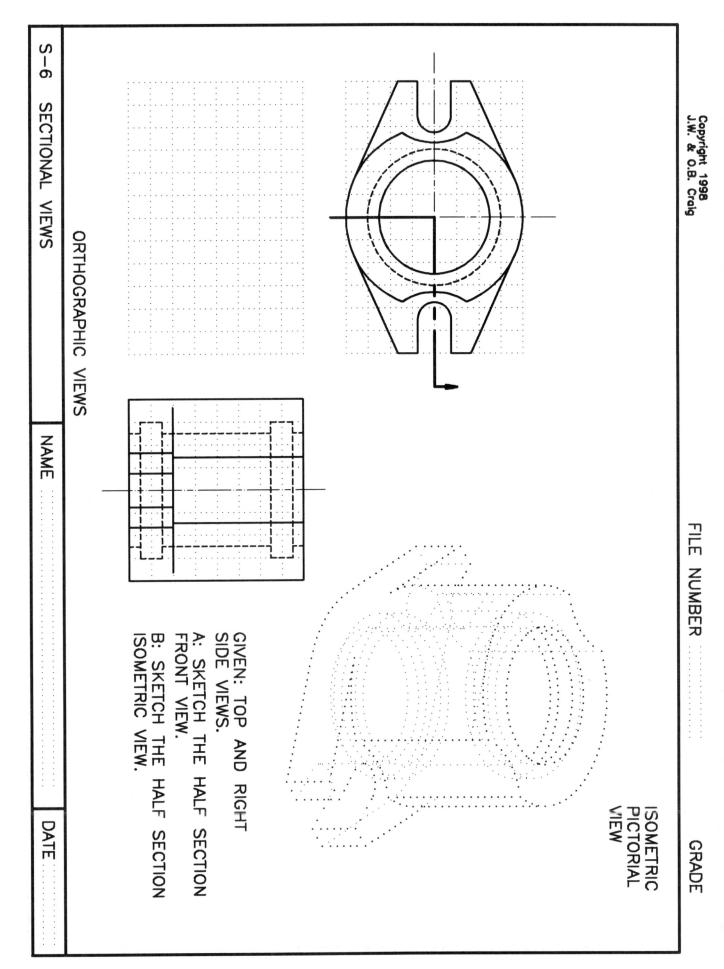

Copyright 1998
J.W. & O.B. Craig

S-6

SECTIONAL VIEWS

ORTHOGRAPHIC VIEWS

NAME

DATE

FILE NUMBER

ISOMETRIC
PICTORIAL
VIEW

GRADE

GIVEN: TOP AND RIGHT
SIDE VIEWS.
A: SKETCH THE HALF SECTION
FRONT VIEW.
B: SKETCH THE HALF SECTION
ISOMETRIC VIEW.

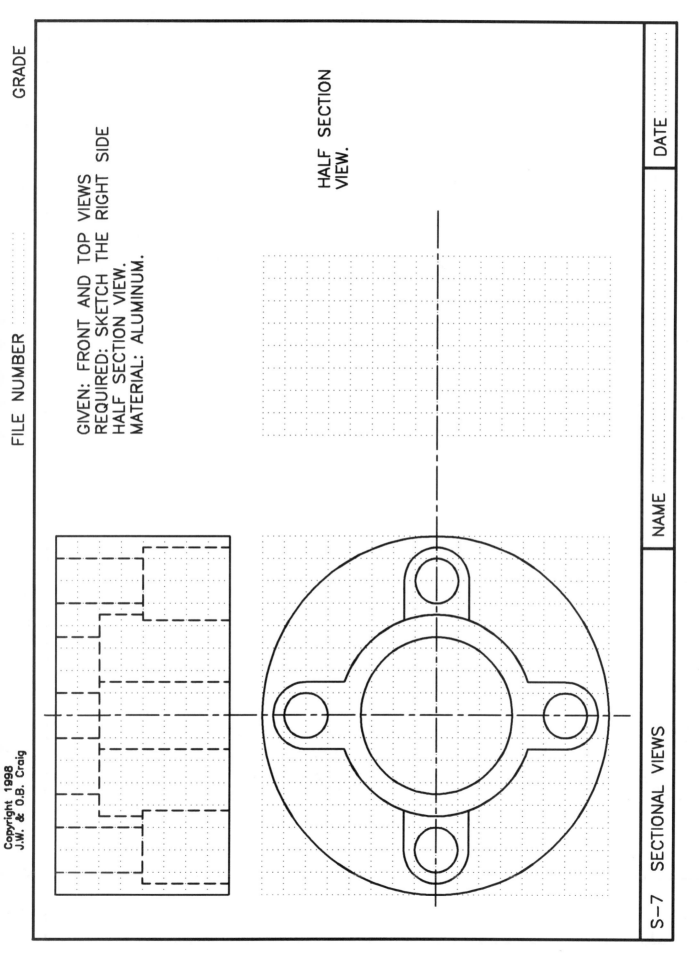

GIVEN: FRONT AND TOP VIEWS
REQUIRED: SKETCH THE RIGHT SIDE
HALF SECTION VIEW.
MATERIAL: ALUMINUM.

HALF SECTION
VIEW.

FILE NUMBER

GRADE

NAME

DATE

SECTIONAL VIEWS

S—7

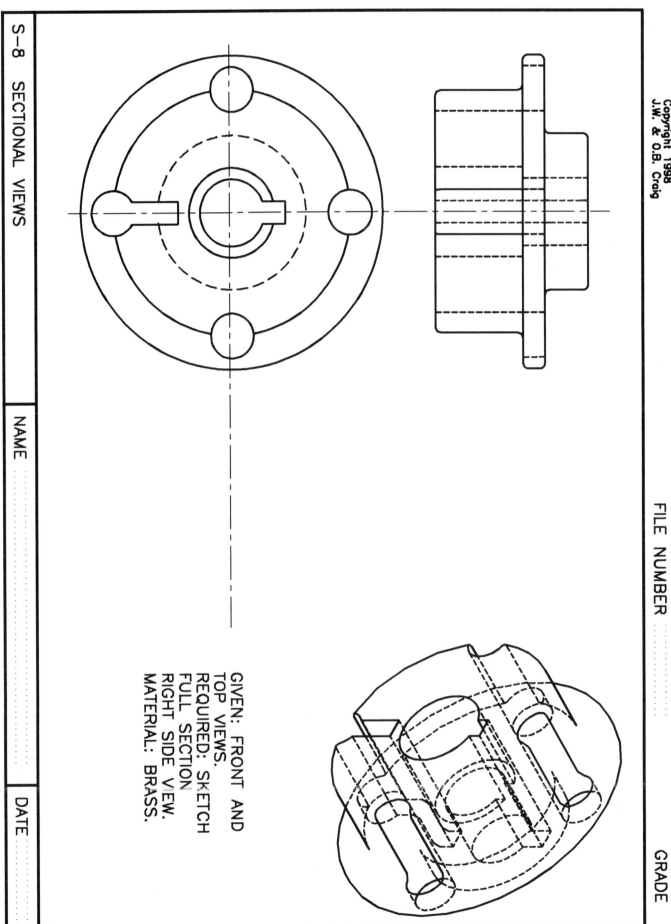

S-8 SECTIONAL VIEWS

NAME

DATE

FILE NUMBER

GRADE

GIVEN: FRONT AND
TOP VIEWS.
REQUIRED: SKETCH
FULL SECTION
RIGHT SIDE VIEW.
MATERIAL: BRASS.

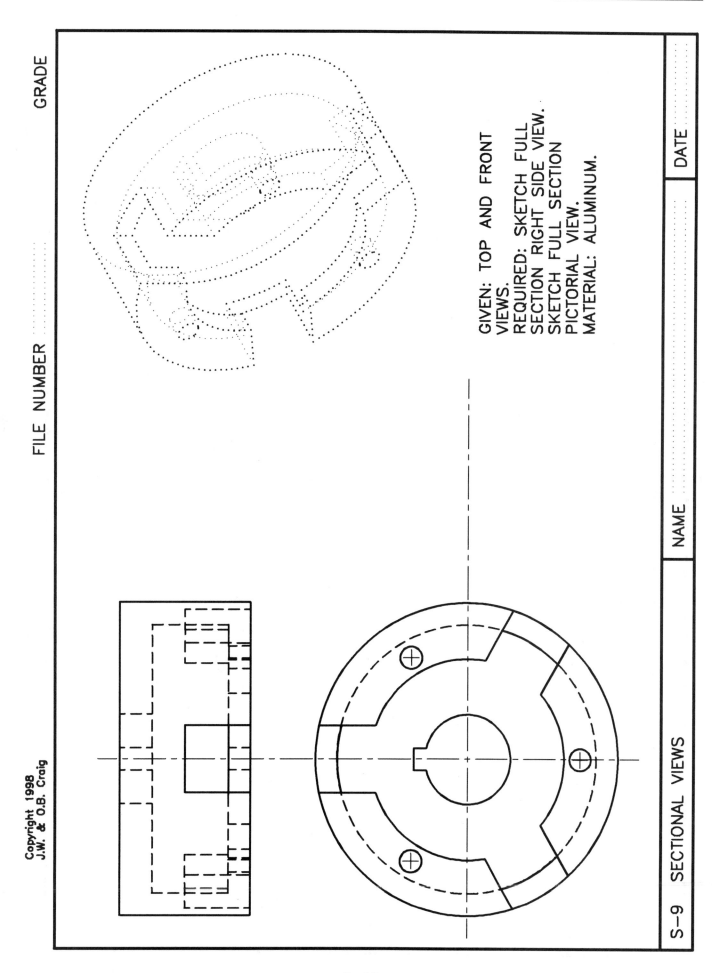

GRADE

FILE NUMBER

GIVEN: TOP AND FRONT VIEWS.
REQUIRED: SKETCH FULL SECTION RIGHT SIDE VIEW.
SKETCH FULL SECTION PICTORIAL VIEW.
MATERIAL: ALUMINUM.

NAME

DATE

S—9   SECTIONAL VIEWS

NOTE: SKETCH CENTER LINES IN TOP, FRONT AND RIGHT SIDE VIEWS.

FILE NUMBER ....

GRADE

S-10   SECTIONAL VIEWS

NAME ....

DATE ....

GIVEN: VIEWS OF
SPEED REDUCER
COVER.
REQUIRED: SKETCH
THE FULL SECTION
FRONT VIEW.
MATERIAL: CAST IRON.

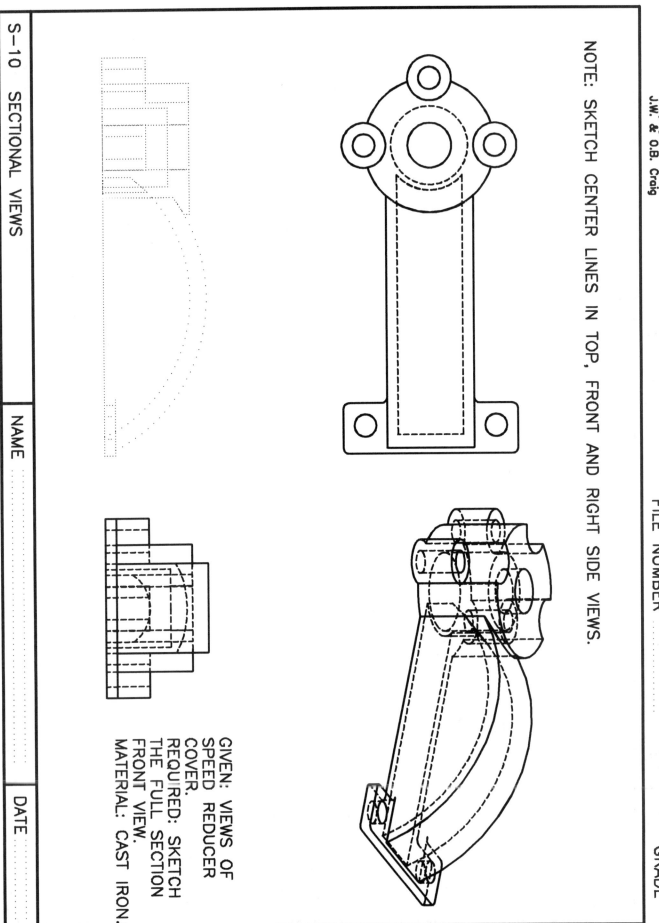

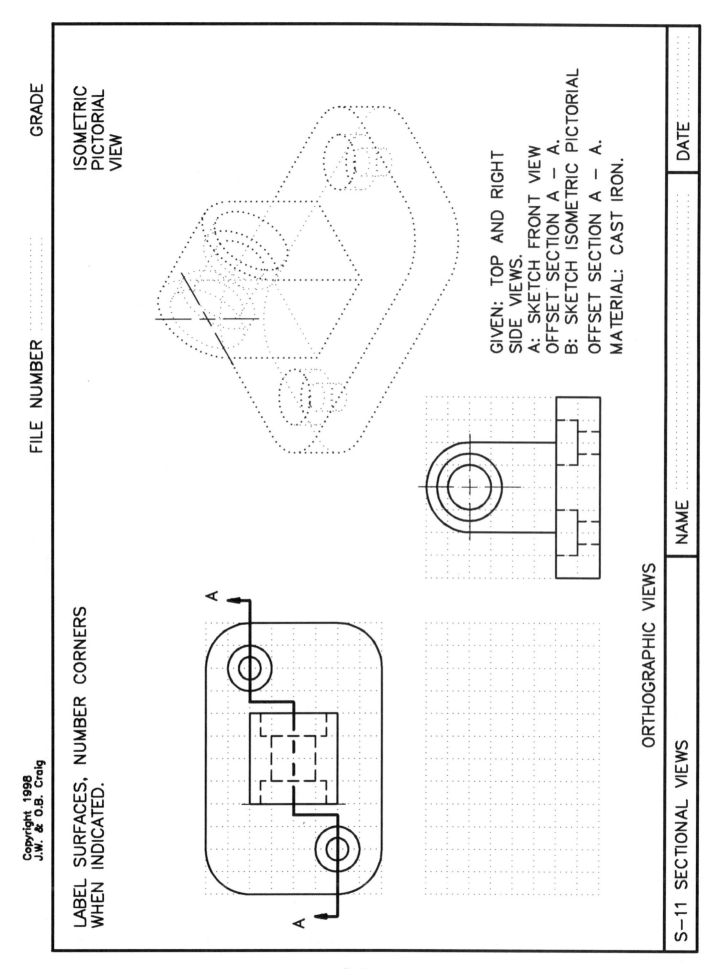

GRADE

ISOMETRIC
PICTORIAL
VIEW

FILE NUMBER

GIVEN: TOP AND RIGHT
SIDE VIEWS.
A: SKETCH FRONT VIEW
OFFSET SECTION A – A.
B: SKETCH ISOMETRIC PICTORIAL
OFFSET SECTION A – A.
MATERIAL: CAST IRON.

LABEL SURFACES, NUMBER CORNERS
WHEN INDICATED.

A

A

ORTHOGRAPHIC VIEWS

NAME

DATE

S—11 SECTIONAL VIEWS

ISOMETRIC
PICTORIAL
VIEW

Copyright 1998
J.W. & O.B. Craig

FILE NUMBER

GRADE

GIVEN: TOP AND LEFT SIDE
VIEWS.
A: SKETCH FRONT OFFSET
VIEW A- A.
B: SKETCH ISOMETRIC PICTORIAL
SECTION A - A.
MATERIAL: STEEL.

S-12   SECTIONAL VIEWS

ORTHOGRAPHIC VIEWS

NAME

DATE

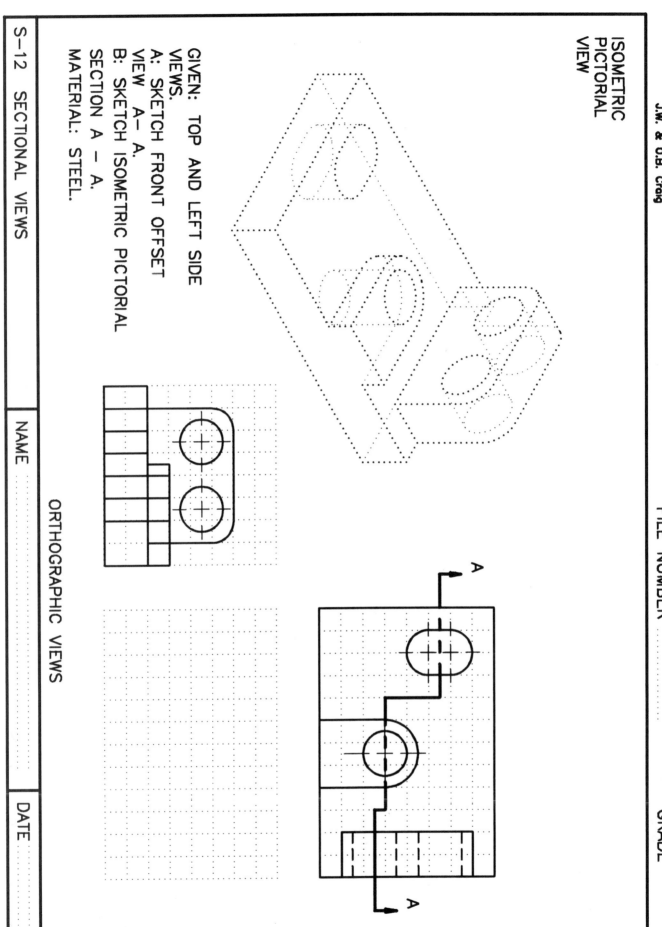

GRADE

FILE NUMBER

GIVEN: FRONT AND RIGHT
SIDE VIEWS.
SKETCH: TOP VIEW
OFFSET SECTION A – A.

MATERIAL: ALUMINUM.

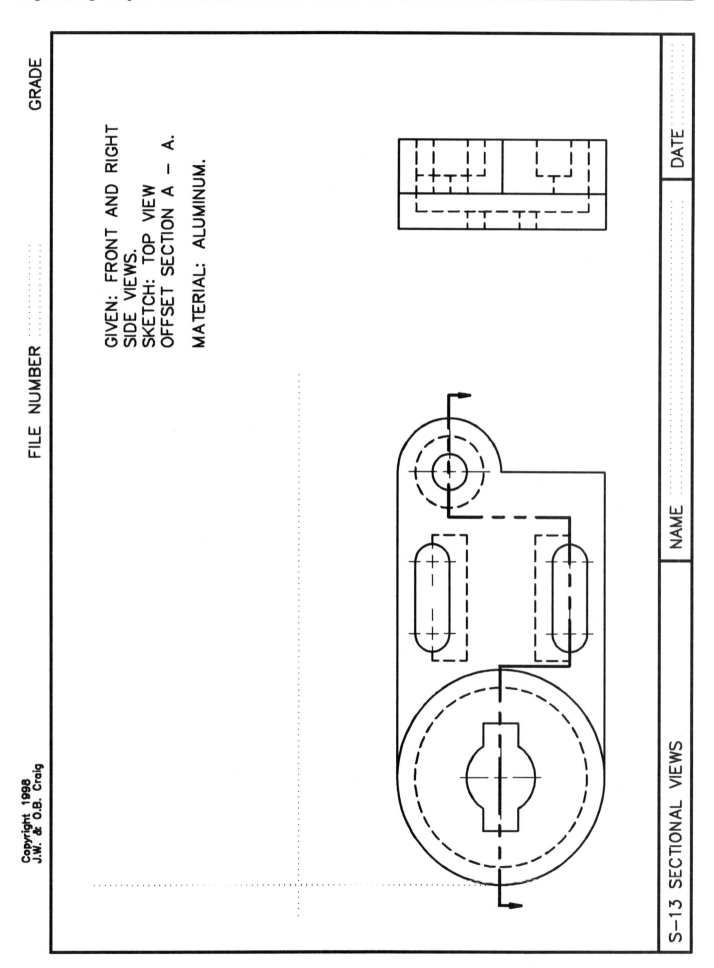

DATE

NAME

S–13 SECTIONAL VIEWS

S—14   SECTIONAL VIEWS

NAME

DATE

FILE NUMBER

GRADE

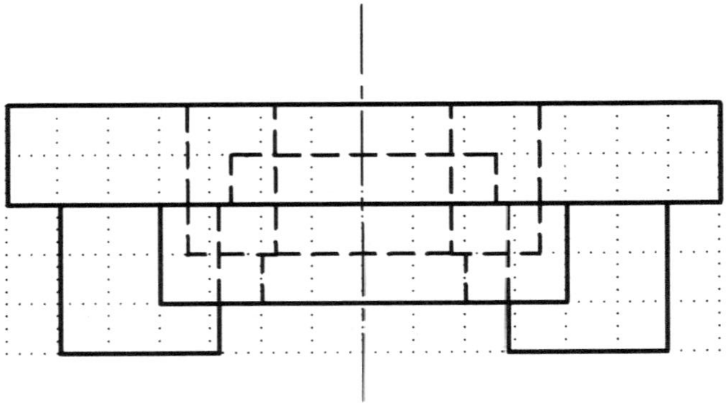

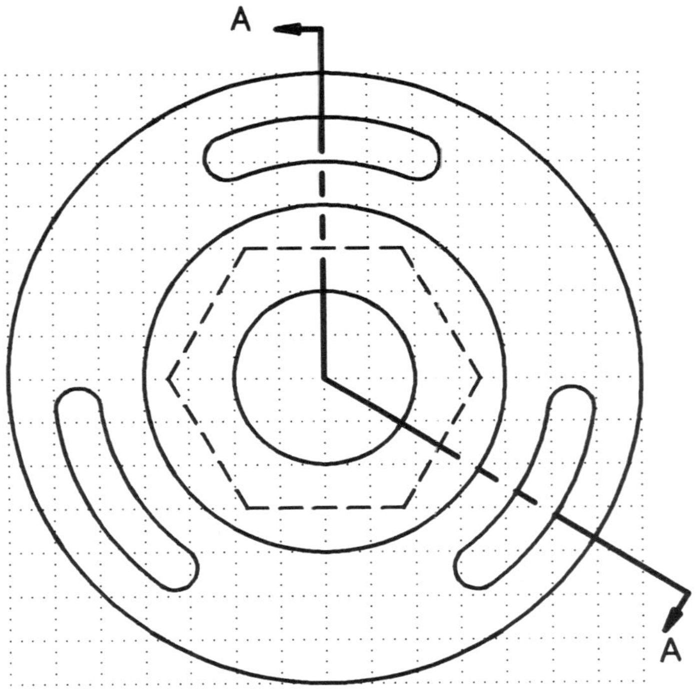

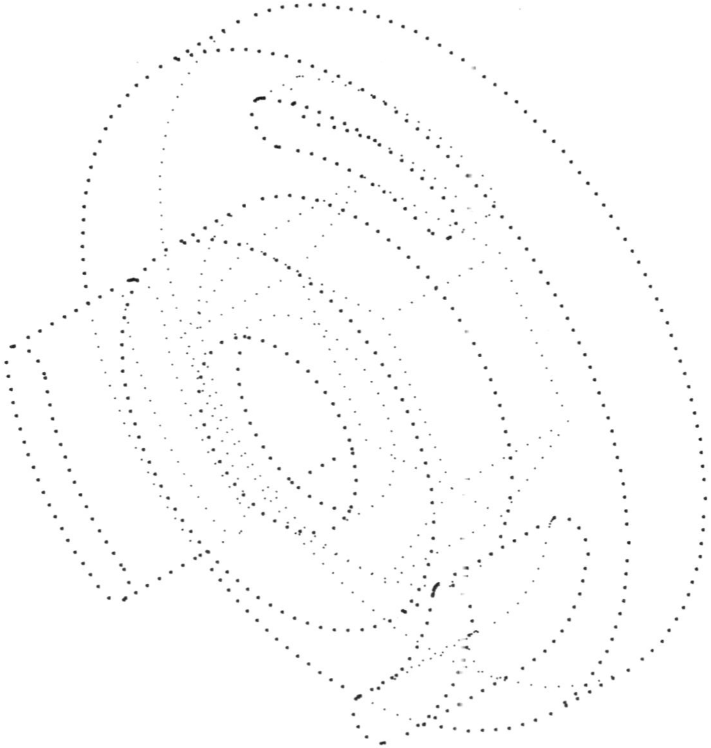

GIVEN: FRONT AND TOP VIEWS.
A: SKETCH RIGHT SIDE VIEW
ALIGNED SECTION A – A.
B: SKETCH PICTORIAL VIEW
SECTION A – A.
MATERIAL: ALUMINUM.

SKETCH CENTER LINES IN
FRONT AND RIGHT SIDE VIEWS.

A

A

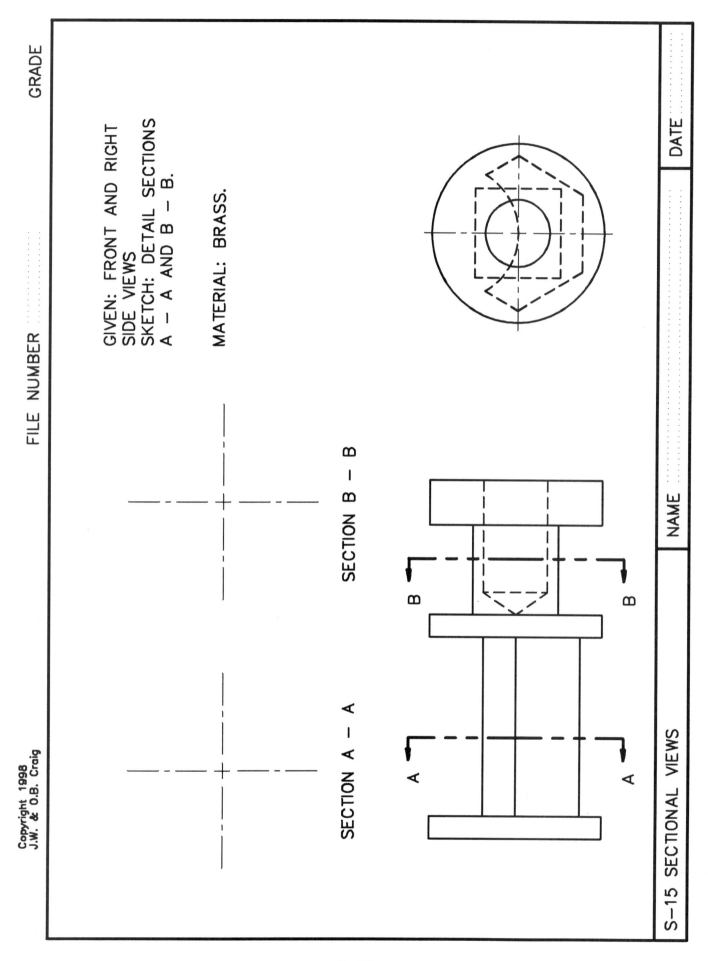

GRADE

FILE NUMBER

GIVEN: FRONT AND RIGHT
SIDE VIEWS
SKETCH: DETAIL SECTIONS
A – A AND B – B.

MATERIAL: BRASS.

SECTION B – B

SECTION A – A

B

B

A

A

DATE

NAME

S–15 SECTIONAL VIEWS

FILE NUMBER .... GRADE ....

GIVEN: FRONT AND
RIGHT VIEWS.
A: SKETCH TOP VIEW.
B: SKETCH REVOLVED
SECTIONS A–A AND B–B.

SECTION A – A

SECTION B – B

SPECIAL WRENCH
MATERIAL:
MANGANESE STEEL.

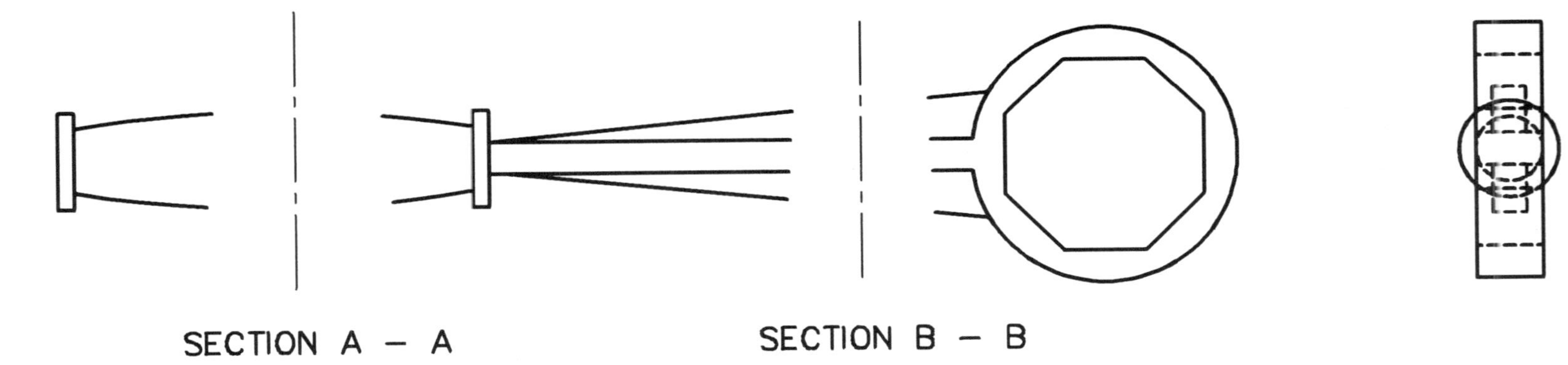

S–16 SECTIONAL VIEWS

NAME .... DATE ....

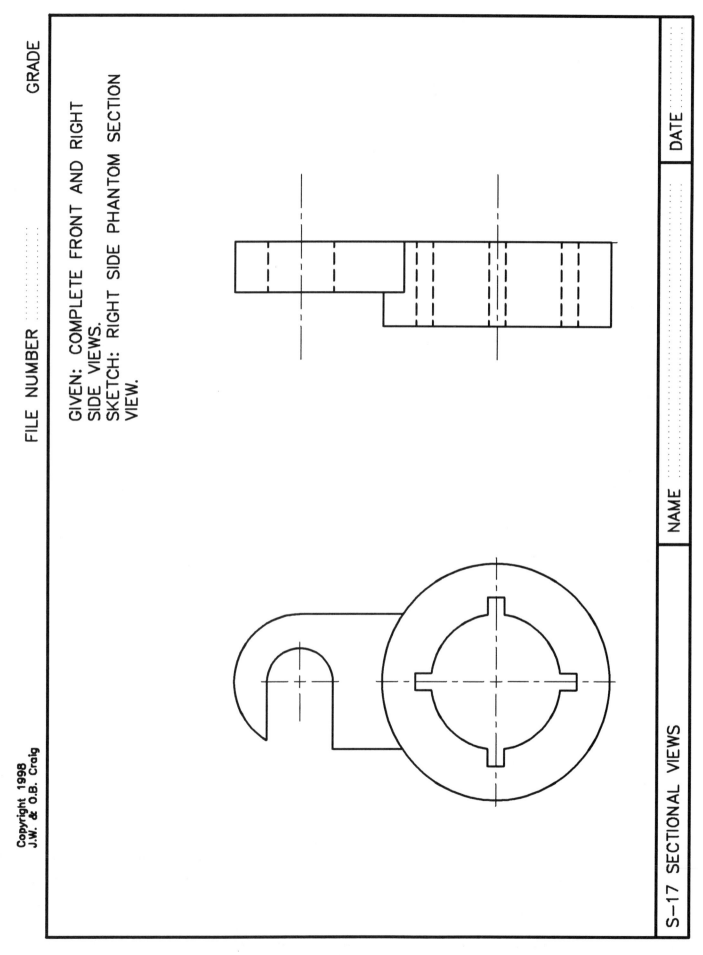

GRADE

FILE NUMBER

GIVEN: COMPLETE FRONT AND RIGHT
SIDE VIEWS.
SKETCH: RIGHT SIDE PHANTOM SECTION
VIEW.

DATE

NAME

S—17 SECTIONAL VIEWS

IF SURFACES OR CORNERS ARE LABELED
IN THE GIVEN VIEWS, SHOW THE LABELS
IN ALL VIEWS. PROVE YOUR ANSWER.

FILE NUMBER   GRADE

ISOMETRIC
PICTORIAL
VIEW

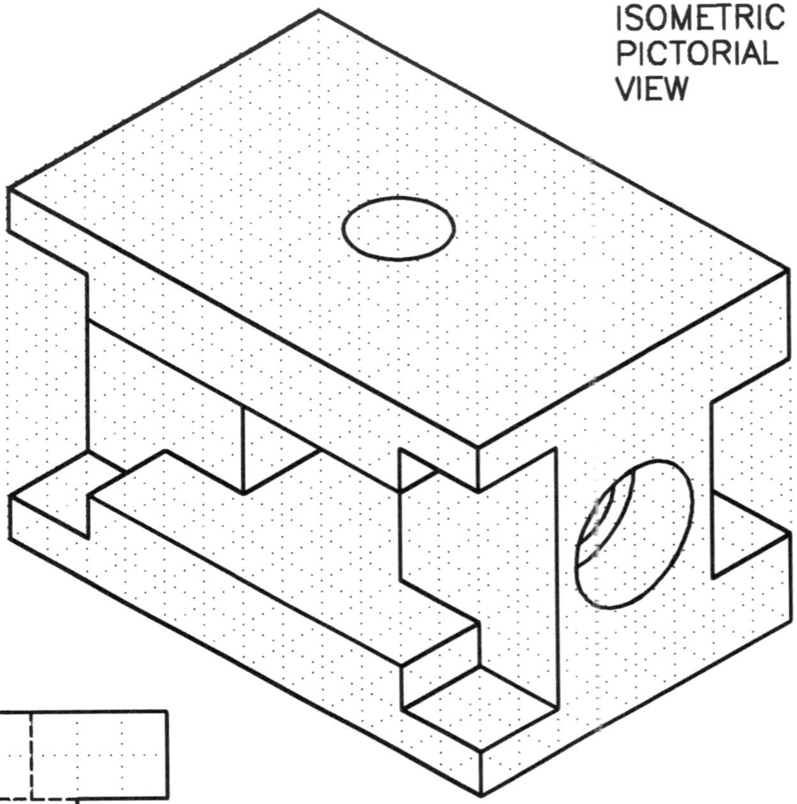

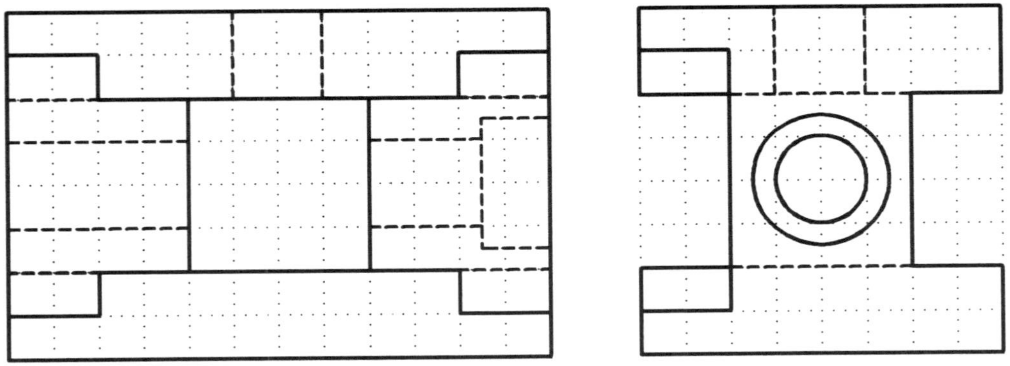

S—18 SECTIONAL VIEWS

ORTHOGRAPHIC VIEWS

NAME   DATE

GIVEN: FRONT AND RIGHT SIDE
VIEWS.
REQUIRED: SKETCH THE
PHANTOM SECTION TOP VIEW.

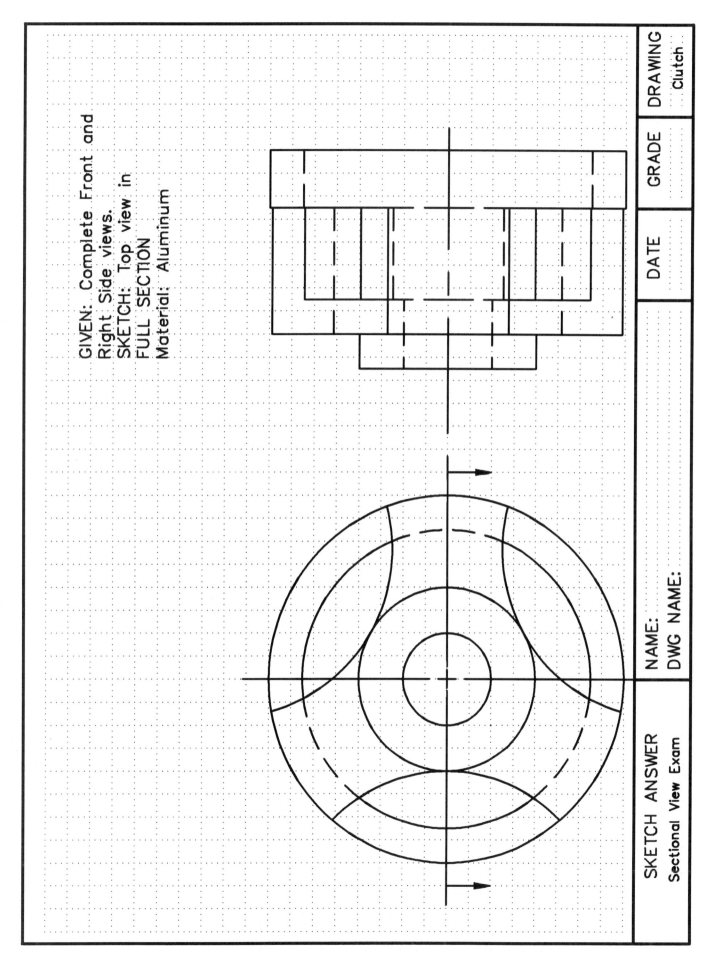

GIVEN: Complete Front and
Right Side views.
SKETCH: Top view in
FULL SECTION
Material: Aluminum

DRAWING
Clutch

GRADE

DATE

NAME:
DWG NAME:

SKETCH ANSWER
Sectional View Exam

NAME

DATE

NOTE: Use this grid format
in horizontal direction.

FILE NUMBER

GRADE

Threaded Fasteners

Parts may be assembled using permanent methods. Welding, brazing or chemical bonding are common processes. Other parts may be bolted together forming a semi-permanent assembly. When items must be taken apart for service or inspection, bolted assemblies are preferred. Many types of bolts, nuts, washers and special fasteners exist. A few of the more common types will be shown.

Fasteners must be specified on drawings. Except for very special purpose applications, most threaded fasteners are purchased from another source. Specifications must be complete so the proper size, strength, finish, etc. are known. When assemblies of parts are designed, every item -- even the smallest pin or washer -- must be described and accounted for in the parts list.

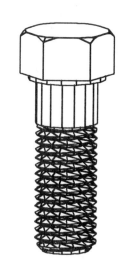

Threads are based on a helix. In this example, a triangular shape is swept in a spiral form. The thread advances for each turn. Two turns are shown. This is a right hand helix -- turning the helix clockwise causes advancement.

Threads are specified by giving the Nominal diameter and the number of Pitches per inch or Pitches per millimeter.

Thread terms are shown. Because of manufacturing strength and safety factors, the Root points are rounded and the Crest points are flattened. The Pitch Diameter is needed for precise measurement.

Pitch is the distance from one thread profile to the next.

A Chamfer on the end of the thread makes for easier engagement with a nut.

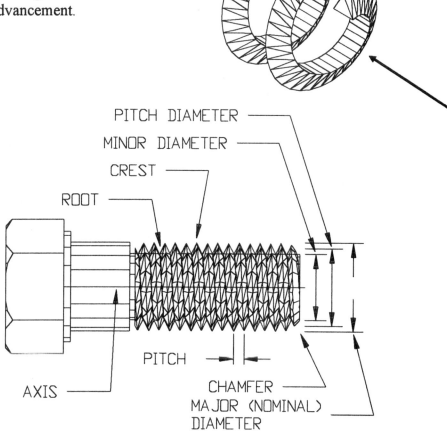

PITCH DIAMETER

MINOR DIAMETER

CREST

ROOT

PITCH

AXIS

CHAMFER

MAJOR (NOMINAL) DIAMETER

External and Internal Sharp-V Threads

External threads may be cut using a Die as shown. For hand-threading the Die is held in a Die Handle. Some dies may be purchased with a hexagonal outer shape for use with a mechanic's wrench .

A set screw adjustment in a split Die allows for slight changes in size when cutting close fitting threads.

Typical External Thread note:

__ **1/2 - 13UNC** (Inch system)
__**M5 x .8** (Metric).

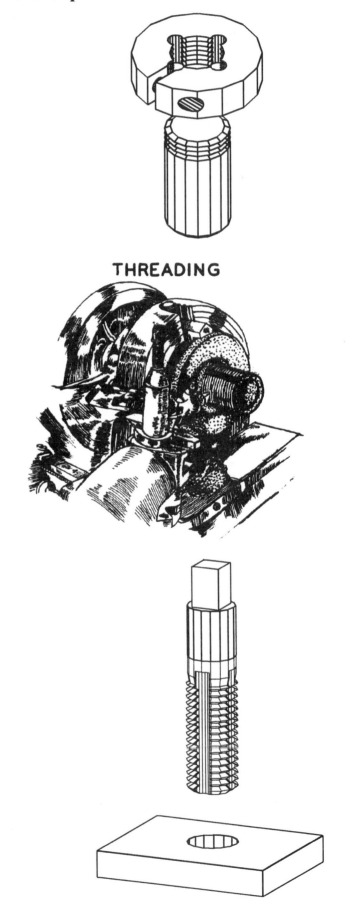

THREADING

Both external and internal threads may be cut using a Lathe. This a slow, expensive process. Special thread diameters, thread pitches and multiple start threads may be cut this way.

A Tap is used to cut smaller diameter internal threads. A hole must be drilled the correct size prior to threading. These drill sizes are shown in tables and are referred to as Tap Drills. Just enough material must be left inside the hole for threading. If the hole is too small, the tap will catch and break. If the hole is drilled too large, there will not be enough material for a full strength thread. Typical Tap Drill - Thread Note:
__ **27/64 DRILL - 1/2 - 13UNC**
__**M5 x .8** (Metric - just specify thread size)

Tap Drill calculation based on 75% thread depth:
(Inch system)
Tap drill size= NOMINAL DIAMETER - (1.08253 x .75 / Thds per in.)
(Metric system)
Tap drill size= NOMINAL DIAMETER - (1.08253 x Pitch x .75)

Special Thread Forms

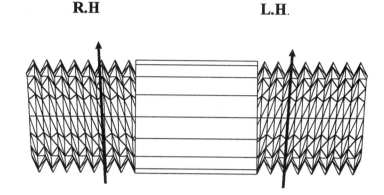

Sharp "V" Right Hand threads are standard. Left Hand threads are sometimes needed for special designs. A Left Hand thread must be noted:

1/2 - 13UNC - L.H.

Left hand threads are used on items like tanks of dangerous gas, turnbuckles, lug bolts for some vehicles and water faucets. They must be special-ordered from suppliers.

Power Threads are used on larger parts where heavy forces are encountered. They must be specially designed and manufactured in most cases.

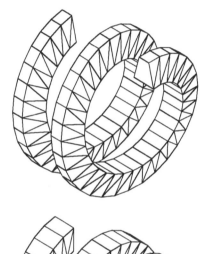

ACME threads have a heavier cross-section. They have a slight angle on each side. This makes cutting the thread easier and allows for wear-compensation.

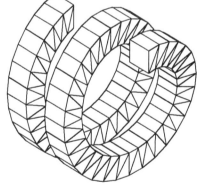

SQUARE threads are obsolete. The ACME form (above) is preferred. Some older designs may have this thread form.

BUTTRESS threads are designed to handle a heavy force in one direction.

These threads are often used on heavy lifting machinery -- house jacks, truck jacks, etc.

Design information for special threads may be found in standard references like "Machinery's Handbook".

FORCE

Special Thread Forms - continued

Multiple start threads are used in special applications. Many starts are possible. The example shows a double start thread where two helixes are cut 180 degrees apart. This design causes more rapid advancement per turn. Cameras might use 20 starts to move the lens rapidly in or out for a short twist of the focusing nut. Lead is the advancement per turn.
LEAD = PITCH x MULTIPLE

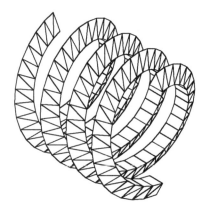

Thread Representation

Sharp - "V" threads may be represented on drawings using detailed, schematic or simplified representations. Simplified is preferred. Examples of external, internal and hidden views are shown. Also, schematic and simplified examples of holes which are drilled and threaded part way through are shown.

THREAD SYMBOLS

I. DETAILED SYMBOLS

Detailed threads are not common. Too much time is required to draw this form. Patent Drawings are more artistic and may use this representation

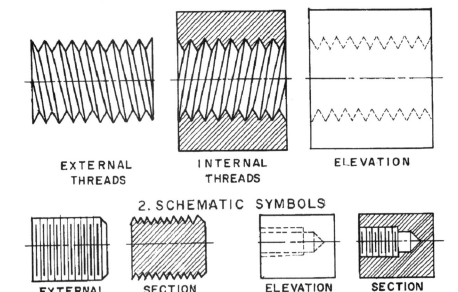

EXTERNAL THREADS   INTERNAL THREADS   ELEVATION

2. SCHEMATIC SYMBOLS

Schematic symbols are common on older drawings.
The internal threads are not drilled and threaded through. These are "blind tapped" holes.

EXTERNAL   SECTION   ELEVATION   SECTION
EXTERNAL THREADS   INTERNAL THREADS

3. SIMPLIFED SYMBOLS

Simplified thread representation is preferred. Dashed lines are used to represent threaded areas. Simplified threads require much less time to draw.

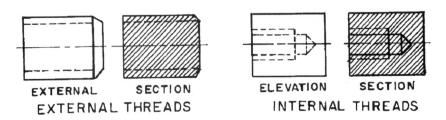

EXTERNAL   SECTION   ELEVATION   SECTION
EXTERNAL THREADS   INTERNAL THREADS

Standard Thread Sizes

Thread sizes in the <u>inch system</u> are shown. Unified National Coarse (UNC) is the top number. Unified National Fine (UNF) is the bottom number in each row. Tap Drill sizes may be fractional size, number size or letter size. Specify: Thread size - Thds/in Thread series.　**6 - 32 UNC** or **1/2 - 13UNC**

Inch System. Small sizes to 1/4 inch.

Thread Size	Nominal Diameter	Threads Per Inch	Tap Drill Size
0	.060	80	3/64
1	.073	64UNC 72UNF	53 53
2	.086	56UNC 64UNF	50 50
3	.099	48UNC 56UNF	47 45
4	.112	40UNC 48UNF	43 42
5	.125	40UNC 44UNF	38 37
6	.138	32UNC 40UNF	36 33
8	.164	32UNC 36UNF	16 14
10	.190	24UNC 32UNF	25 21
12	.216	24UNC 28UNF	16 14

Fractional inch sizes 1/4" to 1.00" UNC/UNF

Fraction Size	Nominal Diameter	Threads Per Inch	Tap Drill Size
1/4	.250	20UNC 28UNF	7 3
5/16	.3125	18UNC 24UNF	F I
3/8	.375	16UNC 24UNF	5/16 Q
7/16	.4375	14UNC 20UNF	U 25/64
1/2	.500	13UNC 20UNF	27/64 29/64
9/16	.5625	12UNC 18UNF	31/64 33/64
5/8	.625	11UNC 18UNF	17/32 37/64
3/4	.750	10UNC 16UNF	21/32 11/16
7/8	.875	9UNC 14UNF	49/64 13/16
1"	1.000	8UNC 12UNF	7/8 59/64

<u>Metric threads.</u> Specify: M(size in mm) Pitches/mm.　(Sizes based on Aerospace specifications)

Nominal Size (mm)	Designation (Preferred sizes)
1.6	M1.6 x .35
2	M2 x .4
2.5	M2.5 x .45
3	M3 x .5
3.5	M3.5 x .6
4	M4 x .7
5	M5 x .8
6	M6 x 1
7	M7 x 1

8	M8 x 1
10	M10 x 1.25
12	M12 x 1.25
14	M14 x 1.5
16	M16 x 1.5
18	M18 x 1.5
20	M20 x 1.5
22	M22 x 1.5
24	M24 x 2
27	M27 x 2

Hexagon Head Bolt and Nut

A hexagon head bolt and nut are shown in a typical application. The bolt and nut are used to clamp parts together. Notice that there must be a clearance hole drilled slightly larger than the bolt nominal size. Add about 1/32 inch to the nominal size to determine the clearance hole size.

HEXAGON HEAD BOLT AND NUT
SIMPLIFIED THREAD SYMBOLS

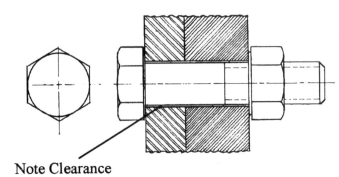

Note Clearance

Hexagon head bolts are preferred.

When drawing hexagon head bolts and nuts, use the "across corners" form shown at "A". The hexagon bolt at "B" and the square bolt at "C" are easily confused.

Use figure "S" when drawing square head bolts.

(Simplified threads are preferred.)

REGULAR HEXAGON AND SQUARE BOLTS

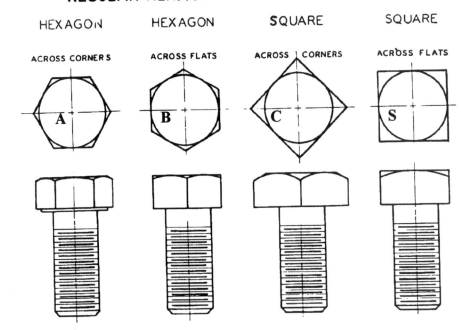

Features of bolts, nuts, set screws, etc. are proportional to the Nominal diameter "D". Sizes are calculated by multiplying the ratio shown times "D".
 __Head dia = 3/4 x "D".
 __Head thickness = 2/3 x "D".
  To draw the hexagon head:
1. Draw the end view hexagon as shown. Project corners to the front view.
2. Front view - measure head thickness. Draw 60 degree equilateral triangles to locate radius centers. Draw small radius in foreshortened faces. Draw large radius in true size face.

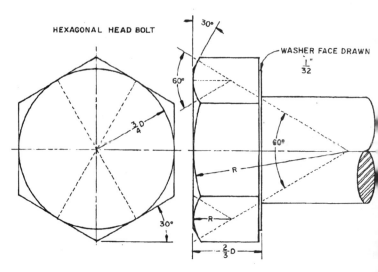

Hexagon Nuts

General drawing sizes for standard hexagon nuts are shown. All ratios are based on the nominal diameter of the thread. Many variations on these sizes exist. Some of the more common sizes are shown below.

__Metric sizes are not quite the same as these ratios.

__Jam nuts are thinner. Jam nuts are often used to lock other nuts. By tightening one nut on top of another, extra friction in the threads will prevent loosening of the assembly.

__Typical callout:

1/2 - 20UNF STD NUT or M5 x .8 NUT

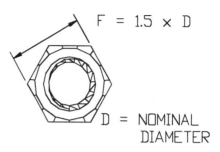

$F = 1.5 \times D$

$D = $ NOMINAL DIAMETER

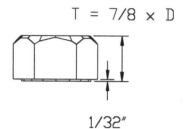

$T = 7/8 \times D$

1/32"

Inch nut size tables: (Sizes are approximate)

Nominal Thd Diameter	"F" Across Flats	"T" Thickness
0	5/32	.050
1	5/32	.050
2	3/16	.066
3	3/16	.066
4	1/4	.098
5	5/16	.114
6	5/16	.114
8	11/32	.130
10	3/8	.130
12	7/16	.161

Nominal Thd Diameter	"F" Across Flats	"T" Std Nut Thickness	Jam Nut Thickness
1/4	7/16	7/32	5/32
5/16	1/2	17/64	3/16
3/8	9/16	21/64	7/32
7/16	11/16	3/8	1/4
1/2	3/4	7/16	5/16
9/16	7/8	31/64	5/16
5/8	15/16	35/64	3/8
3/4	1-1/8	41/64	27/64
7/8	1-5/16	3/4	31/64
1.00	1-1/2	55/64	35/64

Metric nut size tables: (mm)

Nominal Size	"F" Across Flats	"T" Thickness
M1.6	3.20	1.30
M2	4.00	1.60
M2.5	5.00	2.00
M3	5.50	2.40
M3.5	6.00	2.80
M4	7.00	3.20
M5	8.00	4.70

M6	10.00	5.20
M8	13.00	6.80
M10	16	8.40
M12	18.00	10.80
M14	21.00	12.80
M16	24.00	14.80
M20	30.00	18.00
M24	36.00	21.50
M30	45.00	25.60

Hexagon Head Bolts

Inch sizes are shown at the top of the page. Approximate ratios are shown in the picture. Table sizes are rounded for drawing purposes.

__Step by step drawing instructions are shown on page K - 6. Length is from bottom of head to end of bolt.

Typical callout:

__Thread size

__Thread Pitch (and UNC/UNF)

__Class of fit (optional)

__Bolt length

__Head type

1/2 - 13UNC -2A x 1-1/2 HEX HD BOLT

M5 x .8 x16 HEX HD MACHINE SCREW

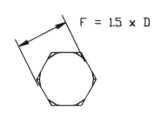

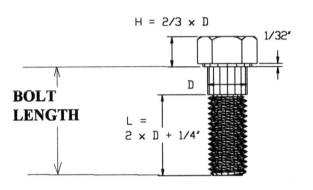

Fractional inch tables: (Sizes are approximate)

Nominal Thd Diameter	"F" Across Flats	"T" Head Thickness
1	.125	.044
2	.125	.050
3	.188	.055
4	.188	.060
5	.188	.070
6	.250	.093
8	.250	.110
10	.312	.120
12	.312	.155

Nominal Thd Diameter	"F" Across Flats	"T" Head Thickness
1/4	7/16	5/32
5/16	1/2	13/64
3/8	9/16	15/64
7/16	11/16	9/32
1/2	3/4	5/16
9/16	7/8	23/64
5/8	15/16	25/64
3/4	1-1/8	15/32
7/8	1-5/16	35/64
1.00	1-1/2	39/64

Metric size tables: (mm)

Nominal Size	"F" Across Flats	"T" Head Thickness
M2	4.00	1.6
M2.5	5.00	2.1
M3	5.50	2.3
M3.5	6.00	2.6
M4	7.00	3.0
M5	8.00	3.6

M6	10.00	4.2
M8	13.00	5.5
M10	16	6.6
M12	18.00	7.8
M14	21.00	9.1
M16	24.00	10.3
M20	30.00	12.9
M24	36.00	15.4
M30	45.00	19.5

Flat Head Machine Screws

Flat Head bolts are designed to be countersunk as shown in the detail drawing. Add 1/32" to 1/8 " to the head diameter to specify the countersink diameter. Head angle is 82 degrees in this chart.

Typical callout:
1/2 - 13UNC x 1-1/4 FLAT HD BOLT
M10 x 1.25 x 20 FLAT HEAD BOLT

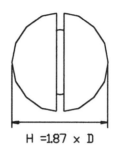

H =1.87 × D

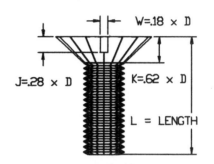
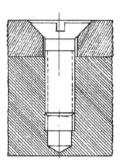

W=.18 × D

J=.28 × D   K=.62 × D

L = LENGTH

Nominal Thd Diameter	"H" Head Diameter	"K" Hea Height
0	.119	.035
1	.146	.043
2	.172	.051
3	.199	..059
4	.225	.067
5	.252	.075
6	.279	.083
8	.332	.100
10	.385	.116
12	.438	.132

Nominal Thd Diameter	"H" Head Diameter	"K" Head Height
1/4	.507	.153
5/16	.635	.191
3/8	.762	.230
7/16	.812	.223
1/2	.875	.223
9/16	1.00	.260
5/8	1.125	.298
3/4	1.375	.372

Metric size tables: (mm)

Nominal Size	"H" Head Diameter	K" Head Height
M1.6	3.20	.80
M2	4.00	1.00
M2.5	5.00	1.25
M3	5.50	1.50
M3.5	7.00	1.75
M4	8.00	2.00
M5	10.00	2.50

M6	12.00	3.00
M8	16.00	4.00
M10	20.00	5.00
M12	24.00	6.00
M14	28.00	7.00
M16	32.00	8.00
M20	40.00	10.00

Note: Sizes in tables are rounded for drawing purposes.

Fillister and Hexagon Socket Head Machine Screws

Hexagon Socket and Fillister head machine and cap screws are often designed in assemblies as recessed head types as shown in the insert. Add about 1/16" to the head diameter and to the head height for counter bore sizes.

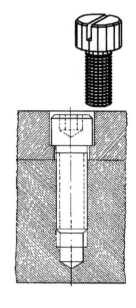

Typical callout:

5/16 - 18UNC x 1.5 FIL HD MACH SCREW
M8 x 1 x 12 HEX SOC HD MACH SCREW

Note: Hexagon Socket (flat to flat) = 3/4 x D

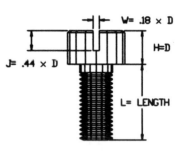

Inch size table: (Sizes are approximate)

Nominal Thd Diameter	"A" Head Diameter	"H" Head Height
0	.090	.055
1	.118	.066
2	.140	.083
3	.161	.095
4	.183	.107
5	.205	.120
6	.226	.132
8	.270	.156
10	.313	..180
12	.357	.205

Nominal Thd Diameter	"A" Head Diameter	"H" Head Height
1/4	.414	.237
5/16	.518	.295
3/8	.622	.355
7/16	.625	.368
1/2	.750	.412
9/16	.812	.466
5/8	.875	.521
3/4	1.000	.612

Metric size tables: (mm)

Nominal Size	"A" Head Diameter	"H" Head Height
M1.6	3.00	1.60
M2	4.00	2.00
M2.5	4.50	2.50
M3	5.50	3.00
M3.5	n/a	n/a
M4	7.00	4.00
M5	8.50	5.00

M6	10.00	6.00
M8	13.00	8.00
M10	16.00	10.00
M12	18.00	12.00
M14	21.00	14.00
M16	24.00	16.00
M20	30.00	20.00

Note: Sizes in tables are rounded for drawing purposes.

Round Head Machine Screw

Round Head Machine Screws are shown in the tables.

Typical callout:
3/8 - 24UNF x 3/4 RND HD MACH SCREW
M4 x .7 x 10 PAN HD MACH SCREW

Nominal Thd Diameter	"A" Head Diameter	"H" Head Height
0	.113	.053
1	.138	.060
2	.162	.070
3	.190	.080
4	.210	.090
5	.235	.095
6	.260	.100
8	.300	.120
10	.360	.140
12	.408	.153

Nominal Thd Diameter	"A" Head Diameter	"H" Head Height
1/4	.472	.175
5/16	.590	.216
3/8	.708	.256
7/16	.750	.328
1/2	.813	.355
9/16	.938	.410
5/8	1.000	.438
3/4	1.250	.547

Metric PAN HEAD size tables: (mm)

Nominal Size	"A" Head Diameter	"H" Head Height
M1.6	n/a	n/a
M2	4.00	1.60
M2.5	5.00	2.10
M3	5.60	2.40
M3.5	7.00	2.60
M4	8.00	3.10
M5	9.50	3.70

M6	12.00	4.60
M8	16.00	6.00
M10	20.00	7.50
M12	18.00	12.00
M14	n/a	n/a
M16	n/a	n/a
M20	n/a	n/a

Note: Sizes in tables are rounded for drawing purposes.

Set Screws

Set Screws are headless type fasteners. They are usually made from very hard steel. Hexagon sockets, slotted head and a variety of fluted sockets are available.

Many point styles are also used. Examples are shown below.
Callout should include:

__Thread size and series
__Length
__Head type
__Point type

1/4 - 20UNC x 7*-/8 HEX SOC HD CONE POINT SET SCREW

M5 x .8 x 5 SLOTTED HD CUP POINT SET SCREW

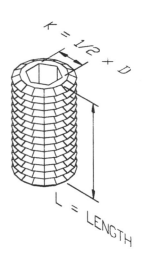

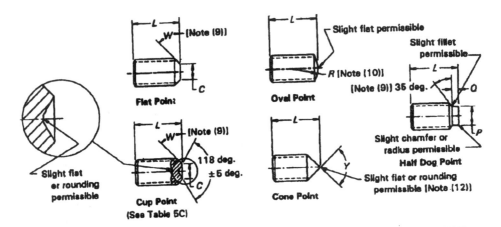

Flat Point

Cup Point (See Table 5C)

Oval Point

Cone Point

Half Dog Point

TABLE 5A   DIMENSIONS OF HEXAGON AND SPLINE SOCKET SET SCREWS

Nominal Size or Basic Screw Diameter		P Half Dog Point Diameter		Q Half Dog Point Length		B Shortest Optimum Nominal Length to Which T_N Applies			B_1 Shortest Optimum Nominal Length to Which T_S Applies		
		Max.	Min.	Max.	Min.	Cup and Flat Points	90 deg. Cone and Oval Points	Half Dog Point	Cup and Flat Points	90 deg. Cone and Oval Points	Half Dog Point
0	0.0600	0.040	0.037	0.017	0.013	0.13	0.13	0.13	0.06	0.13	0.13
1	0.0730	0.049	0.045	0.021	0.017	0.13	0.19	0.13	0.13	0.19	0.13
2	0.0860	0.057	0.053	0.024	0.020	0.13	0.19	0.19	0.13	0.19	0.19
3	0.0990	0.066	0.062	0.027	0.023	0.19	0.19	0.19	0.13	0.19	0.19
4	0.1120	0.075	0.070	0.030	0.026	0.19	0.19	0.19	0.13	0.19	0.19
5	0.1250	0.083	0.078	0.033	0.027	0.19	0.19	0.19	0.13	0.19	0.19
6	0.1380	0.092	0.087	0.038	0.032	0.19	0.25	0.19	0.19	0.25	0.25
8	0.1640	0.109	0.103	0.043	0.037	0.19	0.25	0.25	0.19	0.25	0.25
10	0.1900	0.127	0.120	0.049	0.041	0.19	0.25	0.25	0.19	0.25	0.25
1/4	0.2500	0.156	0.149	0.067	0.059	0.25	0.31	0.31	0.26	0.31	0.31
5/16	0.3125	0.203	0.195	0.082	0.074	0.31	0.44	0.38	0.31	0.44	0.38
3/8	0.3750	0.250	0.241	0.099	0.089	0.38	0.44	0.44	0.38	0.44	0.44
7/16	0.4375	0.297	0.287	0.114	0.104	0.44	0.63	0.50	0.44	0.63	0.50
1/2	0.5000	0.344	0.334	0.130	0.120	0.50	0.63	0.63	0.50	0.63	0.63
5/8	0.6250	0.469	0.456	0.164	0.148	0.63	0.88	0.88	0.63	0.88	0.88
3/4	0.7500	0.562	0.549	0.196	0.180	0.75	1.00	1.0	0.75	1.00	1.00

Set Screws - continued

Two examples of the use of set screws are shown. The pulley is locked in place by the first set screw. Then, the first set screw is locked by the second.

The second example uses a full dog point set screw to allow linear motion of the shaft, but no circular motion.

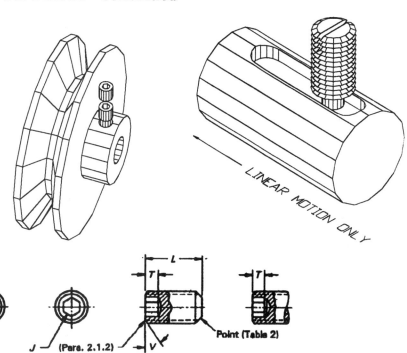

LINEAR MOTION ONLY

M   J   (Para. 2.1.2)   V   Point (Table 2)

TABLE 1   DIMENSIONS OF METRIC SOCKET SET SCREWS

D	Thread Pitch	J	M	L	T					
					Minimum Key Engagement					
					Cup and Flat Points		Cone and Oval Points		Half Dog Points	
Nominal Size or Basic Screw Diameter	Thread Pitch	Hexagon Socket Size	Spline Socket Size	Nominal Screw Lengths	Hex. T_h	Spl. T_s	Hex. T_h	Spl. T_s	Hex. T_h	Spl. T_s
		Nom.	Nom.		Min.	Min.	Min.	Min.	Min.	Min.
1.6	0.35	0.7	0.84	1.5	0.6	0.6	0.6	0.6	...	...
				2	0.8	0.7	0.8	0.7	0.6	0.6
				2.5	1.0	0.7	1.0	0.7	0.7	0.7
				3	1.25	0.7	1.25	0.7	1.25	0.7
2	0.4	0.9	0.84	1.5	0.6	0.6	0.6	0.6	...	...
				2	0.8	0.7	0.8	0.7	...	...
				2.5	1.0	0.7	1.0	0.7	0.6	0.7
				3	1.2	0.7	1.2	0.7	1.2	0.7
				4	1.5	0.7	1.5	0.7	1.5	0.7
2.5	0.45	1.3	1.22	2	0.7	0.7	0.7	0.7	...	...
				2.5	1.1	1.0	1.0	1.0	0.8	0.9
				3	1.5	1.0	1.3	1.0	1.2	1.0
				4	1.8	1.0	1.8	1.0	1.8	1.0
3	0.5	1.5	1.52	2	0.6	0.6	...	...	...	...
				2.5	1.1	1.1	0.7	0.7	...	...
				3	1.5	1.2	1.0	1.0	1.0	1.0
				4	2.1	1.2	1.5	1.2	2.0	1.2
				5	2.1	1.2	2.1	1.2	2.1	1.2
4	0.7	2	2.44	2.5	1.0	1.0	...	...	...	...
				3	1.3	1.3	1.0	1.0	1.0	1.0
				4	1.8	1.8	1.5	1.5	1.5	1.5
				5	2.3	2.0	2.0	2.0	2.0	2.0
				6	2.3	2.0	2.3	2.0	2.3	2.0
5	0.8	2.5	2.82	3	1.2	1.2	...	...	...	...
				4	2.0	2.0	1.2	1.2	...	...
				5	2.7	2.3	1.7	1.7	2.0	2.0
				6	2.7	2.3	2.0	2.0	2.5	2.3
				8	2.7	2.3	2.7	2.3	2.7	2.3
See para.		2.2.1	2.2.1		2.2.2					

D	Thread Pitch	J	M	L	T					
					Minimum Key Engagement					
					Cup and Flat Points		Cone and Oval Points		Half Dog Points	
Nominal Size or Basic Screw Diameter	Thread Pitch	Hexagon Socket Size	Spline Socket Size	Nominal Screw Lengths	Hex. T_h	Spl. T_s	Hex. T_h	Spl. T_s	Hex. T_h	Spl. T_s
		Nom.	Nom.		Min.	Min.	Min.	Min.	Min.	Min.
6	1	3	3.68	4	1.8	1.8	...	...	...	...
				5	2.5	2.5	1.8	1.8	1.5	1.5
				6	3.0	3.0	2.7	2.7	2.0	2.0
				8	3.0	3.0	3.0	3.0	3.0	3.0
8	1.25	4	4.65	5	1.8	1.8	...	...	...	...
				6	2.5	2.5	2.3	2.3	1.8	1.8
				8	4.0	4.0	3.5	3.5	3.0	3.0
				10	4.0	4.0	4.0	4.0	4.0	4.0
10	1.5	5	5.49	6	2.0	2.0	...	...	...	...
				8	3.6	3.6	3.0	3.0	2.5	2.5
				10	5.0	5.0	4.0	4.0	4.0	4.0
				12	5.0	5.0	5.0	5.0	5.0	5.0
12	1.75	6	6.38	8	3.0	3.0	...	...	...	...
				10	4.5	4.5	3.8	3.8	3.5	3.5
				12	6.0	6.0	5.0	5.0	5.0	5.0
				16	6.0	6.0	6.0	6.0	6.0	6.0
16	2	8	9.45	10	3.0	3.0	...	...	...	...
				12	4.8	4.8	3.0	3.0	3.0	3.0
				16	8.0	8.0	6.0	6.0	6.0	6.0
				20	8.0	8.0	8.0	8.0	8.0	8.0
20	2.5	10	11.53	12	...	...	...	...	...	...
				16	6.0	6.0	5.0	5.0	5.0	5.0
				20	8.0	8.0	8.0	8.0	8.0	8.0
				25	10.0	10.0	10.0	10.0	10.0	10.0
24	3	12	15.11	16	5.0	5.0	...	...	...	...
				20	8.0	8.0	7.0	7.0	6.0	6.0
				25	12.0	12.0	10.0	10.0	10.0	10.0
				30	12.0	12.0	12.0	12.0	12.0	12.0
See para.		2.2.1	2.2.1		2.2.2					

Keys and Pins

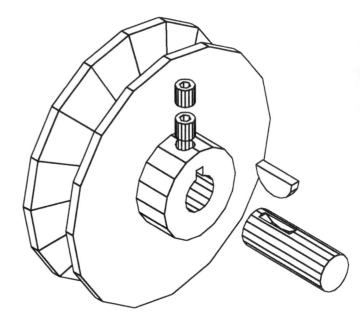

A Woodruff key is used to lock parts together in the example. The key extends between the shaft and the pulley to prevent slippage. Flat keys are also used, but they have a tendency to work loose.

Woodruff key numbers relate to the key size in inches:

__The last two numbers are the key diameter in 8ths.
__The numbers before the last two digits are the key thickness in 32nds

A 1008 key is 1" diameter and 5/16" thick.

Woodruff Keys: (examples)

Key Number	Size
202	1/16 x 1/4
303	3/32 x 3/8
403	1/8 x 3/8
204	1/16 x 1/2
404	1/8 x 1/2
406	1/8 x 3/4
606	3/16 x 3/4
707	7/32 x7/8
808	1/4 x 1.00
1008	5/16 x 1.00
1010	5/16 x 1-1/4
1212	3/8 x 1-1/2

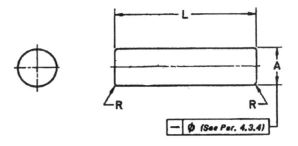

Table 3   Dimensions of Hardened Ground Production Dowel Pins

Nominal Size¹ or Nominal Pin Diameter		A Pin Diameter			R Corner Radius		Double Shear Load Min, Lb Material Carbon Steel
		Basic	Max	Min	Max	Min	
1/16	0.0625	0.0627	0.0628	0.0626	0.020	0.010	790
3/32	0.0938	0.0939	0.0940	0.0938	0.020	0.010	1,400
7/64	0.1094	0.1095	0.1096	0.1094	0.020	0.010	1,900
1/8	0.1250	0.1252	0.1253	0.1251	0.020	0.010	2,600
5/32	0.1562	0.1564	0.1565	0.1563	0.020	0.010	4,100
3/16	0.1875	0.1877	0.1878	0.1876	0.020	0.010	5,900
7/32	0.2188	0.2189	0.2190	0.2188	0.020	0.010	7,600
1/4	0.2500	0.2602	0.2603	0.2501	0.020	0.010	10,000
5/16	0.3125	0.3127	0.3128	0.3126	0.020	0.010	16,000
3/8	0.3750	0.3752	0.3753	0.3751	0.020	0.010	23,000

Cotter Pins

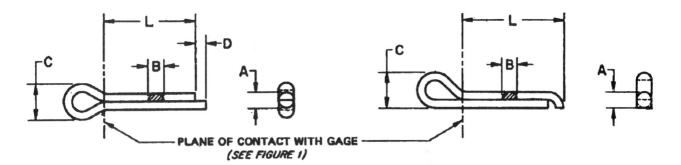

**EXTENDED PRONG
SQUARE CUT TYPE**

PLANE OF CONTACT WITH GAGE
(SEE FIGURE 1)

HAMMER LOCK TYPE

Table 2 Dimensions of Cotter Pins

Nominal Size [1] or Basic Pin Diameter	A Total Shank Diameter		B Wire Width		C Head Diameter	D Extended Prong Length	Recommended Hole Size
	Max	Min	Max	Min	Min	Min	
1/32 0.031	0.032	0.028	0.032	0.022	0.06	0.01	0.047
3/64 0.047	0.048	0.044	0.048	0.035	0.09	0.02	0.062
1/16 0.062	0.060	0.056	0.060	0.044	0.12	0.03	0.078
5/64 0.078	0.076	0.072	0.076	0.057	0.16	0.04	0.094
3/32 0.094	0.090	0.086	0.090	0.069	0.19	0.04	0.109
7/64 0.109	0.104	0.100	0.104	0.080	0.22	0.05	0.125
1/8 0.125	0.120	0.116	0.120	0.093	0.25	0.06	0.141
9/64 0.141	0.134	0.130	0.134	0.104	0.28	0.06	0.156
5/32 0.156	0.150	0.146	0.150	0.116	0.31	0.07	0.172
3/16 0.188	0.176	0.172	0.176	0.137	0.38	0.09	0.203
7/32 0.219	0.207	0.202	0.207	0.161	0.44	0.10	0.234
1/4 0.250	0.225	0.220	0.225	0.176	0.50	0.11	0.266
5/16 0.312	0.280	0.275	0.280	0.220	0.62	0.14	0.312
3/8 0.375	0.335	0.329	0.335	0.263	0.75	0.16	0.375
7/16 0.438	0.406	0.400	0.406	0.320	0.88	0.20	0.438
1/2 0.500	0.473	0.467	0.473	0.373	1.00	0.23	0.500
5/8 0.625	0.598	0.590	0.598	0.472	1.25	0.30	0.625
3/4 0.750	0.723	0.715	0.723	0.572	1.50	0.36	0.750

[1] Where specifying nominal size in decimals, zeros preceding decimal shall be omitted.

For additional requirements refer to General Data for Cotter Pins on Pages 4 and 5.

Lock Washers - Inch Series

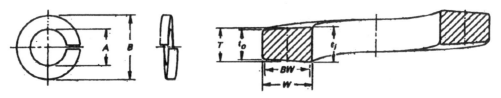

Enlarged Section

TABLE 2　DIMENSIONS OF REGULAR HELICAL SPRING LOCK WASHERS

Nominal Washer Size	A Inside Diameter		B Outside Diameter	T Mean Section Thickness $(t_i+t_o)/2$	W Section Width	$t_i - t_o$ Increase in Thickness (O.D. to I.D.)		BW Bearing Width
	Max.	Min.	Max.	Min.	Min.	Max.	Min.	Min.
No. 2 (0.086)	0.094	0.088	0.172	0.020	0.035	0.0022	0.0011	0.024
No. 3 (0.099)	0.107	0.101	0.195	0.025	0.040	0.0026	0.0013	0.028
No. 4 (0.112)	0.120	0.114	0.209	0.025	0.040	0.0026	0.0013	0.028
No. 5 (0.125)	0.133	0.127	0.236	0.031	0.047	0.0030	0.0015	0.033
No. 6 (0.138)	0.148	0.141	0.250	0.031	0.047	0.0030	0.0015	0.033
No. 8 (0.164)	0.174	0.167	0.293	0.040	0.055	0.0036	0.0018	0.038
No. 10 (0.190)	0.200	0.193	0.334	0.047	0.062	0.0040	0.0020	0.043
No. 12 (0.216)	0.227	0.220	0.377	0.056	0.070	0.0044	0.0022	0.049
1/4 (0.250)	0.260	0.252	0.487	0.062	0.109	0.0070	0.0035	0.076
5/16 (0.3125)	0.322	0.314	0.583	0.078	0.125	0.0080	0.0040	0.087
3/8 (0.375)	0.385	0.377	0.680	0.094	0.141	0.0090	0.0045	0.099
7/16 (0.4375)	0.450	0.440	0.776	0.109	0.156	0.0100	0.0050	0.109
1/2 (0.500)	0.512	0.502	0.869	0.125	0.171	0.0110	0.0055	0.120
9/16 (0.5625)	0.574	0.564	0.965	0.141	0.188	0.0120	0.0060	0.132
5/8 (0.625)	0.640	0.628	1.072	0.156	0.203	0.0130	0.0065	0.142
11/16 (0.6875)	0.703	0.691	1.169	0.172	0.219	0.0140	0.0070	0.153
3/4 (0.750)	0.765	0.753	1.264	0.188	0.234	0.0150	0.0075	0.164
13/16 (0.8125)	0.828	0.816	1.359	0.203	0.250	0.0160	0.0080	0.175
7/8 (0.875)	0.890	0.878	1.455	0.219	0.266	0.0170	0.0085	0.186
15/16 (0.9375)	0.953	0.941	1.551	0.234	0.281	0.0180	0.0090	0.197
1 (1.000)	1.015	1.003	1.647	0.250	0.297	0.0190	0.0095	0.208
1 1/16 (1.0625)	1.080	1.066	1.742	0.266	0.312	0.0200	0.0100	0.218
1 1/8 (1.125)	1.144	1.129	1.838	0.281	0.328	0.0210	0.0105	0.230
1 3/16 (1.1875)	1.208	1.192	1.934	0.297	0.344	0.0220	0.0110	0.241
1 1/4 (1.250)	1.272	1.254	2.028	0.312	0.359	0.0230	0.0115	0.251
1 5/16 (1.3125)	1.335	1.317	2.124	0.328	0.375	0.0240	0.0120	0.262
1 3/8 (1.375)	1.399	1.379	2.210	0.344	0.391	0.0250	0.0125	0.274
1 7/16 (1.4375)	1.462	1.442	2.314	0.359	0.406	0.0260	0.0130	0.284
1 1/2 (1.500)	1.524	1.504	2.409	0.375	0.422	0.0270	0.0135	0.295
1 5/8 (1.625)	1.653	1.633	2.543	0.389	0.424	0.0272	0.0136	0.297
1 3/4 (1.750)	1.778	1.758	2.668	0.389	0.424	0.0272	0.0136	0.297
1 7/8 (1.875)	2.003	1.883	2.800	0.422	0.427	0.0272	0.0136	0.299
2 (2.000)	2.028	2.008	2.925	0.422	0.427	0.0272	0.0136	0.299
2 1/4 (2.250)	2.287	2.262	3.215	0.440	0.442	0.0282	0.0141	0.309
2 1/2 (2.500)	2.537	2.512	3.465	0.440	0.442	0.0282	0.0141	0.309
2 3/4 (2.750)	2.787	2.762	3.818	0.458	0.491	0.0304	0.0157	0.344
3 (3.000)	3.037	3.012	4.068	0.458	0.491	0.0304	0.0157	0.344

GENERAL NOTE: For additional requirements refer to Section 2, General Data for Helical Spring Lock Washers.

4

Detailing Design - Bolt Clearances

Counterbored holes are designed to recess bolt heads below the surface of a part. This gets the bolt head out of the way of other parts. Fillister and Hexagon Socket Head bolt heads are typically recessed this way. The drill hole, counterbore diameter and counterbore depth must be slightly larger than the actual bolt head size to provide clearances.

Counterbore tool.

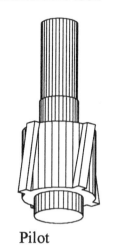

Counterbored hole.

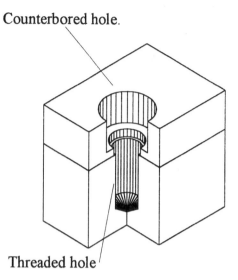

Pilot   Threaded hole

DRILL AND COUNTERBORE SIZES

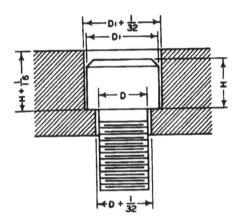

CLEARANCE HOLE DIAMETER:
In the top half of the assembly, a clearance hole for the threaded body is needed. Typically this diameter is:
BOLT NOMINAL DIAMETER + 1/32".

COUNTERBORE DIAMETER = BOLT HEAD DIAMETER + 1/32".

COUNTERBORE DEPTH = BOLT HEAD HEIGHT + 1/16".

Countersunk holes are required for Flat Head fasteners. The depth of the countersunk hole is determined by the diameter at the top of the hole.
(Typically bolt head diameter + 1/8")

Countersink tool.

Countersunk hole

DRILL AND COUNTERSINK SIZES

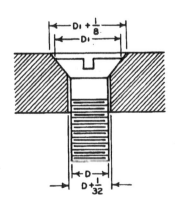

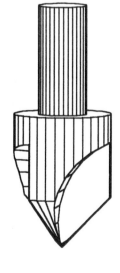

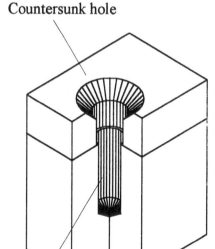

Threaded hole

Tables referenced in Chapter K are exerpted from ANSI/ASME standards. Used by permission. The American National Standards Institute. 11 W 42nd St., New York, New York. 10036.

Students are also encouraged to consult "Machinery's Handbook". Industrial Press, Inc. 200 Madison Avenue, New Your, New York. 10016-4078.

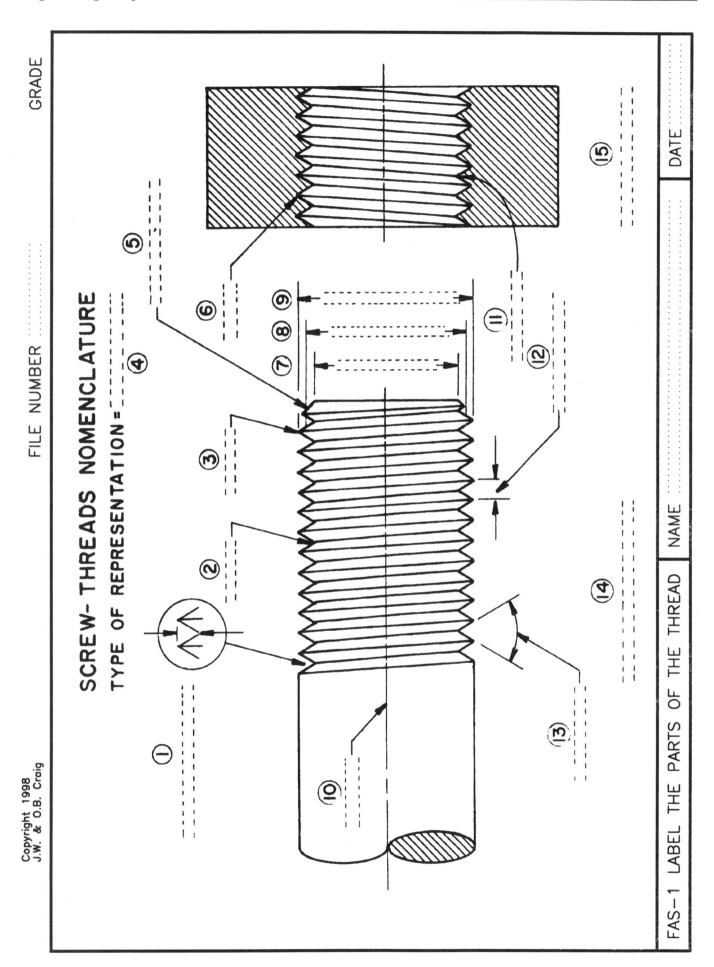

SCREW-THREADS NOMENCLATURE

TYPE OF REPRESENTATION =

GRADE

FILE NUMBER

DATE   NAME

FAS—1 LABEL THE PARTS OF THE THREAD

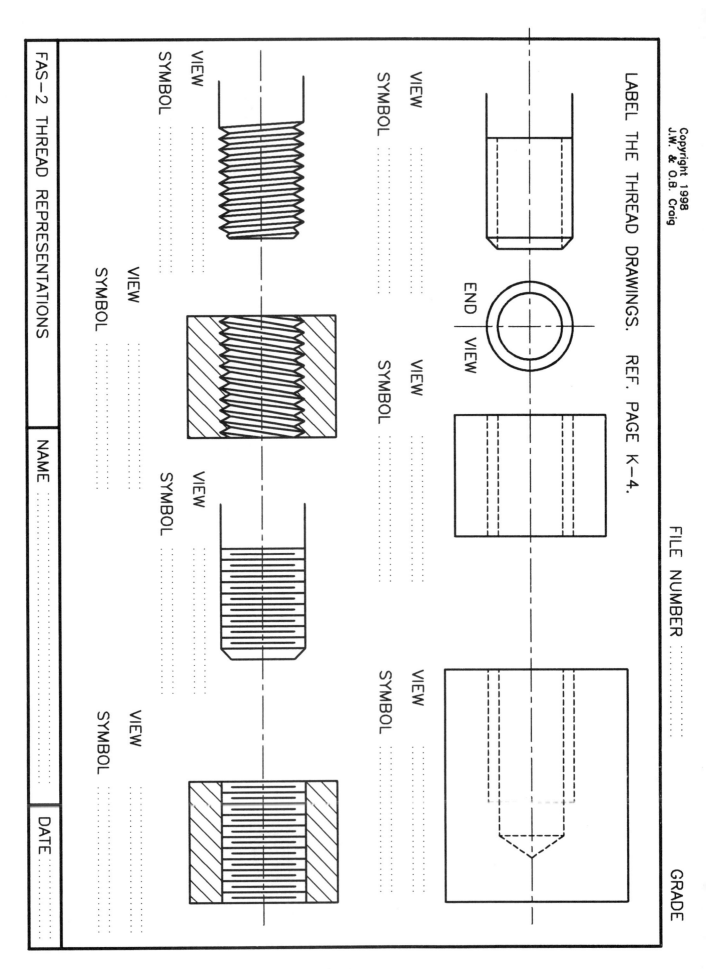

LABEL THE THREAD DRAWINGS. REF. PAGE K-4.

FILE NUMBER ....

GRADE

END | VIEW

SYMBOL ....
VIEW ....

SYMBOL ....
VIEW ....

SYMBOL ....
VIEW ....

SYMBOL ....
VIEW ....

SYMBOL ....
VIEW ....

SYMBOL ....
VIEW ....

FAS-2 THREAD REPRESENTATIONS

NAME ....

DATE ....

GRADE

FILE NUMBER ....

REF: PAGE K-2 AND TABLES PAGE K-5.

AMERICAN STANDARD GIVE:
NOMINAL DIAMETER, THREADS PER INCH, THREAD SERIES.
NOTE: A CLASS OF FIT 1A, 2A OR 3A MAY BE APPENDED
FOR PRECISION THREADS.

WRITE EXTERNAL THREAD NOTES FOR THE FOLLOWING:

1. NOMINAL DIA = 1/2"   SERIES = UNC

2. NOMINAL DIA = 3/4"   SERIES = UNF

3. NOMINAL DIA = #8   SERIES = UNC

4. NOMINAL DIA = 5/16"   SERIES = UNF

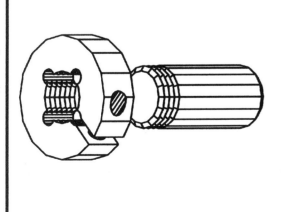

FAS-3 EXTERNAL THREADS - INCH   NAME ....   DATE ....

FILE NUMBER ....

GRADE

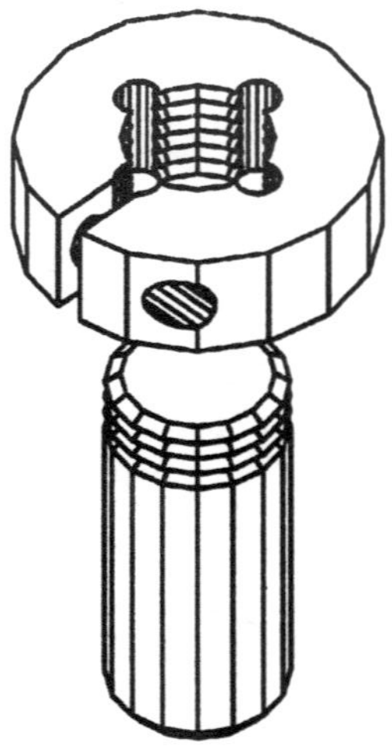

REF: PAGE K-2 AND TABLES PAGE K-5.

METRIC THREADS GIVE:
NOMINAL DIAMETER, THREADS PER MILLIMETER

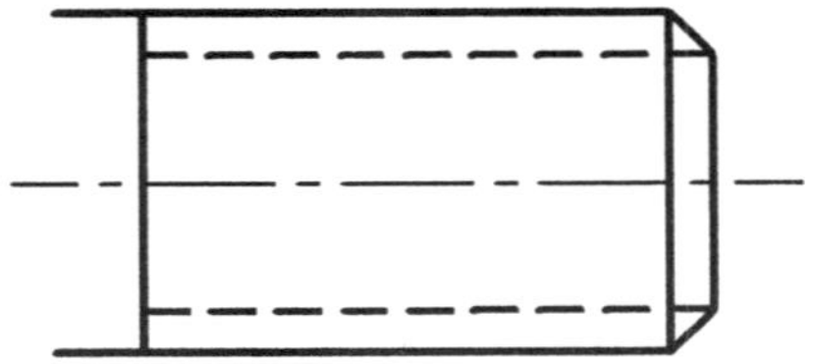

WRITE EXTERNAL THREAD NOTES FOR THE FOLLOWING:

1. NOMINAL DIA = 24 MM
   ....

2. NOMINAL DIA = 6 MM
   ....

3. NOMINAL DIA = 12 MM
   ....

4. NOMINAL DIA = 2 MM
   ....

FAS-4 EXTERNAL THREADS – METRIC

NAME ....

DATE ....

K - 22

GRADE

FILE NUMBER ....

REF: PAGE K-2 AND TABLES PAGE K-5.

AMERICAN STANDARD INTERNAL THREADS GIVE:
DRILL DIAMETER
DRILL DEPTH (IF NOT THRU)
THREAD DIAMETER, THREAD PITCH, THREAD SERIES
THREAD DEPTH (IF NOT THRU).

DESIGN NOTE:
DRILL DEPTH = THREAD DEPTH + THREAD DIAMETER

A CLASS OF FIT 1B, 2B OR 3B MAY BE APPENDED
FOR PRECISION THREADS.

WRITE INTERNAL THREAD NOTES FOR THE FOLLOWING:

1. NOMINAL DIA = 1/2"   SERIES = UNC. THREAD DEPTH = 1.5"

2. NOMINAL DIA = 3/4"   SERIES = UNF. THREAD DEPTH = 2.0"

3. NOMINAL DIA = #8   SERIES = UNC. THREAD DEPTH = 1.0"

4. NOMINAL DIA = 5/16"   SERIES = UNF. THREAD DEPTH = THRU.

THREAD DEPTH

DRILL DEPTH

BLIND TAPPED HOLE

FAS-5 INTERNAL THREADS - INCH

NAME ....

DATE ....

FILE NUMBER ....

GRADE

REF: PAGE K-2 AND TABLES PAGE K-5.

METRIC INTERNAL THREADS GIVE:
DRILL DIAMETER (CALCULATE - SEE FORMULA BELOW).
DRILL DEPTH (IF NOT THRU).
THREAD DIAMETER, THREAD PITCH
THREAD DEPTH (IF NOT THRU).

DESIGN NOTE:
DRILL DEPTH = THREAD DEPTH + THREAD DIAMETER

TAP DRILL DIAMETER =　　　{CALCULATE TO 2 DECIMAL PLACES
BASIC MAJOR DIAMETER - (1.08253 × PITCH × .75)

WRITE INTERNAL THREAD NOTES FOR THE FOLLOWING:

1. NOMINAL DIA = 12 MM. THREAD DEPTH = 30 MM.

....

2. NOMINAL DIA = 24 MM. THREAD DEPTH = 45 MM.

....

3. NOMINAL DIA = 5 MM. THREAD DEPTH = 16MM.

....

4. NOMINAL DIA = 2 MM. THREAD DEPTH = THRU.

....

DRILL
DEPTH

THREAD
DEPTH

BLIND TAPPED HOLE

FAS-6 INTERNAL THREADS - METRIC

NAME	DATE

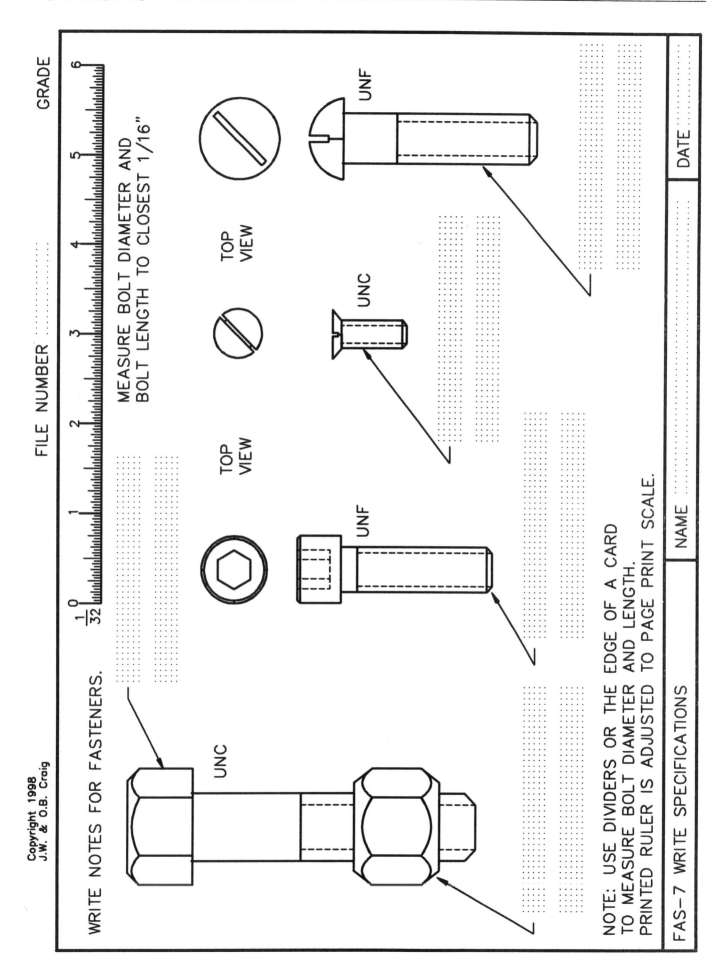

GRADE

FILE NUMBER

DATE

Copyright 1998
J.W. & O.B. Craig

WRITE NOTES FOR FASTENERS.

MEASURE BOLT DIAMETER AND
BOLT LENGTH TO CLOSEST 1/16"

TOP
VIEW

TOP
VIEW

UNF

UNC

UNF

UNC

UNC

NOTE: USE DIVIDERS OR THE EDGE OF A CARD
TO MEASURE BOLT DIAMETER AND LENGTH.
PRINTED RULER IS ADJUSTED TO PAGE PRINT SCALE.

FAS-7 WRITE SPECIFICATIONS

NAME

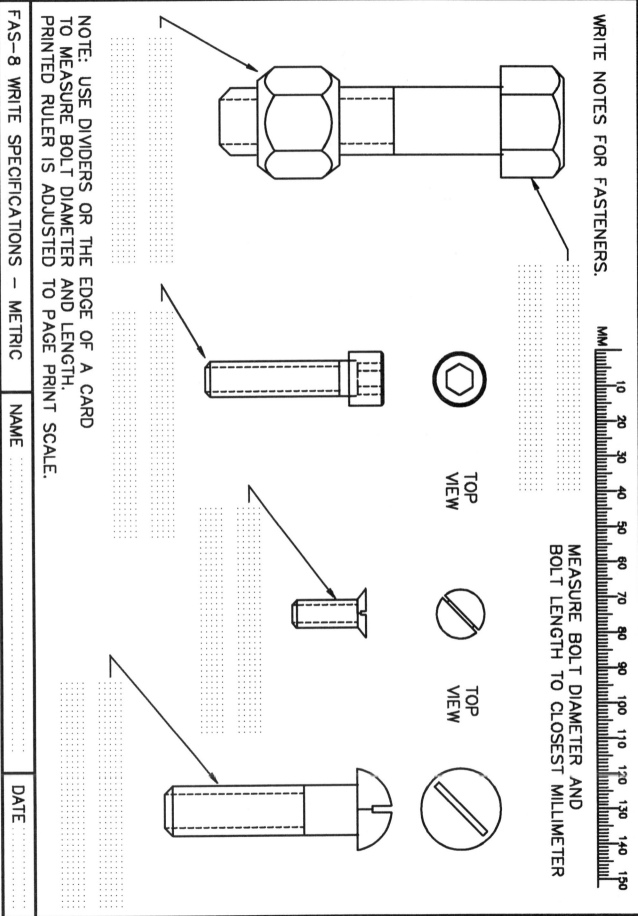

WRITE NOTES FOR FASTENERS.

FILE NUMBER ....

GRADE

MM

TOP VIEW

TOP VIEW

MEASURE BOLT DIAMETER AND
BOLT LENGTH TO CLOSEST MILLIMETER

NOTE: USE DIVIDERS OR THE EDGE OF A CARD
TO MEASURE BOLT DIAMETER AND LENGTH.
PRINTED RULER IS ADJUSTED TO PAGE PRINT SCALE.

FAS-8 WRITE SPECIFICATIONS — METRIC

NAME

DATE

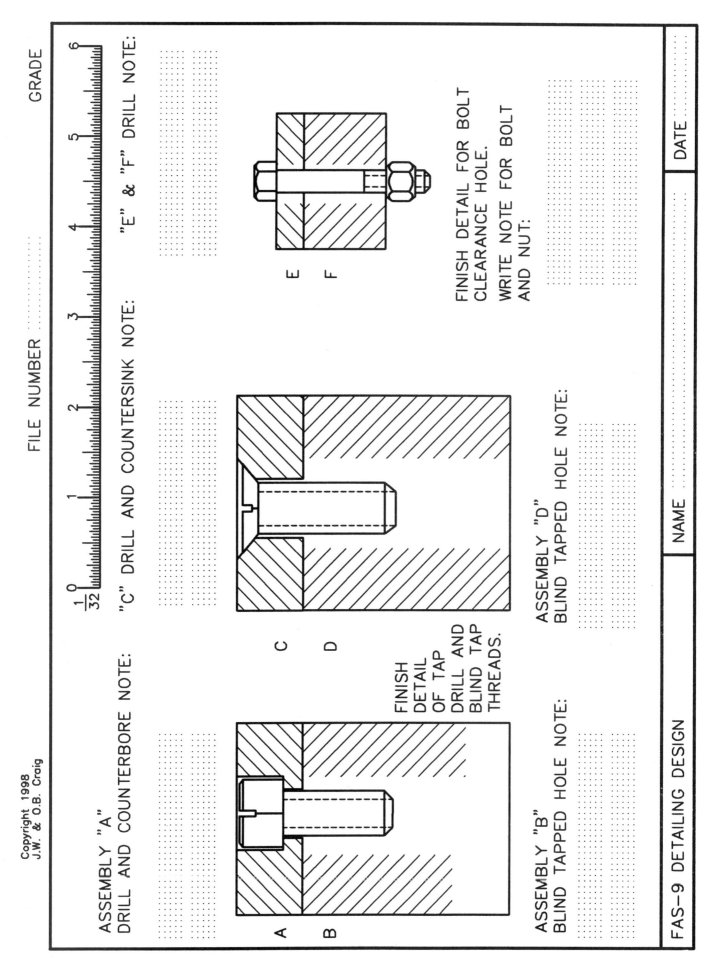

GRADE

FILE NUMBER

Copyright 1998
J.W. & O.B. Craig

"E" & "F" DRILL NOTE:

"C" DRILL AND COUNTERSINK NOTE:

ASSEMBLY "A"
DRILL AND COUNTERBORE NOTE:

FINISH DETAIL FOR BOLT
CLEARANCE HOLE.

WRITE NOTE FOR BOLT
AND NUT:

E

F

ASSEMBLY "D"
BLIND TAPPED HOLE NOTE:

C

D

FINISH
DETAIL
OF TAP
DRILL AND
BLIND TAP
THREADS.

ASSEMBLY "B"
BLIND TAPPED HOLE NOTE:

A

B

$\frac{1}{32}$

NAME

DATE

FAS-9 DETAILING DESIGN

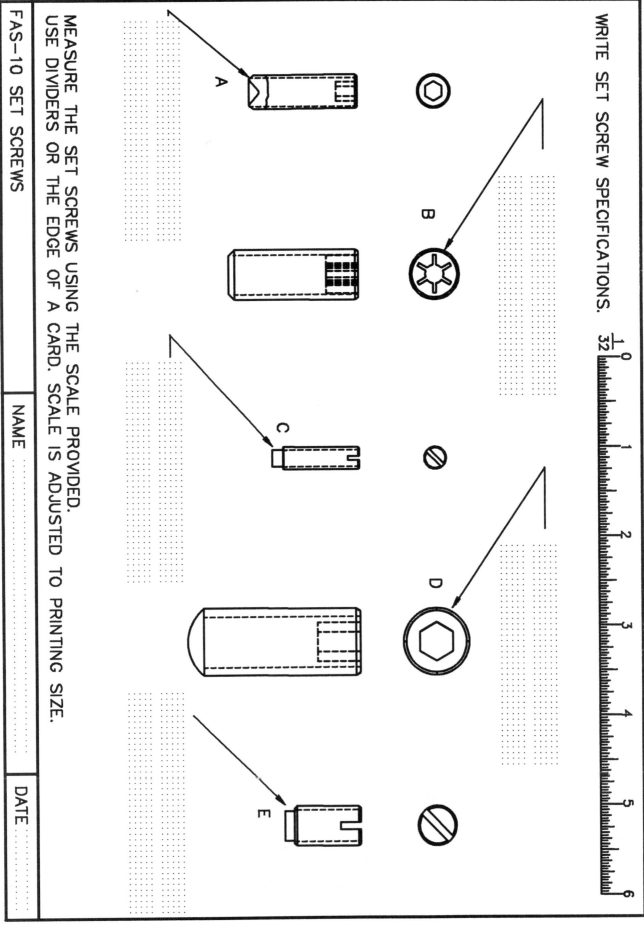

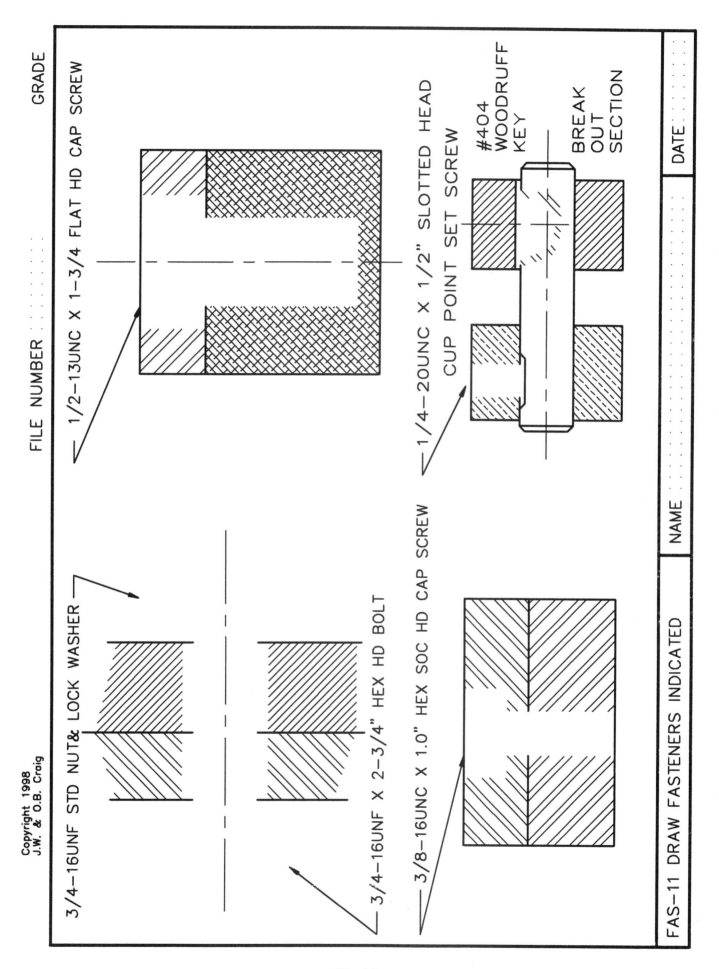

GRADE

FILE NUMBER

1/2–13UNC X 1–3/4 FLAT HD CAP SCREW

#404 WOODRUFF KEY

BREAK OUT SECTION

1/4–20UNC X 1/2" SLOTTED HEAD CUP POINT SET SCREW

3/4–16UNF STD NUT& LOCK WASHER

3/4–16UNF X 2–3/4" HEX HD BOLT

3/8–16UNC X 1.0" HEX SOC HD CAP SCREW

NAME

DATE

FAS–11 DRAW FASTENERS INDICATED

name

date

NOTE: Use this grid format
in horizontal direction.

FILE NUMBER

GRADE

Dimensioning Basics

Dimensions are placed on a drawing to convey the size and location of features. Choosing dimensions involves many decisions based on how the part must function while following standard practices. There may be several ways to place a dimension so the concept of "Engineering Intent" will often point to the most logical selection. What the part is for and how it fits with other parts will narrow the options.

There are many standard forms and practices based on A.N.S.I requirements, contractual agreements and local preferences within a given company. Often, the drafter must look up a particular method or form -- no one is allowed to make up their own rules.

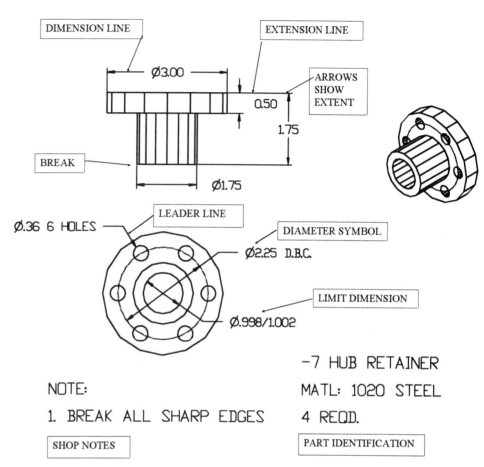

NOTE:

1. BREAK ALL SHARP EDGES

SHOP NOTES

-7 HUB RETAINER

MATL: 1020 STEEL

4 REQD.

PART IDENTIFICATION

__Dimension lines_ extend exactly between Extension lines. The extent of the dimension is terminated by arrows or other end marks.

__ Extension lines_ should have a slight break between the object and the start of the Extension line.

__Leader lines_ point toward the centers of circles, but they stop at the circle.

__Parts must be identified with a _part number_ (-7 in this example), material specifications and the number required per assembly..

__Shop Notes_ provide general information.

All dimensions have a tolerance (unless they are marked as some type of reference dimension -- REF, BSC, MIN, MAX).

Often, the number of decimal places in a dimension is linked to a _tolerance block_. In the example drawing, 2 decimal places equates to +/- .03 inches for general dimensions.

The _limit dimension_ shown gives the tolerance directly. No smaller than .998, no bigger than 1.002 inches diameter.

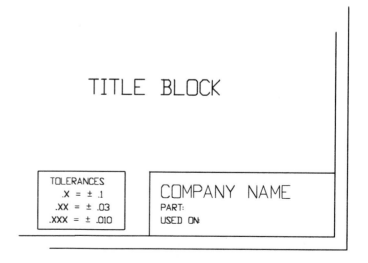

Examples of horizontal dimensions are shown.
__A. Two decimal places with arrows and " (inch) marks.
__B. Alternate style using tick endmarks.
__C. Dual dimensioning with both decimal inch and metric equivalents [102] .
__D. Dimension placed above dimension line.
__E. Narrow space. Arrows inside, numbers outside.
__F. Very narrow space. Arrows outside pointing in.

Arrowheads have a 3.1 ratio -- approximately .125" long and .05" wide. (3mm long and 1 mm wide) on small drawings.

Vertical direction dimensions are shown.
__G. Fractional inch -- narrow space.
__H. Fractional inch -- engineering form.
__J. Fractional inch -- architectural form. Text is above the line and rotated with the line.

__K. Preferred form for lettering fractions. Examples G, H and J are computer drawn. Many CAD software systems use a "/" to denote a fraction. On crowded or small drawings the "/" could be mistaken for a "1".

Place shortest dimensions closest to the object.

Leave .25 to .40 minimum space between dimensions.

Dimension text must be very clear. Use more room between dimensions if needed. Experienced drafters will sketch an overlay or plot a test plot. Then, they sketch freehand the choice of dimensions and the placement. This helps to define the best location for dimensions and the best place to fit each in. A freehand sketch will also help locate missing dimensions which may be very difficult to fit at a later time..

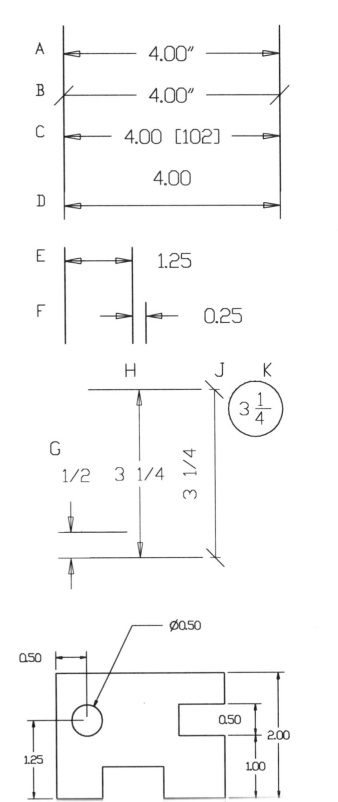

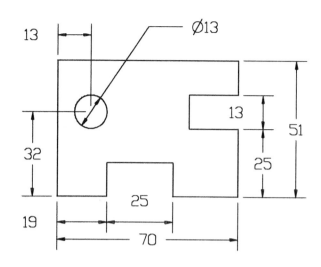

METRIC DIMENSIONS MM

Metric dimensions are usually specified to the closest millimeter for general sizes. The Tolerance Block might show +/- .5mm variation for non-critical features. As industry slowly changes over to the metric system, drafters must incorporate slightly different dimensioning techniques. Dual dimensioning is a transition step.

If the system of measurement is not clear, include a note specifying the units.

METRIC DRAWING SYMBOLS

Metric drawings often use the SI symbols shown to indicate metric dimensions as well as the view placement.

   3rd angle drawings are used mostly in the U.S.A. This seems to be a logical placement of views. The front view is the key view. Top is above the front. Right side is to the right of the front..

   1st angle drawings are used by the rest of the world. The front is the key view. Top is below the front. Right side is to the left of the front. Same views -- just different locations on the page. The SI symbols tell quickly how the drawing is presented.

SI ◎ ◁   3RD ANGLE

SI ◁ ◎   1ST ANGLE

Special symbols may be used with dimensions. REF, (...) or an underline indicates a reference value. These dimensions are placed on the drawing mostly to archive information. Reference dimensions are never used for part production.

BSC (basic size) may be specified in a manner similar to REF. MAX and MIN are special modifiers that give a range of permissible sizes. .998 MIN / 1.002 MAX per the example on page L-1.

Other symbols are shown. (There are many more.) Symbols save drawing time and space while transferring common information.

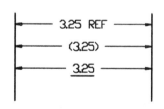

∅ = DIAMETER
R = RADIUS
□ = SQUARE
⊔ = COUNTERBORE
▽ = DEPTH
∨ = COUNTERSINK
◁ = SLOPE
▷ = CONICAL TAPER
S = SPHERICAL DIAMETER
SR = SPHERICAL RADIUS

Types of Dimensions

Size dimensions are needed for all geometric forms. In this example, sizes for cylinders (negative and positive), prisms (hexagonal shape) and pyramids (middle area) are needed. We must know the size in order to create the basic shape.

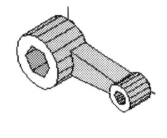

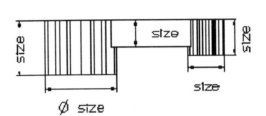

Location dimensions show <u>where</u> the geometric shapes are located in relation to the entire part. Beginners often forget to include location dimensions.

Both size and location for every geometric shape must be shown to define the geometry.

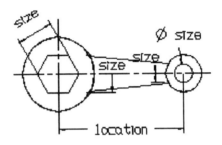

Parts of this type are often made by casting. Once the rough shape is formed then certain areas of the part are machined to accurate size.

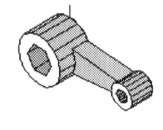

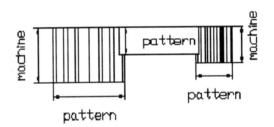

Pattern dimensions are used only by a Pattern Maker to create a wood model of the part. The actual pattern is slightly over size to account for shrinkage as the hot metal cools.

Machine dimensions are needed for the final production. Thicknesses must be machined to size and holes must be machined true, parallel or perpendicular to other surfaces and holes.

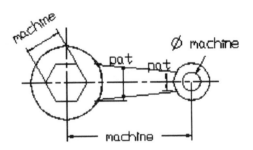

Mating dimensions occur where parts must interface. Usually they are the common faces between parts in an assembly. The hexagonal prism may be force-fit into the hexagonal hole. The cylindrical bolt must slide freely through the cylindrical hole.

Dimensioning Arcs, Circles and Cylinders

Dimension the radius if less than a full circle. (In some situations an arc over 180 degrees should be dimensioned as a diameter.)

Dimension the diameter for full circles.

Precede the radius size with a "R". Precede the diameter with the diameter symbol. Older drawings may use the form: 1.50 DIA.

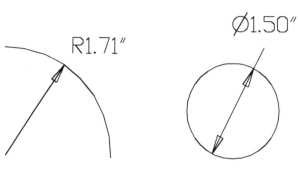

Parts may have many rounds and fillets the same size.
__A. Leader line with note.

TYP (typical) may be used where the geometry is the same.
__B. Single dimension with "TYP".

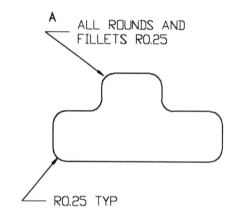

Grooves may be dimensioned one of two ways depending on the method of manufacture. Where the size and shape is not critical, the overall length and width may be specified. Note the use of the "R" without a value. This groove might be punched with a punch-press.

Dimensionless dimensions may be used to eliminate duplications. Where a radius is defined by another dimension, just specify "R" with no numbers.

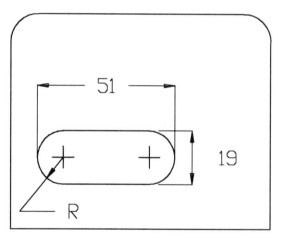

This groove is machined to shape using accurate cutting tools such as an endmill. Because the tool automatically cuts the radius, no radius need be specified. The center to center distance (32mm) is the length of table travel during machining. Tool diameter (20mm) is shown because endmills are sized by diameter.

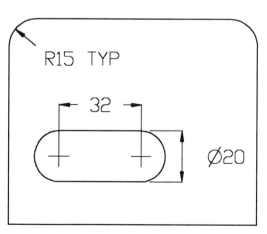

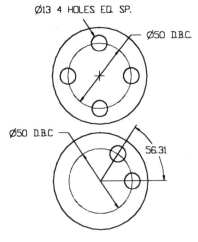

Circular hole patterns may be dimensioned using "Diameter of Bolt Circle" size. This is given with the "D.B.C." designation. Holes which are equally spaced do not require an angular offset. When holes are randomly spaced about a circular center line, specify the angles between centers.

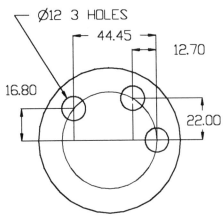

Locate the center of a circle, then give the diameter.

More precise hole locations may require offset dimensions, giving the "X" and "Y" distances to each center.

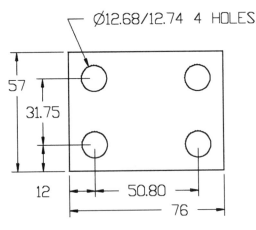

Where hole patterns on one part must align with similar hole patterns on another part, the most accurate locations are obtained by giving the center-to-center dimensions.

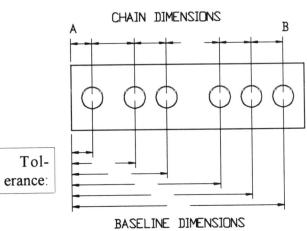

Since each dimension has a tolerance, errors on hole locations can accumulate. This affects how parts fit together. Each chain dimension from one point to another may be accurate. But, the "stack" error from point A to point B can be significant.
   Chain stack error +/- 6mm (total 12mm).

Without increasing accuracy requirements (and cost) the baseline method decreases error:
   Baseline stack error +/- 1mm (2 mm total).

Common hole types are shown:
__A. Drilled through.
__B. Blind drilled (not through).
__C. Counterbored hole.
__D. Countersunk hole.
__E. Threaded hole.

Each of these hole types requires a stand-ard-form note. Information is given in the order needed during manufacture. Tools are sized by diameter, so <u>diameter</u> must be specified.

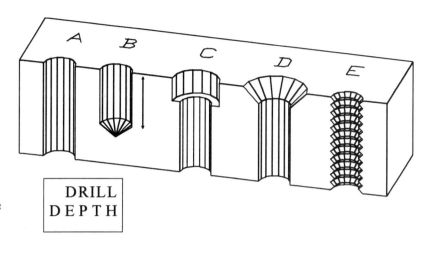

DRILL
D E P T H

<u>Drilled holes</u> are assumed to be drilled through unless a depth is given.
<u>Drill depth does not include the point.</u>
Drills are available in:
__Fraction sizes. 1/64" to several inches diameter.
__Number sizes. #1 to #80.
__Letter sizes "A" to "Z".
__Decimal inch sizes.
__Metric sizes.

Ø 3/8 – 3 HOLES
Ø 3/8 (.375) – 3 HOLES
#30(.1285) ALL HOLES MARKED 'D'
'F'(.257) 1-1/4 DEEP – 4 HOLES
Ø.250 3/4 DP.
Ø5 TYP (metric example)

5/32 DRILL – 21/32 C'BORE 1/2 DEEP
Ø 5/32 ⊔ 21/32 ↧ 1/2
(BOTH NOTES ABOVE ARE THE SAME)

For <u>counterbored</u> holes specify:
__drill diameter
__counterbore diameter
__counterbore depth
__number of holes (if applicable).

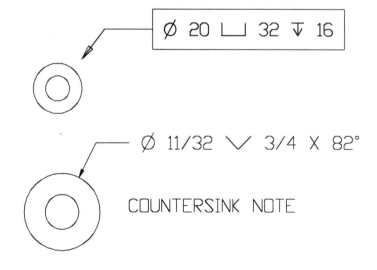

Ø 20 ⊔ 32 ↧ 16

<u>Countersink.</u> Specify:
__drill diameter
__diameter at top of countersunk hole (this controls the depth).
__angle of countersink (82 or 110 degrees)

Ø 11/32 ∨ 3/4 X 82°

COUNTERSINK NOTE

<u>Threaded hole.</u> Thru hole.
__tap drill size (from tables)
__thread nominal size
__threads per inch (or mm)
__thread series (if USA)
__class of fit (optional)

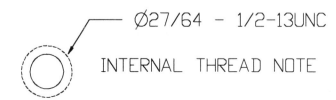

Ø27/64 – 1/2-13UNC

INTERNAL THREAD NOTE

Preferred methods for dimensioning cylinders:
__Negative cylinders (holes) are dimensioned in
the circular view.
__Positive cylinders (mass) are dimensioned in
the rectangular view.

Because the full circle exists, the diameter should
be given.

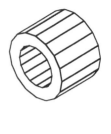

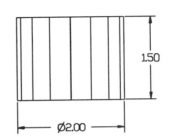

1.50

Ø2.00

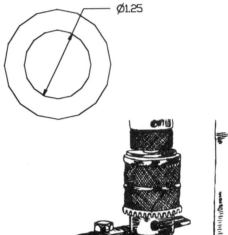

Ø1.25

Drilling a hole often produces an irregular shape.
Drills do not produce a very true, accurate or
smooth holes. In order to machine a true cylindrical shape a second machining step might include
the use of a reamer.

Reaming can produce accurate diameters within a
few thousandths of an inch. Typical note:

REAM .499/.501 - 4 HOLES

BORING

Large diameter holes may be machined by boring. The part in this example is chucked in a
lathe. A lathe tool is clamped into a boring bar
which is positioned by the lathe compound rest.
This operation can be accurate to within a few
thousandths of an inch. Typical callout:

BORE 6.222/6.228 - 3.00 DEEP

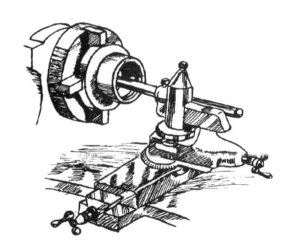

TURNING

Turning on a lathe is used to produce both cylindrical and tapered (conical) parts. Accuracy can be on the order of a few thousandths of an inch.

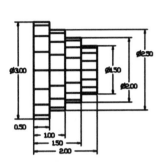

A cylindrical grinder may be used to produce very smooth, accurate cylinders and tapers. Accuracy to a few ten-thousandths of an inch is possible.

GRINDING

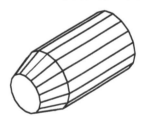

Tapered (conical) features are dimensioned in several possible ways:
__Specify taper-per-unit such as taper per foot or taper per meter, etc.
__Specify large diameter, small diameter and length of taper.
__Specify taper as a ratio of taper to length. In the example, the end tapers at a ratio of 1 unit taper to 3 units length.

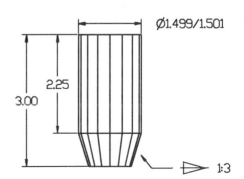

Rectangular Shapes and Rectangular Solids

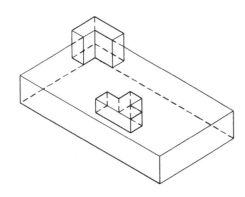

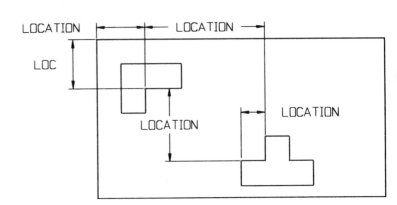

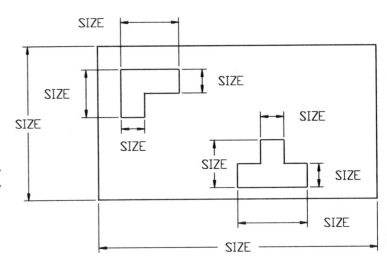

Location and size dimensions are shown for a series of rectangular objects. Often, locations should be planned first. These dimensions may relate features on this part to features on mating parts which must fit.

Size dimensions must be complete so all geometric shapes can be fabricated.

Just the right number of dimensions are needed -- too many may cause accuracy problems -- too few cause delays.

Place dimensions where the shape shows best:

__A&B. Dimension the material thickness. Solid thickness is easier to measure.

__C. This is a groove. Dimension the width and depth. Same with the groove in the front view.

__D,E&F. Show overall width, height and depth. Show depth only once -- either in the top view or the side view, but not both.

__G. Break the "chain". Include two of the three dimensions under D and two of the three next to E.

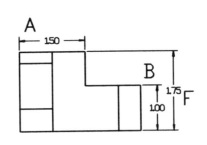

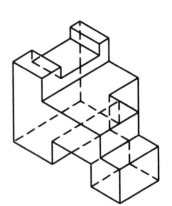

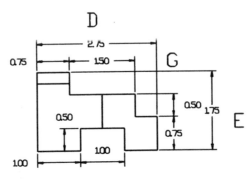

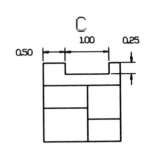

Angular Dimensions

Offset dimensions are preferred when dimensioning angles. They are easier to measure without special tools. In example A, specify the "X" and "Y" offsets.

When accuracy is required, use angular form as in example B.

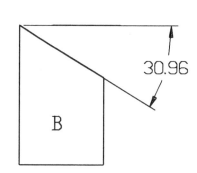

Two methods of dimensioning an angular groove are shown in C and D. Figure C uses offsets to locate the vertex of the angle and each end of the angled lines.

Figure D assures the groove is correctly located and aligned with the part. Locate the vertex by offsets. Give the half-angle to one side then the full angle between sides.

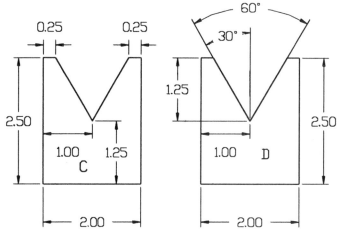

For some types of work, angled features may be specified as a ratio. The slope symbol and a ratio may be used. The slope is expressed as RISE / RUN. In architectural construction this would mean a rise of 3" for a run of 12" This angular form can be measured using a carpenter's framing square.

Angles may be expressed as a percent. Grades for roads are an example of this form.

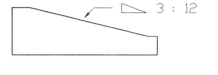

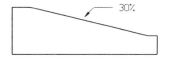

Aligned dimensions may be needed for accurate location of geometric features. The preferred form is to align the numbers horizontally as shown.

A Chamfer is a small bevel on the edge of a part.
__Specify W x H CHAMFER
    8 mm x 12mm CHAMFER
__Specify DIST x ANGLE
    1/8 x 45 CHAMFER

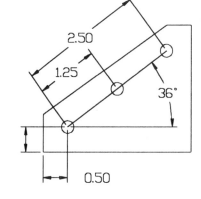

Dimensioning Details

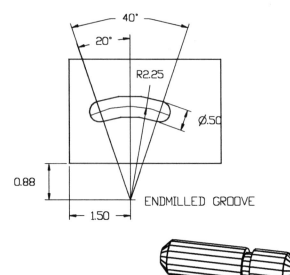

Endmilled circular groove. Locate center, give radius to center of groove, give half and full angle and diameter of milling cutter.

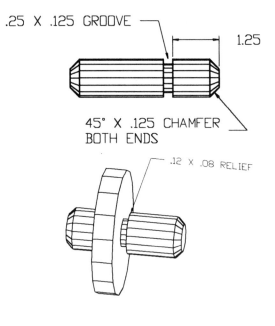

In many cases, cylindrical shafts and parts should have a chamfer on each end. The chamfers will remove dangerous sharp edges and also make the parts easier to assemble.

Grooves and Reliefs are notches cut into a cylinder. The dimension should specify WIDTH X DEPTH in that order.

Grooves may be cut to allow the assembly of C-clips.

Reliefs, grooves or undercuts cannot be used on highly-stressed parts.

A relief is often needed to facilitate turning or grinding multiple diameter areas on a common shaft. It is almost impossible to turn or grind a sharp internal corner.

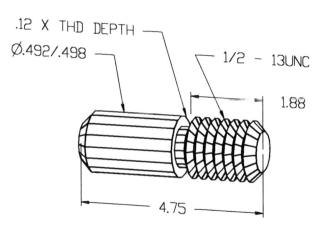

A relief is needed for threading to allow the threading tool to be extracted durning multiple passes. Dimension the length of good threads.

Dimensioning Details -- continued

An <u>Undercut</u> is an internal groove cut inside a cylindrical hole. They are needed for machining internal surfaces, threading runouts, etc. They may also be needed for lubrication.

Specify: W x D UNDERCUT

<u>Keys and keyways</u> are used to lock a shaft to a mating part to prevent slippage. The key is recessed into a groove in the shaft. The key extends upward into the keyway in the mating part.
__Specify: W x D KEYWAY.
For a Woodruff keyseat (per example)
__Specify:
 KEYSEAT FOR #XXX WOODRUFF KEY

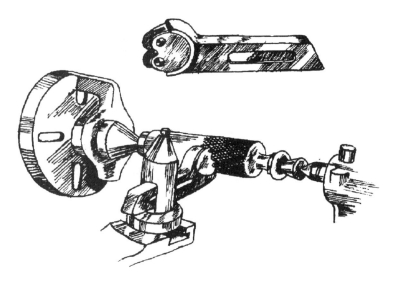

KNURLING

The Knurling operation roughens the surface of the part for a better grip. A micrometer has several knurled surfaces and locks.
Notes:
__FINE KNURL
__MEDIUM KNURL
__COARSE KNURL

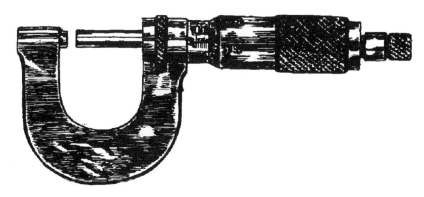

MICROMETER

Dimensioning Solids

Pyramidal shape. Specify base width X, base depth
Y and height Z.

Truncated pyramid. Give base size, projected
height "Z" and height "HT" to cut.

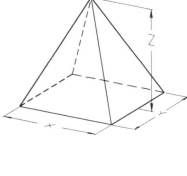

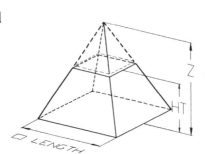

Cone. Specify base diameter and height.

Truncated cone. Specify base diameter,
top diameter and height. Taper dimensions also could be specified.

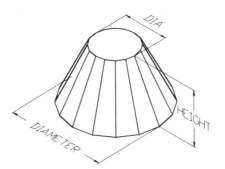

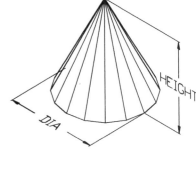

Torus. Specify radius from axis to center of circular cross-section. Specify diameter of circular
cross-section.

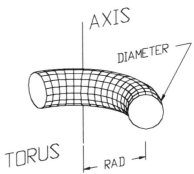

Spherical shape. For a full sphere, specify the diameter.
__Example: S40.

For less than a full sphere, specify the radius with
SR prefix as shown.
__Example SR 50 as shown.

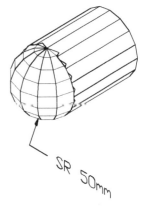

Special Dimensioning Forms

When single view drawings are used, dimensions may have to be placed on hidden features or non-standard locations. Single view drawings save time and space. They should only be used where the the shapes they depict are very clear.

**General Rule:** Do not dimension to hidden lines. Dimensions should be placed where features are seen as visible lines and the shape is clearly defined.

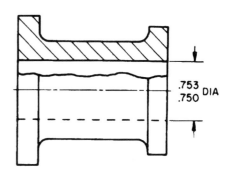

Irregular curves may have to be dimensioned by locating coordinate points on the curve.

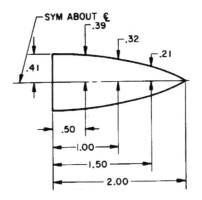

This drawing uses _ordinate_ dimensions referenced to X and Y datum lines.

Hole sizes are labeled on the field of the drawing and sizes are shown in a tabulated chart.

Tabulated drawings may be used for many types of work. Computer spread-sheets may be used to assemble the data.

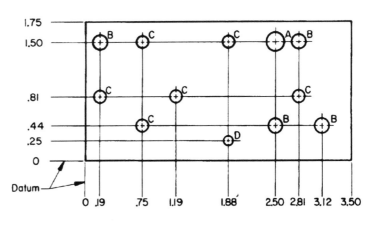

SIZE SYMBOL	A	B	C	D
HOLE DIA	.250	.188	.156	.125

Examples are from ANSI Y14.5. The American National Standards Association. With permission.

NAME

DATE

FILE NUMBER

GRADE

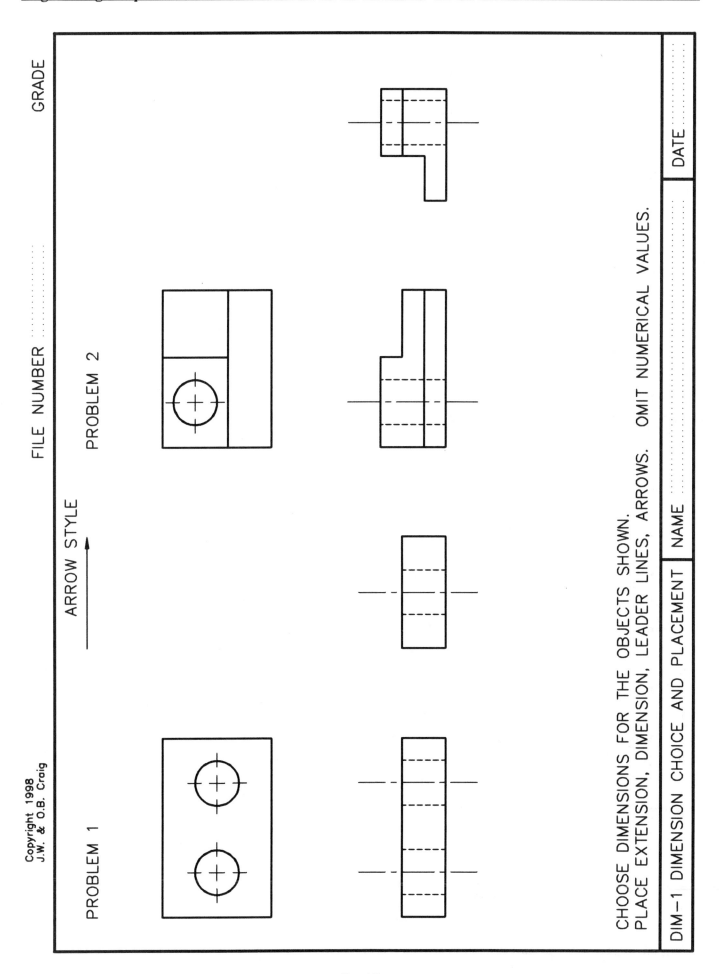

GRADE

FILE NUMBER

PROBLEM 2

ARROW STYLE

PROBLEM 1

CHOOSE DIMENSIONS FOR THE OBJECTS SHOWN.
PLACE EXTENSION, DIMENSION, LEADER LINES, ARROWS.   OMIT NUMERICAL VALUES.

DIM—1 DIMENSION CHOICE AND PLACEMENT | NAME | DATE

PROBLEM 3

Copyright 1998
J.W. & O.B. Craig

FILE NUMBER

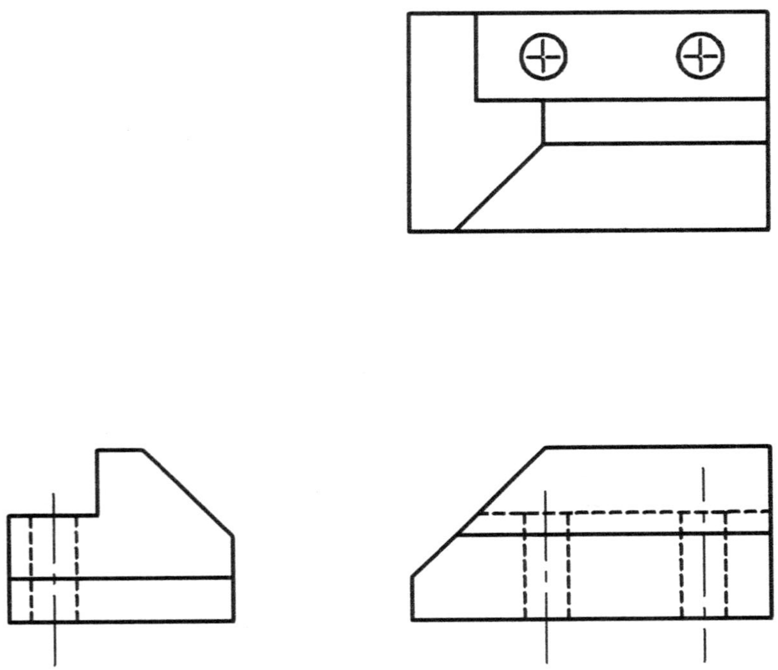

PROBLEM 4

GRADE

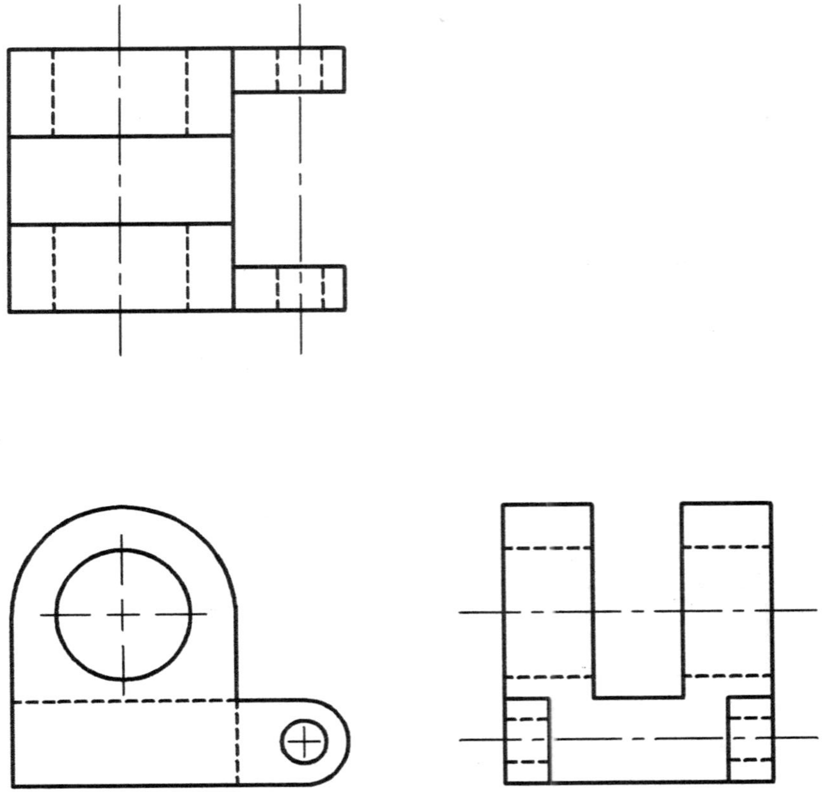

CHOOSE DIMENSIONS FOR OBJECTS SHOWN.
PLACE EXTENSION, DIMENSION, LEADER LINES, ARROWS. OMIT NUMERICAL VALUES.

DIM-2 DIMENSION CHOICE AND PLACEMENT | NAME | DATE

FILE NUMBER ....

GRADE

PROBLEM 5

NOTE: TOP VIEW
WOULD NOT SHOW
ANY USEFUL SHAPE.

PROBLEM 6

NOTE: SINGLE VIEW DRAWING.
NO OTHER VIEWS NEEDED.

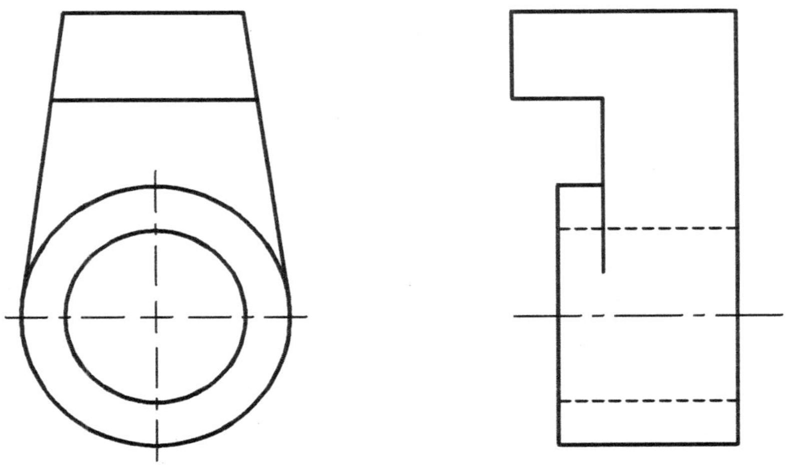

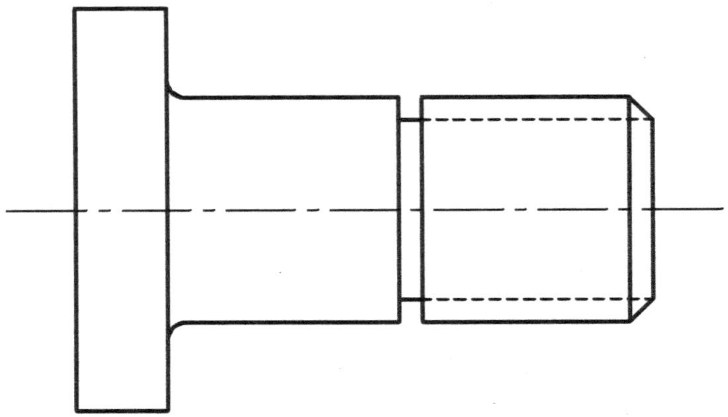

CHOOSE DIMENSIONS FOR THE OBJECTS SHOWN.
PLACE EXTENSION, DIMENSION, LEADER LINES AND ARROWS. OMIT NUMERICAL VALUES.

DIM–3 DIMENSION CHOICE AND PLACEMENT	NAME	DATE ....

PROBLEM 7

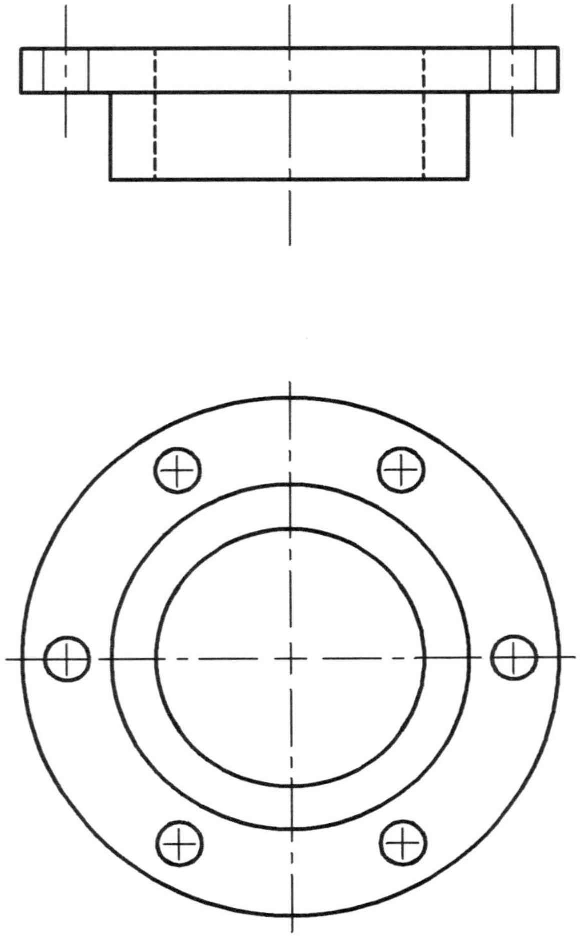

PROBLEM 8

FILE NUMBER

GRADE

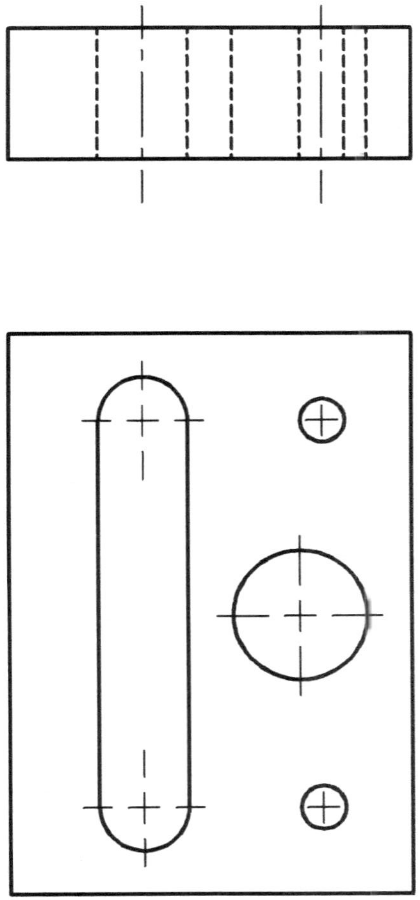

CHOOSE DIMENSIONS FOR THE OBJECTS SHOWN.
PLACE EXTENSION, DIMENSION, LEADER LINES AND ARROWS. OMIT NUMERICAL VALUES.

DIM-4 CHOOSE AND PLACE DIMENSIONS

NAME

DATE

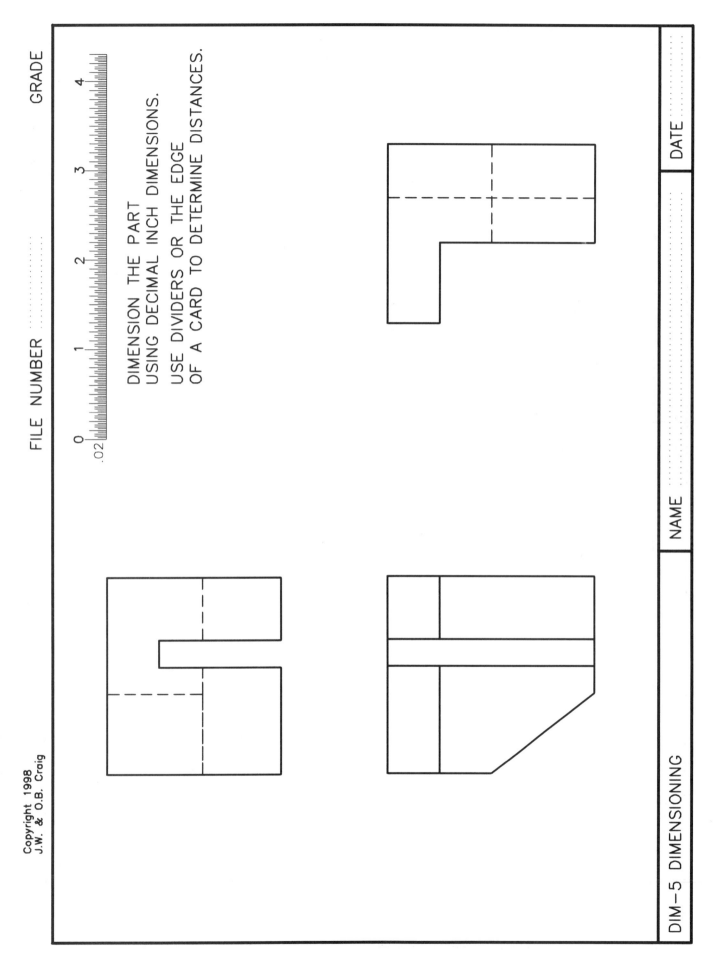

DIMENSION THE PART
USING DECIMAL INCH DIMENSIONS.

USE DIVIDERS OR THE EDGE
OF A CARD TO DETERMINE DISTANCES.

FILE NUMBER

GRADE

NAME

DATE

DIM—5 DIMENSIONING

FILE NUMBER ....   GRADE

DIM−6 DIMENSIONING

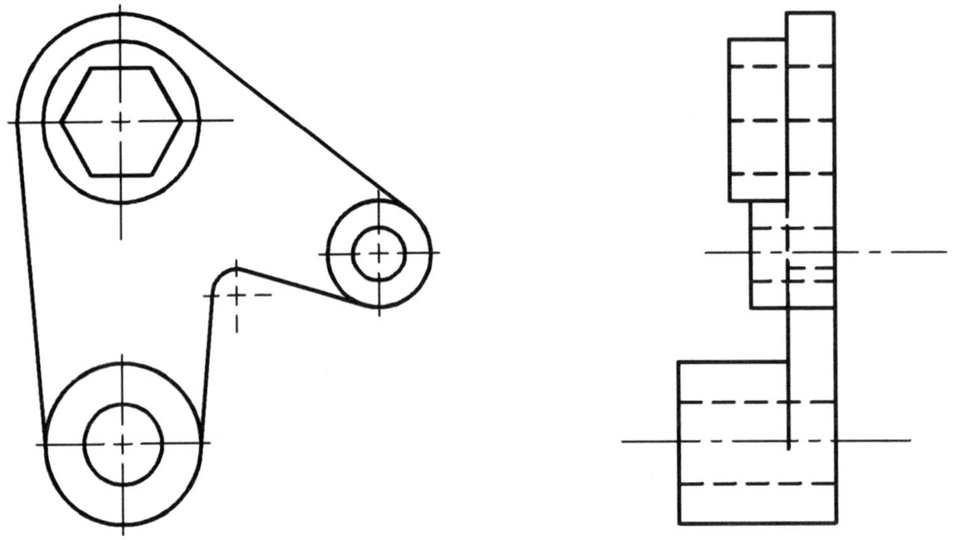

NAME ....   DATE ....

DIMENSION THE PART USING
METRIC MEASUREMENTS.
USE DIVIDERS OR THE EDGE OF
A CARD TO DETERMINE DISTANCES.

MM
10
20
30
40
50
60
70
80
90
100

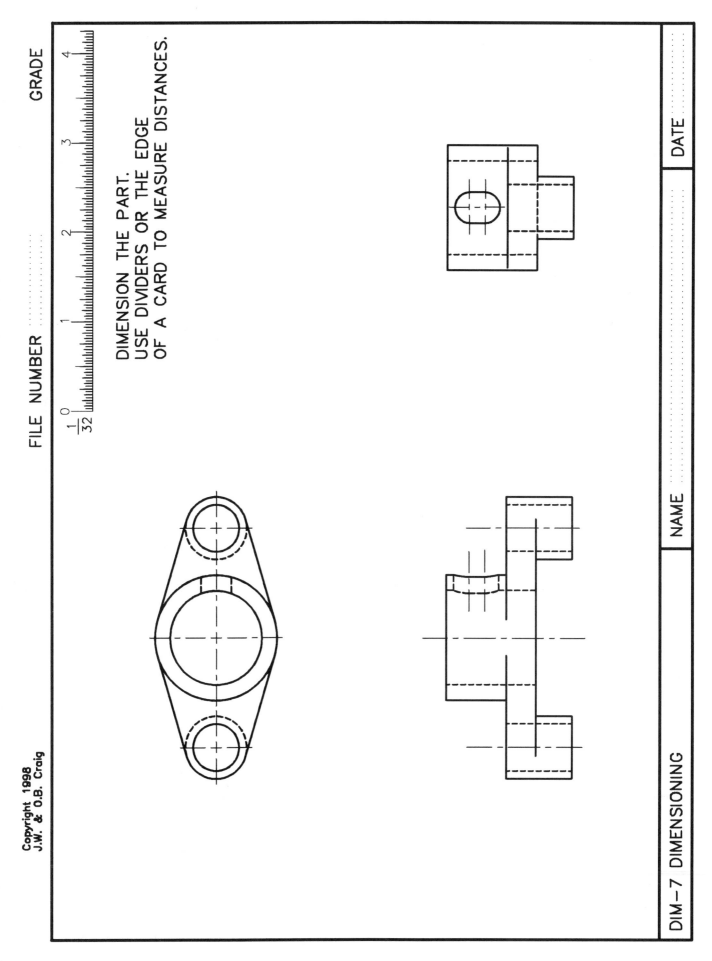

DIMENSION THE PART.
USE DIVIDERS OR THE EDGE
OF A CARD TO MEASURE DISTANCES.

GRADE

FILE NUMBER

DATE

NAME

DIM—7 DIMENSIONING

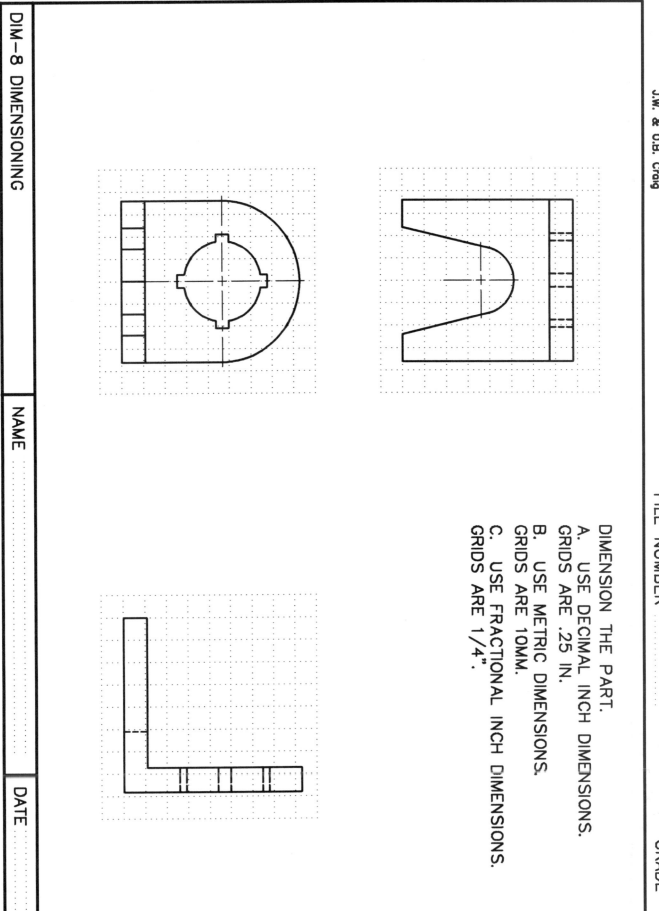

DIM-8 DIMENSIONING

NAME

DATE

FILE NUMBER

GRADE

DIMENSION THE PART.
A. USE DECIMAL INCH DIMENSIONS.
GRIDS ARE .25 IN.
B. USE METRIC DIMENSIONS.
GRIDS ARE 10MM.
C. USE FRACTIONAL INCH DIMENSIONS.
GRIDS ARE 1/4".

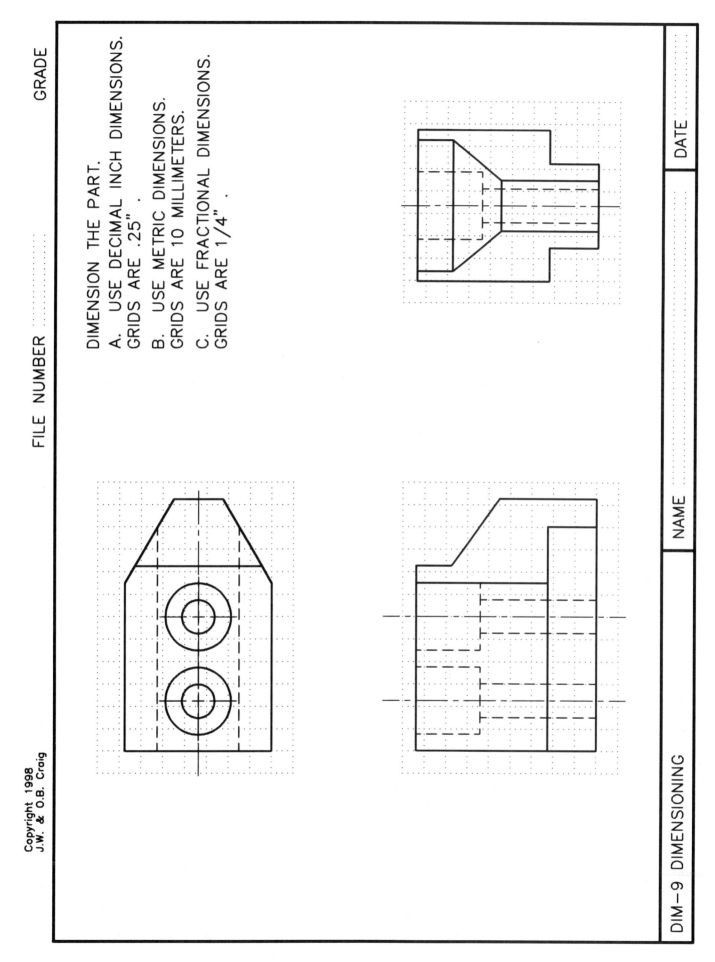

GRADE

FILE NUMBER

DIMENSION THE PART.
A. USE DECIMAL INCH DIMENSIONS.
    GRIDS ARE .25".
B. USE METRIC DIMENSIONS.
    GRIDS ARE 10 MILLIMETERS.
C. USE FRACTIONAL DIMENSIONS.
    GRIDS ARE 1/4".

DATE

NAME

DIM—9 DIMENSIONING

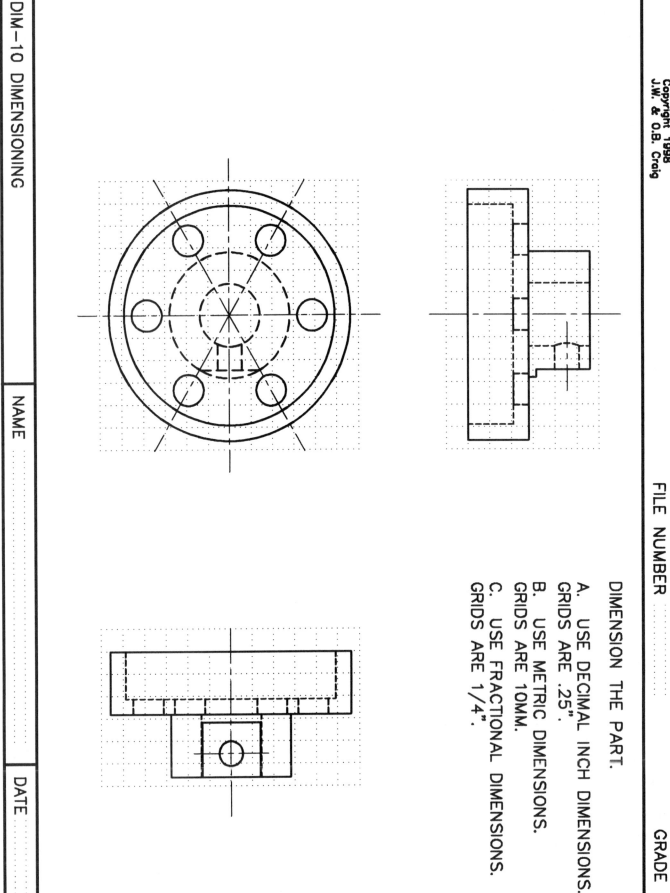

FILE NUMBER ....   GRADE ....

DIMENSION THE PART.

A. USE DECIMAL INCH DIMENSIONS.
    GRIDS ARE .25".

B. USE METRIC DIMENSIONS.
    GRIDS ARE 10MM.

C. USE FRACTIONAL DIMENSIONS.
    GRIDS ARE 1/4".

DIM-10 DIMENSIONING

NAME ....

DATE ....

Tolerance Basics

All dimensions have a tolerance. Exceptions are those dimensions labeled REF, BSC, MIN or MAX. Building parts to very close sizes is expensive. Some areas of each part have a critical relation to mating parts which requires high accuracy. Other areas of parts may be more for appearance or strength. Part of the dimensioning process is to control the location and size of each feature to only the accuracy necessary to assure the part will function properly.

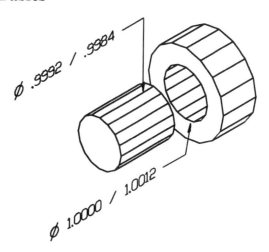

Three levels of tolerances may be identified.

__1. General tolerances. These are keyed to a TOLERANCE BLOCK in the drawing title block. (Page M - 3).

__2. Shop. Local practice based on machines and craftsmen available. These tolerances are chosen from tables or information provided by the shop. (Page M - 4).

__3. Functional. Very close tolerances which must be specified regardless of cost. These are used where the function of the parts is the overriding factor. These sizes are selected from the ANSI Limits and Fits Tables.

There is no sharp line between each of the types of tolerances. Any set of dimensions on a part may contain sizes relating to the three types.

```
TOLERANCES (IN.)
.X   = ± .1
.XX  = ± .03
.XXX = ± .010

TOLERANCES (METRIC)
NO DECIMALS  = ± .8MM
ONE DECIMAL  = ± .3MM

TOLERANCES (ANGULAR)
± 1/2 °
UNLESS OTHERWISE
NOTED
```

Tolerance is the allowable variation from the nominal size. Tolerances may be expressed in several ways:

__Bilateral. 1.000 +/- .002

__Unilateral 1.000 +000 / -.004

__Limit 1.000 / .996 or 1.000MAX .996MIN

Nominal size is the design size. Some calculations use the Nominal size to determine the actual maximum and minimum. In the example above, the Nominal size is "one inch".

```
NOTE TO DESIGNERS:
REL 7-5-XX
MINIMUM MILLING TOLERANCES
TO .5 IN -- .003
.5 TO 1.00 -- .004
1.00 TO 3.00 -- .005
3.00 TO 4.50 -- .006
4.50 TO 8.00 -- .007
```

A <u>Clearance Fit</u> occurs when two parts slide together freely. In this example, the groove in "2" is always wider than the thickness of "1". Limit dimensions must be calculated so that "1" can never be thicker than the minimum width of the groove.

<u>Allowance (for clearance fits)</u> is the minimum clearance between the two parts.

__If the width of the groove is the basis for calculation, then the width will be the nominal size or slightly wider.

__Example: Nominal = 1.000   Allowance = .001
               Tolerance = .004
__Groove = 1.000 MIN to 1.004 MAX
__Maximum thickness of "1" is .999
__Thickness of "1" = .999 MAX to .995 MIN

__Best case clearance = .001
__Worst case clearance = .009

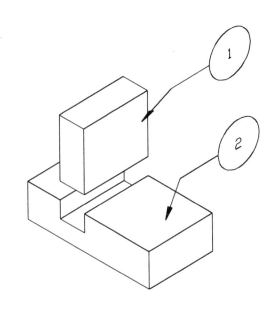

An <u>Interference fit</u> occurs when the two parts must be forced together. The groove in this case is always narrower than the thickness of "1". Limit dimensions must be calculated so that the width of the groove can never be wider than "1" is thick.

<u>Allowance (for force fits)</u> is the maximum interference permissible.

__Example: Nominal 1.000   Allowance = .009
              Tolerance = .004
__Groove = 1.000 MIN to 1.004 MAX
__Maximum thickness of "1" = 1.009
__Thickness of "1" = 1.009 MAX to 1.005 MIN
__Maximum interference is .009
__Minimum interference is .001

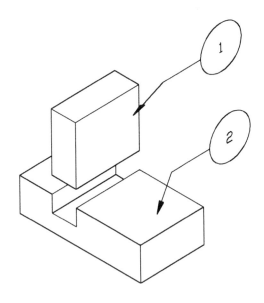

<u>Allowance is defined as the tightest permissible fit</u>. Study the examples above to verify this concept. Allowance is very important in setting up the calculations which determine the actual limit dimensions.

When many parts are manufactured and assembled at random, pairs of parts may by chance come close to the extremes for best case or worst case. These pairs of parts may not function properly. So, manufacturers must expect a percentage of warranty problems.

Other fits are used between the extremes shown. <u>Transition fits</u> permit ranges from close sliding to light interference between mating parts.

General -- Tolerance Block -- Tolerances

Fractional inch dimensions may have a title block tolerance of +/- 1/64".

The 2 1/4" dimension could be:
__2 15/64 MIN
__2 17/64 MAX
and still pass inspection.

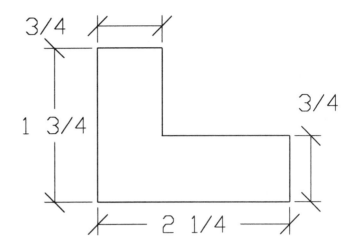

(Note: See Tolerance Block page M - 1.)

Decimal inch dimensions. The number of decimal places shown is keyed to the tolerance block to indicate the tolerance..

When converting fractions to decimals, be careful how many decimal places you show.

__Dimension A. The 2.2 indicates a tolerance of +/- .1 in. 2.1 MIN 2.3 MAX
__Dimension B. The 1.76 indicates a tolerance of +/- .03 in. 1.73 MIN 1.79 MAX.
__Dimension C. The 0.750 indicates a tolerance of +/- .010 in. .740 MIN .760 MAX.

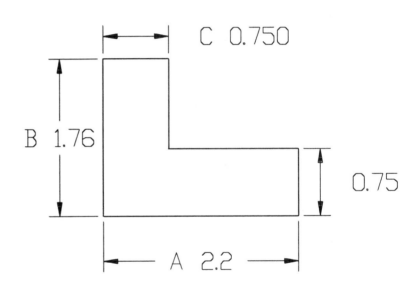

(Note: See Tolerance Block page M-1).

Metric dimensions are most often shown to the closest millimeter for general sizes.
__Dimension A. The tolerance for a no decimal place dimension might be +/- .8mm. Or, 57.2 MIN 58.8 MAX.
__Dimension B. The tolerance on a one decimal place dimension might be +/- .3mm. Or, 43.9 MIN 44.5 MAX.

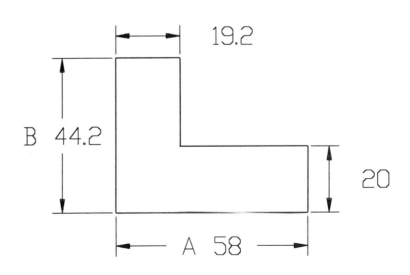

Shop Tolerances

Shop Tolerances relate to local manufacturing capabilities. These capabilities include the age and condition of machine tools, the experience and expertise of machinists and the quality of materials, tools, fixtures, coolants, etc. Many companies will issue recommended minimum tolerances for use by designers. These might balance tolerance ranges based on the needs of the design while keeping costs down.

USA STANDARD

Tolerance values are in thousandths of an inch. Data in bold face are in accordance with ABC agreements.

Nominal Size Range Inches Over To	Grade 4	Grade 5	Grade 6	Grade 7	Grade 8	Grade 9	Grade 10	Grade 11	Grade 12	Grade 13
0 — 0.12	0.12	0.15	0.25	0.4	0.6	1.0	1.6	2.5	4	6
0.12 — 0.24	0.15	0.20	0.3	0.5	0.7	1.2	1.8	3.0	5	7
0.24 — 0.40	0.15	0.25	0.4	0.6	0.9	1.4	2.2	3.5	6	9
0.40 — 0.71	0.2	0.3	0.4	0.7	1.0	1.6	2.8	4.0	7	10
0.71 — 1.19	0.25	0.4	0.5	0.8	1.2	2.0	3.5	5.0	8	12
1.19 — 1.97	0.3	0.4	0.6	1.0	1.6	2.5	4.0	6	10	16
1.97 — 3.15	0.3	0.5	0.7	1.2	1.8	3.0	4.5	7	12	18
3.15 — 4.73	0.4	0.6	0.9	1.4	2.2	3.5	5	9	14	22
4.73 — 7.09	0.5	0.7	1.0	1.6	2.5	4.0	6	10	16	25
7.09 — 9.85	0.6	0.8	1.2	1.8	2.8	4.5	7	12	18	28
9.85 — 12.41	0.6	0.9	1.2	2.0	3.0	5.0	8	12	20	30
12.41 — 15.75	0.7	1.0	1.4	2.2	3.5	6	9	14	22	35
15.75 — 19.69	0.8	1.0	1.6	2.5	4	6	10	16	25	40
19.69 — 30.09	0.9	1.2	2.0	3	5	8	12	20	30	50
30.09 — 41.49	1.0	1.6	2.5	4	6	10	16	25	40	60
41.49 — 56.19	1.2	2.0	3	5	8	12	20	30	50	80
56.19 — 76.39	1.6	2.5	4	6	10	16	25	40	60	100
76.39 — 100.9	2.0	3	5	8	12	20	30	50	80	125
100.9 — 131.9	2.5	4	6	10	16	25	40	60	100	160
131.9 — 171.9	3	5	8	12	20	30	50	80	125	200
171.9 — 200	4	6	10	16	25	40	60	100	160	250

Shop Process: Costly ....Economical

Lapping and Honing

Cylindrical Grinding

Broaching

Reaming

Turning

Boring

Milling

Drilling

Shop Tolerances -- continued

Note: Table page M - 4. Find the nominal size in the left column. Look across for the tolerance in thousandths on an inch.

3/4" dia. holes are to be drilled in a plate. What is a reasonable economical tolerance specification?
See chart page M - 4.
__Grade 13 tolerance would be .012 so .750 +/- .006 would work.
__Grade 12 tolerance would be .008 so a closer tolerance would be .750 +/- .004.

Similar unilateral tolerances could be applied.

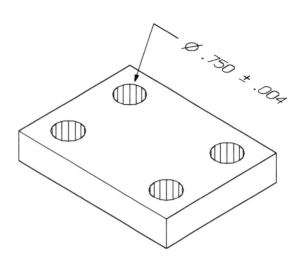

A close fitting 1/2" diameter hole must be reamed in the part shown. What is a reasonable drill size and ream tolerance?

When a hole is to be reamed it must be drilled undersize then reamed to the necessary diameter.
__The closest drill size is 31/64
__From the chart on M - 4, the tolerance might be .0007.
__Note: 31/64 DRILL .5000 +/- .0004 REAM

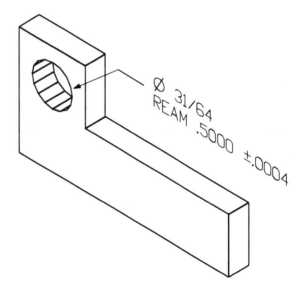

Two diameters are to be machined. A .800 diameter is to be turned and a 1.250 diameter is to be cylindrical ground. See chart page M - 4.

__A reasonable tolerance for turning the .800 diameter - Grade 11 - might be .005 (or .006). So, .800 +/- .003

__Cylindrical grinding tolerance for a 1.250 diameter - Grade 7 - might be .001 so, 1.250 +/- .0005 would work.

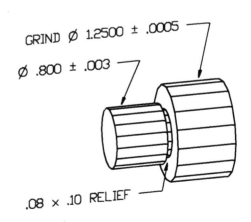

Functional Tolerances -- ANSI Limits and Fits --Inch System

ANSI Limits and Fits are divided into types as shown below. These examples are exerpted by permission.

8.2 Designation of Standard Fits. Standard fits are designated by means of the symbols given below to facilitate reference to classes of fit for educational purposes. These symbols are not intended to be shown on manufacturing drawings; instead, sizes should be specified on drawings.

The letter symbols used are as follows:

RC Running or Sliding Clearance Fit
LC Locational Clearance Fit .
LT Transition Clearance or Interference Fit
LN Locational Interference Fit
FN Force or Shrink Fit

These letter symbols are used in conjunction with numbers representing the class of fit; thus "FN 4" represents a class 4, force fit.

Each of these symbols (two letters and a number) represents a complete fit, for which the minimum and maximum clearance or interference, and the limits of size for the mating parts, are given directly in the tables.

A sample of the RC table is shown below. Using the RC4 column for a nominal 1.000 diameter. Note that the numbers in the table are in <u>thousandths</u>.

Hole: 1.0000 +.0012 - .0000
      1.0012 MAX 1.0000 MIN
Shaft 1.0000 - .0008 = .9992
Shaft 1.0000 - .0016 = .9984
      .9992 MAX .9984 MIN

These fits may be described briefly as follows:

RC1 *Close sliding fits* are intended for the accurate location of parts which must assemble without perceptible play.

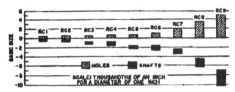

FIG. 1 GRAPHICAL REPRESENTATION OF STANDARD RUNNING OR SLIDING CLEARANCE FITS (SHOWN IN TABLE 5)

RC 2 *Sliding fits* are intended for accurate location but with greater maximum clearance than class RC1. Parts made to this fit move and turn easily but are not intended to run freely, and in the larger sizes may seize with small temperature changes.

RC 3 *Precision running fits* are about the closest fits which can be expected to run freely, and are intended for precision work at slow speeds and light journal pressures, but are not suitable where appreciable temperature differences are likely to be encountered

RC 4 *Close running fits* are intended chiefly for running fits on accurate machinery with moderate surface speeds and journal pressures, where accurate location and minimum play is desired.

RC 5 } *Medium running fits* are intended for higher running speeds, or heavy journal pressures,
RC 6 } or both.

RC 7 *Free running fits* are intended for use where accuracy is not essential, or where large temperature variations are likely to be encountered, or under both of these conditions.

RC 8 } *Loose running fits* are intended for use where wide commercial tolerances may be necessary, together with an allowance, on
RC 9 } the external member.

TABLE 5 RUNNING AND SLIDING FITS

Limits are in thousandths of an inch.

Limits for hole and shaft are applied algebraically to the basic size to obtain the limits of size for the parts.

Data in bold face are in accordance with ABC agreements.

Symbols H5, g5, etc., are Hole and Shaft designations used in ABC System (Appendix I).

Nominal
1.0000 →

Nominal Size Range Inches		Class RC 1			Class RC 2			Class RC 3			Class RC 4		
		Limits of Clearance	Standard Limits		Limits of Clearance	Standard Limits		Limits of Clearance	Standard Limits		Limits of Clearance	Standard Limits	
Over	To		Hole H5	Shaft g4		Hole H6	Shaft g5		Hole H7	Shaft f6		Hole H8	Shaft f7
0	— 0.12	0.1 0.45	+ 0.2 0	− 0.1 − 0.25	0.1 0.55	+ 0.25 0	− 0.1 − 0.3	0.3 0.95	+ 0.4 0	− 0.3 − 0.55	0.3 1.3	+ 0.6 0	− 0.3 − 0.7
0.12	— 0.24	0.15 0.5	+ 0.2 0	− 0.15 − 0.3	0.15 0.65	+ 0.3 0	− 0.15 − 0.35	0.4 1.2	+ 0.5 0	− 0.4 − 0.7	0.4 1.6	+ 0.7 0	− 0.4 − 0.9
0.24	— 0.40	0.2 0.6	+ 0.25 0	− 0.2 − 0.35	0.2 0.85	+ 0.4 0	− 0.2 − 0.45	0.5 1.5	+ 0.6 0	− 0.5 − 0.9	0.5 2.0	+ 0.9 0	− 0.5 − 1.1
0.40	— 0.71	0.25 0.75	+ 0.3 0	− 0.25 − 0.45	0.25 0.95	+ 0.4 0	− 0.25 − 0.55	0.6 1.7	+ 0.7 0	− 0.6 − 1.0	0.6 2.3	+ 1.0 0	− 0.6 − 1.3
0.71	— 1.19	0.3 0.95	+ 0.4 0	− 0.3 − 0.55	0.3 1.2	+ 0.5 0	− 0.3 − 0.7	0.8 2.1	+ 0.8 0	− 0.8 − 1.3	0.8 2.8	+ 1.2 0	− 0.8 − 1.6
1.19	— 1.97	0.4 1.1	+ 0.4 0	− 0.4 − 0.7	0.4 1.4	+ 0.6 0	− 0.4 − 0.8	1.0 2.6	+ 1.0 0	− 1.0 − 1.6	1.0 3.6	+ 1.6 0	− 1.0 − 2.0
1.97	— 3.15	0.4	+ 0.5	− 0.4	0.4	+ 0.7	− 0.4	1.2	+ 1.2	− 1.2	1.2	+ 1.8	− 1.2

ANSI Limits and Fits -- Metric

Preferred nominal or basic stock sizes are shown in Table 1. These sizes also appear in subsequent tables. Designers should use these sizes when possible.

Metric limits and fits provide two sets of design tables for Functional tolerances. Fig. 1 below depicts the "Basic Hole System" geometry. This is based upon the use of standard size hole cutting tools. Sizes are toleranced from the nominal hole size.

The Hole Size Basis for determining limits and fits is often preferred.

Table 1   Preferred Sizes

First Choice	Second Choice	First Choice	Second Choice	First Choice	Second Choice
1		10		100	
	1.1		11		110
1.2		12		120	
	1.4		14		140
1.6		16		160	
	1.8		18		180
2		20		200	
	2.2		22		220
2.5		25		250	
	2.8		28		280
3		30		300	
	3.5		35		350
4		40		400	
	4.5		45		450
5		50		500	
	5.5		55		550
6		60		600	
	7		70		700
8		80		800	
	9		90		900
				1000	

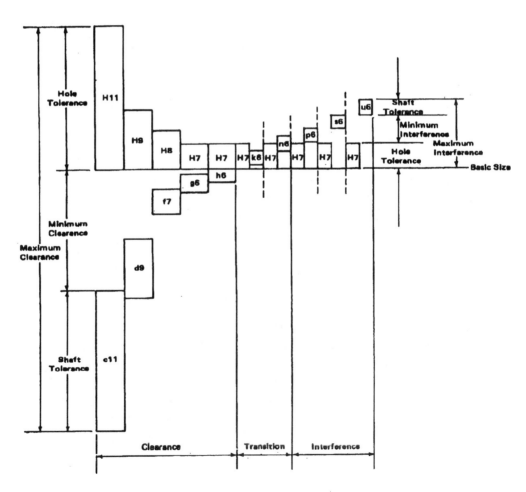

FIG. 4   PREFERRED HOLE BASIS FITS

Metric Tolerances -- continued

Shaft Basis fits may be used when precision size stock is specified. This design system is useful when there are force fits and running fits on the same shaft. The shaft diameter stays the same along the entire length. Hole sizes in mating parts are adjusted for force or running fit.

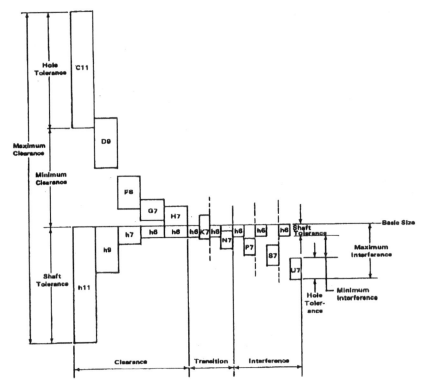

FIG. 5 PREFERRED SHAFT BASIS FITS

Metric Limits and Fits tables may be used for either Hole Basis or Shaft Basis design. Preferred combinations are shown.

Example:
By designating a shaft design of "h6", free running hole sizes may be obtained using a D9 table. Force fit sizes may be obtained using a S7 table.

ISO SYMBOL		DESCRIPTION
Hole Basis	Shaft Basis	
H11/c11	C11/h11	*Loose running* fit for wide commercial tolerances or allowances on external members.
H9/d9	D9/h9	*Free running* fit not for use where accuracy is essential, but good for large temperature variations, high running speeds, or heavy journal pressures.
H8/f7	F8/h7	*Close running* fit for running on accurate machines and for accurate location at moderate speeds and journal pressures.
H7/g6	G7/h6	*Sliding* fit not intended to run freely, but to move and turn freely and locate accurately.
H7/h6	H7/h6	*Locational clearance* fit provides snug fit for locating stationary parts; but can be freely assembled and disassembled.
H7/k6	K7/h6	*Locational transition* fit for accurate location, a compromise between clearance and interference.
H7/n6	N7/h6	*Locational transition* fit for more accurate location where greater interference is permissible.
H7/p6[1]	P7/h6	*Locational interference* fit for parts requiring rigidity and alignment with prime accuracy of location but without special bore pressure requirements.
H7/s6	S7/h6	*Medium drive* fit for ordinary steel parts or shrink fits on light sections, the tightest fit usable with cast iron.
H7/u6	U7/h6	*Force* fit suitable for parts which can be highly stressed or for shrink fits where the heavy pressing forces required are impractical.

Clearance Fits / Transition Fits / Interference Fits

More Clearance / More Interference

[1] Transition fit for basic sizes in range from 0 through 3 mm.

FIG. 6 DESCRIPTION OF PREFERRED FITS

Metric Tolerances -- continued

Metric limits are shown directly in the tables. Locate the Nominal size in the left hand column and look across to find the actual sizes to specify.

In this example, a 3mm Nominal size and a Loose Running fit were chosen.

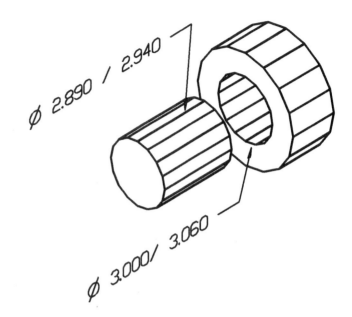

TABLE 2 PREFERRED HOLE BASIS CLEARANCE FITS

BASIC SIZE		LOOSE RUNNING			FREE RUNNING			CLOSE RUNNING		
		Hole H11	Shaft c11	Fit	Hole H9	Shaft d9	Fit	Hole H8	Shaft f7	Fit
1	MAX	1·060	0·940	0·180	1·025	0·980	0·070	1·014	0·994	0·030
	MIN	1·000	0·880	0·060	1·000	0·955	0·020	1·000	0·984	0·006
1·2	MAX	1·260	1·140	0·180	1·225	1·180	0·070	1·214	1·194	0·030
	MIN	1·200	1·080	0·060	1·200	1·155	0·020	1·200	1·184	0·006
1·6	MAX	1·660	1·540	0·180	1·625	1·580	0·070	1·614	1·594	0·030
	MIN	1·600	1·480	0·060	1·600	1·555	0·020	1·600	1·584	0·006
2	MAX	2·060	1·940	0·180	2·025	1·980	0·070	2·014	1·994	0·030
	MIN	2·000	1·880	0·060	2·000	1·955	0·020	2·000	1·984	0·006
2·5	MAX	2·560	2·440	0·180	2·525	2·480	0·070	2·514	2·494	0·030
	MIN	2·500	2·380	0·060	2·500	2·455	0·020	2·500	2·484	0·006
3	MAX	3·060	2·940	0·180	3·025	2·980	0·070	3·014	2·994	0·030
	MIN	3·000	2·880	0·060	3·000	2·955	0·020	3·000	2·984	0·006
4	MAX	4·075	3·930	0·220	4·030	3·970	0·090	4·018	3·990	0·040
	MIN	4·000	3·855	0·070	4·000	3·940	0·030	4·000	3·978	0·010

TABLE 5 RUNNING AND SLIDING FITS
Limits are in thousandths of an inch.

Limits for hole and shaft are applied algebraically to the basic size to obtain the limits of size for the parts.

Data in bold face are in accordance with ABC agreements.

Symbols H5, g5, etc., are Hole and Shaft designations used in ABC System (Appendix I).

Nominal Size Range Inches (Over – To)	RC1 Limits of Clearance	RC1 Hole H5	RC1 Shaft g4	RC2 Limits of Clearance	RC2 Hole H6	RC2 Shaft g5	RC3 Limits of Clearance	RC3 Hole H7	RC3 Shaft f6	RC4 Limits of Clearance	RC4 Hole H8	RC4 Shaft f7
0 – 0.12	0.1 / 0.45	+0.2 / 0	−0.1 / −0.25	0.1 / 0.55	+0.25 / 0	−0.1 / −0.3	0.3 / 0.95	+0.4 / 0	−0.3 / −0.55	0.3 / 1.3	+0.6 / 0	−0.3 / −0.7
0.12 – 0.24	0.15 / 0.5	+0.2 / 0	−0.15 / −0.3	0.15 / 0.65	+0.3 / 0	−0.15 / −0.35	0.4 / 1.2	+0.5 / 0	−0.4 / −0.7	0.4 / 1.6	+0.7 / 0	−0.4 / −0.9
0.24 – 0.40	0.2 / 0.6	+0.25 / 0	−0.2 / −0.35	0.2 / 0.85	+0.4 / 0	−0.2 / −0.45	0.5 / 1.5	+0.6 / 0	−0.5 / −0.9	0.5 / 2.0	+0.9 / 0	−0.5 / −1.1
0.40 – 0.71	0.25 / 0.75	+0.3 / 0	−0.25 / −0.45	0.25 / 0.95	+0.4 / 0	−0.25 / −0.55	0.6 / 1.7	+0.7 / 0	−0.6 / −1.0	0.6 / 2.3	+1.0 / 0	−0.6 / −1.3
0.71 – 1.19	0.3 / 0.95	+0.4 / 0	−0.3 / −0.55	0.3 / 1.2	+0.5 / 0	−0.3 / −0.7	0.8 / 2.1	+0.8 / 0	−0.8 / −1.3	0.8 / 2.8	+1.2 / 0	−0.8 / −1.6
1.19 – 1.97	0.4 / 1.1	+0.4 / 0	−0.4 / −0.7	0.4 / 1.4	+0.6 / 0	−0.4 / −0.8	1.0 / 2.6	+1.0 / 0	−1.0 / −1.6	1.0 / 3.6	+1.6 / 0	−1.0 / −2.0
1.97 – 3.15	0.4 / 1.2	+0.5 / 0	−0.4 / −0.7	0.4 / 1.6	+0.7 / 0	−0.4 / −0.9	1.2 / 3.1	+1.2 / 0	−1.2 / −1.9	1.2 / 4.2	+1.8 / 0	−1.2 / −2.4
3.15 – 4.73	0.5 / 1.5	+0.6 / 0	−0.5 / −0.9	0.5 / 2.0	+0.9 / 0	−0.5 / −1.1	1.4 / 3.7	+1.4 / 0	−1.4 / −2.3	1.4 / 5.0	+2.2 / 0	−1.4 / −2.8
4.73 – 7.09	0.6 / 1.8	+0.7 / 0	−0.6 / −1.1	0.6 / 2.3	+1.0 / 0	−0.6 / −1.3	1.6 / 4.2	+1.6 / 0	−1.6 / −2.6	1.6 / 5.7	+2.5 / 0	−1.6 / −3.2
7.09 – 9.85	0.6 / 2.0	+0.8 / 0	−0.6 / −1.2	0.6 / 2.6	+1.2 / 0	−0.6 / −1.4	2.0 / 5.0	+1.8 / 0	−2.0 / −3.2	2.0 / 6.6	+2.8 / 0	−2.0 / −3.8
9.85 – 12.41	0.8 / 2.3	+0.9 / 0	−0.8 / −1.4	0.7 / 2.8	+1.2 / 0	−0.7 / −1.6	2.5 / 5.7	+2.0 / 0	−2.5 / −3.7	2.2 / 7.2	+3.0 / 0	−2.2 / −4.2
12.41 – 15.75	1.0 / 2.7	+1.0 / 0	−1.0 / −1.7	0.7 / 3.1	+1.4 / 0	−0.7 / −1.7	3.0 / 6.6	+2.2 / 0	−3.0 / −4.4	2.5 / 8.2	+3.5 / 0	−2.5 / −4.7
15.75 – 19.69	1.2 / 3.0	+1.0 / 0	−1.2 / −2.0	0.8 / 3.4	+1.6 / 0	−0.8 / −1.8	4.0 / 8.1	+2.5 / 0	−4.0 / −5.6	2.8 / 9.3	+4.0 / 0	−2.8 / −5.3
19.69 – 30.09	1.6 / 3.7	+1.2 / 0	−1.6 / −2.5	1.6 / 4.8	+2.0 / 0	−1.6 / −2.8	5.0 / 10.0	+3.0 / 0	−5.0 / −7.0	5.0 / 13.0	+5.0 / 0	−5.0 / −8.0
30.09 – 41.49	2.0 / 4.6	+1.6 / 0	−2.0 / −3.0	2.0 / 6.1	+2.5 / 0	−2.0 / −3.6	6.0 / 12.5	+4.0 / 0	−6.0 / −8.5	6.0 / 16.0	+6.0 / 0	−6.0 / −10.0
41.49 – 56.19	2.5 / 5.7	+2.0 / 0	−2.5 / −3.7	2.5 / 7.5	+3.0 / 0	−2.5 / −4.5	8.0 / 16.0	+5.0 / 0	−8.0 / −11.0	8.0 / 21.0	+8.0 / 0	−8.0 / −13.0
56.19 – 76.39	3.0 / 7.1	+2.5 / 0	−3.0 / −4.6	3.0 / 9.5	+4.0 / 0	−3.0 / −5.5	10.0 / 20.0	+6.0 / 0	−10.0 / −14.0	10.0 / 26.0	+10.0 / 0	−10.0 / −16.0
76.39 – 100.9	4.0 / 9.0	+3.0 / 0	−4.0 / −6.0	4.0 / 12.0	+5.0 / 0	−4.0 / −7.0	12.0 / 25.0	+8.0 / 0	−12.0 / −17.0	12.0 / 32.0	+12.0 / 0	−12.0 / −20.0
100.9 – 131.9	5.0 / 11.5	+4.0 / 0	−5.0 / −7.5	5.0 / 15.0	+6.0 / 0	−5.0 / −9.0	16.0 / 32.0	+10.0 / 0	−16.0 / −22.0	16.0 / 42.0	+16.0 / 0	−16.0 / −26.0
131.9 – 171.9	6.0 / 14.0	+5.0 / 0	−6.0 / −9.0	6.0 / 19.0	+8.0 / 0	−6.0 / −11.0	18.0 / 38.0	+12.0 / 0	−18.0 / −26.0	18.0 / 50.0	+20.0 / 0	−18.0 / −30.0
171.9 – 200	8.0 / 18.0	+6.0 / 0	−8.0 / −12.0	8.0 / 22.0	+10.0 / 0	−8.0 / −12.0	22.0 / 48.0	+16.0 / 0	−22.0 / −32.0	22.0 / 63.0	+25.0 / 0	−22.0 / −38.0

Continued on page 7

TABLE 5 RUNNING AND SLIDING FITS (continued from page 10)

Limits are in thousandths of an inch.

Limits for hole and shaft are applied algebraically to the basic size to obtain the limits of size for the parts

Data in bold face are in accordance with ABC agreements

Symbols H8, e7, etc., are Hole and Shaft designations used in ABC System (Appendix I).

Class RC 5			Class RC 6			Class RC 7			Class RC 8			Class RC 9			Nominal Size Range Inches	
Limits of Clearance	Standard Limits		Limits of Clearance	Standard Limits		Limits of Clearance	Standard Limits		Limits of Clearance	Standard Limits		Limits of Clearance	Standard Limits			
	Hole H8	Shaft e7		Hole H9	Shaft e8		Hole H9	Shaft d8		Hole H10	Shaft c9		Hole H11	Shaft	Over	To
0.6 / 1.6	+0.6 / -0	-0.6 / -1.0	0.6 / 2.2	+1.0 / -0	-0.6 / -1.2	1.0 / 2.6	+1.0 / 0	-1.0 / -1.6	2.5 / 5.1	+1.6 / 0	-2.5 / -3.5	4.0 / 8.1	+2.5 / 0	-4.0 / -5.6	0 -	0.12
0.8 / 2.0	+0.7 / -0	-0.8 / -1.3	0.8 / 2.7	+1.2 / -0	-0.8 / -1.5	1.2 / 3.1	+1.2 / 0	-1.2 / -1.9	2.8 / 5.8	+1.8 / 0	-2.8 / -4.0	4.5 / 9.0	+3.0 / 0	-4.5 / -6.0	0.12-	0.24
1.0 / 2.5	+0.9 / -0	-1.0 / -1.6	1.0 / 3.3	+1.4 / -0	-1.0 / -1.9	1.6 / 3.9	+1.4 / 0	-1.6 / -2.5	3.0 / 6.6	+2.2 / 0	-3.0 / -4.4	5.0 / 10.7	+3.5 / 0	-5.0 / -7.2	0.24-	0.40
1.2 / 2.9	+1.0 / -0	-1.2 / -1.9	1.2 / 3.8	+1.6 / -0	-1.2 / -2.2	2.0 / 4.6	+1.6 / 0	-2.0 / -3.0	3.5 / 7.9	+2.8 / 0	-3.5 / -5.1	6.0 / 12.8	+4.0 / -0	-6.0 / -8.8	0.40-	0.71
1.6 / 3.6	+1.2 / -0	-1.6 / -2.4	1.6 / 4.8	+2.0 / -0	-1.6 / -2.8	2.5 / 5.7	+2.0 / 0	-2.5 / -3.7	4.5 / 10.0	+3.5 / 0	-4.5 / -6.5	7.0 / 15.5	+5.0 / 0	-7.0 / -10.5	0.71-	1.19
2.0 / 4.6	+1.6 / -0	-2.0 / -3.0	2.0 / 6.1	+2.5 / -0	-2.0 / -3.6	3.0 / 7.1	+2.5 / 0	-3.0 / -4.6	5.0 / 11.5	+4.0 / 0	-5.0 / -7.5	8.0 / 18.0	+6.0 / 0	-8.0 / -12.0	1.19-	1.97
2.5 / 5.5	+1.8 / -0	-2.5 / -3.7	2.5 / 7.3	+3.0 / -0	-2.5 / -4.3	4.0 / 8.8	+3.0 / 0	-4.0 / -5.8	6.0 / 13.5	+4.5 / 0	-6.0 / -9.0	9.0 / 20.5	+7.0 / 0	-9.0 / -13.5	1.97-	3.15
3.0 / 6.6	+2.2 / -0	-3.0 / -4.4	3.0 / 8.7	+3.5 / -0	-3.0 / -5.2	5.0 / 10.7	+3.5 / 0	-5.0 / -7.2	7.0 / 15.5	+5.0 / 0	-7.0 / -10.5	10.0 / 24.0	+9.0 / 0	-10.0 / -15.0	3.15-	4.73
3.5 / 7.6	+2.5 / -0	-3.5 / -5.1	3.5 / 10.0	+4.0 / -0	-3.5 / -6.0	6.0 / 12.5	+4.0 / 0	-6.0 / -8.5	8.0 / 18.0	+6.0 / 0	-8.0 / -12.0	12.0 / 28.0	+10.0 / 0	-12.0 / -18.0	4.73-	7.09
4.0 / 8.6	+2.8 / -0	-4.0 / -5.8	4.0 / 11.3	+4.5 / 0	-4.0 / -6.8	7.0 / 14.3	+4.5 / 0	-7.0 / -9.8	10.0 / 21.5	+7.0 / 0	-10.0 / -14.5	15.0 / 34.0	+12.0 / 0	-15.0 / -22.0	7.09-	9.85
5.0 / 10.0	+3.0 / 0	-5.0 / -7.0	5.0 / 13.0	+5.0 / 0	-5.0 / -8.0	8.0 / 16.0	+5.0 / 0	-8.0 / -11.0	12.0 / 25.0	+8.0 / 0	-12.0 / -17.0	18.0 / 38.0	+12.0 / 0	-18.0 / -26.0	9.85-	12.41
6.0 / 11.7	+3.5 / 0	-6.0 / -8.2	6.0 / 15.5	+6.0 / 0	-6.0 / -9.5	10.0 / 19.5	+6.0 / 0	-10.0 / -13.5	14.0 / 29.0	+9.0 / 0	-14.0 / -20.0	22.0 / 45.0	+14.0 / 0	-22.0 / -31.0	12.41-	15.75
8.0 / 14.5	+4.0 / 0	-8.0 / -10.5	8.0 / 18.0	+6.0 / 0	-8.0 / -12.0	12.0 / 22.0	+6.0 / 0	-12.0 / -16.0	16.0 / 32.0	+10.0 / 0	-16.0 / -22.0	25.0 / 51.0	+16.0 / 0	-25.0 / -35.0	15.75-	19.69
10.0 / 18.0	+5.0 / 0	-10.0 / -13.0	10.0 / 23.0	+8.0 / 0	-10.0 / -15.0	16.0 / 29.0	+8.0 / 0	-16.0 / -21.0	20.0 / 40.0	+12.0 / 0	-20.0 / -28.0	30.0 / 62.0	+20.0 / 0	-30.0 / -42.0	19.69-	30.09
12.0 / 22.0	+6.0 / 0	-12.0 / -16.0	12.0 / 28.0	+10.0 / 0	-12.0 / -18.0	20.0 / 36.0	+10.0 / 0	-20.0 / -26.0	25.0 / 51.0	+16.0 / 0	-25.0 / -35.0	40.0 / 81.0	+25.0 / 0	-40.0 / -56.0	30.09-	41.49
16.0 / 29.0	+8.0 / 0	-16.0 / -21.0	16.0 / 36.0	+12.0 / 0	-16.0 / -24.0	25.0 / 45.0	+12.0 / 0	-25.0 / -33.0	30.0 / 62.0	+20.0 / 0	-30.0 / -42.0	50.0 / 100	+30.0 / 0	-50.0 / -70.0	41.49-	56.19
20.0 / 36.0	+10.0 / 0	-20.0 / -26.0	20.0 / 46.0	+16.0 / 0	-20.0 / -30.0	30.0 / 56.0	+16.0 / 0	-30.0 / -40.0	40.0 / 81.0	+25.0 / 0	-40.0 / -56.0	60.0 / 125	+40.0 / 0	-60.0 / -85.0	56.19-	76.39
25.0 / 45.0	+12.0 / 0	-25.0 / -33.0	25.0 / 57.0	+20.0 / 0	-25.0 / -37.0	40.0 / 72.0	+20.0 / 0	-40.0 / -52.0	50.0 / 100	+30.0 / 0	-50.0 / -70.0	80.0 / 160	+50.0 / 0	-80.0 / -110	76.39-	100.9
30.0 / 56.0	+16.0 / 0	-30.0 / -40.0	30.0 / 71.0	+25.0 / 0	-30.0 / -46.0	50.0 / 91.0	+25.0 / 0	-50.0 / -66.0	60.0 / 125	+40.0 / 0	-60.0 / -85.0	100 / 200	+60.0 / 0	-100 / -140	100.9 -	131.9
35.0 / 67.0	+20.0 / 0	-35.0 / -47.0	35.0 / 85.0	+30.0 / 0	-35.0 / -55.0	60.0 / 110.0	+30.0 / 0	-60.0 / -80.0	80.0 / 160	+50.0 / 0	-80.0 / -110	130 / 260	+80.0 / 0	-130 / -180	131.9 -	171.9
45.0 / 86.0	+25.0 / 0	-45.0 / -61.0	45.0 / 110.0	+40.0 / 0	-45.0 / -70.0	80.0 / 145.0	+40.0 / 0	-80.0 / -105.0	100 / 200	+60.0 / 0	-100 / -140	150 / 310	+100 / 0	-150 / -210	171.9 -	200

End of Table 5

TABLE 6 LOCATIONAL CLEARANCE FITS
Limits are in thousandths of an inch.

Limits for hole and shaft are applied algebraically to the basic size to obtain the limits of size for the parts.

Data in bold face are in accordance with ABC agreements.

Symbols H6, h5, etc., are Hole and Shaft designations used in ABC System (Appendix I).

Nominal Size Range Inches Over	To	Class LC 1 Limits of Clearance	Std Hole H6	Std Shaft h5	Class LC 2 Limits of Clearance	Std Hole H7	Std Shaft h6	Class LC 3 Limits of Clearance	Std Hole H8	Std Shaft h7	Class LC 4 Limits of Clearance	Std Hole H10	Std Shaft h9	Class LC 5 Limits of Clearance	Std Hole H7	Std Shaft g6
0 –	0.12	0 / 0.45	+0.25 / –0	+0 / –0.2	0 / 0.65	+0.4 / –0	+0 / –0.25	0 / 1	+0.6 / –0	+0 / –0.4	0 / 2.6	+1.6 / –0	+0 / –1.0	0.1 / 0.75	+0.4 / –0	–0.1 / –0.35
0.12–	0.24	0 / 0.5	+0.3 / –0	+0 / –0.2	0 / 0.8	+0.5 / –0	+0 / –0.3	0 / 1.2	+0.7 / –0	+0 / –0.5	0 / 3.0	+1.8 / –0	+0 / –1.2	0.15 / 0.95	+0.5 / –0	–0.15 / –0.45
0.24–	0.40	0 / 0.65	+0.4 / –0	+0 / –0.25	0 / 1.0	+0.6 / –0	+0 / –0.4	0 / 1.5	+0.9 / –0	+0 / –0.6	0 / 3.6	+2.2 / –0	+0 / –1.4	0.2 / 1.2	+0.6 / –0	–0.2 / –0.6
0.40–	0.71	0 / 0.7	+0.4 / –0	+0 / –0.3	0 / 1.1	+0.7 / –0	+0 / –0.4	0 / 1.7	+1.0 / –0	+0 / –0.7	0 / 4.4	+2.8 / –0	+0 / –1.6	0.25 / 1.35	+0.7 / –0	–0.25 / –0.65
0.71–	1.19	0 / 0.9	+0.5 / –0	+0 / –0.4	0 / 1.3	+0.8 / –0	+0 / –0.5	0 / 2	+1.2 / –0	+0 / –0.8	0 / 5.5	+3.5 / –0	+0 / –2.0	0.3 / 1.6	+0.8 / –0	–0.3 / –0.8
1.19–	1.97	0 / 1.0	+0.6 / –0	+0 / –0.4	0 / 1.6	+1.0 / –0	+0 / –0.6	0 / 2.6	+1.6 / –0	+0 / –1	0 / 6.5	+4.0 / –0	+0 / –2.5	0.4 / 2.0	+1.0 / –0	–0.4 / –1.0
1.97–	3.15	0 / 1.2	+0.7 / –0	+0 / –0.5	0 / 1.9	+1.2 / –0	+0 / –0.7	0 / 3	+1.8 / –0	+0 / –1.2	0 / 7.5	+4.5 / –0	+0 / –3	0.4 / 2.3	+1.2 / –0	–0.4 / –1.1
3.15–	4.73	0 / 1.5	+0.9 / –0	+0 / –0.6	0 / 2.3	+1.4 / –0	+0 / –0.9	0 / 3.6	+2.2 / –0	+0 / –1.4	0 / 8.5	+5.0 / –0	+0 / –3.5	0.5 / 2.8	+1.4 / –0	–0.5 / –1.4
4.73–	7.09	0 / 1.7	+1.0 / –0	+0 / –0.7	0 / 2.6	+1.6 / –0	+0 / –1.0	0 / 4.1	+2.5 / –0	+0 / –1.6	0 / 10	+6.0 / –0	+0 / –4	0.6 / 3.2	+1.6 / –0	–0.6 / –1.6
7.09–	9.85	0 / 2.0	+1.2 / –0	+0 / –0.8	0 / 3.0	+1.8 / –0	+0 / –1.2	0 / 4.6	+2.8 / –0	+0 / –1.8	0 / 11.5	+7.0 / –0	+0 / –4.5	0.6 / 3.6	+1.8 / –0	–0.6 / –1.8
9.85–	12.41	0 / 2.1	+1.2 / –0	+0 / –0.9	0 / 3.2	+2.0 / –0	+0 / –1.2	0 / 5	+3.0 / –0	+0 / –2.0	0 / 13	+8.0 / –0	+0 / –5	0.7 / 3.9	+2.0 / –0	–0.7 / –1.9
12.41–	15.75	0 / 2.4	+1.4 / –0	+0 / –1.0	0 / 3.6	+2.2 / –0	+0 / –1.4	0 / 5.7	+3.5 / –0	+0 / –2.2	0 / 15	+9.0 / –0	+0 / –6	0.7 / 4.3	+2.2 / –0	–0.7 / –2.1
15.75–	19.69	0 / 2.8	+1.6 / –0	+0 / –1.0	0 / 4.1	+2.5 / –0	+0 / –1.6	0 / 6.5	+4 / –0	+0 / –2.5	0 / 16	+10.0 / –0	+0 / –6	0.8 / 4.9	+2.5 / –0	–0.8 / –2.4
19.69–	30.09	0 / 3.2	+2.0 / –0	+0 / –1.2	0 / 5.0	+3 / –0	+0 / –2	0 / 8	+5 / –0	+0 / –3	0 / 20	+12.0 / –0	+0 / –8	0.9 / 5.9	+3.0 / –0	–0.9 / –2.9
30.09–	41.49	0 / 4.1	+2.5 / –0	+0 / –1.6	0 / 6.5	+4 / –0	+0 / –2.5	0 / 10	+6 / –0	+0 / –4	0 / 26	+16.0 / –0	+0 / –10	1.0 / 7.5	+4.0 / –0	–1.0 / –3.5
41.49–	56.19	0 / 5.0	+3.0 / –0	+0 / –2.0	0 / 8.0	+5 / –0	+0 / –3	0 / 13	+8 / –0	+0 / –5	0 / 32	+20.0 / –0	+0 / –12	1.2 / 9.2	+5.0 / –0	–1.2 / –4.2
56.19–	76.39	0 / 6.5	+4.0 / –0	+0 / –2.5	0 / 10	+6 / –0	+0 / –4	0 / 16	+10 / –0	+0 / –6	0 / 41	+25.0 / –0	+0 / –16	1.2 / 11.2	+6.0 / –0	–1.2 / –5.2
76.39–	100.9	0 / 8.0	+5.0 / –0	+0 / –3.0	0 / 13	+8 / –0	+0 / –5	0 / 20	+12 / –0	+0 / –8	0 / 50	+30.0 / –0	+0 / –20	1.4 / 14.4	+8.0 / –0	–1.4 / –6.4
100.9 –	131.9	0 / 10.0	+6.0 / –0	+0 / –4.0	0 / 16	+10 / –0	+0 / –6	0 / 26	+16 / –0	+0 / –10	0 / 65	+40.0 / –0	+0 / –25	1.6 / 17.6	+10.0 / –0	–1.6 / –7.6
131.9 –	171.9	0 / 13.0	+8.0 / –0	+0 / –5.0	0 / 20	+12 / –0	+0 / –8	0 / 32	+20 / –0	+0 / –12	0 / 8	+50.0 / –0	+0 / –30	1.8 / 21.8	+12.0 / –0	–1.8 / –9.8
171.9 –	200	0 / 16.0	+10.0 / –0	+0 / –6.0	0 / 26	+16 / –0	+0 / –10	0 / 41	+25 / –0	+0 / –16	0 / 100	+60.0 / –0	+0 / –40	1.8 / 27.8	+16.0 / –0	–1.8 / –11.8

Continued on page 13

TABLE 6 LOCATIONAL CLEARANCE FITS (continued from page 12)

Limits are in thousandths of an inch.

Limits for hole and shaft are applied algebraically to the basic size to obtain the limits of size for the parts.

Data in bold face are in accordance with ABC agreements.

Symbols II9, f8, etc., are Hole and Shaft designations used in ABC System (Appendix I).

Class LC 6			Class LC 7			Class LC 8			Class LC 9			Class LC 10			Class LC 11			Nominal Size Range Inches	
Limits of Clearance	Hole H9	Shaft f8	Limits of Clearance	Hole H10	Shaft e9	Limits of Clearance	Hole H10	Shaft d9	Limits of Clearance	Hole H11	Shaft c10	Limits of Clearance	Hole H12	Shaft	Limits of Clearance	Hole H13	Shaft	Over	To
0.3 / 1.9	+1.0 / 0	−0.3 / −0.9	0.6 / 3.2	+1.6 / 0	−0.6 / −1.6	1.0 / 3.6	+1.6 / −0	−1.0 / −2.0	2.5 / 6.6	+2.5 / −0	−2.5 / −4.1	4 / 12	+4 / −0	−4 / −8	5 / 17	+6 / −0	−5 / −11	0	0.12
0.4 / 2.3	+1.2 / 0	−0.4 / −1.1	0.8 / 3.8	+1.8 / 0	−0.8 / −2.0	1.2 / 4.2	+1.8 / −0	−1.2 / −2.4	2.8 / 7.6	+3.0 / −0	−2.8 / −4.6	4.5 / 14.5	+5 / −0	−4.5 / −9.5	6 / 20	+7 / −0	−6 / −13	0.12	0.24
0.5 / 2.8	+1.4 / 0	−0.5 / −1.4	1.0 / 4.6	+2.2 / 0	−1.0 / −2.4	1.6 / 5.2	+2.2 / −0	−1.6 / −3.0	3.0 / 8.7	+3.5 / −0	−3.0 / −5.2	5 / 17	+6 / −0	−5 / −11	7 / 25	+9 / −0	−7 / −16	0.24	0.40
0.6 / 3.2	+1.6 / 0	−0.6 / −1.6	1.2 / 5.6	+2.8 / 0	−1.2 / −2.8	2.0 / 6.4	+2.8 / −0	−2.0 / −3.6	3.5 / 10.3	+4.0 / −0	−3.5 / −6.3	6 / 20	+7 / −0	−6 / −13	8 / 28	+10 / −0	−8 / −18	0.40	0.71
0.8 / 4.0	+2.0 / 0	−0.8 / −2.0	1.6 / 7.1	+3.5 / 0	−1.6 / −3.6	2.5 / 8.0	+3.5 / −0	−2.5 / −4.5	4.5 / 13.0	+5.0 / −0	−4.5 / −8.0	7 / 23	+8 / −0	−7 / −15	10 / 34	+12 / −0	−10 / −22	0.71	1.19
1.0 / 5.1	+2.5 / 0	−1.0 / −2.6	2.0 / 8.5	+4.0 / 0	−2.0 / −4.5	3.0 / 9.5	+4.0 / −0	−3.0 / −5.5	5 / 15	+6 / −0	−5 / −9	8 / 28	+10 / −0	−8 / −18	12 / 44	+16 / −0	−12 / −28	1.19	1.97
1.2 / 6.0	+3.0 / 0	−1.2 / −3.0	2.5 / 10.0	+4.5 / 0	−2.5 / −5.5	4.0 / 11.5	+4.5 / −0	−4.0 / −7.0	6 / 17.5	+7 / −0	−6 / −10.5	10 / 34	+12 / −0	−10 / −22	14 / 50	+18 / −0	−14 / −32	1.97	3.15
1.4 / 7.1	+3.5 / 0	−1.4 / −3.6	3.0 / 11.5	+5.0 / 0	−3.0 / −6.5	5.0 / 13.5	+5.0 / −0	−5.0 / −8.5	7 / 21	+9 / −0	−7 / −12	11 / 39	+14 / −0	−11 / −25	16 / 60	+22 / −0	−16 / −38	3.15	4.73
1.6 / 8.1	+4.0 / 0	−1.6 / −4.1	3.5 / 13.5	+6.0 / 0	−3.5 / −7.5	6 / 16	+6 / −0	−6 / −10	8 / 24	+10 / −0	−8 / −14	12 / 44	+16 / −0	−12 / −28	18 / 68	+25 / −0	−18 / −43	4.73	7.09
2.0 / 9.3	+4.5 / 0	−2.0 / −4.8	4.0 / 15.5	+7.0 / 0	−4.0 / −8.5	7 / 18.5	+7 / −0	−7 / −11.5	10 / 29	+12 / −0	−10 / −17	16 / 52	+18 / −0	−16 / −34	22 / 78	+28 / −0	−22 / −50	7.09	9.85
2.2 / 10.2	+5.0 / 0	−2.2 / −5.2	4.5 / 17.5	+8.0 / 0	−4.5 / −9.5	7 / 20	+8 / −0	−7 / −12	12 / 32	+12 / −0	−12 / −20	20 / 60	+20 / −0	−20 / −40	28 / 88	+30 / −0	−28 / −58	9.85	12.41
2.5 / 12.0	+6.0 / 0	−2.5 / −6.0	5.0 / 20.0	+9.0 / 0	−5 / −11	8 / 23	+9 / −0	−8 / −14	14 / 37	+14 / −0	−14 / −23	22 / 66	+22 / −0	−22 / −44	30 / 100	+35 / −0	−30 / −65	12.41	15.75
2.8 / 12.8	+6.0 / 0	−2.8 / −6.8	5.0 / 21.0	+10.0 / 0	−5 / −11	9 / 25	+10 / −0	−9 / −15	16 / 42	+16 / −0	−16 / −26	25 / 75	+25 / −0	−25 / −50	35 / 115	+40 / −0	−35 / −75	15.75	19.69
3.0 / 16.0	+8.0 / 0	−3.0 / −8.0	6.0 / 26.0	+12.0 / −0	−6 / −14	10 / 30	+12 / −0	−10 / −18	18 / 50	+20 / −0	−18 / −30	28 / 88	+30 / −0	−28 / −58	40 / 140	+50 / −0	−40 / −90	19.69	30.09
3.5 / 19.5	+10.0 / 0	−3.5 / −9.5	7.0 / 33.0	+16.0 / −0	−7 / −17	12 / 38	+16 / −0	−12 / −22	20 / 61	+25 / −0	−20 / −36	30 / 110	+40 / −0	−30 / −70	45 / 165	+60 / −0	−45 / −105	30.09	41.49
4.0 / 24.0	+12.0 / 0	−4.0 / −12.0	8.0 / 40.0	+20.0 / −0	−8 / −20	14 / 46	+20 / −0	−14 / −26	25 / 75	+30 / −0	−25 / −45	40 / 140	+50 / −0	−40 / −90	60 / 220	+80 / −0	−60 / −140	41.49	56.19
4.5 / 30.5	+16.0 / 0	−4.5 / −14.5	9.0 / 50.0	+25.0 / −0	−9 / −25	16 / 57	+25 / −0	−16 / −32	30 / 95	+40 / −0	−30 / −55	50 / 170	+60 / −0	−50 / 110	70 / 270	+100 / −0	−70 / −170	56.19	76.39
5.0 / 37.0	+20.0 / 0	−5 / −17	10.0 / 60.0	+30.0 / −0	−10 / −30	18 / 68	+30 / −0	−18 / −38	35 / 115	+50 / −0	−35 / −65	50 / 210	+80 / −0	−50 / −130	80 / 330	+125 / −0	−80 / −205	76.39	100.9
6.0 / 47.0	+25.0 / 0	−6 / −22	12.0 / 67.0	+40.0 / −0	−12 / −27	20 / 85	+40 / −0	−20 / −45	40 / 140	+60 / −0	−40 / −80	60 / 260	+100 / −0	−60 / −160	90 / 410	+160 / −0	−90 / −250	100.9	131.9
7.0 / 57.0	+30.0 / 0	−7 / −27	14.0 / 94.0	+50.0 / −0	−14 / −44	25 / 105	+50 / −0	−25 / −55	50 / 180	+80 / −0	−50 / −100	80 / 330	+125 / −0	−80 / −205	100 / 500	+200 / −0	−100 / −300	131.9	171.9
7.0 / 72.0	+40.0 / 0	−7 / −32	14.0 / 114.0	+60.0 / −0	−14 / −54	25 / 125	+60 / −0	−25 / −65	50 / 210	+100 / −0	−50 / −110	90 / 410	+160 / −0	−90 / −250	125 / 625	+250 / −0	−125 / −375	171.9	200

End of Table 6

9

M - 13

TABLE 7 LOCATIONAL TRANSITION FITS

Limits are in thousandths of an inch.

Limits for hole and shaft are applied algebraically to the basic size to obtain the limits of size for the mating parts.

Data in bold face are in accordance with ABC agreements.

"Fit" represents the maximum interference (minus values) and the maximum clearance (plus values).

Symbols H7, js6, etc., are Hole and Shaft designations used in ABC System (Appendix D).

Nominal Size Range Inches Over – To	Class LT 1 Fit	Class LT 1 Hole H7	Class LT 1 Shaft js6	Class LT 2 Fit	Class LT 2 Hole H8	Class LT 2 Shaft js7	Class LT 3 Fit	Class LT 3 Hole H7	Class LT 3 Shaft k6	Class LT 4 Fit	Class LT 4 Hole H8	Class LT 4 Shaft k7	Class LT 5 Fit	Class LT 5 Hole H7	Class LT 5 Shaft n6	Class LT 6 Fit	Class LT 6 Hole H7	Class LT 6 Shaft n7
0 – 0.12	−0.10 / +0.50	+0.4 / −0	+0.10 / −0.10	−0.2 / +0.8	+0.6 / −0	+0.2 / −0.2							−0.5 / +0.15	+0.4 / −0	+0.5 / +0.25	−0.65 / +0.15	+0.4 / −0	+0.65 / +0.25
0.12 – 0.24	−0.15 / +0.65	+0.5 / −0	+0.15 / −0.15	−0.25 / +0.95	+0.7 / −0	+0.25 / −0.25							−0.6 / +0.2	+0.5 / −0	+0.6 / +0.3	−0.8 / +0.2	+0.5 / −0	+0.8 / +0.3
0.24 – 0.40	−0.2 / +0.8	+0.6 / −0	+0.2 / −0.2	−0.3 / +1.2	+0.9 / −0	+0.3 / −0.3	−0.5 / +0.5	+0.6 / −0	+0.5 / +0.1	−0.7 / +0.8	+0.9 / −0	+0.7 / +0.1	−0.8 / +0.2	+0.6 / −0	+0.8 / +0.4	−1.0 / +0.2	+0.6 / −0	+1.0 / +0.4
0.40 – 0.71	−0.2 / +0.9	+0.7 / −0	+0.2 / −0.2	−0.35 / +1.35	+1.0 / −0	+0.35 / −0.35	−0.5 / +0.6	+0.7 / −0	+0.5 / +0.1	−0.8 / +0.9	+1.0 / −0	+0.8 / +0.1	−0.9 / +0.2	+0.7 / −0	+0.9 / +0.5	−1.2 / +0.2	+0.7 / −0	+1.2 / +0.5
0.71 – 1.19	−0.25 / +1.05	+0.8 / −0	+0.25 / −0.25	−0.4 / +1.6	+1.2 / −0	+0.4 / −0.4	−0.6 / +0.7	+0.8 / −0	+0.6 / +0.1	−0.9 / +1.1	+1.2 / −0	+0.9 / +0.1	−1.1 / +0.2	+0.8 / −0	+1.1 / +0.6	−1.4 / +0.2	+0.8 / −0	+1.4 / +0.6
1.19 – 1.97	−0.3 / +1.3	+1.0 / −0	+0.3 / −0.3	−0.5 / +2.1	+1.6 / −0	+0.5 / −0.5	−0.7 / +0.9	+1.0 / −0	+0.7 / +0.1	−1.1 / +1.5	+1.6 / −0	+1.1 / +0.1	−1.3 / +0.3	+1.0 / −0	+1.3 / +0.7	−1.7 / +0.3	+1.0 / −0	+1.7 / +0.7
1.97 – 3.15	−0.3 / +1.5	+1.2 / −0	+0.3 / −0.3	−0.6 / +2.4	+1.8 / −0	+0.6 / −0.6	−0.8 / +1.1	+1.2 / −0	+0.8 / +0.1	−1.3 / +1.7	+1.8 / −0	+1.3 / +0.1	−1.5 / +0.4	+1.2 / −0	+1.5 / +0.8	−2.0 / +0.4	+1.2 / −0	+2.0 / +0.8
3.15 – 4.73	−0.4 / +1.8	+1.4 / −0	+0.4 / −0.4	−0.7 / +2.9	+2.2 / −0	+0.7 / −0.7	−1.0 / +1.3	+1.4 / −0	+1.0 / +0.1	−1.5 / +2.1	+2.2 / −0	+1.5 / +0.1	−1.9 / +0.4	+1.4 / −0	+1.9 / +1.0	−2.4 / +0.4	+1.4 / −0	+2.4 / +1.0
4.73 – 7.09	−0.5 / +2.1	+1.6 / −0	+0.5 / −0.5	−0.8 / +3.3	+2.5 / −0	+0.8 / −0.8	−1.1 / +1.5	+1.6 / −0	+1.1 / +0.1	−1.7 / +2.4	+2.5 / −0	+1.7 / +0.1	−2.2 / +0.4	+1.6 / −0	+2.2 / +1.2	−2.8 / +0.4	+1.6 / −0	+2.8 / +1.2
7.09 – 9.85	−0.6 / +2.4	+1.8 / −0	+0.6 / −0.6	−0.9 / +3.7	+2.8 / −0	+0.9 / −0.9	−1.4 / +1.6	+1.8 / −0	+1.4 / +0.2	−2.0 / +2.6	+2.8 / −0	+2.0 / +0.2	−2.6 / +0.4	+1.8 / −0	+2.6 / +1.4	−3.2 / +0.4	+1.8 / −0	+3.2 / +1.4
9.85 – 12.41	−0.6 / +2.6	+2.0 / −0	+0.6 / −0.6	−1.0 / +4.0	+3.0 / −0	+1.0 / −1.0	−1.4 / +1.8	+2.0 / −0	+1.4 / +0.2	−2.2 / +2.8	+3.0 / −0	+2.2 / +0.2	−2.6 / +0.6	+2.0 / −0	+2.6 / +1.4	−3.4 / +0.6	+2.0 / −0	+3.4 / +1.4
12.41 – 15.75	−0.7 / +2.9	+2.2 / −0	+0.7 / −0.7	−1.0 / +4.5	+3.5 / −0	+1.0 / −1.0	−1.6 / +2.0	+2.2 / −0	+1.6 / +0.2	−2.4 / +3.3	+3.5 / −0	+2.4 / +0.2	−3.0 / +0.6	+2.2 / −0	+3.0 / +1.6	−3.8 / +0.6	+2.2 / −0	+3.8 / +1.6
15.75 – 19.69	−0.8 / +3.3	+2.5 / −0	+0.8 / −0.8	−1.2 / +5.2	+4.0 / −0	+1.2 / −1.2	−1.8 / +2.3	+2.5 / −0	+1.8 / +0.2	−2.7 / +3.8	+4.0 / −0	+2.7 / +0.2	−3.4 / +0.7	+2.5 / −0	+3.4 / +1.8	−4.3 / +0.7	+2.5 / −0	+4.3 / +1.8

End of Table 7

TABLE 8 LOCATIONAL INTERFERENCE FITS

Limits are in thousandths of an inch.

Limits for hole and shaft are applied algebraically to the basic size to obtain the limits of size for the parts.

Data in bold face are in accordance with ABC agreements,
Symbols H7, p6, etc., are Hole and Shaft designations
used in ABC System (Appendix I).

Nominal Size Range Inches (Over — To)	Class LN 1			Class LN 2			Class LN 3		
	Limits of Interference	Standard Limits		Limits of Interference	Standard Limits		Limits of Interference	Standard Limits	
		Hole H6	Shaft n5		Hole H7	Shaft p6		Hole H7	Shaft r6
0 — 0.12	0 / 0.45	+0.25 / −0	+0.45 / +0.25	0 / 0.65	+0.4 / −0	+0.65 / +0.4	0.1 / 0.75	+0.4 / −0	+0.75 / +0.5
0.12 — 0.24	0 / 0.5	+0.3 / −0	+0.5 / +0.3	0 / 0.8	+0.5 / −0	+0.8 / +0.5	0.1 / 0.9	+0.5 / 0	+0.9 / +0.6
0.24 — 0.40	0 / 0.65	+0.4 / 0	+0.65 / +0.4	0 / 1.0	+0.6 / −0	+1.0 / +0.6	0.2 / 1.2	+0.6 / −0	+1.2 / +0.8
0.40 — 0.71	0 / 0.8	+0.4 / −0	+0.8 / +0.4	0 / 1.1	+0.7 / −0	+1.1 / +0.7	0.3 / 1.4	+0.7 / −0	+1.4 / +1.0
0.71 — 1.19	0 / 1.0	+0.5 / −0	+1.0 / +0.5	0 / 1.3	+0.8 / −0	+1.3 / +0.8	0.4 / 1.7	+0.8 / −0	+1.7 / +1.2
1.19 — 1.97	0 / 1.1	+0.6 / −0	+1.1 / +0.6	0 / 1.6	+1.0 / −0	+1.6 / +1.0	0.4 / 2.0	+1.0 / −0	+2.0 / +1.4
1.97 — 3.15	0.1 / 1.3	+0.7 / −0	+1.3 / +0.7	0.2 / 2.1	+1.2 / −0	+2.1 / +1.4	0.6 / 2.3	+1.2 / −0	+2.3 / +1.6
3.15 — 4.73	0.1 / 1.6	+0.9 / −0	+1.6 / +1.0	0.2 / 2.5	+1.4 / −0	+2.5 / +1.6	0.6 / 2.9	+1.4 / −0	+2.9 / +2.0
4.73 — 7.09	0.2 / 1.9	+1.0 / −0	+1.9 / +1.2	0.2 / 2.8	+1.6 / −0	+2.8 / +1.8	0.9 / 3.5	+1.6 / −0	+3.5 / +2.5
7.09 — 9.85	0.2 / 2.2	+1.2 / −0	+2.2 / +1.4	0.2 / 3.2	+1.8 / −0	+3.2 / +2.0	1.2 / 4.2	+1.8 / −0	+4.2 / +3.0
9.85 — 12.41	0.2 / 2.3	+1.2 / −0	+2.3 / +1.4	0.2 / 3.4	+2.0 / −0	+3.4 / +2.2	1.5 / 4.7	+2.0 / −0	+4.7 / +3.5
12.41 — 15.75	0.2 / 2.6	+1.4 / −0	+2.6 / +1.6	0.3 / 3.9	+2.2 / −0	+3.9 / +2.5	2.3 / 5.9	+2.2 / −0	+5.9 / +4.5
15.75 — 19.69	0.2 / 2.8	+1.6 / −0	+2.8 / +1.8	0.3 / 4.4	+2.5 / −0	+4.4 / +2.8	2.5 / 6.6	+2.5 / −0	+6.6 / +5.0
19.69 — 30.09		+2.0 / −0		0.5 / 5.5	+3 / −0	+5.5 / +3.5	4 / 9	+3 / −0	+9 / +7
30.09 — 41.49		+2.5 / −0		0.5 / 7.0	+4 / −0	+7.0 / +4.5	5 / 11.5	+4 / −0	+11.5 / +9
41.49 — 56.19		+3.0 / −0		1 / 9	+5 / −0	+9 / +6	7 / 15	+5 / −0	+15 / +12
56.19 — 76.39		+4.0 / −0		1 / 11	+6 / −0	+11 / +7	10 / 20	+6 / −0	+20 / +16
76.39 — 100.9		+5.0 / −0		1 / 14	+8 / −0	+14 / +9	12 / 25	+8 / −0	+25 / +20
100.9 — 131.9		+6.0 / −0		2 / 18	+10 / −0	+18 / +12	15 / 31	+10 / −0	+31 / +25
131.9 — 171.9		+8.0 / −0		4 / 24	+12 / −0	+24 / +16	18 / 38	+12 / −0	+38 / +30
171.9 — 200		+10.0 / −0		4 / 30	+16 / −0	+30 / +20	24 / 50	+16 / −0	+50 / +40

11　　　　　　　　　　　　　　　　　　**End of Table 8**

USA STANDARD

TABLE 9 FORCE AND SHRINK FITS

Limits are in thousandths of an inch.

Limits for hole and shaft are applied algebraically to the basic size to obtain the limits of size for the parts.

Data in bold face are in accordance with ABC agreements.

Symbols H7, s6, etc., are Hole and Shaft designations used in ABC System (Appendix I).

Nominal Size Range Inches (Over – To)	Class FN 1 Limits of Interference	Class FN 1 Hole H6	Class FN 1 Shaft	Class FN 2 Limits of Interference	Class FN 2 Hole H7	Class FN 2 Shaft s6	Class FN 3 Limits of Interference	Class FN 3 Hole H7	Class FN 3 Shaft t6	Class FN 4 Limits of Interference	Class FN 4 Hole H7	Class FN 4 Shaft u6	Class FN 5 Limits of Interference	Class FN 5 Hole H8	Class FN 5 Shaft x7
0 – 0.12	0.05 / 0.5	+0.25 / −0	+0.5 / +0.3	0.2 / 0.85	+0.4 / −0	+0.85 / +0.6				0.3 / 0.95	+0.4 / −0	+0.95 / +0.7	0.3 / 1.3	+0.6 / −0	+1.3 / +0.9
0.12 – 0.24	0.1 / 0.6	+0.3 / −0	+0.6 / +0.4	0.2 / 1.0	+0.5 / −0	+1.0 / +0.7				0.4 / 1.2	+0.5 / −0	+1.2 / +0.9	0.5 / 1.7	+0.7 / −0	+1.7 / +1.2
0.24 – 0.40	0.1 / 0.75	+0.4 / −0	+0.75 / +0.5	0.4 / 1.4	+0.6 / −0	+1.4 / +1.0				0.6 / 1.6	+0.6 / −0	+1.6 / +1.2	0.5 / 2.0	+0.9 / −0	+2.0 / +1.4
0.40 – 0.56	0.1 / 0.8	−0.4 / −0	+0.8 / +0.5	0.5 / 1.6	+0.7 / −0	+1.6 / +1.2				0.7 / 1.8	+0.7 / −0	+1.8 / +1.4	0.6 / 2.3	+1.0 / −0	+2.3 / +1.6
0.56 – 0.71	0.2 / 0.9	+0.4 / −0	+0.9 / +0.6	0.5 / 1.6	+0.7 / −0	+1.6 / +1.2				0.7 / 1.8	+0.7 / −0	+1.8 / +1.4	0.8 / 2.5	+1.0 / −0	+2.5 / +1.8
0.71 – 0.95	0.2 / 1.1	+0.5 / −0	+1.1 / +0.7	0.6 / 1.9	+0.8 / −0	+1.9 / +1.4				0.8 / 2.1	+0.8 / −0	+2.1 / +1.6	1.0 / 3.0	+1.2 / −0	+3.0 / +2.2
0.95 – 1.19	0.3 / 1.2	+0.5 / −0	+1.2 / +0.8	0.6 / 1.9	+0.8 / −0	+1.9 / +1.4	0.8 / 2.1	+0.8 / −0	+2.1 / +1.6	1.0 / 2.3	+0.8 / −0	+2.3 / +1.8	1.3 / 3.3	+1.2 / −0	+3.3 / +2.5
1.19 – 1.58	0.3 / 1.3	+0.6 / −0	+1.3 / +0.9	0.8 / 2.4	+1.0 / −0	+2.4 / +1.8	1.0 / 2.6	+1.0 / −0	+2.6 / +2.0	1.5 / 3.1	+1.0 / −0	+3.1 / +2.5	1.4 / 4.0	+1.6 / −0	+4.0 / +3.0
1.58 – 1.97	0.4 / 1.4	+0.6 / −0	+1.4 / +1.0	0.8 / 2.4	+1.0 / −0	+2.4 / +1.8	1.2 / 2.8	+1.0 / −0	+2.8 / +2.2	1.8 / 3.4	+1.0 / −0	+3.4 / +2.8	2.4 / 5.0	+1.6 / −0	+5.0 / +4.0
1.97 – 2.56	0.6 / 1.8	+0.7 / −0	+1.8 / +1.3	0.8 / 2.7	+1.2 / −0	+2.7 / +2.0	1.3 / 3.2	+1.2 / −0	+3.2 / +2.5	2.3 / 4.2	+1.2 / −0	+4.2 / +3.5	3.2 / 6.2	+1.8 / −0	+6.2 / +5.0
2.56 – 3.15	0.7 / 1.9	+0.7 / −0	+1.9 / +1.4	1.0 / 2.9	+1.2 / −0	+2.9 / +2.2	1.8 / 3.7	+1.2 / −0	+3.7 / +3.0	2.8 / 4.7	+1.2 / −0	+4.7 / +4.0	4.2 / 7.2	+1.8 / −0	+7.2 / +6.0
3.15 – 3.94	0.9 / 2.4	+0.9 / −0	+2.4 / +1.8	1.4 / 3.7	+1.4 / −0	+3.7 / +2.8	2.1 / 4.4	+1.4 / −0	+4.4 / +3.5	3.6 / 5.9	+1.4 / −0	+5.9 / +5.0	4.8 / 8.4	+2.2 / −0	+8.4 / +7.0
3.94 – 4.73	1.1 / 2.6	+0.9 / −0	+2.6 / +2.0	1.6 / 3.9	+1.4 / −0	+3.9 / +3.0	2.6 / 4.9	+1.4 / −0	+4.9 / +4.0	4.6 / 6.9	+1.4 / −0	+6.9 / +6.0	5.8 / 9.4	+2.2 / −0	+9.4 / +8.0
4.73 – 5.52	1.2 / 2.9	+1.0 / −0	+2.9 / +2.2	1.9 / 4.5	+1.6 / −0	+4.5 / +3.5	3.4 / 6.0	+1.6 / −0	+6.0 / +5.0	5.4 / 8.0	+1.6 / −0	+8.0 / +7.0	7.5 / 11.6	+2.5 / −0	+11.6 / +10.0
5.52 – 6.30	1.5 / 3.2	+1.0 / −0	+3.2 / +2.5	2.4 / 5.0	+1.6 / −0	+5.0 / +4.0	3.4 / 6.0	+1.6 / −0	+6.0 / +5.0	5.4 / 8.0	+1.6 / −0	+8.0 / +7.0	9.5 / 13.6	+2.5 / −0	+13.6 / +12.0
6.30 – 7.09	1.8 / 3.5	+1.0 / −0	+3.5 / +2.8	2.9 / 5.5	+1.6 / −0	+5.5 / +4.5	4.4 / 7.0	+1.6 / −0	+7.0 / +6.0	6.4 / 9.0	+1.6 / −0	+9.0 / +8.0	9.5 / 13.6	+2.5 / −0	+13.6 / +12.0
7.09 – 7.88	1.8 / 3.8	+1.2 / −0	+3.8 / +3.0	3.2 / 6.2	+1.8 / −0	+6.2 / +5.0	5.2 / 8.2	+1.8 / −0	+8.2 / +7.0	7.2 / 10.2	+1.8 / −0	+10.2 / +9.0	11.2 / 15.8	+2.8 / −0	+15.8 / +14.0
7.88 – 8.86	2.3 / 4.3	+1.2 / −0	+4.3 / +3.5	3.2 / 6.2	+1.8 / −0	+6.2 / +5.0	5.2 / 8.2	+1.8 / −0	+8.2 / +7.0	8.2 / 11.2	+1.8 / −0	+11.2 / +10.0	13.2 / 17.8	+2.8 / −0	+17.8 / +16.0
8.86 – 9.85	2.3 / 4.3	+1.2 / −0	+4.3 / +3.5	4.2 / 7.2	+1.8 / −0	+7.2 / +6.0	6.2 / 9.2	+1.8 / −0	+9.2 / +8.0	10.2 / 13.2	+1.8 / −0	+13.2 / +12.0	13.2 / 17.8	+2.8 / −0	+17.8 / +16.0
9.85 – 11.03	2.8 / 4.9	+1.2 / −0	+4.9 / +4.0	4.0 / 7.2	+2.0 / −0	+7.2 / +6.0	7.0 / 10.2	+2.0 / −0	+10.2 / +9.0	10.0 / 13.2	+2.0 / −0	+13.2 / +12.0	15.0 / 20.0	+3.0 / −0	+20.0 / +18.0
11.03 – 12.41	2.8 / 4.9	+1.2 / −0	+4.9 / +4.0	5.0 / 8.2	+2.0 / −0	+8.2 / +7.0	7.0 / 10.2	+2.0 / −0	+10.2 / +9.0	12.0 / 15.2	+2.0 / −0	+15.2 / +14.0	17.0 / 22.0	+3.0 / −0	+22.0 / +20.0
12.41 – 13.98	3.1 / 5.5	+1.4 / −0	+5.5 / +4.5	5.8 / 9.4	+2.2 / −0	+9.4 / +8.0	7.8 / 11.4	+2.2 / −0	+11.4 / +10.0	13.8 / 17.4	+2.2 / −0	+17.4 / +16.0	18.5 / 24.2	+3.5 / +0	+24.2 / +22.0
13.98 – 15.75	3.6 / 6.1	+1.4 / −0	+6.1 / +5.0	5.8 / 9.4	+2.2 / −0	+9.4 / +8.0	9.8 / 13.4	+2.2 / −0	+13.4 / +12.0	15.8 / 19.4	+2.2 / −0	+19.4 / +18.0	21.5 / 27.2	+3.5 / −0	+27.2 / +25.0
15.75 – 17.72	4.4 / 7.0	+1.6 / −0	+7.0 / +6.0	6.5 / 10.6	+2.5 / −0	+10.6 / +9.0	9.5 / 13.6	+2.5 / −0	+13.6 / +12.0	17.5 / 21.6	+2.5 / −0	+21.6 / +20.0	24.0 / 30.5	+4.0 / −0	+30.5 / +28.0
17.72 – 19.69	4.4 / 7.0	+1.6 / −0	+7.0 / +6.0	7.5 / 11.6	+2.5 / −0	+11.6 / +10.0	11.5 / 15.6	+2.5 / −0	+15.6 / +14.0	19.5 / 23.6	+2.5 / −0	+23.6 / +22.0	26.0 / 32.5	+4.0 / −0	+32.5 / +30.0

Continued on page 19

14

M - 16

**AMERICAN NATIONAL STANDARD
PREFERRED METRIC LIMITS AND FITS**   ANSI B4.2-1978

Dimensions in mm.

TABLE 2 PREFERRED HOLE BASIS CLEARANCE FITS

BASIC SIZE		LOOSE RUNNING			FREE RUNNING			CLOSE RUNNING			SLIDING			LOCATIONAL CLEARANCE		
		Hole H11	Shaft c11	Fit	Hole H9	Shaft d9	Fit	Hole H8	Shaft f7	Fit	Hole H7	Shaft g6	Fit	Hole H7	Shaft h6	Fit
1	MAX	1.060	0.940	0.180	1.025	0.980	0.070	1.014	0.994	0.030	1.010	0.998	0.018	1.010	1.000	0.016
	MIN	1.000	0.880	0.060	1.000	0.955	0.020	1.000	0.984	0.006	1.000	0.992	0.002	1.000	0.994	0.000
1.2	MAX	1.260	1.140	0.180	1.225	1.180	0.070	1.214	1.194	0.030	1.210	1.198	0.018	1.210	1.200	0.016
	MIN	1.200	1.080	0.060	1.200	1.155	0.020	1.200	1.184	0.006	1.200	1.192	0.002	1.200	1.194	0.000
1.6	MAX	1.660	1.540	0.180	1.625	1.580	0.070	1.614	1.594	0.030	1.610	1.598	0.018	1.610	1.600	0.016
	MIN	1.600	1.480	0.060	1.600	1.555	0.020	1.600	1.584	0.006	1.600	1.592	0.002	1.600	1.594	0.000
2	MAX	2.060	1.940	0.180	2.025	1.980	0.070	2.014	1.994	0.030	2.010	1.998	0.018	2.010	2.000	0.016
	MIN	2.000	1.880	0.060	2.000	1.955	0.020	2.000	1.984	0.006	2.000	1.992	0.002	2.000	1.994	0.000
2.5	MAX	2.560	2.440	0.180	2.525	2.480	0.070	2.514	2.494	0.030	2.510	2.498	0.018	2.510	2.500	0.016
	MIN	2.500	2.380	0.060	2.500	2.455	0.020	2.500	2.484	0.006	2.500	2.492	0.002	2.500	2.494	0.000
3	MAX	3.060	2.940	0.180	3.025	2.980	0.070	3.014	2.994	0.030	3.010	2.998	0.018	3.010	3.000	0.016
	MIN	3.000	2.880	0.060	3.000	2.955	0.020	3.000	2.984	0.006	3.000	2.992	0.002	3.000	2.994	0.000
4	MAX	4.075	3.930	0.220	4.030	3.970	0.090	4.018	3.990	0.040	4.012	3.996	0.024	4.012	4.000	0.020
	MIN	4.000	3.855	0.070	4.000	3.940	0.030	4.000	3.978	0.010	4.000	3.988	0.004	4.000	3.992	0.000
5	MAX	5.075	4.930	0.220	5.030	4.970	0.090	5.018	4.990	0.040	5.012	4.996	0.024	5.012	5.000	0.020
	MIN	5.000	4.855	0.070	5.000	4.940	0.030	5.000	4.978	0.010	5.000	4.988	0.004	5.000	4.992	0.000
6	MAX	6.075	5.930	0.220	6.030	5.970	0.090	6.018	5.990	0.040	6.012	5.996	0.024	6.012	6.000	0.020
	MIN	6.000	5.855	0.070	6.000	5.940	0.030	6.000	5.978	0.010	6.000	5.988	0.004	6.000	5.992	0.000
8	MAX	8.090	7.920	0.260	8.036	7.960	0.112	8.022	7.987	0.050	8.015	7.995	0.029	8.015	8.000	0.024
	MIN	8.000	7.830	0.080	8.000	7.924	0.040	8.000	7.972	0.013	8.000	7.986	0.005	8.000	7.991	0.000
10	MAX	10.090	9.920	0.260	10.036	9.960	0.112	10.022	9.987	0.050	10.015	9.995	0.029	10.015	10.000	0.024
	MIN	10.000	9.830	0.080	10.000	9.924	0.040	10.000	9.972	0.013	10.000	9.986	0.005	10.000	9.991	0.000
12	MAX	12.110	11.905	0.315	12.043	11.950	0.136	12.027	11.984	0.061	12.018	11.994	0.035	12.018	12.000	0.029
	MIN	12.000	11.795	0.095	12.000	11.907	0.050	12.000	11.966	0.016	12.000	11.983	0.006	12.000	11.989	0.000
16	MAX	16.110	15.905	0.315	16.043	15.950	0.136	16.027	15.984	0.061	16.018	15.994	0.035	16.018	16.000	0.029
	MIN	16.000	15.795	0.095	16.000	15.907	0.050	16.000	15.966	0.016	16.000	15.983	0.006	16.000	15.989	0.000
20	MAX	20.130	19.890	0.370	20.052	19.935	0.169	20.033	19.980	0.074	20.021	19.993	0.041	20.021	20.000	0.034
	MIN	20.000	19.760	0.110	20.000	19.883	0.065	20.000	19.959	0.020	20.000	19.980	0.007	20.000	19.987	0.000
25	MAX	25.130	24.890	0.370	25.052	24.935	0.169	25.033	24.980	0.074	25.021	24.993	0.041	25.021	25.000	0.034
	MIN	25.000	24.760	0.110	25.000	24.883	0.065	25.000	24.959	0.020	25.000	24.980	0.007	25.000	24.987	0.000
30	MAX	30.130	29.890	0.370	30.052	29.935	0.169	30.033	29.980	0.074	30.021	29.993	0.041	30.021	30.000	0.034
	MIN	30.000	29.760	0.110	30.000	29.883	0.065	30.000	29.959	0.020	30.000	29.980	0.007	30.000	29.987	0.000

8

TABLE 2 PREFERRED HOLE BASIS CLEARANCE FITS (Continued)

Dimensions in mm.

BASIC SIZE		LOOSE RUNNING			FREE RUNNING			CLOSE RUNNING			SLIDING			LOCATIONAL CLEARANCE		
		Hole H11	Shaft c11	Fit	Hole H9	Shaft d9	Fit	Hole H8	Shaft f7	Fit	Hole H7	Shaft g6	Fit	Hole H7	Shaft h6	Fit
40	MAX	40.160	39.880	0.440	40.062	39.920	0.204	40.039	39.975	0.089	40.025	39.991	0.050	40.025	40.000	0.041
	MIN	40.000	39.720	0.120	40.000	39.858	0.080	40.000	39.950	0.025	40.000	39.975	0.009	40.000	39.984	0.000
50	MAX	50.160	49.870	0.450	50.062	49.920	0.204	50.039	49.975	0.089	50.025	49.991	0.050	50.025	50.000	0.041
	MIN	50.000	49.710	0.130	50.000	49.858	0.080	50.000	49.950	0.025	50.000	49.975	0.009	50.000	49.984	0.000
60	MAX	60.190	59.860	0.520	60.074	59.900	0.248	60.046	59.970	0.106	60.030	59.990	0.059	60.030	60.000	0.049
	MIN	60.000	59.670	0.140	60.000	59.826	0.100	60.000	59.940	0.030	60.000	59.971	0.010	60.000	59.981	0.000
80	MAX	80.190	79.850	0.530	80.074	79.900	0.248	80.046	79.970	0.106	80.030	79.990	0.059	80.030	80.000	0.049
	MIN	80.000	79.660	0.150	80.000	79.826	0.100	80.000	79.940	0.030	80.000	79.971	0.010	80.000	79.981	0.000
100	MAX	100.220	99.830	0.610	100.087	99.880	0.294	100.054	99.964	0.125	100.035	99.988	0.069	100.035	100.000	0.057
	MIN	100.000	99.610	0.170	100.000	99.793	0.120	100.000	99.929	0.036	100.000	99.966	0.012	100.000	99.978	0.000
120	MAX	120.220	119.820	0.620	120.087	119.880	0.294	120.054	119.964	0.125	120.035	119.988	0.069	120.035	120.000	0.057
	MIN	120.000	119.600	0.180	120.000	119.793	0.120	120.000	119.929	0.036	120.000	119.966	0.012	120.000	119.978	0.000
160	MAX	160.250	159.790	0.710	160.100	159.855	0.345	160.063	159.957	0.146	160.040	159.986	0.079	160.040	160.000	0.065
	MIN	160.000	159.540	0.210	160.000	159.755	0.145	160.000	159.917	0.043	160.000	159.961	0.014	160.000	159.975	0.000
200	MAX	200.290	199.760	0.820	200.115	199.830	0.400	200.072	199.950	0.168	200.046	199.985	0.090	200.046	200.000	0.075
	MIN	200.000	199.470	0.240	200.000	199.715	0.170	200.000	199.904	0.050	200.000	199.956	0.015	200.000	199.971	0.000
250	MAX	250.290	249.720	0.860	250.115	249.830	0.400	250.072	249.950	0.168	250.046	249.985	0.090	250.046	250.000	0.075
	MIN	250.000	249.430	0.280	250.000	249.715	0.170	250.000	249.904	0.050	250.000	249.956	0.015	250.000	249.971	0.000
300	MAX	300.320	299.670	0.970	300.130	299.810	0.450	300.081	299.944	0.189	300.052	299.983	0.101	300.052	300.000	0.084
	MIN	300.000	299.350	0.330	300.000	299.680	0.190	300.000	299.892	0.056	300.000	299.951	0.017	300.000	299.968	0.000
400	MAX	400.360	399.600	1.120	400.140	399.790	0.490	400.089	399.938	0.208	400.057	399.982	0.111	400.057	400.000	0.093
	MIN	400.000	399.240	0.400	400.000	399.650	0.210	400.000	399.881	0.062	400.000	399.946	0.018	400.000	399.964	0.000
500	MAX	500.400	499.520	1.280	500.155	499.770	0.540	500.097	499.932	0.228	500.063	499.980	0.123	500.063	500.000	0.103
	MIN	500.000	499.120	0.480	500.000	499.615	0.230	500.000	499.869	0.068	500.000	499.940	0.020	500.000	499.960	0.000

AMERICAN NATIONAL STANDARD
PREFERRED METRIC LIMITS AND FITS

AMERICAN NATIONAL STANDARD
PREFERRED METRIC LIMITS AND FITS

ANSI B4.2-1978

Dimensions in mm.

TABLE 3 PREFERRED HOLE BASIS TRANSITION AND INTERFERENCE FITS

BASIC SIZE		LOCATIONAL TRANSN. Hole H7	Shaft k6	Fit	LOCATIONAL TRANSN. Hole H7	Shaft n6	Fit	LOCATIONAL INTERF. Hole H7	Shaft p6	Fit	MEDIUM DRIVE Hole H7	Shaft s6	Fit	FORCE Hole H7	Shaft u6	Fit
1	MAX	1.010	1.006	0.010	1.010	1.010	0.006	1.010	1.012	0.004	1.010	1.020	-0.004	1.010	1.024	-0.008
	MIN	1.000	1.000	-0.006	1.000	1.004	-0.010	1.000	1.006	-0.012	1.000	1.014	-0.020	1.000	1.018	-0.024
1.2	MAX	1.210	1.206	0.010	1.210	1.210	0.006	1.210	1.212	0.004	1.210	1.220	-0.004	1.210	1.224	-0.008
	MIN	1.200	1.200	-0.006	1.200	1.204	-0.010	1.200	1.206	-0.012	1.200	1.214	-0.020	1.200	1.218	-0.024
1.6	MAX	1.610	1.606	0.010	1.610	1.610	0.006	1.610	1.612	0.004	1.610	1.620	-0.004	1.610	1.624	-0.008
	MIN	1.600	1.600	-0.006	1.600	1.604	-0.010	1.600	1.606	-0.012	1.600	1.614	-0.020	1.600	1.618	-0.024
2	MAX	2.010	2.006	0.010	2.010	2.010	0.006	2.010	2.012	0.004	2.010	2.020	-0.004	2.010	2.024	-0.008
	MIN	2.000	2.000	-0.006	2.000	2.004	-0.010	2.000	2.006	-0.012	2.000	2.014	-0.020	2.000	2.018	-0.024
2.5	MAX	2.510	2.506	0.010	2.510	2.510	0.006	2.510	2.512	0.004	2.510	2.520	-0.004	2.510	2.524	-0.008
	MIN	2.500	2.500	-0.006	2.500	2.504	-0.010	2.500	2.506	-0.012	2.500	2.514	-0.020	2.500	2.518	-0.024
3	MAX	3.010	3.006	0.010	3.010	3.010	0.006	3.010	3.012	0.004	3.010	3.020	-0.004	3.010	3.024	-0.008
	MIN	3.000	3.000	-0.006	3.000	3.004	-0.010	3.000	3.006	-0.012	3.000	3.014	-0.020	3.000	3.018	-0.024
4	MAX	4.012	4.009	0.011	4.012	4.016	0.004	4.012	4.020	0.000	4.012	4.027	-0.007	4.012	4.031	-0.011
	MIN	4.000	4.001	-0.009	4.000	4.008	-0.016	4.000	4.012	-0.020	4.000	4.019	-0.027	4.000	4.023	-0.031
5	MAX	5.012	5.009	0.011	5.012	5.016	0.004	5.012	5.020	0.000	5.012	5.027	-0.007	5.012	5.031	-0.011
	MIN	5.000	5.001	-0.009	5.000	5.008	-0.016	5.000	5.012	-0.020	5.000	5.019	-0.027	5.000	5.023	-0.031
6	MAX	6.012	6.009	0.011	6.012	6.016	0.004	6.012	6.020	0.000	6.012	6.027	-0.007	6.012	6.031	-0.011
	MIN	6.000	6.001	-0.009	6.000	6.008	-0.016	6.000	6.012	-0.020	6.000	6.019	-0.027	6.000	6.023	-0.031
8	MAX	8.015	8.010	0.014	8.015	8.019	0.005	8.015	8.024	0.000	8.015	8.032	-0.008	8.015	8.037	-0.013
	MIN	8.000	8.001	-0.010	8.000	8.010	-0.019	8.000	8.015	-0.024	8.000	8.023	-0.032	8.000	8.028	-0.037
10	MAX	10.015	10.010	0.014	10.015	10.019	0.005	10.015	10.024	0.000	10.015	10.032	-0.008	10.015	10.037	-0.013
	MIN	10.000	10.001	-0.010	10.000	10.010	-0.019	10.000	10.015	-0.024	10.000	10.023	-0.032	10.000	10.028	-0.037
12	MAX	12.018	12.012	0.017	12.018	12.023	0.006	12.018	12.025	0.000	12.018	12.039	-0.010	12.018	12.044	-0.015
	MIN	12.000	12.001	-0.012	12.000	12.012	-0.023	12.000	12.018	-0.029	12.000	12.028	-0.039	12.000	12.033	-0.044
16	MAX	16.018	16.012	0.017	16.018	16.023	0.006	16.018	16.029	0.000	16.018	16.039	-0.010	16.018	16.044	-0.015
	MIN	16.000	16.001	-0.012	16.000	16.012	-0.023	16.000	16.018	-0.029	16.000	16.028	-0.039	16.000	16.033	-0.044
20	MAX	20.021	20.015	0.019	20.021	20.028	0.006	20.021	20.035	-0.001	20.021	20.048	-0.014	20.021	20.054	-0.020
	MIN	20.000	20.002	-0.015	20.000	20.015	-0.028	20.000	20.022	-0.035	20.000	20.035	-0.048	20.000	20.041	-0.054
25	MAX	25.021	25.015	0.019	25.021	25.028	0.006	25.021	25.035	-0.001	25.021	25.048	-0.014	25.021	25.061	-0.027
	MIN	25.000	25.002	-0.015	25.000	25.015	-0.028	25.000	25.022	-0.035	25.000	25.035	-0.048	25.000	25.048	-0.061
30	MAX	30.021	30.015	0.019	30.021	30.028	0.006	30.021	30.035	-0.001	30.021	30.048	-0.014	30.021	30.061	-0.027
	MIN	30.000	30.002	-0.015	30.000	30.015	-0.028	30.000	30.022	-0.035	30.000	30.035	-0.048	30.000	30.048	-0.061

TABLE 3   PREFERRED HOLE BASIS TRANSITION AND INTERFERENCE FITS (Continued)

Dimensions in mm.

BASIC SIZE		LOCATIONAL TRANSN. Hole H7	Shaft k6	Fit	LOCATIONAL TRANSN. Hole H7	Shaft n6	Fit	LOCATIONAL INTERF. Hole H7	Shaft p6	Fit	MEDIUM DRIVE Hole H7	Shaft s6	Fit	FORCE Hole H7	Shaft u6	Fit
40	MAX	40.025	40.018	0.023	40.025	40.033	0.008	40.025	40.042	0.001	40.025	40.059	-0.018	40.025	40.076	-0.035
	MIN	40.000	40.002	-0.018	40.000	40.017	-0.033	40.000	40.026	-0.042	40.000	40.043	-0.059	40.000	40.060	-0.076
50	MAX	50.025	50.018	0.023	50.025	50.033	0.008	50.025	50.042	0.001	50.025	50.059	-0.018	50.025	50.086	-0.045
	MIN	50.000	50.002	-0.018	50.000	50.017	-0.033	50.000	50.026	-0.042	50.000	50.043	-0.059	50.000	50.070	-0.086
60	MAX	60.030	60.021	0.028	60.030	60.039	0.010	60.030	60.051	0.002	60.030	60.072	-0.023	60.030	60.106	-0.057
	MIN	60.000	60.002	-0.021	60.000	60.020	-0.039	60.000	60.032	-0.051	60.000	60.053	-0.072	60.000	60.087	-0.106
80	MAX	80.030	80.021	0.028	80.030	80.039	0.010	80.030	80.051	0.002	80.030	80.078	-0.029	80.030	80.121	-0.072
	MIN	80.000	80.002	-0.021	80.000	80.020	-0.039	80.000	80.032	-0.051	80.000	80.059	-0.078	80.000	80.102	-0.121
100	MAX	100.035	100.025	0.032	100.035	100.045	0.012	100.035	100.059	0.002	100.035	100.093	-0.036	100.035	100.146	-0.089
	MIN	100.000	100.003	-0.025	100.000	100.023	-0.045	100.000	100.037	-0.059	100.000	100.071	-0.093	100.000	100.124	-0.146
120	MAX	120.035	120.025	0.032	120.035	120.045	0.012	120.035	120.059	0.002	120.035	120.101	-0.044	120.035	120.166	-0.109
	MIN	120.000	120.003	-0.025	120.000	120.023	-0.045	120.000	120.037	-0.059	120.000	120.079	-0.101	120.000	120.144	-0.166
160	MAX	160.040	160.028	0.037	160.040	160.052	0.013	160.040	160.068	0.003	160.040	160.125	-0.060	160.040	160.215	-0.150
	MIN	160.000	160.003	-0.028	160.000	160.027	-0.052	160.000	160.043	-0.068	160.000	160.100	-0.125	160.000	160.190	-0.215
200	MAX	200.046	200.033	0.042	200.046	200.060	0.015	200.046	200.079	-0.004	200.046	200.151	-0.076	200.046	200.265	-0.190
	MIN	200.000	200.004	-0.033	200.000	200.031	-0.060	200.000	200.050	-0.079	200.000	200.122	-0.151	200.000	200.236	-0.265
250	MAX	250.046	250.033	0.042	250.046	250.060	0.015	250.046	250.079	-0.004	250.046	250.169	-0.094	250.046	250.313	-0.238
	MIN	250.000	250.004	-0.033	250.000	250.031	-0.060	250.000	250.050	-0.079	250.000	250.140	-0.169	250.000	250.284	-0.313
300	MAX	300.052	300.036	0.048	300.052	300.066	0.018	300.052	300.088	-0.004	300.052	300.202	-0.118	300.052	300.382	-0.298
	MIN	300.000	300.004	-0.036	300.000	300.034	-0.066	300.000	300.056	-0.088	300.000	300.170	-0.202	300.000	300.350	-0.382
400	MAX	400.057	400.040	0.053	400.057	400.073	0.020	400.057	400.098	-0.005	400.057	400.244	-0.151	400.057	400.471	-0.378
	MIN	400.000	400.004	-0.040	400.000	400.037	-0.073	400.000	400.062	-0.098	400.000	400.208	-0.244	400.000	400.435	-0.471
500	MAX	500.063	500.045	0.058	500.063	500.080	0.023	500.063	500.108	-0.005	500.063	500.292	-0.189	500.063	500.580	-0.477
	MIN	500.000	500.005	-0.045	500.000	500.040	-0.080	500.000	500.068	-0.108	500.000	500.252	-0.292	500.000	500.540	-0.580

AMERICAN NATIONAL STANDARD
PREFERRED METRIC LIMITS AND FITS

AMERICAN NATIONAL STANDARD
PREFERRED METRIC LIMITS AND FITS

ANSI B4.2-1978

Dimensions in mm.

TABLE 4 PREFERRED SHAFT BASIS CLEARANCE FITS

BASIC SIZE		LOOSE RUNNING Hole C11	Shaft h11	Fit	FREE RUNNING Hole D9	Shaft h9	Fit	CLOSE RUNNING Hole F8	Shaft h7	Fit	SLIDING Hole G7	Shaft h6	Fit	LOCATIONAL CLEARANCE Hole H7	Shaft h6	Fit
1	MAX	1.120	1.000	0.180	1.045	1.000	0.070	1.020	1.000	0.030	1.012	1.000	0.018	1.010	1.000	0.016
	MIN	1.060	0.940	0.060	1.020	0.975	0.020	1.006	0.990	0.006	1.002	0.994	0.002	1.000	0.994	0.000
1.2	MAX	1.320	1.200	0.180	1.245	1.200	0.070	1.220	1.200	0.030	1.212	1.200	0.018	1.210	1.200	0.016
	MIN	1.260	1.140	0.060	1.220	1.175	0.020	1.206	1.190	0.006	1.202	1.194	0.002	1.200	1.194	0.000
1.6	MAX	1.720	1.600	0.180	1.645	1.600	0.070	1.620	1.600	0.030	1.612	1.600	0.018	1.610	1.600	0.016
	MIN	1.660	1.540	0.060	1.620	1.575	0.020	1.606	1.590	0.006	1.602	1.594	0.002	1.600	1.594	0.000
2	MAX	2.120	2.000	0.180	2.045	2.000	0.070	2.020	2.000	0.030	2.012	2.000	0.018	2.010	2.000	0.016
	MIN	2.060	1.940	0.060	2.020	1.975	0.020	2.006	1.990	0.006	2.002	1.994	0.002	2.000	1.994	0.000
2.5	MAX	2.620	2.500	0.180	2.545	2.500	0.070	2.520	2.500	0.030	2.512	2.500	0.018	2.510	2.500	0.016
	MIN	2.560	2.440	0.060	2.520	2.475	0.020	2.506	2.490	0.006	2.502	2.494	0.002	2.500	2.494	0.000
3	MAX	3.120	3.000	0.180	3.045	3.000	0.070	3.020	3.000	0.030	3.012	3.000	0.018	3.010	3.000	0.016
	MIN	3.060	2.940	0.060	3.020	2.975	0.020	3.006	2.990	0.006	3.002	2.994	0.002	3.000	2.994	0.000
4	MAX	4.145	4.000	0.220	4.060	4.000	0.090	4.028	4.000	0.040	4.016	4.000	0.024	4.012	4.000	0.020
	MIN	4.070	3.925	0.070	4.030	3.970	0.030	4.010	3.988	0.010	4.004	3.992	0.004	4.000	3.992	0.000
5	MAX	5.145	5.000	0.220	5.060	5.000	0.090	5.028	5.000	0.040	5.016	5.000	0.024	5.012	5.000	0.020
	MIN	5.070	4.925	0.070	5.030	4.970	0.030	5.010	4.988	0.010	5.004	4.992	0.004	5.000	4.992	0.000
6	MAX	6.145	6.000	0.220	6.060	6.000	0.090	6.028	6.000	0.040	6.016	6.000	0.024	6.012	6.000	0.020
	MIN	6.070	5.925	0.070	6.030	5.970	0.030	6.010	5.988	0.010	6.004	5.992	0.004	6.000	5.992	0.000
8	MAX	8.170	8.000	0.260	8.076	8.000	0.112	8.035	8.000	0.050	8.020	8.000	0.029	8.015	8.000	0.024
	MIN	8.080	7.910	0.080	8.040	7.964	0.040	8.013	7.985	0.013	8.005	7.991	0.005	8.000	7.991	0.000
10	MAX	10.170	10.000	0.260	10.076	10.000	0.112	10.035	10.000	0.050	10.020	10.000	0.029	10.015	10.000	0.024
	MIN	10.080	9.910	0.080	10.040	9.964	0.040	10.013	9.985	0.013	10.005	9.991	0.005	10.000	9.991	0.000
12	MAX	12.205	12.000	0.315	12.093	12.000	0.136	12.043	12.000	0.061	12.024	12.000	0.035	12.018	12.000	0.029
	MIN	12.095	11.890	0.095	12.050	11.957	0.050	12.016	11.982	0.016	12.006	11.989	0.006	12.000	11.989	0.000
16	MAX	16.205	16.000	0.315	16.093	16.000	0.136	16.043	16.000	0.061	16.024	16.000	0.035	16.018	16.000	0.029
	MIN	16.095	15.890	0.095	16.050	15.957	0.050	16.016	15.982	0.016	16.006	15.989	0.006	16.000	15.989	0.000
20	MAX	20.240	20.000	0.370	20.117	20.000	0.169	20.053	20.000	0.074	20.028	20.000	0.041	20.021	20.000	0.034
	MIN	20.110	19.870	0.110	20.065	19.948	0.065	20.020	19.979	0.020	20.007	19.987	0.007	20.000	19.987	0.000
25	MAX	25.240	25.000	0.370	25.117	25.000	0.169	25.053	25.000	0.074	25.028	25.000	0.041	25.021	25.000	0.034
	MIN	25.110	24.870	0.110	25.065	24.948	0.065	25.020	24.979	0.020	25.007	24.987	0.007	25.000	24.987	0.000
30	MAX	30.240	30.000	0.370	30.117	30.000	0.169	30.053	30.000	0.074	30.028	30.000	0.041	30.021	30.000	0.034
	MIN	30.110	29.870	0.110	30.065	29.948	0.065	30.020	29.979	0.020	30.007	29.987	0.007	30.000	29.987	0.000

12

13

TABLE 4   PREFERRED SHAFT BASIS CLEARANCE FITS (Continued)

Dimensions in mm.

BASIC SIZE		LOOSE RUNNING			FREE RUNNING			CLOSE RUNNING			SLIDING			LOCATIONAL CLEARANCE		
		Hole C11	Shaft h11	Fit	Hole D9	Shaft h9	Fit	Hole F8	Shaft h7	Fit	Hole G7	Shaft h6	Fit	Hole H7	Shaft h6	Fit
40	MAX	40.280	40.000	0.440	40.142	40.000	0.204	40.064	40.000	0.089	40.034	40.000	0.050	40.025	40.000	0.041
	MIN	40.120	39.840	0.120	40.080	39.938	0.080	40.025	39.975	0.025	40.009	39.984	0.009	40.000	39.984	0.000
50	MAX	50.290	50.000	0.450	50.142	50.000	0.204	50.064	50.000	0.089	50.034	50.000	0.050	50.025	50.000	0.041
	MIN	50.130	49.840	0.130	50.080	49.938	0.080	50.025	49.975	0.025	50.009	49.984	0.009	50.000	49.984	0.000
60	MAX	60.330	60.000	0.520	60.174	60.000	0.248	60.076	60.000	0.106	60.040	60.000	0.059	60.030	60.000	0.049
	MIN	60.140	59.810	0.140	60.100	59.926	0.100	60.030	59.970	0.030	60.010	59.981	0.010	60.000	59.981	0.000
80	MAX	80.340	80.000	0.530	80.174	80.000	0.248	80.076	80.000	0.106	80.040	80.000	0.059	80.030	80.000	0.049
	MIN	80.150	79.810	0.150	80.100	79.926	0.100	80.030	79.970	0.030	80.010	79.981	0.010	80.000	79.981	0.000
100	MAX	100.390	100.000	0.610	100.207	100.000	0.294	100.090	100.000	0.125	100.047	100.000	0.069	100.035	100.000	0.057
	MIN	100.170	99.780	0.170	100.120	99.913	0.120	100.036	99.965	0.036	100.012	99.978	0.012	100.000	99.978	0.000
120	MAX	120.400	120.000	0.620	120.207	120.000	0.294	120.090	120.000	0.125	120.047	120.000	0.069	120.035	120.000	0.057
	MIN	120.180	119.780	0.180	120.120	119.913	0.120	120.036	119.965	0.036	120.012	119.978	0.012	120.000	119.978	0.000
160	MAX	160.460	160.000	0.710	160.245	160.000	0.345	160.106	160.000	0.146	160.054	160.000	0.079	160.040	160.000	0.065
	MIN	160.210	159.750	0.210	160.145	159.900	0.145	160.043	159.960	0.043	160.014	159.975	0.014	160.000	159.975	0.000
200	MAX	200.530	200.000	0.820	200.285	200.000	0.400	200.122	200.000	0.168	200.061	200.000	0.090	200.046	200.000	0.075
	MIN	200.240	199.710	0.240	200.170	199.885	0.170	200.050	199.954	0.050	200.015	199.971	0.015	200.000	199.971	0.000
250	MAX	250.570	250.000	0.860	250.285	250.000	0.400	250.122	250.000	0.168	250.061	250.000	0.090	250.046	250.000	0.075
	MIN	250.280	249.710	0.280	250.170	249.885	0.170	250.050	249.954	0.050	250.015	249.971	0.015	250.000	249.971	0.000
300	MAX	300.650	300.000	0.970	300.320	300.000	0.450	300.137	300.000	0.189	300.069	300.000	0.101	300.052	300.000	0.084
	MIN	300.330	299.680	0.330	300.190	299.870	0.190	300.056	299.948	0.056	300.017	299.968	0.017	300.000	299.968	0.000
400	MAX	400.760	400.000	1.120	400.350	400.000	0.490	400.151	400.000	0.208	400.075	400.000	0.111	400.057	400.000	0.093
	MIN	400.400	399.640	0.400	400.210	399.860	0.210	400.062	399.943	0.062	400.018	399.964	0.018	400.000	399.964	0.000
500	MAX	500.880	500.000	1.280	500.385	500.000	0.540	500.165	500.000	0.228	500.083	500.000	0.123	500.063	500.000	0.103
	MIN	500.480	499.600	0.480	500.230	499.845	0.230	500.068	499.937	0.068	500.020	499.960	0.020	500.000	499.960	0.000

AMERICAN NATIONAL STANDARD PREFERRED METRIC LIMITS AND FITS

AMERICAN NATIONAL STANDARD
PREFERRED METRIC LIMITS AND FITS

ANSI B4.2-1978

TABLE 5   PREFERRED SHAFT BASIS TRANSITION AND INTERFERENCE FITS

Dimensions in mm.

BASIC SIZE		LOCATIONAL TRANSN. Hole K7	Shaft h6	Fit	LOCATIONAL TRANSN. Hole N7	Shaft h6	Fit	LOCATIONAL INTERF. Hole P7	Shaft h6	Fit	MEDIUM DRIVE Hole S7	Shaft h6	Fit	FORCE Hole U7	Shaft h6	Fit
1	MAX	1.000	1.000	0.006	0.996	1.000	0.002	0.994	1.000	0.000	0.986	1.000	-0.008	0.982	1.000	-0.012
	MIN	0.990	0.994	-0.010	0.986	0.994	-0.014	0.984	0.994	-0.016	0.976	0.994	-0.024	0.972	0.994	-0.028
1.2	MAX	1.200	1.200	0.006	1.196	1.200	0.002	1.194	1.200	0.000	1.186	1.200	-0.008	1.182	1.200	-0.012
	MIN	1.190	1.194	-0.010	1.186	1.194	-0.014	1.184	1.194	-0.016	1.176	1.194	-0.024	1.172	1.194	-0.028
1.6	MAX	1.600	1.600	0.006	1.596	1.600	0.002	1.594	1.600	0.000	1.586	1.600	-0.008	1.582	1.600	-0.012
	MIN	1.590	1.594	-0.010	1.586	1.594	-0.014	1.584	1.594	-0.016	1.576	1.594	-0.024	1.572	1.594	-0.028
2	MAX	2.000	2.000	0.006	1.996	2.000	0.002	1.994	2.000	0.000	1.986	2.000	-0.008	1.982	2.000	-0.012
	MIN	1.990	1.994	-0.010	1.986	1.994	-0.014	1.984	1.994	-0.016	1.976	1.994	-0.024	1.972	1.994	-0.028
2.5	MAX	2.500	2.500	0.006	2.496	2.500	0.002	2.494	2.500	0.000	2.486	2.500	-0.008	2.482	2.500	-0.012
	MIN	2.490	2.494	-0.010	2.486	2.494	-0.014	2.484	2.494	-0.016	2.476	2.494	-0.024	2.472	2.494	-0.028
3	MAX	3.000	3.000	0.006	2.996	3.000	0.002	2.994	3.000	0.000	2.986	3.000	-0.008	2.982	3.000	-0.012
	MIN	2.990	2.994	-0.010	2.986	2.994	-0.014	2.984	2.994	-0.016	2.976	2.994	-0.024	2.972	2.994	-0.028
4	MAX	4.003	4.000	0.011	3.996	4.000	0.004	3.992	4.000	0.000	3.985	4.000	-0.007	3.981	4.000	-0.011
	MIN	3.991	3.992	-0.009	3.984	3.992	-0.016	3.980	3.992	-0.020	3.973	3.992	-0.027	3.969	3.992	-0.031
5	MAX	5.003	5.000	0.011	4.996	5.000	0.004	4.992	5.000	0.000	4.985	5.000	-0.007	4.981	5.000	-0.011
	MIN	4.991	4.992	-0.009	4.984	4.992	-0.016	4.980	4.992	-0.020	4.973	4.992	-0.027	4.969	4.992	-0.031
6	MAX	6.003	6.000	0.011	5.996	6.000	0.004	5.992	6.000	0.000	5.985	6.000	-0.007	5.981	6.000	-0.011
	MIN	5.991	5.992	-0.009	5.984	5.992	-0.016	5.980	5.992	-0.020	5.973	5.992	-0.027	5.969	5.992	-0.031
8	MAX	8.005	8.000	0.014	7.996	8.000	0.005	7.991	8.000	0.000	7.983	8.000	-0.008	7.978	8.000	-0.013
	MIN	7.990	7.991	-0.010	7.981	7.991	-0.019	7.976	7.991	-0.024	7.968	7.991	-0.032	7.963	7.991	-0.037
10	MAX	10.005	10.000	0.014	9.996	10.000	0.005	9.991	10.000	0.000	9.983	10.000	-0.008	9.978	10.000	-0.013
	MIN	9.990	9.991	-0.010	9.981	9.991	-0.019	9.976	9.991	-0.024	9.968	9.991	-0.032	9.963	9.991	-0.037
12	MAX	12.006	12.000	0.017	11.995	12.000	0.006	11.989	12.000	0.000	11.979	12.000	-0.010	11.974	12.000	-0.015
	MIN	11.988	11.989	-0.012	11.977	11.989	-0.023	11.971	11.989	-0.029	11.961	11.989	-0.039	11.956	11.989	-0.044
16	MAX	16.006	16.000	0.017	15.995	16.000	0.006	15.989	16.000	0.000	15.979	16.000	-0.010	15.974	16.000	-0.015
	MIN	15.988	15.989	-0.012	15.977	15.989	-0.023	15.971	15.989	-0.029	15.961	15.989	-0.039	15.956	15.989	-0.044
20	MAX	20.006	20.000	0.019	19.993	20.000	0.006	19.986	20.000	-0.001	19.973	20.000	-0.014	19.967	20.000	-0.020
	MIN	19.985	19.987	-0.015	19.972	19.987	-0.028	19.965	19.987	-0.035	19.952	19.987	-0.048	19.946	19.987	-0.054
25	MAX	25.006	25.000	0.019	24.993	25.000	0.006	24.986	25.000	-0.001	24.973	25.000	-0.014	24.960	25.000	-0.027
	MIN	24.985	24.987	-0.015	24.972	24.987	-0.028	24.965	24.987	-0.035	24.952	24.987	-0.048	24.939	24.987	-0.061
30	MAX	30.006	30.000	0.019	29.993	30.000	0.006	29.986	30.000	-0.001	29.973	30.000	-0.014	29.960	30.000	-0.027
	MIN	29.985	29.987	-0.015	29.972	29.987	-0.028	29.965	29.987	-0.035	29.952	29.987	-0.048	29.939	29.987	-0.061

14

Tolerance Problems

The parts shown in the picture are assembled as follows:

__Bearing "B" has an Interference fit with member "M".

__Shaft "S" rotates in bearing "B".

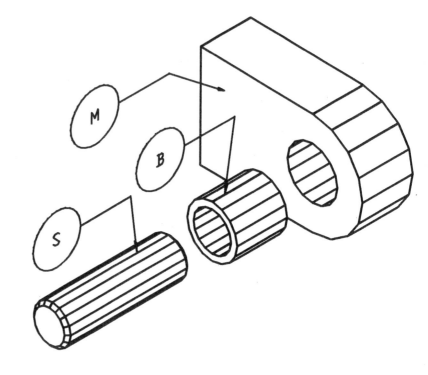

TOL-1 Bearing O.D. = 1.40, bearing I.D. = .75 inches

1. Neatly sketch the parts on isometric grid as shown. Use appropriate scale.

2. Use light drive fit for the bearing and free running fit for the shaft. Calculate dimensions. Show calculations. Use Preferred Hole Basis Charts.

3. Fully dimension the parts using your grid scale to determine sizes. Include all size and location dimensions.

TOL-2 Bearing O.D. = 40mm, bearing I.D. = 26mm {METRIC dimensions}

1. Neatly sketch the parts on isometric grid as shown. Use appropriate scale.

2. Use light drive fit for the bearing and free running fit for the shaft. Calculate dimensions. Show calculations. Use Preferred Hole Basis Charts.

3. Fully dimension the parts using your grid scale to determine sizes. Include all size and location dimensions.

Tolerance Problems -- continued

Description:

Arm "A" must rotate in Block "B".

The assembly is held together with Washer "W" and Nut "N".

Design the Limit dimensions for the assembly so that it is impossible to lock the Arm by over-tightening Nut "N".

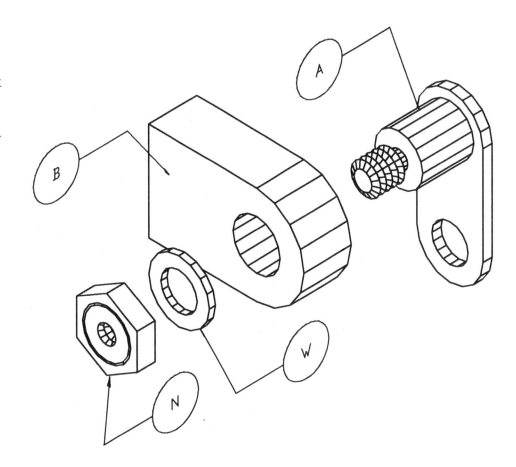

TOL-3. Diameter of shaft "A" is .5625 IN. Thickness of Block "B" is 1.08 IN.
1. Neatly sketch the assembly on isometric grid to scale.
2. Calculate the Limit dimensions per description. Show calculations.
3. Dimension the sketch. Use scale of sketch to determine size and location dimension values.

TOL-4. Diameter of shaft "A" is 20mm. Thickness of Block "B" is 36.5 mm.
1. Neatly sketch the assembly on isometric grid to scale.
2. Calculate the Limit dimensions per description. Show calculations.
3. Dimension the sketch. Use scale of sketch to determine size and location dimension values.

Tolerance Problems -- continued

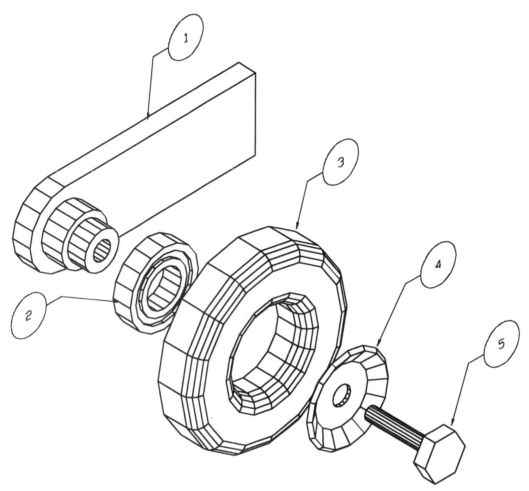

Belt tightener assembly -- Idler Wheel "3" runs against the outside of a serpentine belt.
Bearing "2" is a sealed roller-bearing. Bearing "2" is forced tightly into the inside hole in "3".
Bearing "2" slips closely over the cylindrical boss on Arm "1".
Bolt "5" and Flare Washer "4" hold the assembly together.

TOL-5. Bearing "2" O.D. = 2.125 IN. I.D. = 1.15 IN.
1. Neatly sketch the assembly on isometric or rectangular grid as assigned.
2. Calculate the limit dimensions for the mating parts. Show calculations.
3. Place the limit dimensions on the sketch. Using the sketch scale, place size and locations.

TOL-6. Bearing "2" O.D. = 85 mm. I.D. = 28mm.
1. Neatly sketch the assembly on isometric or rectangular grid as assigned.
2. Calculate the limit dimensions for the mating parts. Show calculations.
3. Place the limit dimensions on the sketch. Using the sketch scale, place size and locations.

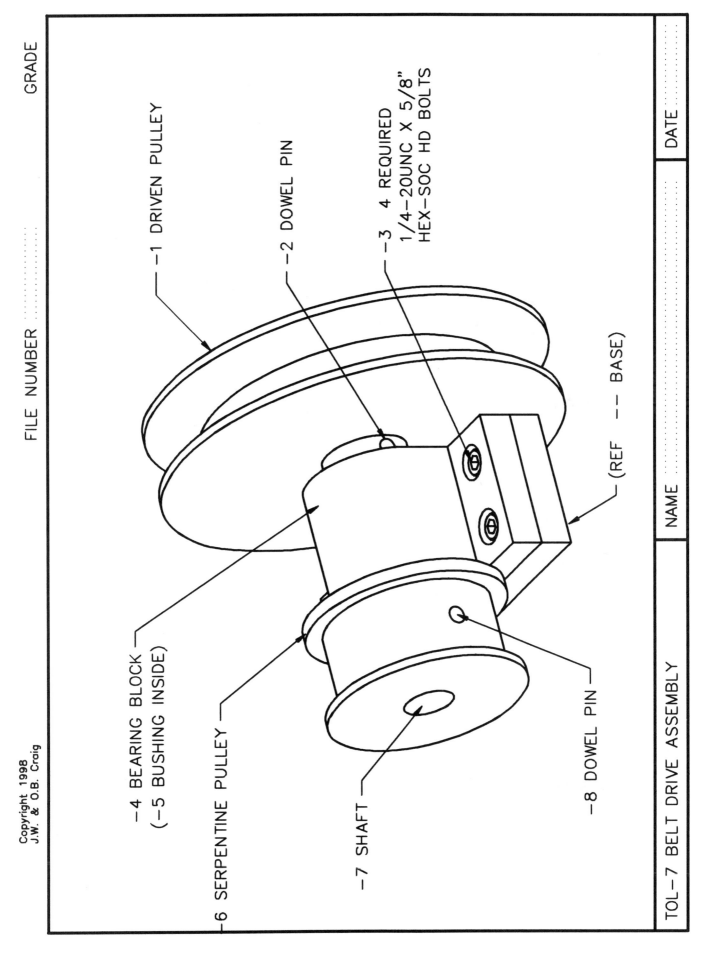

GRADE

FILE NUMBER

DATE

NAME

—1 DRIVEN PULLEY

—2 DOWEL PIN

—3 4 REQUIRED
1/4—20UNC X 5/8"
HEX—SOC HD BOLTS

(REF — — BASE)

—4 BEARING BLOCK
(—5 BUSHING INSIDE)

6 SERPENTINE PULLEY

—7 SHAFT

—8 DOWEL PIN

TOL—7 BELT DRIVE ASSEMBLY

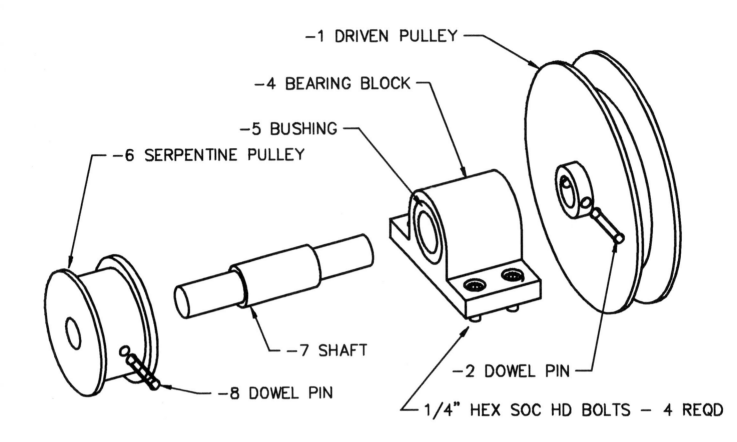

-1 DRIVEN PULLEY

-4 BEARING BLOCK

-5 BUSHING

-6 SERPENTINE PULLEY

-7 SHAFT

-8 DOWEL PIN

-2 DOWEL PIN

1/4" HEX SOC HD BOLTS – 4 REQD

NOTES ON THE BELT DRIVE ASSEMBLY:

1. Pulleys (-1) and (-6) have a sliding fit with the shaft (-7).

2. The shaft (-7) has a running fit with the bronze bushing (-5).

3. Bushing (-5) has a force fit with the bearing block (-4).

4. 1/4" hexagon socket head bolts are counterbored into and fit into clearance holes in the bearing block (-4).

5. Dowel pins (-2) and (-8) have a force fit with the shaft (-7) and the pulleys.

6. There are six critical (mating) dimensions on the shaft (-7). Be sure to consider the design carefully.

Dimension the parts using either decimal inch or metric dimensions as assigned.

Fully dimension all parts. Use instruments or freehand sketching as assigned.
Determine nominal sizes using the scales printed on each page. Use dividers or the edge of a card to measure features.

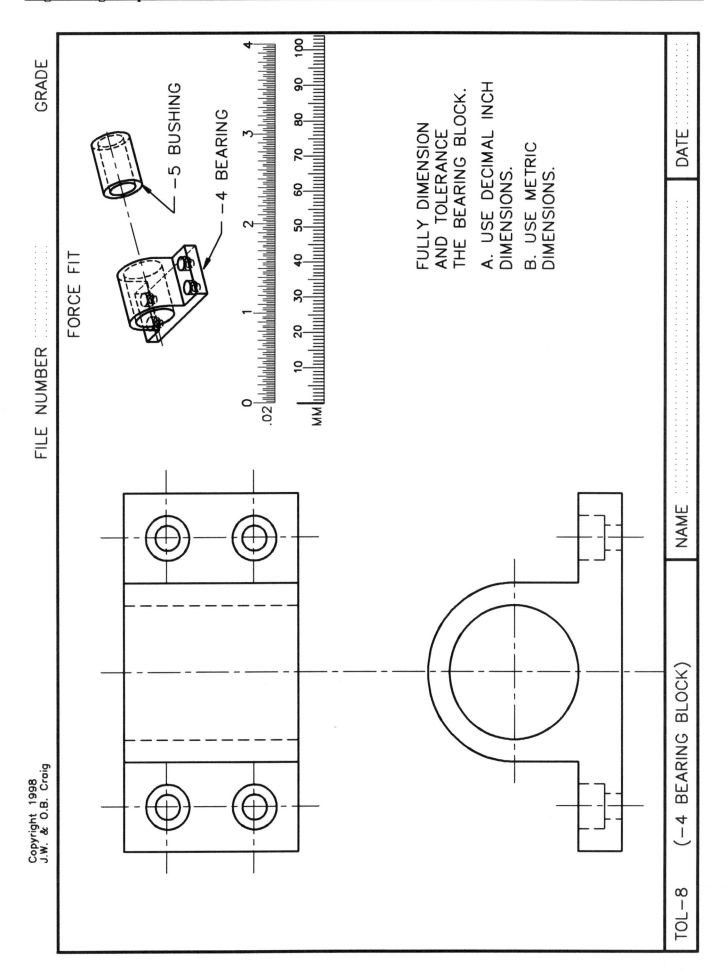

GRADE

FILE NUMBER

FORCE FIT

—5 BUSHING

—4 BEARING

FULLY DIMENSION
AND TOLERANCE
THE BEARING BLOCK.

A. USE DECIMAL INCH
DIMENSIONS.

B. USE METRIC
DIMENSIONS.

.02

MM

NAME

DATE

TOL—8   (—4 BEARING BLOCK)

NOTE: Use this grid format
in horizontal direction.

name

date

FILE NUMBER

GRADE

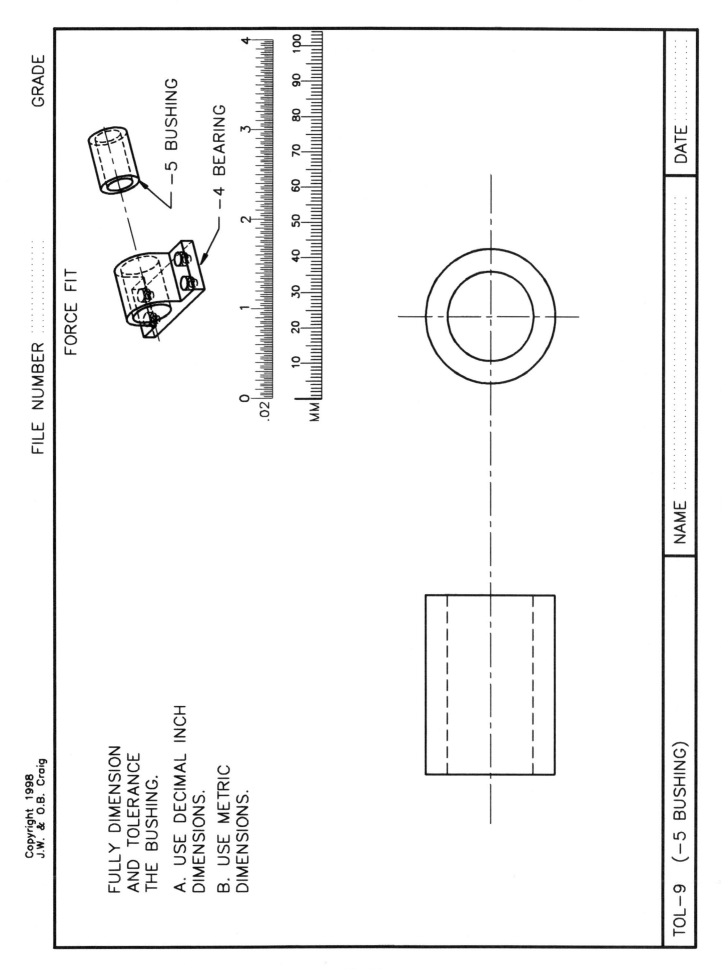

GRADE

FILE NUMBER

FORCE FIT

—5 BUSHING

—4 BEARING

FULLY DIMENSION
AND TOLERANCE
THE BUSHING.

A. USE DECIMAL INCH
DIMENSIONS.

B. USE METRIC
DIMENSIONS.

MM

.02

0   10   20   30   40   50   60   70   80   90   100

0   1   2   3   4

NAME

DATE

TOL—9   (—5 BUSHING)

RECTANGULAR GRID

NAME

DATE

FILE NUMBER

GRADE

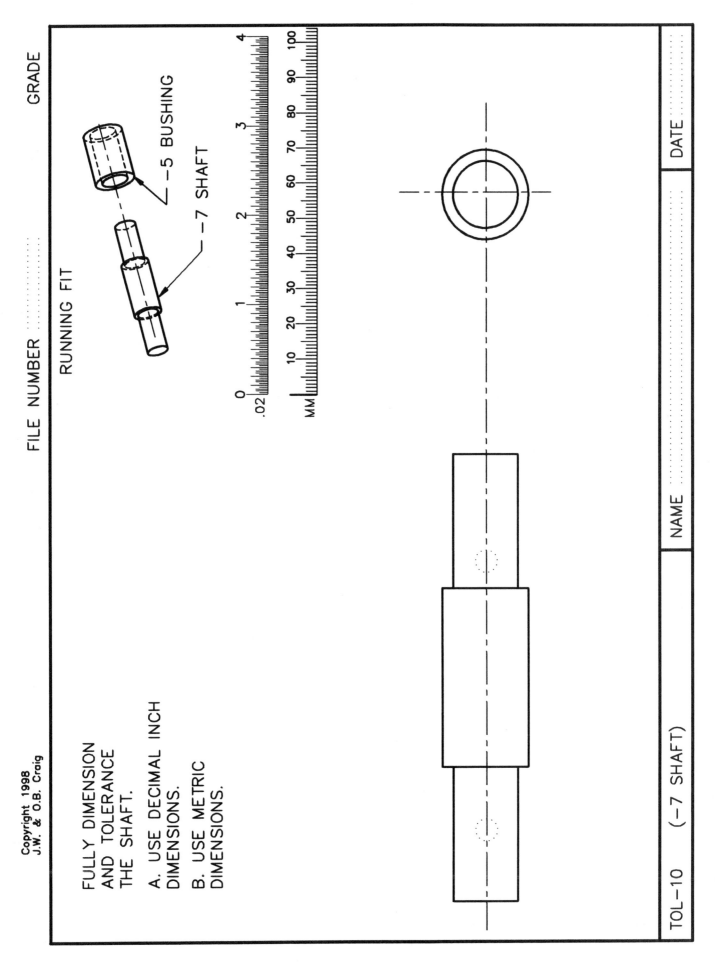

FILE NUMBER

GRADE

RUNNING FIT

FULLY DIMENSION
AND TOLERANCE
THE SHAFT.

A. USE DECIMAL INCH
DIMENSIONS.

B. USE METRIC
DIMENSIONS.

−5 BUSHING

−7 SHAFT

NAME

DATE

TOL−10   (−7 SHAFT)

name

date

NOTE: Use this grid format
in horizontal direction.

FILE NUMBER

GRADE

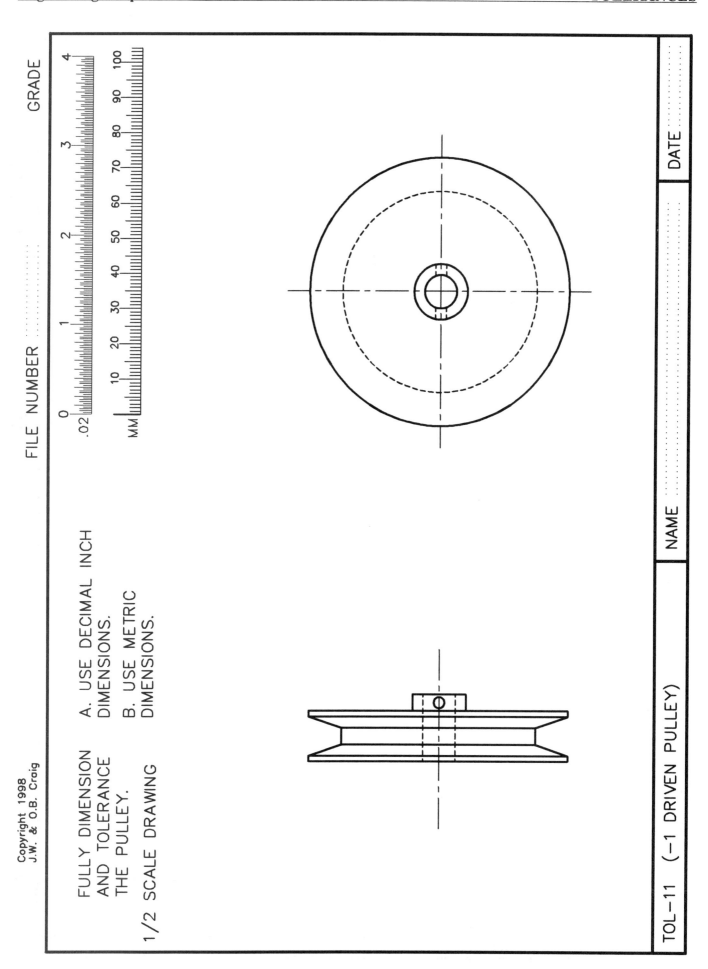

GRADE

FILE NUMBER

FULLY DIMENSION
AND TOLERANCE
THE PULLEY.

A. USE DECIMAL INCH
DIMENSIONS.

B. USE METRIC
DIMENSIONS.

1/2 SCALE DRAWING

TOL−11   (−1 DRIVEN PULLEY)

NAME

DATE

RECTANGULAR GRID

NAME

DATE

FILE NUMBER

GRADE

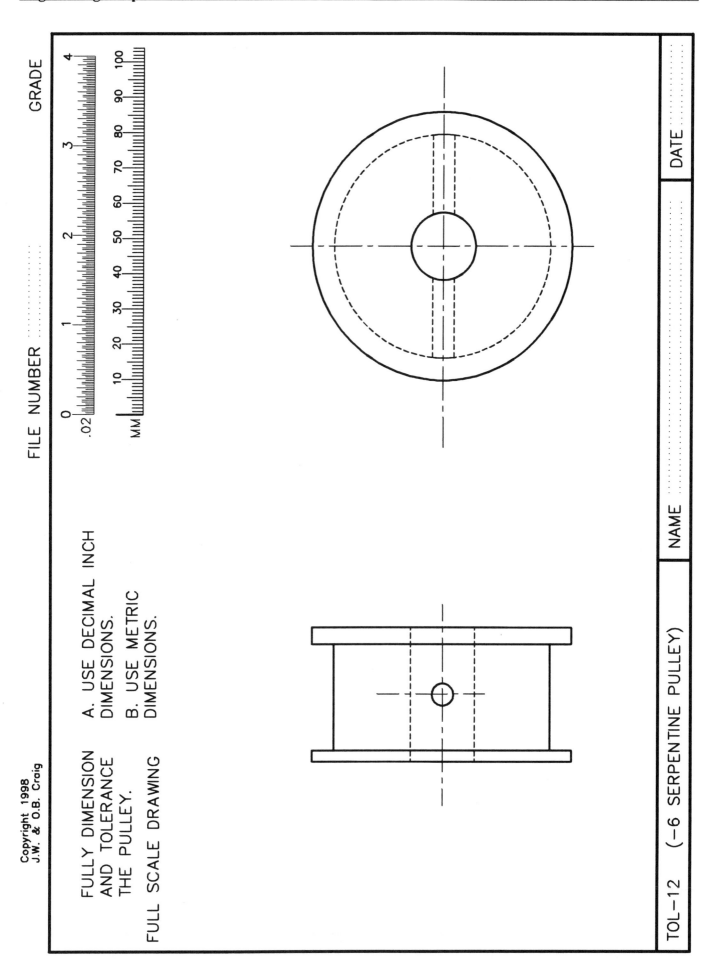

GRADE

FILE NUMBER

FULLY DIMENSION
AND TOLERANCE
THE PULLEY.

A. USE DECIMAL INCH
DIMENSIONS.

B. USE METRIC
DIMENSIONS.

FULL SCALE DRAWING

DATE

NAME

TOL-12   (-6 SERPENTINE PULLEY)

name

date

NOTE: Use this grid format
in horizontal direction.

FILE NUMBER

GRADE

Third Angle and First Angle Projection

Three orthogonal planes in space are used to define the primary drawing views. These planes are each 90 degrees to the other two planes. Most machine tools operate using these axes. Also, most building and engineering projects rely on these planes as the basis for construction.

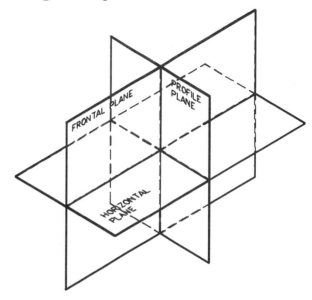

Early mathemeticians labeled the quadrants between the planes counterclockwise as shown. The 1st angle, 2nd angle, 3rd angle and 4th angle are refered to often in plotting points on a graph.

These quandrants are also used as the basis for creating three dimensional objects in space. The individual surfaces are the basis for creating a series of two dimensional views of the three dimensional objects.

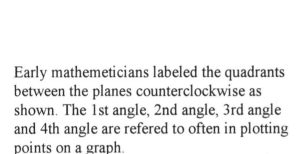

First Angle Projection

In Europe drawings were created by placing an object in the first angle as shown. Two dimensional views are drawn on the planes behind or under the object.

This type of drawing is the World Standard. While not common in the United States, virtually all drawings created in the rest of the industrial coutries follow this form.

With diversification, U.S. companies must create these drawings and technical people must read first angle drawings

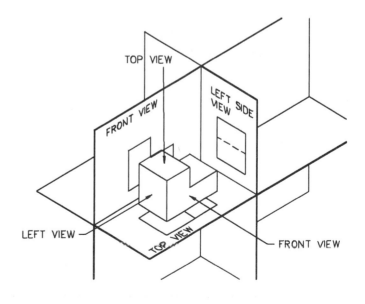

First Angle Views.

On flat paper the views appear as shown:

The front view is the key view.
The top view is placed below the front.
The right view is placed to the left of the front.
The left view is placed to the right of the front, etc.

Older Engineers often refer to this representation as "a Dutch Projection".

Third Angle projection.

Placing the object in the 3rd quadrant results in the arrangement of views which is more familiar in the United States. Views are placed on projection planes above, in front of or to the right of the object.

The adoption of different projection systems was probably due to the isolation of America and Europe at the time of the Industrial Revolution.

Third angle arrangement of views:

Notice that 2nd angle or 4th angle projections could be created also.

What would be the view arrangement for a 2nd angle projection?

What would be the view arrangement for a 4th angle projection?

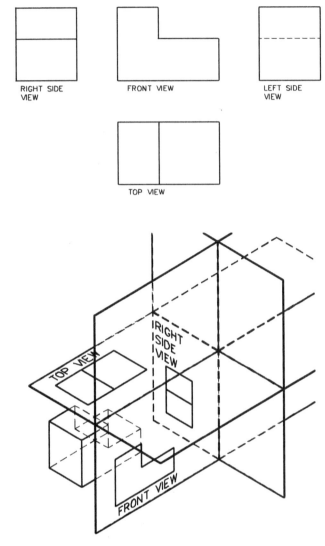

ORTHOGRAPHIC PROJECTION

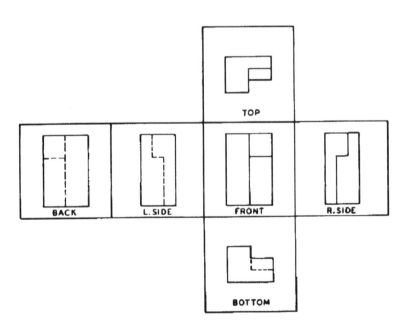

GIVEN: ISOMETRIC PICTORIAL VIEW.

SKETCH: FIRST ANGLE FRONT, RIGHT AND TOP VIEWS.

FILE NUMBER .... GRADE

LABEL SURFACES, NUMBER CORNERS WHEN INDICATED.

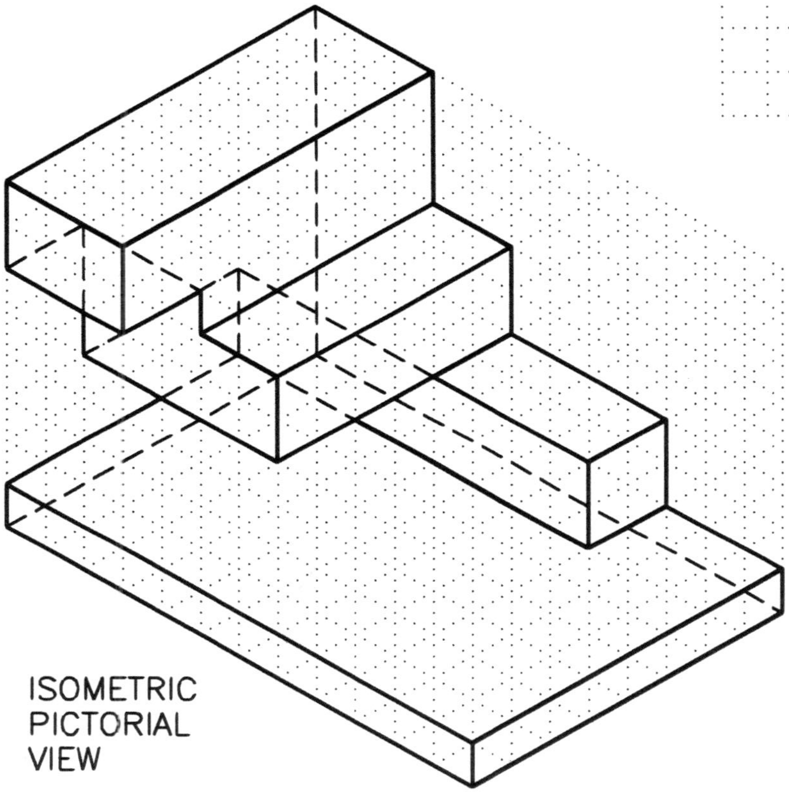

FIRST ANGLE ORTHOGRAPHIC VIEWS

NAME .... DATE ....

ISOMETRIC PICTORIAL VIEW

FIRST ANGLE —1

Copyright 1998
J.W. & O.B. Craig

GIVEN: ISOMETRIC PICTORIAL VIEW.
SKETCH FRONT, RIGHT, TOP
FIRST ANGLE PROJECTION VIEWS.

FILE NUMBER

GRADE

LABEL SURFACES, NUMBER CORNERS
WHEN INDICATED.

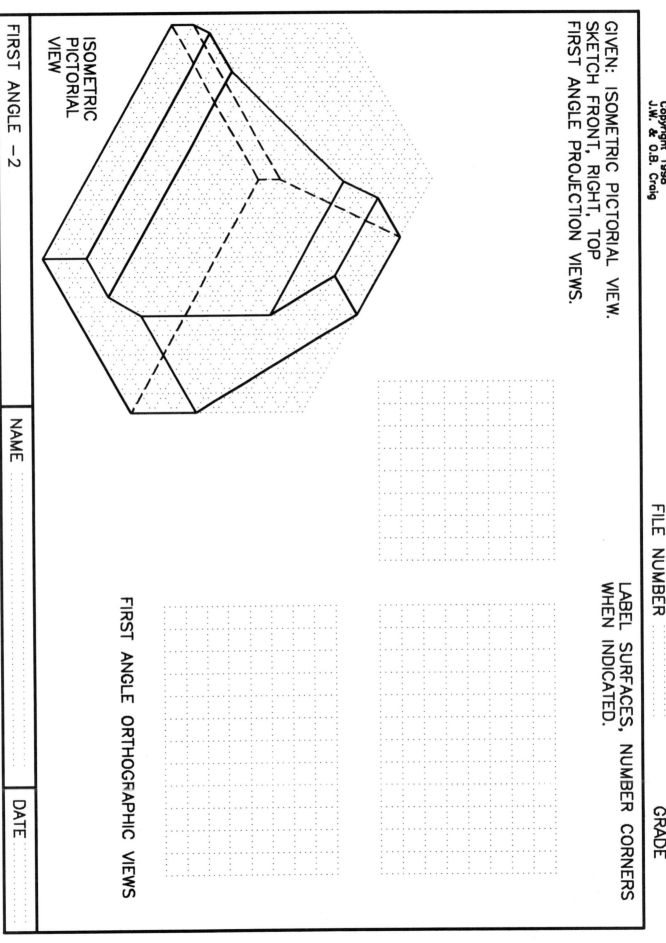

ISOMETRIC
PICTORIAL
VIEW

FIRST ANGLE ORTHOGRAPHIC VIEWS

FIRST ANGLE -2

NAME

DATE

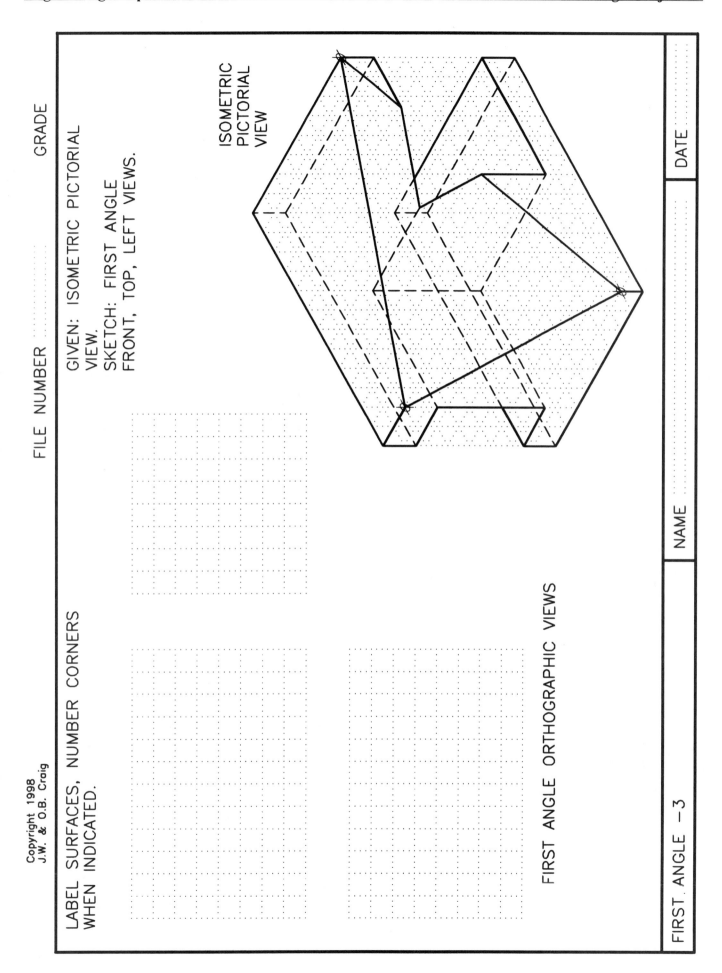

GRADE

FILE NUMBER

GIVEN: ISOMETRIC PICTORIAL VIEW.

SKETCH: FIRST ANGLE FRONT, TOP, LEFT VIEWS.

ISOMETRIC PICTORIAL VIEW

LABEL SURFACES, NUMBER CORNERS WHEN INDICATED.

FIRST ANGLE ORTHOGRAPHIC VIEWS

NAME

DATE

FIRST ANGLE −3

FIRST ANGLE —4

ORTHOGRAPHIC VIEWS

NAME

DATE

FILE NUMBER

GRADE

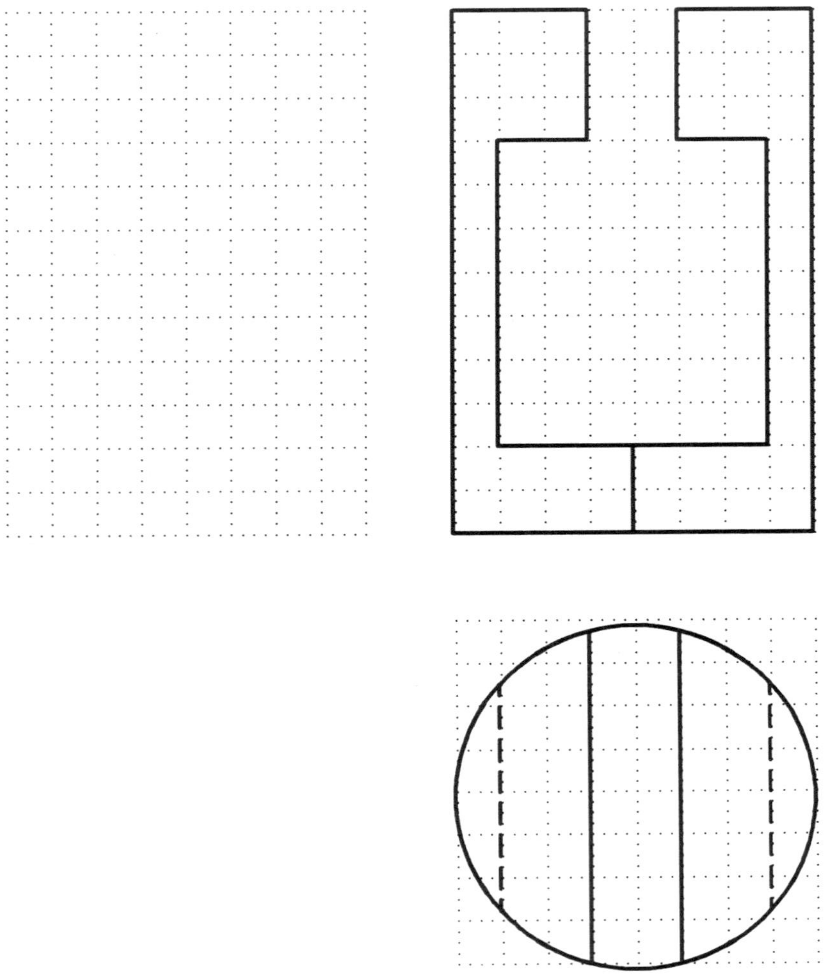

ISOMETRIC
PICTORIAL
VIEW

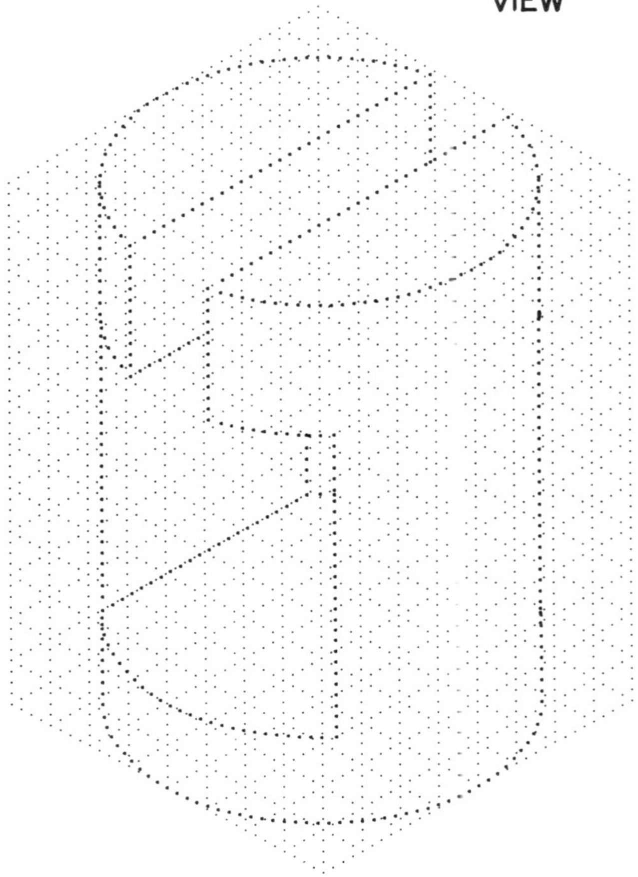

GIVEN: FRONT AND TOP VIEWS.
SKETCH: FIRST ANGLE
RIGHT SIDE VIEW.
SKETCH: ISOMETRIC PICTORIAL VIEW.

GRADE

FILE NUMBER

LABEL SURFACES, NUMBER CORNERS
WHEN INDICATED.

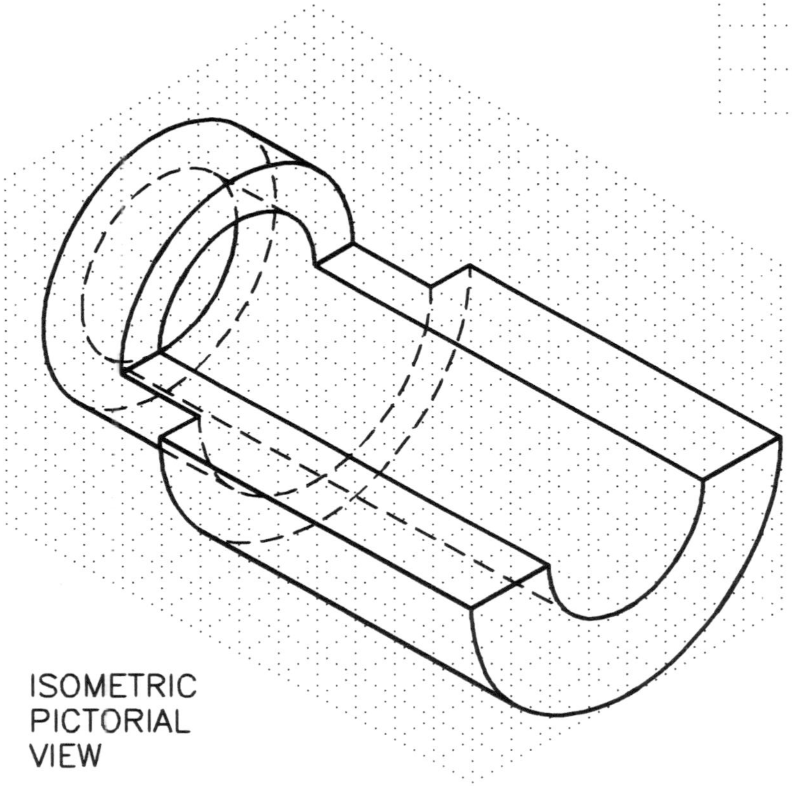

FIRST ANGLE ORTHOGRAPHIC VIEWS

Copyright 1998
J.W. & O.B. Craig

GIVEN:
SKETCH: FIRST ANGLE VIEWS
1. RIGHT SIDE VIEW.
2. FRONT VIEW FULL SECTION
3. TOP VIEW.
MATERIAL: STEEL.

ISOMETRIC
PICTORIAL
VIEW

FIRST ANGLE −5

NAME

DATE

Copyright 1998
J.W. & O.B. Craig

GIVEN: FIRST ANGLE PROJECTION
FRONT AND RIGHT SIDE VIEWS.
SKETCH: TOP AND ISOMETRIC
PICTORIAL VIEWS.

FILE NUMBER

LABEL SURFACES, NUMBER CORNERS
WHEN INDICATED.

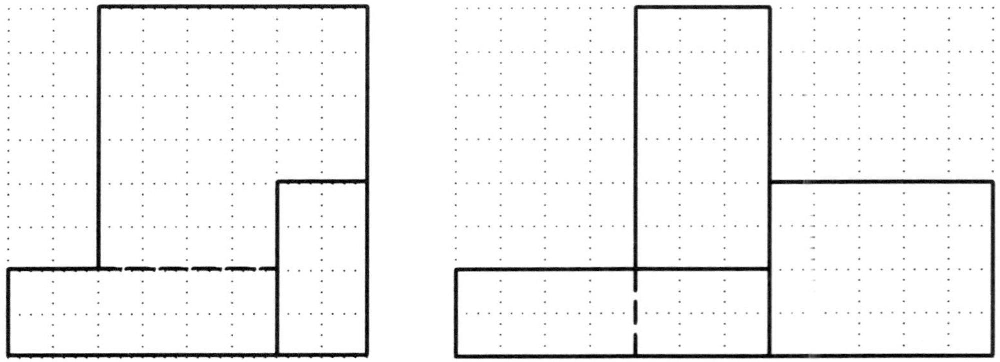

GRADE

ISOMETRIC
PICTORIAL
VIEW

FIRST ANGLE ORTHOGRAPHIC VIEWS

FIRST ANGLE —6

NAME

DATE

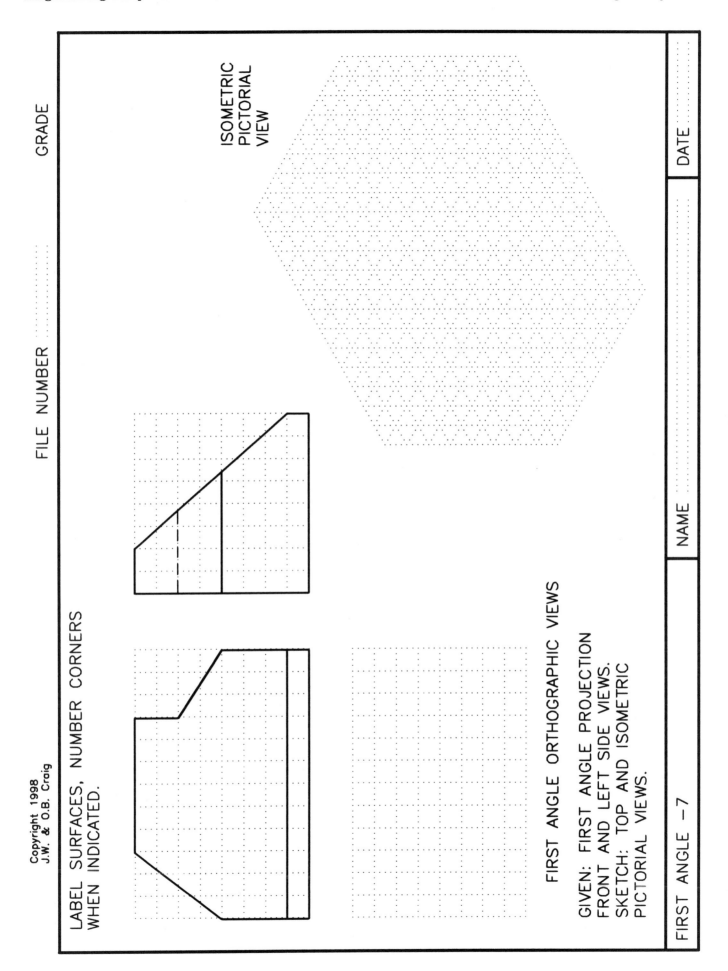

GRADE

FILE NUMBER

ISOMETRIC
PICTORIAL
VIEW

Copyright 1998
J.W. & O.B. Craig

LABEL SURFACES, NUMBER CORNERS
WHEN INDICATED.

FIRST ANGLE ORTHOGRAPHIC VIEWS

GIVEN: FIRST ANGLE PROJECTION
FRONT AND LEFT SIDE VIEWS.
SKETCH: TOP AND ISOMETRIC
PICTORIAL VIEWS.

FIRST ANGLE −7

NAME

DATE

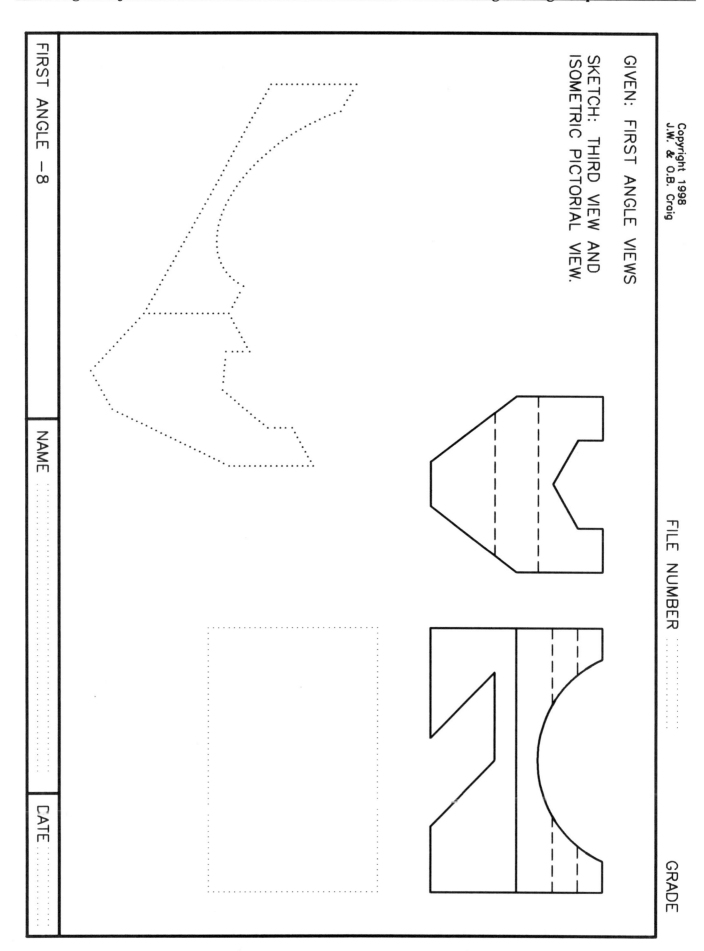

GIVEN: FIRST ANGLE VIEWS

SKETCH: THIRD VIEW AND
ISOMETRIC PICTORIAL VIEW.

FILE NUMBER

GRADE

FIRST ANGLE −8

NAME

DATE

GEOMETRY
O F
DRAWING

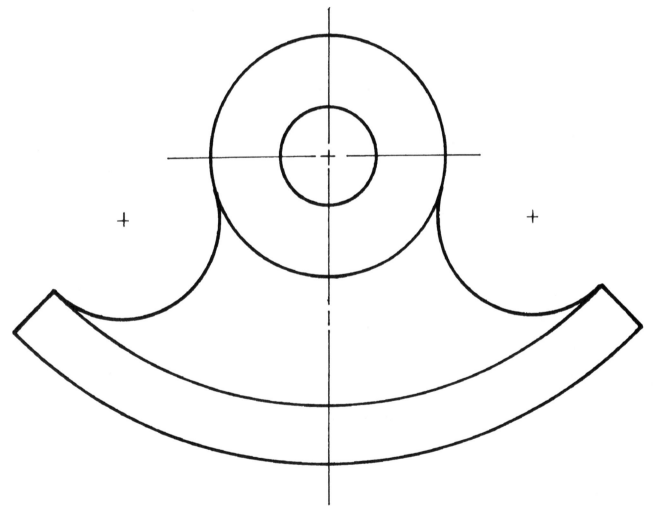

ORVAL B. CRAIG

GEOMETRIC SHAPES

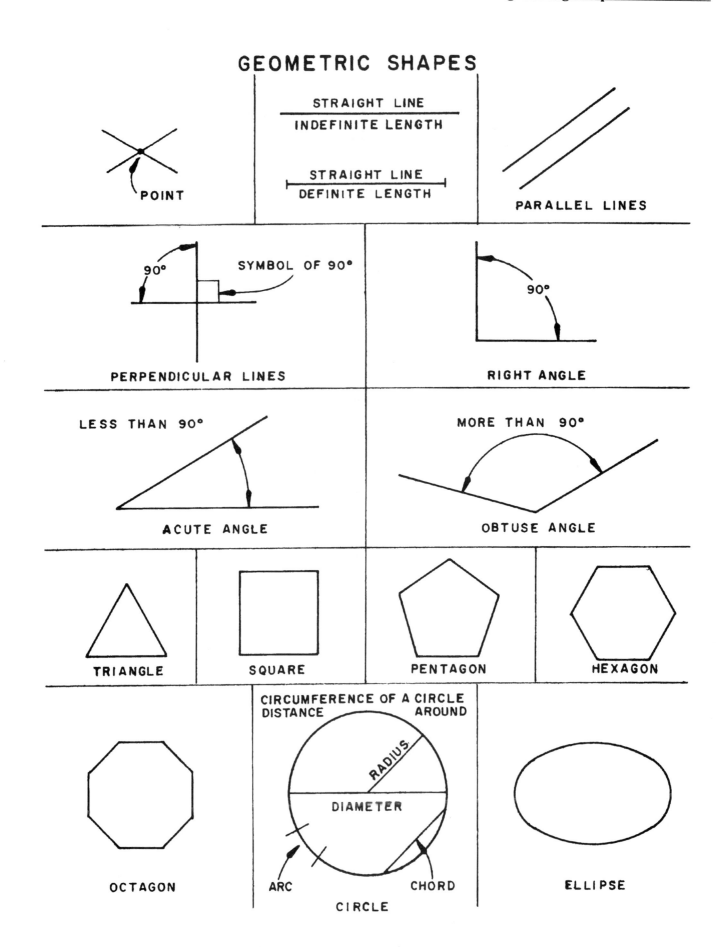

POINT

STRAIGHT LINE
INDEFINITE LENGTH

STRAIGHT LINE
DEFINITE LENGTH

PARALLEL LINES

90°   SYMBOL OF 90°

PERPENDICULAR LINES

90°

RIGHT ANGLE

LESS THAN 90°

ACUTE ANGLE

MORE THAN 90°

OBTUSE ANGLE

TRIANGLE

SQUARE

PENTAGON

HEXAGON

OCTAGON

CIRCUMFERENCE OF A CIRCLE
DISTANCE   AROUND

RADIUS

DIAMETER

ARC   CHORD

CIRCLE

ELLIPSE

HOW TO BISECT A LINE

A ├────────────────────┤ B

PROBLEM = BISECT LINE A-B
BISECT = CUT IN HALF

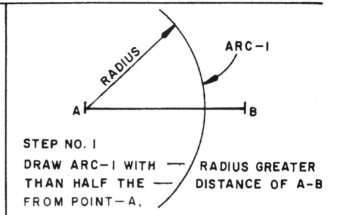

STEP NO. 1
DRAW ARC-1 WITH ── RADIUS GREATER
THAN HALF THE ── DISTANCE OF A-B
FROM POINT-A.

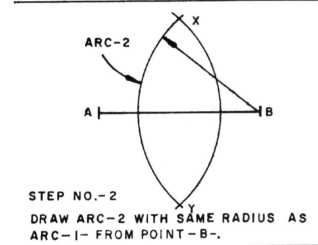

ARC-2

STEP NO.-2
DRAW ARC-2 WITH SAME RADIUS AS
ARC-1- FROM POINT-B-.

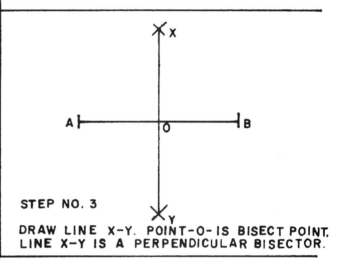

STEP NO. 3
DRAW LINE X-Y. POINT-O- IS BISECT POINT.
LINE X-Y IS A PERPENDICULAR BISECTOR.

PERPENDICULAR TO A LINE

A ───────────┬─────────── B
          X POINT

PROBLEM = DRAW PERPENDICULAR AT
POINT-X- TO LINE A-B

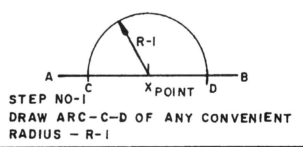

STEP NO-1
DRAW ARC-C-D OF ANY CONVENIENT
RADIUS — R-1

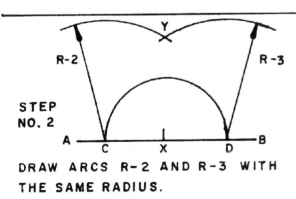

STEP
NO. 2

DRAW ARCS R-2 AND R-3 WITH
THE SAME RADIUS.

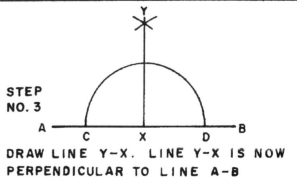

STEP
NO. 3

DRAW LINE Y-X. LINE Y-X IS NOW
PERPENDICULAR TO LINE A-B

BISECT AN ANGLE

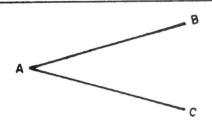

PROBLEM = BISECT AN ANGLE
     ANGLE   B—A—C

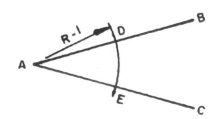

STEP NO. 1
WITH CONVENIENT RADIUS FROM POINT
-A- DRAW ARC-R-1

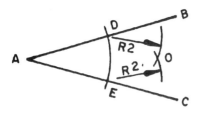

STEP NO. 2
WITH CONVENIENT RADIUS FROM POINTS
D AND E - DRAW ARC R2 - LOCATE POINT-O-

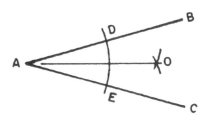

STEP NO. 3
DRAW LINE O-A. THIS LINE IS THE
BISECTING LINE.

CIRCLE THROUGH - 3 - POINTS

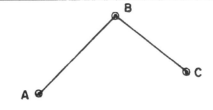

PROBLEM = DRAW CIRCLE THRU - 3 - POINTS

STEP NO. 1
DRAW LINES A-B AND B-C

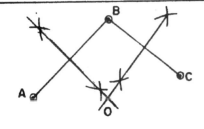

STEP NO. 2
BISECT LINE A-B AND B-C. EXTEND LINES
TO INTERSECT AT POINT-O-.

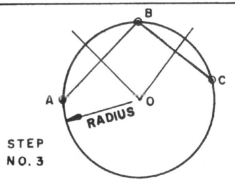

STEP
NO. 3

WITH O-A AS THE RADIUS DRAW CIRCLE.

FIND THE CENTER OF A CIRCLE

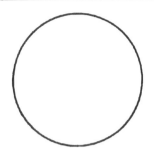

PROBLEM = FIND THE CENTER OF CIRCLE
USE THE CHORD METHOD.

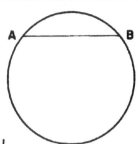

STEP NO. I
DRAW HORIZONTAL LINE A-B ACROSS
THE TOP OF THE CIRCLE.

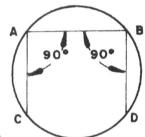

STEP NO. 2
DRAW PERPENDICULAR LINES DOWN
FROM POINTS A AND B.

CHORD METHOD

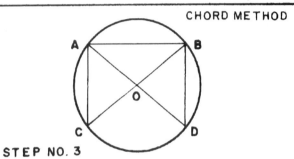

STEP NO. 3
DRAW LINES A-D AND B-C. POINT -O-
IS THE CENTER OF THE CIRCLE.

FIND THE CENTER OF A CIRCLE

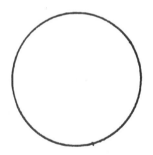

PROBLEM = FIND THE CENTER OF CIRCLE

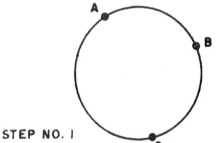

STEP NO. I
LOCATE -3- CONVENIENT POINTS ON
THE CIRCLE A-B-C

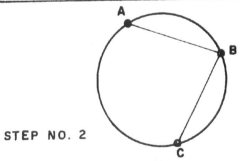

STEP NO. 2

DRAW LINES A-B AND B-C

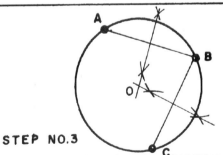

STEP NO. 3
DRAW PERPENDICULAR BISECTOR OF
LINES A-B AND B-C.-O- IS THE CENTER.

TO DRAW A PENTAGON

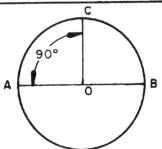

STEP NO.1
DRAW HORIZONTAL LINE A-B
DRAW VERTICAL LINE O-C

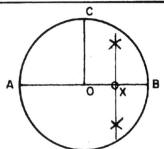

STEP NO. 2
BISECT LINE O-B
LOCATE POINT -X

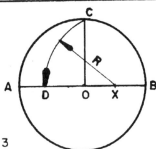

STEP NO. 3
WITH X-C AS THE RADIUS DRAW ARC-C-D.
LOCATE POINT -D-.

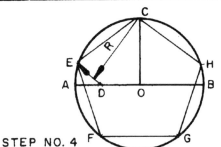

STEP NO. 4
WITH C-D AS THE RADIUS DRAW ARC D-E.
DISTANCE C-E WILL BE ONE SIDE OF THE
PENTAGON. LAY OFF OTHER FOUR SIDES.

TO DRAW A HEXAGON

HEXAGON ACROSS FLATS

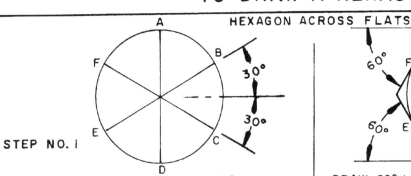

STEP NO. 1

DRAW LINES E-B AND F-C ON 30°
DRAW VERTICAL LINE A-D

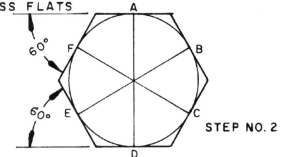

STEP NO. 2

DRAW 60° LINES AT POINTS -F-B-C-E
E-B = DISTANCE ACROSS FLATS

HEXAGON ACROSS CORNERS

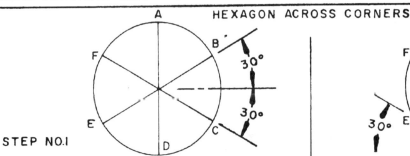

STEP NO.1

DRAW LINES E-B AND F-C ON 30°
DRAW VERTICAL LINE A-D

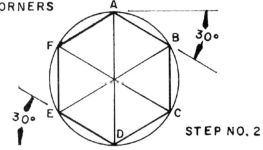

STEP NO. 2

CONNECT POINTS ON INSIDE OF CIRCLE
E-B = DISTANCE ACROSS CORNERS

TO DRAW A OCTAGON

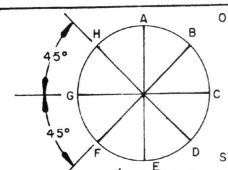

OCTAGON ACROSS FLATS

A=E- B=F- C=G-D=H
DISTANCE ACROSS
FLATS

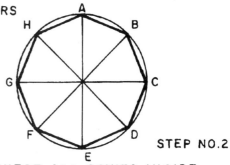

STEP NO.1
DRAW 45° LINES H-D AND B-F. DRAW VERTICAL
LINE A-E AND HORIZONTAL LINE C-G

STEP NO.2
DRAW TANGENT LINES AT POINTS –
A–B–C–D–E–F–G

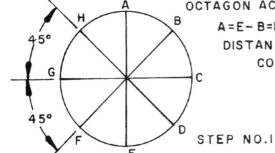

OCTAGON ACROSS CORNERS

A=E- B=F – C=G- D=H
DISTANCE ACROSS
CORNERS

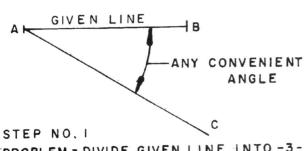

STEP NO.1
DRAW 45° LINES H-D AND B-F. DRAW VERTICAL
LINE A-E AND HORIZONTAL LINE C-G.

STEP NO.2
CONNECT ALL POINTS INSIDE
THE CIRCLE.

DIVIDING A LINE INTO EQUAL PARTS

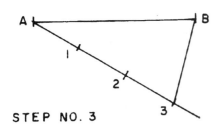

STEP NO. 1
PROBLEM = DIVIDE GIVEN LINE INTO –3–
EQUAL PARTS.

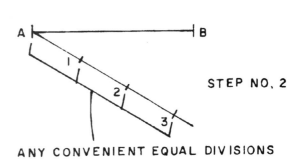

STEP NO. 2

ANY CONVENIENT EQUAL DIVISIONS

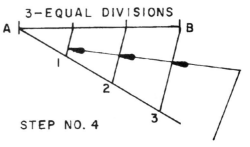

STEP NO. 3

CONNECT POINT –3– WITH POINT–B

STEP NO. 4

DRAW PARALLEL LINES FROM POINTS
I-AND–2 WITH LINE–3–B.

DRAWING ODD SHAPED FIGURES

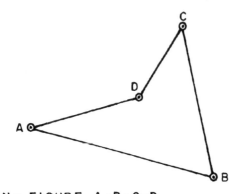

GIVEN = FIGURE A-B-C-D

PROBLEM = TRANSFER ODD SHAPED
FIGURE A-B-C-D

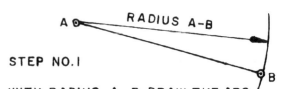

STEP NO. I

WITH RADIUS A-B DRAW THE ARC
LOCATE POINT-B- AT ANY CONVENIENT
PLACE ON THE ARC.

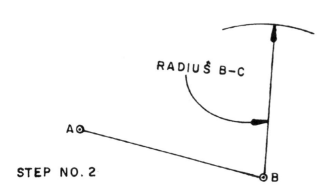

STEP NO. 2

WITH THE DISTANCE B-C DRAW THE
ARC-B-C FROM POINT-B.

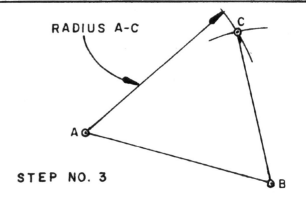

STEP NO. 3

WITH THE DISTANCE A-C DRAW THE
ARC-A-C FROM POINT-A. THE
INTERSECTION LOCATES POINT-C.

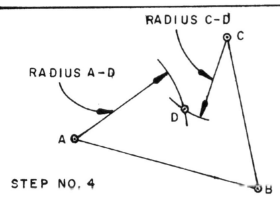

STEP NO. 4

WITH THE DISTANCE A-D DRAW THE
ARC A-D FROM POINT-A. WITH THE
DISTANCE C-D DRAW THE ARC C-D.
THE INTERSECTION LOCATES POINT-D.

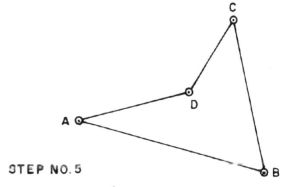

STEP NO. 5

FINISH THE ODD SHAPED FIGURE BY
DRAWING LINES C-D AND A-D

ARC TANGENT TO TWO LINES

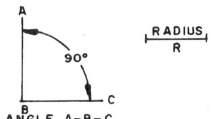

GIVEN= ANGLE A-B-C
PROBLEM= DRAW ARC WITH RADIUS -R-
TANGENT TO ANGLE A-B-C.

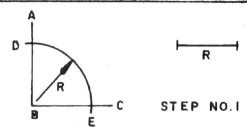

STEP NO.1

FROM POINT-B- WITH RADIUS -R-
DRAW ARC D-E

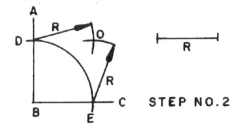

STEP NO.2

FROM POINTS D AND E WITH RADIUS -R-
DRAW ARCS THAT INTERSECT AT -O.

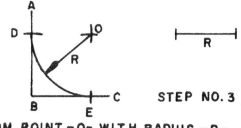

STEP NO.3

FROM POINT -O- WITH RADIUS -R-
DRAW ARC D-E.

ARC TANGENT TO TWO LINES

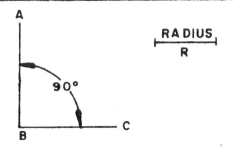

GIVEN= ANGLE A-B-C

PROBLEM= DRAW ARC WITH RADIUS-R-
TANGENT TO ANGLE A-B-C.

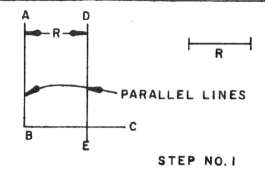

PARALLEL LINES

STEP NO.1

WITH THE DISTANCE OF RADIUS -R-
DRAW LINE D-E PARALLEL TO
LINE A-B.

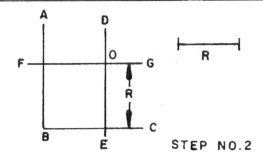

STEP NO.2

WITH THE DISTANCE OF RADIUS -R-
DRAW LINE F-G PARALLEL TO
LINE B-C. LINE F-G AND LINE D-E
INTERSECT AT POINT -O.

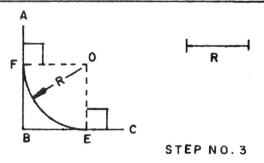

STEP NO.3

FROM POINT -O- WITH THE RADIUS OF
-R- DRAW ARC F-E. POINTS -F AND E-
ARE THE TANGENT POINTS.

ARC TANGENT TO TWO LINES

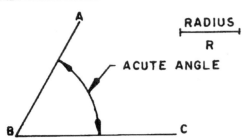

GIVIN = ACUTE ANGLE A—B—C
PROBLEM = DRAW ARC WITH RADIUS —R—
TANGENT TO ANGLE A—B—C.

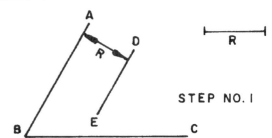

STEP NO. I

WITH THE DISTANCE OF RADIUS —R—
DRAW LINE D—E PARALLEL TO
LINE A—B.

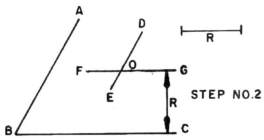

STEP NO.2

WITH THE DISTANCE OF RADIUS —R—
DRAW LINE F—G PARALLEL TO
LINE B—C. NOTE POINT —O—.

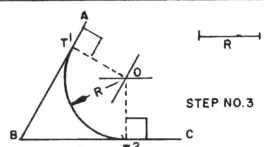

STEP NO.3

FROM POINT—O—WITH RADIUS —R—DRAW
ARC T¹—T². T¹—T² ARE TANGENT POINTS.

ARC TANGENT TO TWO LINES

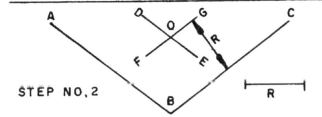

GIVEN = OBTUSE ANGLE A—B—C.
PROBLEM = DRAW ARC WITH RADIUS —R—
TANGENT TO ANGLE A—B—C.

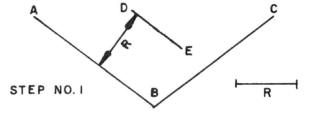

STEP NO. I

WITH THE DISTANCE OF RADIUS —R—
DRAW LINE D—E PARALLEL TO
LINE A—B.

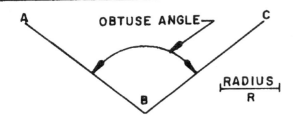

STEP NO. 2

WITH THE DISTANCE OF RADIUS —R—
DRAW LINE F—G PARALLEL TO LINE
B—C. NOTE INTERSECTING POINT —O—.

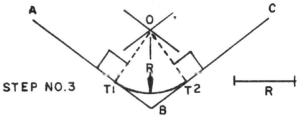

STEP NO.3

FROM POINT —O—WITH RADIUS —R—DRAW
ARC T¹—T². T¹—T² ARE TANGENT POINTS.

ARC TANGENT TO LINE AND ARC

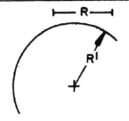

GIVEN = ARC - R¹ AND LINE A-B.
PROBLEM = DRAW 'ARC WITH GIVEN RADIUS
TANGENT TO LINE A-B AND ARC R¹.

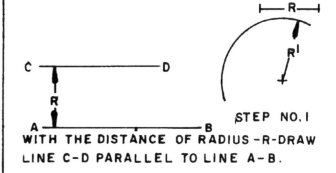

STEP NO. I
WITH THE DISTANCE OF RADIUS -R- DRAW
LINE C-D PARALLEL TO LINE A-B.

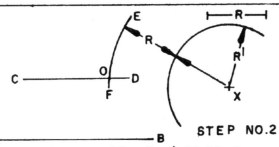

STEP NO. 2
WITH THE DISTANCE OF R¹ PLUS -R-
DRAW ARC E-F FROM POINT-X.
NOTE INTERSECTING POINT-O-.

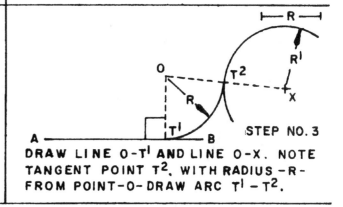

STEP NO. 3
DRAW LINE O-T¹ AND LINE O-X. NOTE
TANGENT POINT T². WITH RADIUS -R-
FROM POINT-O-DRAW ARC T¹ - T².

ARC TANGENT TO TWO ARCS

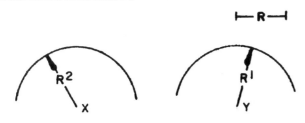

GIVEN = ARCS R¹ AND R².
PROBLEM = DRAW AN ARC WITH THE
RADIUS OF -R- TANGENT TO ARCS R¹ AND R²

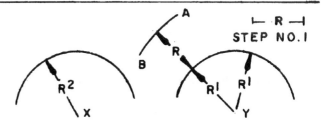

STEP NO. I
WITH THE RADIUS OF -R¹- PLUS -R- DRAW
DRAW ARC A-B.

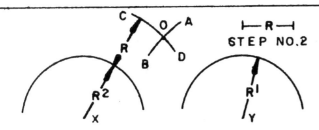

STEP NO. 2
WITH THE RADIUS OF -R² PLUS -R- DRAW
ARC C-D. NOTE THE INTERSECTING
POINT -O- WITH ARCS A-B AND C-D

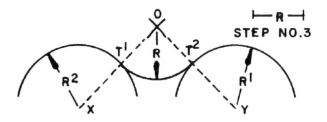

STEP NO. 3
DRAW LINE O-X AND O-Y. NOTE TANGENT
POINTS T¹ AND T². WITH THE RADIUS -R-
FROM POINT -O- DRAW ARC T¹ - T².

ARC TANGENT TO LINE AND ARC

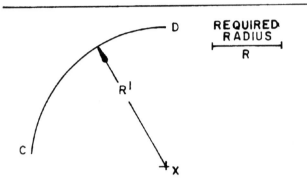

GIVEN = LINE-A-B AND ARC- C-D.
REQUIRED= DRAW ARC WITH RADIUS-R-
TANGENT TO LINE-A-B- AND ARC – C-D.

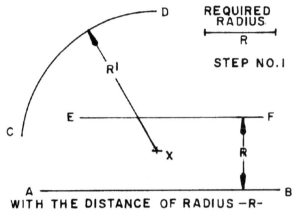

STEP NO.1

WITH THE DISTANCE OF RADIUS –R-
DRAW LINE-E-F-PARALLEL TO LINE
–A–B–.

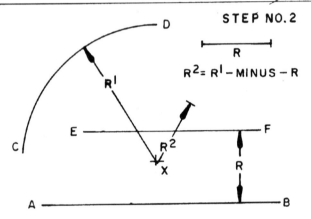

STEP NO.2

$R^2 = R^1 - MINUS - R$

TO FIND THE RADIUS R^2 SUB-TRACT THE
RADIUS – R- FROM THE RADIUS-R^1-.

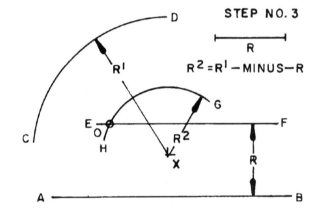

STEP NO. 3

$R^2 = R^1 - MINUS - R$

FROM POINT-X-WITH RADIUS-R^2-DRAW
ARC- G-H-. NOTE INTERSECTING POINT-O-.

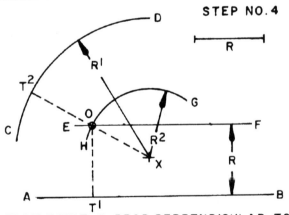

STEP NO. 4

FROM POINT-O-DROP PERPENDICULAR TO
LINE-A-B. THIS IS LINE-O-T^1.
DRAW LINE – X-O-T^2. POINT T^2 IS
THE TANGENT POINT ON ARC – C-D

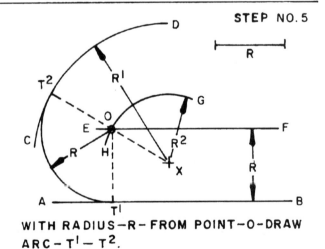

STEP NO. 5

WITH RADIUS-R-FROM POINT-O-DRAW
ARC-T^1 – T^2.

ARC TANGENT TO TWO ARCS

REQUIRED RADIUS
-R-

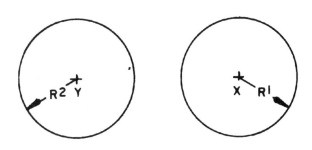

GIVEN = CIRCLE-R¹-AND CIRCLE-R².
    REQUIRED RADIUS -R-.
REQUIRED= DRAW AN ARC WITH THE
GIVEN RADIUS -R- TANGENT TO THE
TOP OF THE TWO CIRCLES.

REQUIRED RADIUS
-R-

STEP NO. 1

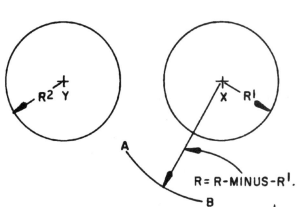

WITH THE RADIUS OF -R- MINUS-R¹.
FROM POINT-X-DRAW ARC-A-B.

REQUIRED RADIUS
-R-

STEP NO. 2

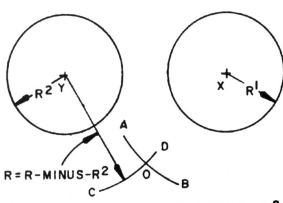

WITH THE RADIUS OF -R-MINUS-R²
FROM POINT-Y-DRAW ARC -C-D.
NOTE THE INTERSECTING POINT-O-
WITH ARCS A-B AND C-D.

REQUIRED RADIUS
-R-

STEP NO. 3

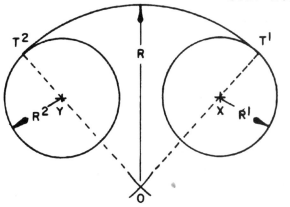

DRAW LINE O-X EXTENDED TO LOCATE
TANGENT POINT T¹.
DRAW LINE O-Y EXTENDED TO LOCATE
TANGENT POINT T².
WITH THE RADIUS -R-FROM POINT-O-
DRAW ARC -T¹-T².

ARC TANGENT TO TWO ARCS

REQUIRED RADIUS
-R-

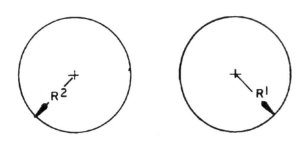

GIVEN = REQUIRED RADIUS -R-
         CIRCLE -R¹ AND CIRCLE -R²

REQUIRED = DRAW AN ARC WITH RADIUS
         -R- TANGENT TO THE TOP
         OF CIRCLE -R¹- AND THE
         BOTTOM OF CIRCLE -R².

REQUIRED RADIUS
-R-

STEP NO. I

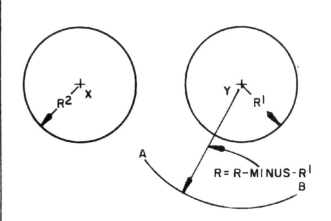

WITH RADIUS -R- MINUS RADIUS -R¹
FROM POINT -Y- DRAW ARC- A-B.

REQUIRED RADIUS
-R-

STEP NO. 2

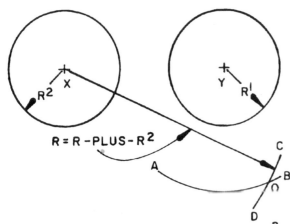

WITH RADIUS -R- PLUS THE RADIUS -R²
FROM POINT -X- DRAW ARC - C-D. NOTE
INTERSECTING POINT -O-.

REQUIRED RADIUS
-R-

STEP NO. 3

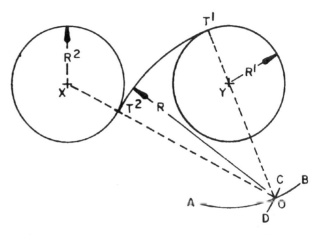

FROM POINT -O- DRAW LINE -O-T²-X.
FROM POINT -O- DRAW LINE -O-Y -T¹.
FROM POINT- O -DRAW ARC -T¹-T²
WITH THE REQUIRED RADIUS -R-.

PROVING TANGENT POINTS

A tangent point is the exact point where one line stops and another line starts. Tangent means to touch. A tangent point is the exact point where a straight line stops being a straight line, and a curved line starts. A tangent point is the exact point where one curved line stops and another curved line starts. Every tangent point can be proved.

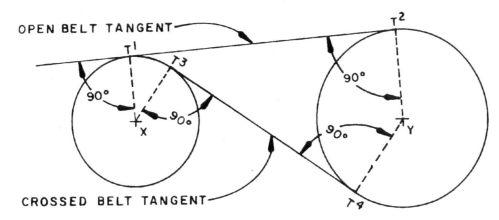

To prove the tangent point when a straight line is tangent to an arc perpendicular is dropped from the center of the circle to the straight line. You always drop a perpendicular when dealing with a straight line. Prove the tangent point before drawing the straight line.

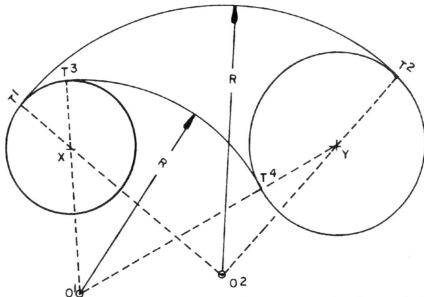

To prove the tangent point when an arc is tangent to another arc, a line is drawn from the center to center of the arcs, and at times the line must be extended to the outside of the circle to prove the tangent point. You always connect centers of circles when proving tangents to curved lines.

Always prove the tangent points before drawing the tangent arc.

APPROXIMATE ELLIPSE

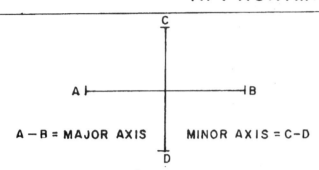

A — B = MAJOR AXIS   MINOR AXIS = C-D

DRAW = APPROXIMATE ELLIPSE USING
THE 15° —30°-60° METHOD.

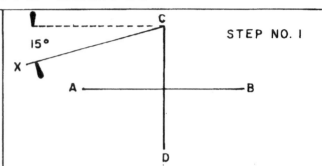

STEP NO. 1

DRAW LINE C—X FROM POINT-C-ON 15°

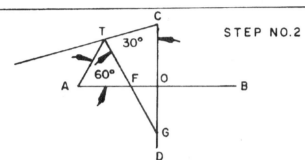

STEP NO.2

DRAW LINE A—T FROM POINT—A—ON 60°
DRAW LINE T-F-G FROM POINT-T-
ON 30°

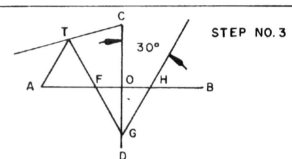

STEP NO.3

DRAW LINE G-H FROM POINT-G-ON 30°
A-T-F =EQUILATERAL TRIANGLE

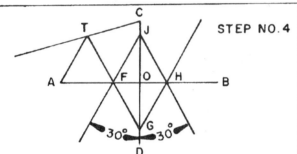

STEP NO. 4

THRU POINTS -F-AND-H- DRAW LINES ON
30°. THIS WILL LOCATE POINT - J.

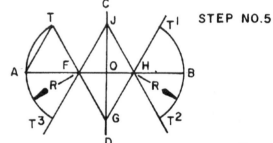

STEP NO.5

WITH RADIUS-F-A-DRAW ARC-T-A-T3.
WITH RADIUS-H-B-DRAW ARC-T1-B-T2

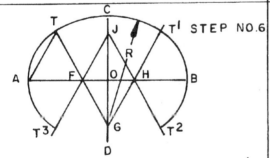

STEP NO.6

WITH RADIUS -G-C-DRAW ARC-T-C-T1
FROM CENTER POINT—G-.

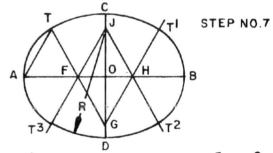

STEP NO.7

WITH RADIUS-J-D-DRAW ARC-T3-C-T2.
FROM CENTER POINT —J-.

TRIANGLE — GIVEN 3 SIDES

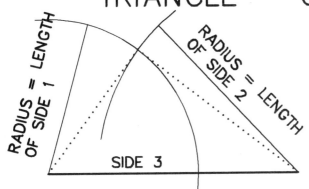

SIDE 1	
SIDE 2	
SIDE 3	

THIS CONSTRUCTION IS USED MANY TIMES IN THE PROCESS OF CONSTRUCTING THE FLAT PATTERN FOR SHEET METAL SURFACES.

ARC THROUGH A POINT
AND TANGENT TO AN ARC

GIVEN (AR)
ARC RADIUS

1. DRAW AN ARC FROM THE GIVEN POINT = AR
2. DRAW AN ARC FROM THE CENTER OF THE CIRCLE = AR + RC
3. WHERE ARCS 1 AND 2 INTERSECT (POINT 3) IS THE CENTER FOR THE REQUIRED ARC.

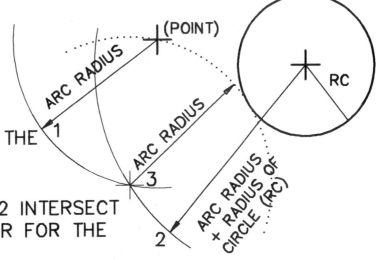

RECTIFY AN ARC

THIS CONSTRUCTION APPROXIMATES THE LENGTH ALONG AN ARC MEASURED ALONG A STRAIGHT LINE.
1. DIVIDE THE ARC INTO EQUAL CHORDS.
2. STEP THE SAME CHORD LENGTH ALONG LINE A – B'
3. MEASURE THE LAST SEGMENT LENGTH

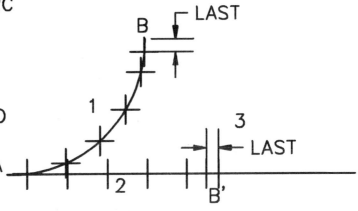

NAME

DATE

FILE NUMBER

GRADE

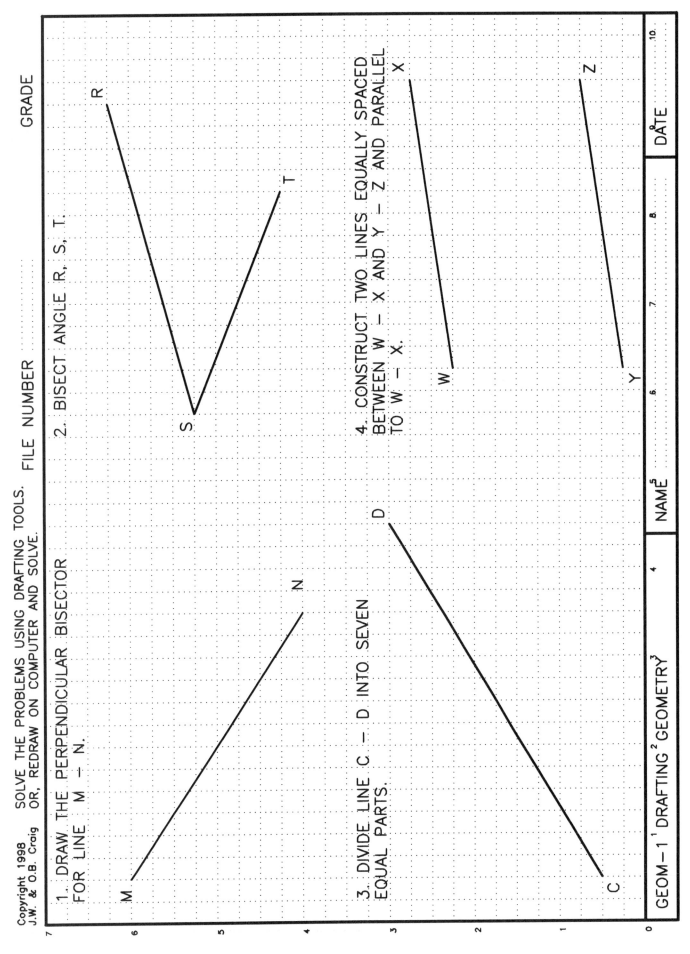

SOLVE THE PROBLEMS USING DRAFTING TOOLS.   FILE NUMBER
OR, REDRAW ON COMPUTER AND SOLVE.

1. DRAW THE PERPENDICULAR BISECTOR
FOR LINE M – N.

2. BISECT ANGLE R, S, T.

M

N

R

S

T

GRADE

3. DIVIDE LINE C – D INTO SEVEN
EQUAL PARTS.

4. CONSTRUCT TWO LINES EQUALLY SPACED
BETWEEN W – X AND Y – Z AND PARALLEL
TO W – X.

C

D

W

X

Y

Z

GEOM–1 DRAFTING ² GEOMETRY³   NAME⁵   DATE⁹

NAME

DATE

FILE NUMBER

GRADE

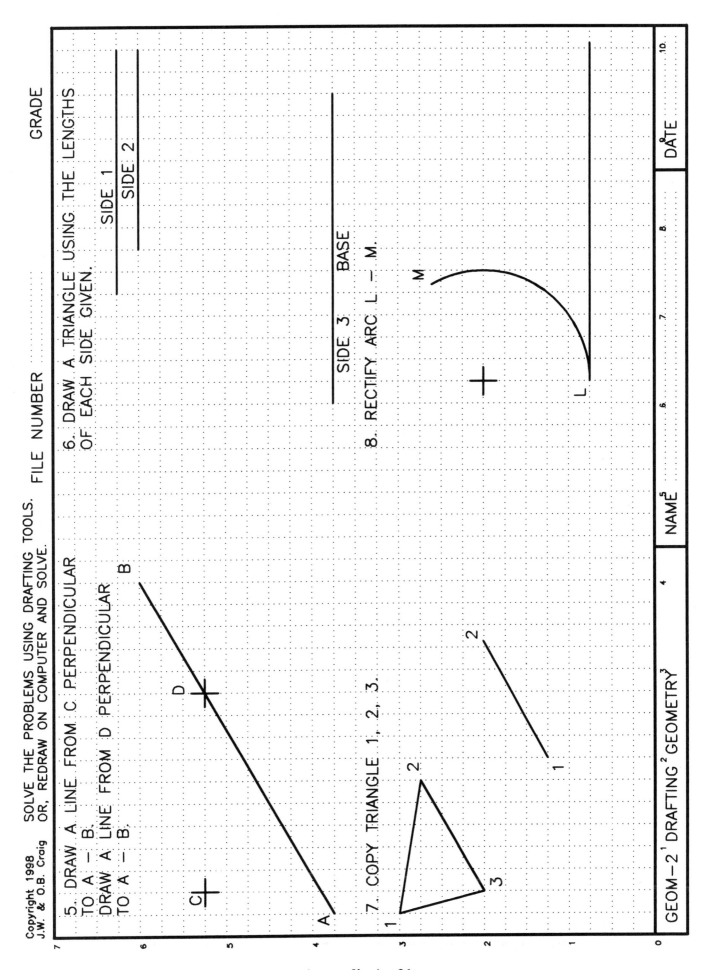

SOLVE THE PROBLEMS USING DRAFTING TOOLS.   FILE NUMBER   GRADE
OR, REDRAW ON COMPUTER AND SOLVE.

5. DRAW A LINE FROM C PERPENDICULAR
   TO A – B.

DRAW A LINE FROM D PERPENDICULAR
TO A – B.

6. DRAW A TRIANGLE USING THE LENGTHS
   OF EACH SIDE GIVEN.

SIDE 1

SIDE 2

SIDE 3   BASE

8. RECTIFY ARC L – M.

7. COPY TRIANGLE 1, 2, 3.

GEOM–2 DRAFTING GEOMETRY   NAME   DATE

NAME

DATE

FILE NUMBER

GRADE

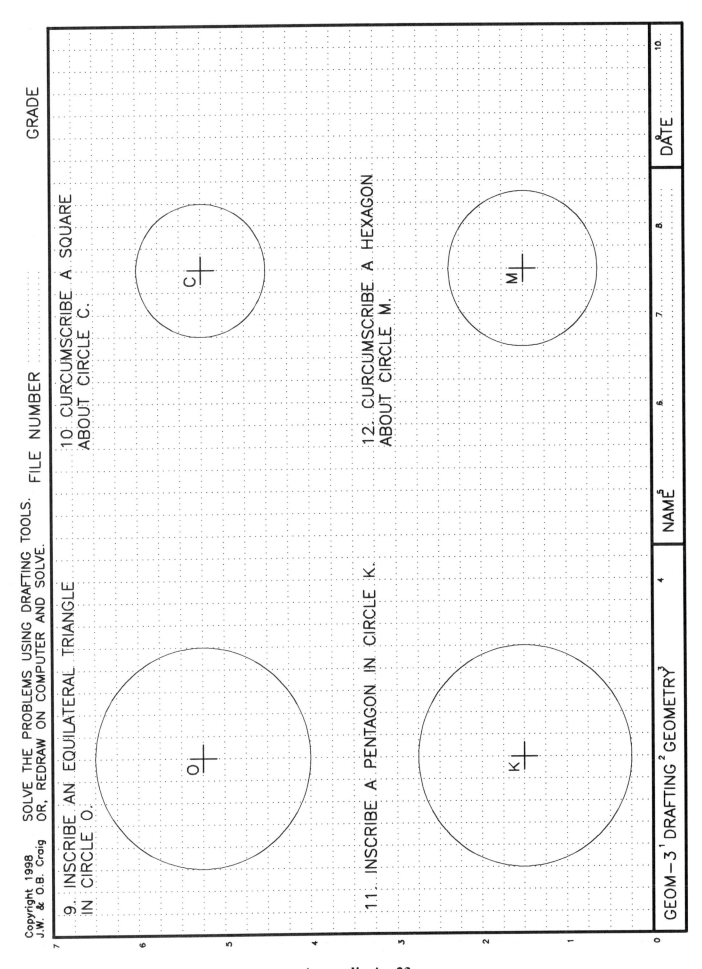

SOLVE THE PROBLEMS USING DRAFTING TOOLS.
OR, REDRAW ON COMPUTER AND SOLVE.

FILE NUMBER

GRADE

9. INSCRIBE AN EQUILATERAL TRIANGLE
IN CIRCLE O.

10. CURCUMSCRIBE A SQUARE
ABOUT CIRCLE C.

11. INSCRIBE A PENTAGON IN CIRCLE K.

12. CURCUMSCRIBE A HEXAGON
ABOUT CIRCLE M.

GEOM−3 DRAFTING GEOMETRY

NAME

DATE

NAME

DATE

FILE NUMBER

GRADE

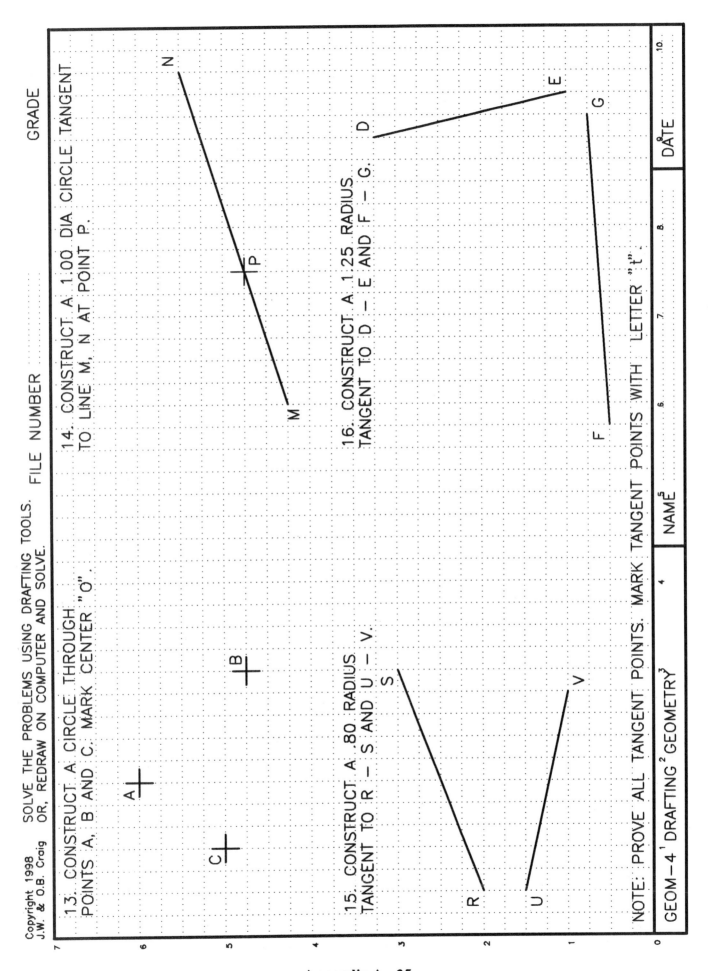

SOLVE THE PROBLEMS USING DRAFTING TOOLS.   FILE NUMBER _____   GRADE _____
OR, REDRAW ON COMPUTER AND SOLVE.

13. CONSTRUCT A CIRCLE THROUGH
POINTS A, B AND C. MARK CENTER "O".

14. CONSTRUCT A 1.00 DIA. CIRCLE TANGENT
TO LINE M, N AT POINT P.

15. CONSTRUCT A .80 RADIUS
TANGENT TO R – S AND U – V.

16. CONSTRUCT A 1.25 RADIUS
TANGENT TO D – E AND F – G.

NOTE: PROVE ALL TANGENT POINTS. MARK TANGENT POINTS WITH LETTER "t".

GEOM–4 DRAFTING GEOMETRY

NAME _____   DATE _____

NAME

DATE

FILE NUMBER

GRADE

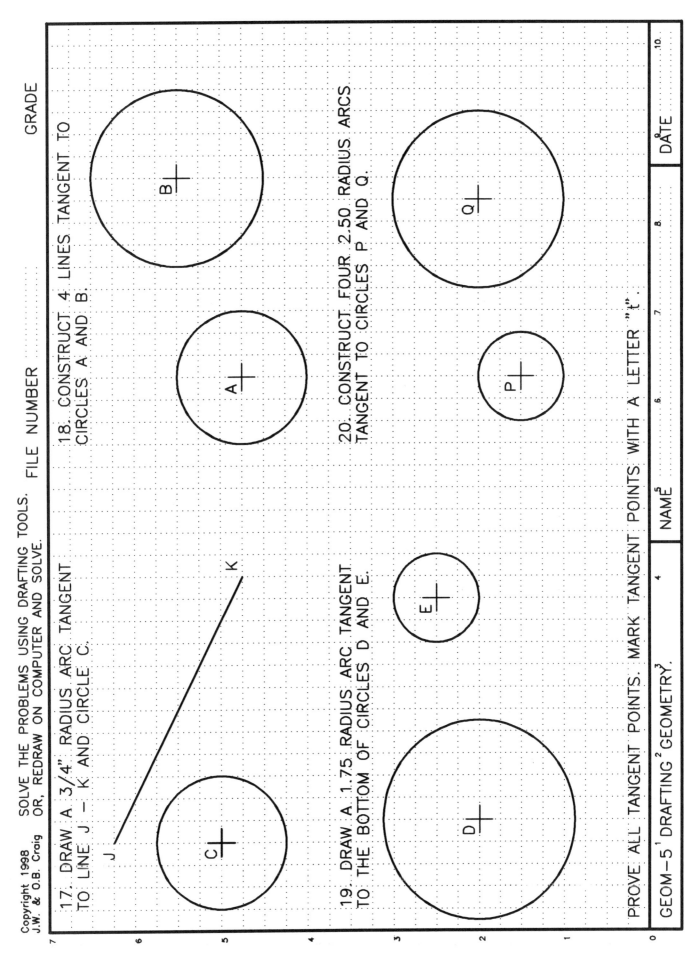

SOLVE THE PROBLEMS USING DRAFTING TOOLS.
OR, REDRAW ON COMPUTER AND SOLVE.

FILE NUMBER

GRADE

17. DRAW A 3/4" RADIUS ARC TANGENT
TO LINE J – K AND CIRCLE C.

18. CONSTRUCT 4 LINES TANGENT TO
CIRCLES A AND B.

19. DRAW A 1.75 RADIUS ARC TANGENT
TO THE BOTTOM OF CIRCLES D AND E.

20. CONSTRUCT FOUR 2.50 RADIUS ARCS
TANGENT TO CIRCLES P AND Q.

PROVE ALL TANGENT POINTS. MARK TANGENT POINTS WITH A LETTER "t".

GEOM–5 DRAFTING GEOMETRY.

NAME

DATE

NAME

DATE

FILE NUMBER

GRADE

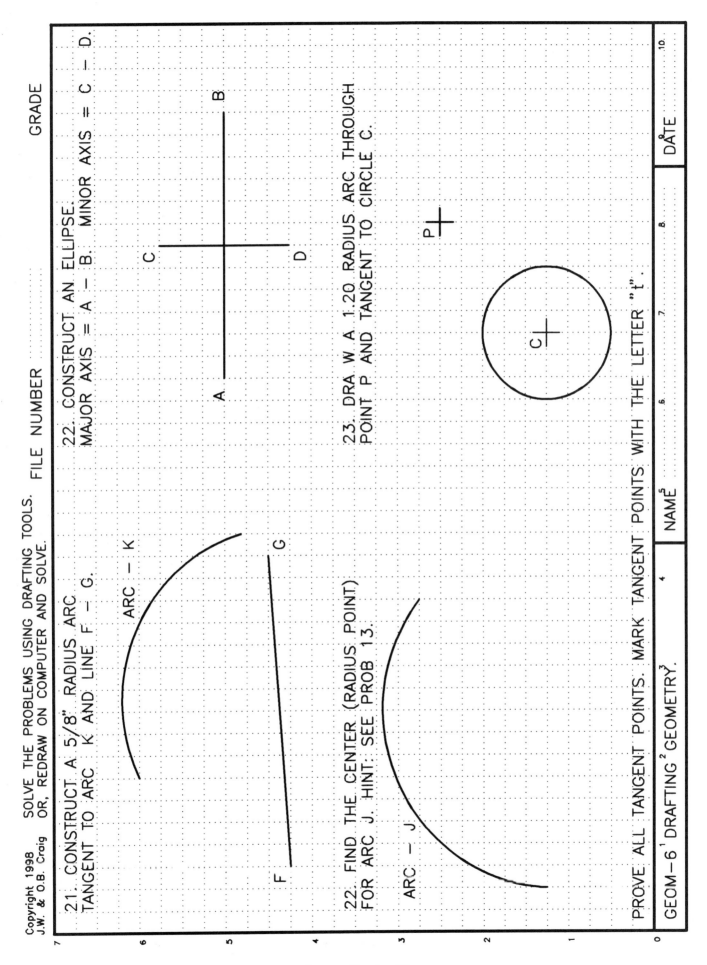

SOLVE THE PROBLEMS USING DRAFTING TOOLS. FILE NUMBER GRADE
OR, REDRAW ON COMPUTER AND SOLVE.

21. CONSTRUCT A 5/8" RADIUS ARC.
TANGENT TO ARC K AND LINE F – G.

ARC – K

F

G

22. FIND THE CENTER (RADIUS POINT.)
FOR ARC J. HINT: SEE PROB 13.

ARC – J

22. CONSTRUCT AN ELLIPSE.
MAJOR AXIS = A – B. MINOR AXIS = C – D.

B

C

A

D

23. DRA W A 1.20 RADIUS ARC THROUGH
POINT P AND TANGENT TO CIRCLE C.

P

C

PROVE ALL TANGENT POINTS. MARK TANGENT POINTS WITH THE LETTER "t".

GEOM–6 DRAFTING GEOMETRY. NAME DATE

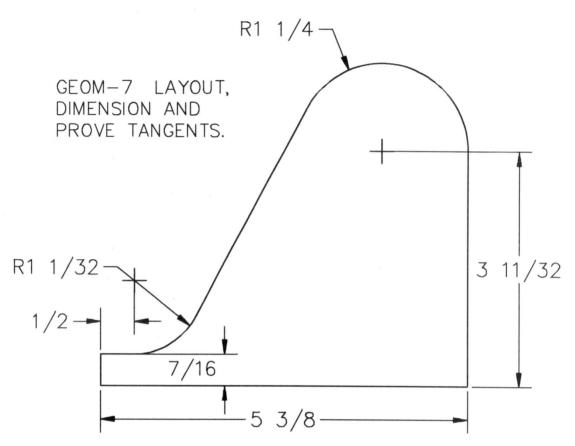

GEOM–7 LAYOUT,
DIMENSION AND
PROVE TANGENTS.

R1 1/4

R1 1/32

1/2

7/16

3 11/32

5 3/8

GEOM–8. OVERUNNING CLUTCH HOUSING.
LAYOUT, DIMENSION AND PROVE TANGENTS.

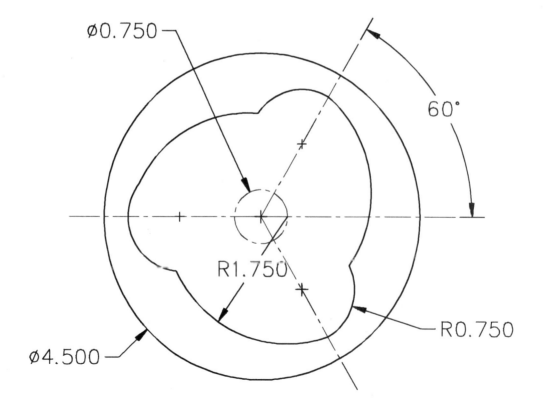

⌀0.750

60°

R1.750

R0.750

⌀4.500

GEOM—9. LAYOUT, DIMENSION AND PROVE ALL TANGENTS.

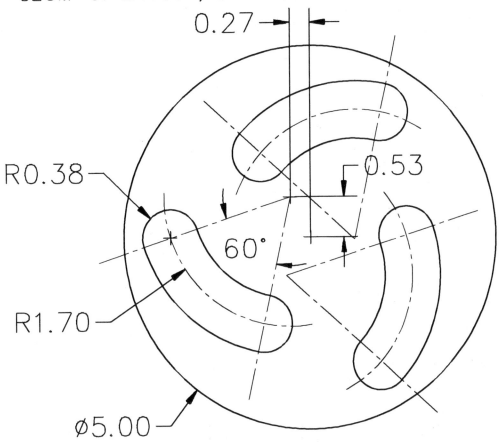

GEOM—10. METRIC MM. LAYOUT, DIMENSION AND PROVE ALL TANGENTS.

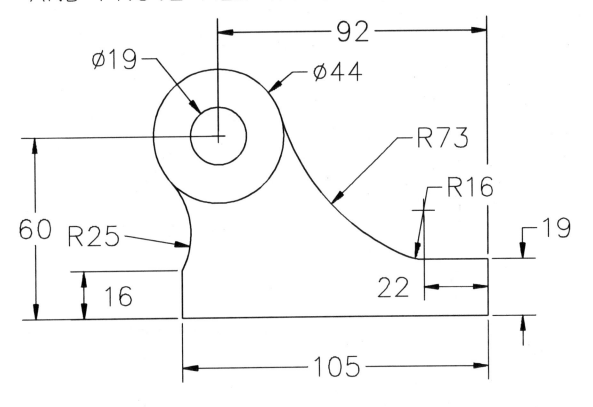

GEOM—11. METRIC MM. LAYOUT, DIMENSION AND PROVE ALL TANGENTS.

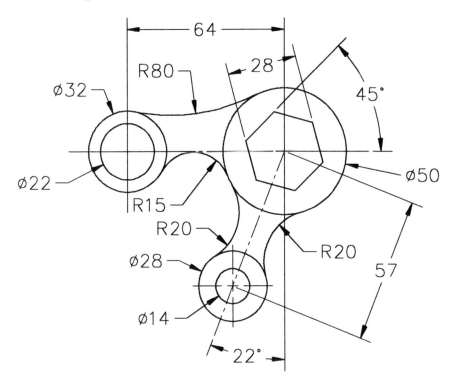

GEOM—12. METRIC MM. LAYOUT, DIMENSION AND PROVE ALL TANGENTS.

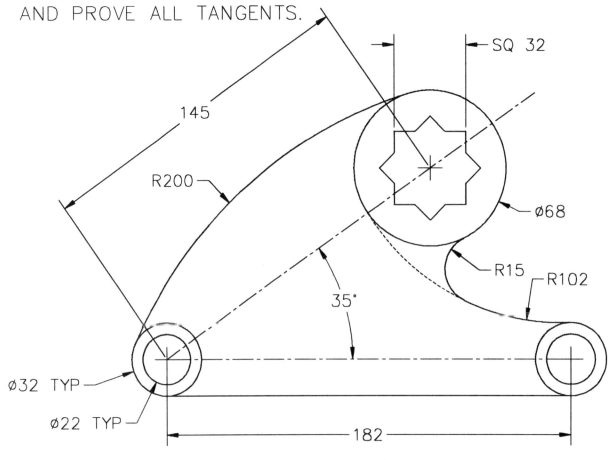

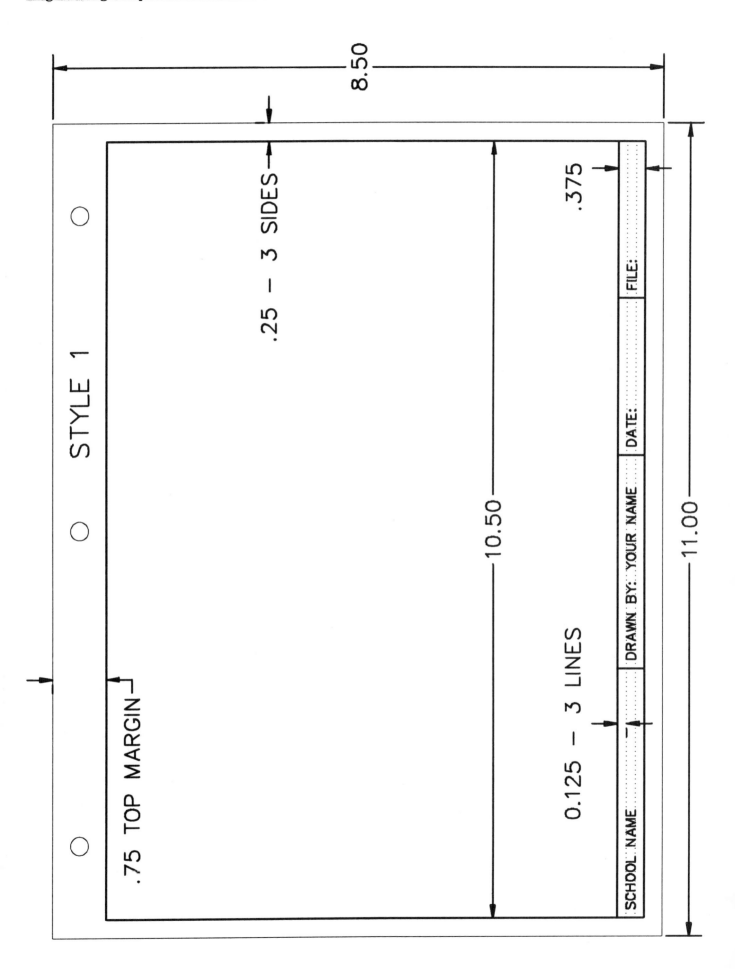

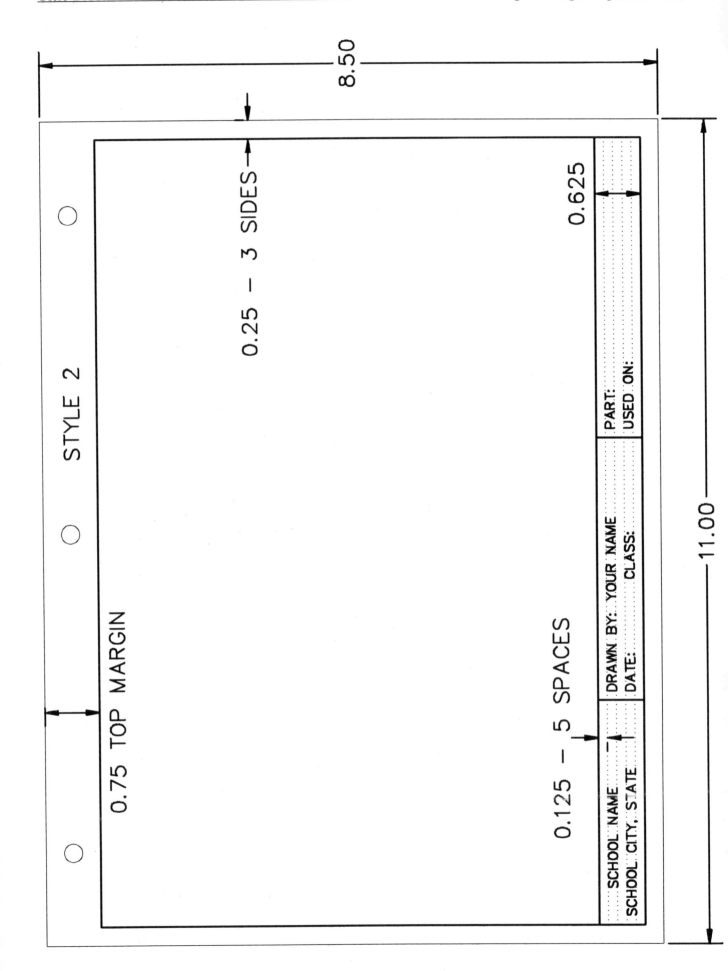

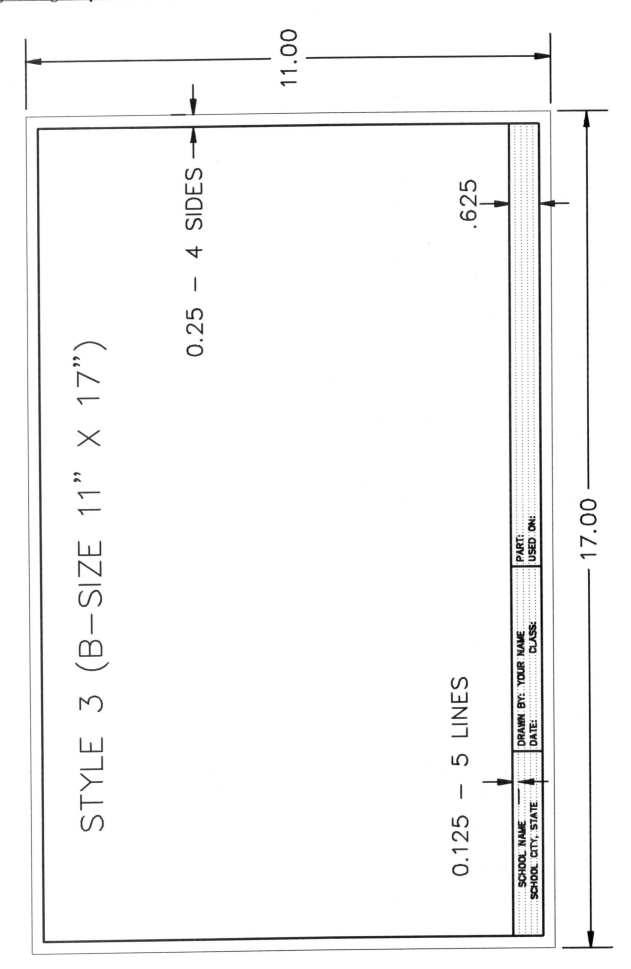

STYLE 3 (B-SIZE 11" X 17")

11.00

0.25 — 4 SIDES

.625

17.00

0.125 — 5 LINES

DRAWN BY: YOUR NAME	PART:
DATE:	CLASS:	USED ON:
SCHOOL NAME	
SCHOOL CITY, STATE	

NAME

DATE

Copyright 1998
J.W & O.B. Craig

NOTE: Use this grid format
in horizontal direction.

FILE NUMBER

GRADE

GRADE

FILE NUMBER

DATE

NAME

NAME

DATE

Copyright 1998
J.W & O.B. Craig

NOTE: Use this grid format
in horizontal direction.

FILE NUMBER

GRADE

GRADE

FILE NUMBER

Copyright 1998
J.W. & O.B. Craig

DATE

NAME

NAME

DATE

Copyright 1998
J.W. & O.B. Craig

NOTE: Turn the page
vertically for use.

FILE NUMBER

GRADE